To my parents

This book is in the **Addison-Wesley Series in**

COMPUTER SCIENCE AND INFORMATION PROCESSING

Richard S. Varga

Edward J. McCluskey, Jr.

Consulting Editors

SHAN S. KUO, *University of New Hampshire*

Numerical Methods and Computers

ADDISON-WESLEY PUBLISHING COMPANY

Reading, Massachusetts · Palo Alto · London · Don Mills, Ontario

PREFACE

During the past six years the author has been giving a course in numerical methods and computers at Yale and Tufts Universities and the University of New Hampshire. This course is designed to acquaint students with the numerical methods used in solving problems by means of a high-speed digital computer. The interests of his audience have included such diverse subjects as biology, chemical engineering, chemistry, civil engineering, economics, electrical engineering, computer science, mechanical engineering, physics, psychology, and pure mathematics.

When I began teaching this course, I found that many excellent texts in numerical methods were available, but most of them were either not computer-based or were too specialized for use in a course of this nature. Furthermore, most books in programming languages touched little on numerical methods. Accordingly, it became necessary to prepare some mimeographed notes from which this book developed.

In preparing these lecture notes, I had two objectives in mind: first, to provide the student with the necessary fundamental knowledge of the computer-oriented numerical methods for basic problems in algebra and analysis which form the building blocks for more complicated problems; second, to acquaint him with a high-speed digital computer. The student was required to program and solve meaningful problems on a computer. Experience in the classroom has indicated that this approach develops an excellent comprehension of the successful application of computer-oriented numerical methods.

This text is divided into three parts. Part I deals with man-machine communication in some detail. Part II describes the various numerical methods that have been proved suitable for electronic computers. Part III is concerned with modern topics in digital computation, including linear programming and the Monte Carlo method. Throughout the book the popular IBM 1620, a medium-size digital computer, is used for illustrative purposes.

The book is suited for courses on the methods of modern computation which are included in the curricula of most universities. The prerequisite in mathematics is a good knowledge of elementary differential equations. It is hoped that this book forms a bridge between programming techniques and methods of numerical analysis. The deliberate emphasis on the flow chart and the presentation of a *tested* FORTRAN program for each numerical method should provide the student with real insight into the techniques of computer problem solving, and scientists and engineers with a guide to the solution of advanced problems.

It is with pleasure that I gratefully acknowledge the help and encouragement of my friends, colleagues, and students. In particular, my thanks go to W. R. Burrows, D. T. Chin, C. S. Chu, W. D'Avanzo, D. S. Fine, Y. W. Hsu, L. P. Kuan, J. Stephenson, E. Vaines, L. A. Walsh, and C. Wolfe for their comments, criticisms, and help in eliminating errors. I also wish to express my appreciation to Drs. A. Wang and S. Chao for helpful comments on Chapter 2. Numerous ideas were drawn from the internal publications of Computation Centers at the Massachusetts Institute of Technology, Yale University, University of Michigan, University of New Hampshire, and Tufts University.

I am also grateful for the expert typing by Jane Kelfer and Mary Lambert. Finally, I wish to thank the staff of Addison-Wesley Publishing Company for their continuous cooperation.

Durham, New Hampshire
June 1965   S.S.K.

CONTENTS

PART II. COMPUTER-ORIENTED NUMERICAL METHODS

CHAPTER 6. Computer Solution of Polynomial and Transcendental Equations

CHAPTER 7. Ordinary Differential Equations with Initial Conditions

CHAPTER 8. Matrix Algebra and Simultaneous Equations

CHAPTER 9. Eigenvalues and Eigenvectors of a Real Symmetric Matrix

PART III. MODERN METHODS

PART **I**

COMMUNICATION
WITH DIGITAL COMPUTERS

The subject matter of Part I is concerned with an introduction of computer components and the general problem of man-machine communication. It is divided into five chapters. Chapter 1 is introductory in aim and content while Chapter 2 deals with the basic units of digital computers. Chapter 3 presents logical flow charting, a graphical representation of a sequence of commands. Chapter 4 is concerned with the floating-point method of arithmetic. Chapter 5 presents the FORTRAN coding system together with many detailed examples.

INTRODUCTION

1.1 CHARACTERISTICS OF DIGITAL COMPUTERS

High-speed electronic computers are triggering a revolution in the solving of engineering and science problems. This revolution will free men from many mentally stultifying computational tasks, and more important, it will make possible the solution of engineering and science problems of greater complexity.

There are two classes of computers: analog or digital. An analog computer, like a slide rule, solves problems by converting numbers into physical quantities such as distance or electrical resistance. On the other hand, a high-speed digital computer is like a desk calculator in that it uses numbers to express all the variables and quantities of a problem. However, it differs from a desk calculator in one important respect: it can automatically perform a long and complete sequence of operations without intervention from the human operator.

This book deals exclusively with digital computations; references to analog computations are listed at the end of the chapter.

We shall now discuss some marked characteristics of digital computers, the first of which is their high speed. In a matter of seconds or minutes, vast quantities of computations can be automatically performed. Computations avoided because of their impracticality prior to the use of digital computers can now be handled as a matter of simple routine. Consider the case of comparative engineering design. The designer, without computers, would either make a "guestimate" from his experience or at best estimate only one or two alternatives. When a digital computer is used, a complete comparative study can be obtained to show the effect of numerous parameters in a short time.

The digital computer is not merely a glorified slide rule; it has the ability to store, or remember, various information for future use. Such information includes the original data, commands of operation, and intermediate results. In addition, digital computers are able to change or modify the commands of operations internally, and

3

frequently the intermediate results obtained are used internally to dictate the path of subsequent computations.

For example, at a point of computation, the answer is tested for zero. Depending on whether or not the answer is zero, the machine will automatically take one of two entirely different courses for subsequent computations. Thus the digital computer is also noted for its ability to make a logical decision.

1.2   A BRIEF HISTORY AND SURVEY OF THE APPLICATION OF DIGITAL COMPUTERS

The first all-electronic digital computer was completed in 1946 at the University of Pennsylvania and was named the Electrical Numerical Integrator and Automatic Computer (ENIAC).

Vacuum tubes were used for most of its functions. This was a great improvement over the Mark I digital computer built at Harvard University in 1944, which made use of electromechanical relays. In the period following the completion of the ENIAC, two significant developments made possible the present-day family of computers. One was the development of a memory device for holding a few hundred to several thousand numbers. The other was the realization that commands could also be stored in this memory device in a manner similar to that in which the numbers are stored. This knowledge made it possible to instruct the computer to follow these commands from each memory space as required. In the meantime, the representation of numbers in the binary system was put in use and since that time the number of basic commands has been steadily increased.

Since 1951 there have been continuous advances in the design and components of digital computers. Among these were the introduction of solid-state or transistorized design, increased number of available memory spaces, faster speed of operation, and a further diversification of commands.

Digital computers are presently being used to store and retrieve information quickly and economically, simulate complex business operations, create a "model" river system, help determine who wrote the Federalist papers whose authorship is disputed, chart the complex interrelations among the hundreds of electric signals reproduced by the living brain, formulate and prove mathematical theorems, take the first step toward translation of languages, forecast the weather, and analyze the decay tracks left by strange particles in bubble chambers.

Computers are also used to calculate spacecraft orbits, process payrolls, update transactions, control chemical blending processes, design structures and machine components, and assist in medical diagnoses. They are simulating aircraft flight characteristics, automating airline reservation procedures, and controlling inventories.

A procedure called *time-sharing* which brings the user closer to the computer is rapidly gaining recognition. In this procedure, a number of consoles scattered in different locations are connected to one central computer so that a number of users can take over control, successively, as they need its services.

Another interesting development is in the area of engineering graphics. By using a light pen on a cathode-ray oscilloscope, one can draw two projections of a given object and ask the computer to straighten out lines or rectify angles. A perspective view can then be produced by the computer. Similarly, the equation of a surface may be read in and a contour plot can readily be made by the computer.

BIBLIOGRAPHY

ALT, F. L., Ed., *Advances in Computers*. Academic Press, New York. This is intended to be a continuing publication, the first volume of which appeared in 1960.

BERKLEY, E. C., *The Computer Revolution*. Doubleday, Garden City, N. Y., 1962.

GRABBE, E. M., S. RAMO, and D. E. WOOLDRIDGE, Eds., *Handbook of Automation, Computation and Control*, **I–III**. John Wiley and Sons, New York, 1958–61.

LIAPUNOV, A. A., "Mathematical Investigations Related to the Use of Electronic Computing Machines," translated by M. D. FRIEDMAN, *Comm. Assoc. Comput. Mach.*, **3,** pp. 107–118 (1960).

MONTGOMERIE, G. A., *Digital Calculating Machines*. Blackie, Glasgow, 1956.

PFEIFFER, J., *The Thinking Machine*. Lippincott, Philadelphia, 1962.

STEGUN, I. A., and M. ABRANOWITZ, "Pitfalls in Computation," *J. Soc. Ind. Appl. Math.*, **4,** pp. 201–219 (1956).

WILKES, M. V., *Automatic Digital Computers*. Methuen, London, 1956.

Analog Computer Techniques

JOHNSON, C. L., *Analog Computer Techniques*. McGraw-Hill, New York, 1956.

KARPLUS, WALTER J., *Analog Simulation Solution of Field Problems*. McGraw-Hill, New York, 1958.

KORN, G. A., and T. M. KORN, *Electronic Analog Computers*. McGraw-Hill, New York, 1956.

ROGERS, A. E., and T. W. CONNOLLY, *Analog Computation in Engineering Design*. McGraw-Hill, 1960.

SOROKA, WALTER W., *Analog Methods in Computation and Simulation*. McGraw-Hill, New York, 1954.

WARFIELD, JOHN N., *Introduction to Electronic Analog Computers*. Prentice-Hall, Englewood Cliffs, N. J., 1959.

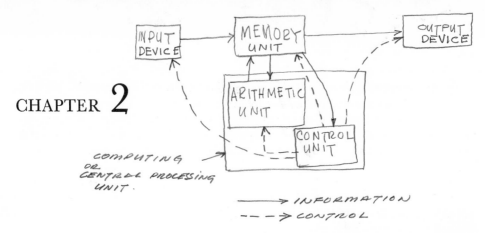

CHAPTER **2**

*COMPUTING
OR
CENTRAL PROCESSING
UNIT.*

$\longrightarrow$ *INFORMATION*
$--\rightarrow$ *CONTROL*

MAIN COMPUTER
COMPONENTS

2.1   FUNCTIONS OF COMPUTER COMPONENTS

A basic computer system consists of the four main components shown in Fig. 2.1: input devices, a memory unit, a central processing unit, and output devices. Physically, they may be either combined into a single unit or separated into several distinct parts.

The main function of input devices is to feed both data and commands into the memory unit. This is accomplished through units such as a keyboard, a punched card reader, a device to read magnetic or paper tape, a telephone, or a teletype line. Among these devices, the magnetic tape reader appears to be the fastest.

After the commands and data are stored in the memory unit, the commands are then used to instruct the computer to proceed with the computation or data processing. It is important to note that intermediate or final answers can also be stored in the memory unit for future use and output.

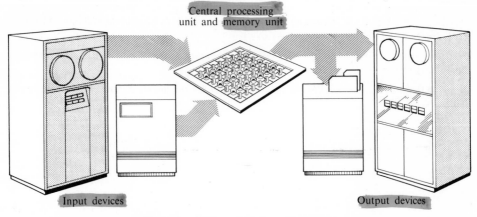

Central processing unit and memory unit

Input devices

Output devices

Fig. 2.1.   Basic computer components.

The central processing unit is needed to locate the proper instruction which will either execute and perform simple arithmetic operations or make some logical decisions. The central processor accomplishes all this by opening and closing various electronic switches (or gates) to allow the stored data to pass from one part of the machine to another and through devices such as adders and magnitude comparaters. In this respect, the central processor is much like a railroad switchyard.

Finally, there are output devices which serve to carry the resultant data outside the computer. These devices include punch printers and magnetic or paper tape units. An oscilloscope resembling a television set or a plotter may also be utilized to display the results in pictorial form.

2.2 MEMORY UNITS

As mentioned in the last section, the memory unit serves to retain (a) initial data or instructions, (b) intermediate results, and (c) final answers. It is convenient to compare the memory unit to an array of post office boxes, with each box storing either a command or a datum. However, there is a basic difference. At any particular time, two or more communications can generally be stored in a single ordinary mail box, while only one command or one datum can be stored in a given memory location. As a second command or datum enters into a given memory location, the existing content is automatically erased. Also, unlike a mailbox, when the content in a given memory location A is transmitted to some other location B, the content in A is not disturbed; that is, it exists in both location A and location B. It cannot be erased from the original location until a new command or datum is fed into this original storage location. Memory location and storage location are synonymous.

There are many types of storage media available for digital computers, including magnetic cores, magnetic drums, thin films, disks, and others.

We shall first discuss the *magnetic core*. Each core is a doughnut-shaped piece of ferromagnetic material about 0.08 in. in diameter. A wire is inserted through its hollow portion, as shown in Fig. 2.2(a), and when an electric current is passed along the wire, it sets up a magnetic field around the wire. The core is magnetized by the field and remains magnetized even if the current is stopped (Fig. 2.2b). Now, if a current is passed along the wire in the opposite direction, the field around the wire is

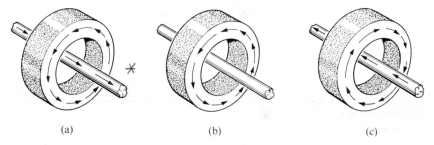

(a)   (b)   (c)

Fig. 2.2. Magnetic core. (a) Core is magnetized. (b) Core remains magnetized. (c) Core is *flipped*.

* note right hand Rule.

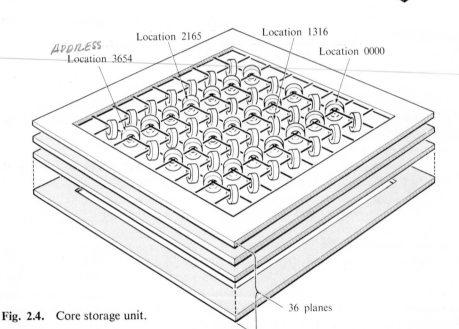

SENSE WIRE

Amplifier

Computer

Fig. 2.3. Amplification of core flipping.

Location 2165   Location 1316

ADDRESS
Location 3654   Location 0000

36 planes

Fig. 2.4. Core storage unit.

reversed, as shown in Fig. 2.2(c). This change of the magnetic state of a core is called *flipping.* Another wire, a sense wire, is also inserted through the hollow portion, and, when a magnetic core flips, a low voltage passes along this sense wire. This voltage is then amplified and used in the computer (Fig. 2.3).

A core storage unit is made of many such magnetic cores arranged in sheets, as shown in Fig. 2.4. The corresponding cores in all sheets can be considered one distinct group. Such a group is usually identified with a unique number commonly known as an *address*, or a *location.*

Thus, in the core storage unit shown in Fig. 2.4, there are 49 addresses, each of which extends downward through the 36 planes. In a digital computer containing 8192 memory locations, the addresses would be numbered consecutively from 0000 to 8191.

address — locates the group of cores that correspond in said slot (handwritten annotation)

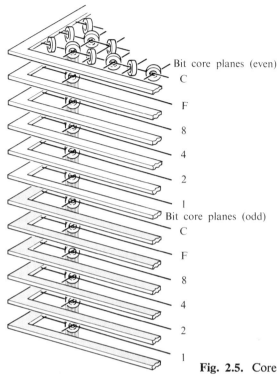

Bit core planes (even)
C
F
8
4
2
1
Bit core planes (odd)
C
F
8
4
2
1

Fig. 2.5. Core array for IBM 1620.

It should be emphasized that the location number is totally different from the information stored in this location. For example, in location 7614 which has 36 cores, the information stored may be

$$101101101110011001111011001101110001.$$ *36 Bits of info* (handwritten)

This information may be a datum or an instruction for future use, but it is not the number 7614 in binary notation. The use of the zeros and ones for the representation of information will be explained later in Sections 2.4 and 2.5.

A similar schematic diagram is given in Fig. 2.5 for the core storage of an IBM 1620. The basic difference between this diagram and the one preceding it is the number of addresses in the series of planes. In the IBM 1620, all the even-numbered addresses are in the top six planes, and the odd-numbered addresses in the bottom six.

Turning now to the second type of memory unit, we examine the *magnetic drum*. This is a metal cylinder with a magnetic coating, which can be demagnetized and magnetized readily, or it can remain magnetized for a period of time.

Two important characteristics of the magnetic drum are worth mentioning. The first is its ability to retain the recorded information even if the power generating the computer is cut off. The second characteristic is its ability to store an input datum or an instruction in any specified location. This information can, of course, be called for from such a location.

Depending on the computer, the number of drum locations varies widely. The locations are numbered consecutively from 0000 to, for instance, 1999 for a 2000-location drum.

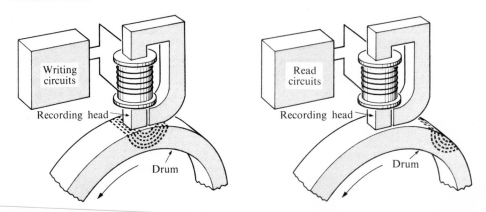

Fig. 2.6.   Writing on a magnetic drum.   **Fig. 2.7.**   Reading from a magnetic drum.

Under operating conditions, the drum is rotating at high speed (in the vicinity of 10,000 rpm). When a magnetic-coated surface is passed directly under an active recording head (Fig. 2.6), the surface becomes magnetized as in a household tape recorder. It is evident that information stored on the drum's surface exists in a mixed pattern of magnetized and nonmagnetized areas. Each area represents a binary digit, that is, either a "0" or a "1." When reading from the drum, the process is just reversed. As the drum surface is passed under the recording head, the magnetized area induces small voltage in the head (Fig. 2.7) which can be amplified and transmitted to the computer for use.

2.3   CENTRAL PROCESSING UNIT

The two basic parts in the central processing unit are the arithmetic section and the control section. The former is the problem-solving section, and the latter controls the sequence of operations and is therefore the "master mind" of the entire system.

The arithmetic section executes such simple arithmetic operations as addition, subtraction, multiplication, and division, as well as the transferring and storing of results.

In computers, the device which serves to locate the proper instruction for execution is called the *instruction sequencer*. This device is also responsible for setting up the conditions for the next instruction. For example, the next instruction to be executed may depend on the sign of the number in the arithmetic unit; if it is minus, the next instruction will be obtained from location 1678, for example. Conversely, if it is positive, then the next instruction might be obtained from another location, say 1296.

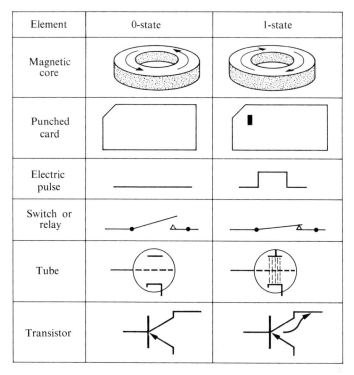

Element	0-state	1-state
Magnetic core		
Punched card		
Electric pulse		
Switch or relay		
Tube		
Transistor		

Fig. 2.8. Bistate elements.

2.4 BISTATE ELEMENTS

A distinguishing characteristic of all computer elements is their ability to represent two (and only two) distinct states. The magnetic core mentioned in Section 2.2 is a typical example. The core may be in either of two magnetized directions. These two distinct conditions can be used to represent the information which the core holds. For instance, one condition may be interpreted as the digit 0; the other, as 1. Similarly, various computer elements may be used to represent yes or no, positive or negative, on or off, etc. Figure 2.8 shows some of the bistate computer elements.

This two-state character is important in that it makes it possible to denote the digits 0 or 1 in a particular storage location. The binary digits 0 and 1 are commonly called *bits*. "Bit" is a contraction of two words, "binary" and "digit." These *bits* are the basic units of information stored in digital computers.

There are two types of digital computers available commercially, binary computers and decimal computers. In a binary computer, data or an internal machine code can be represented simply in the binary system (see Table 2.1); a master computer program is always available to convert decimal input into binary. In a decimal computer, each decimal digit is accepted and automatically converted internally to a fixed group

TABLE 2.1. Typical Representations of Numbers and Symbols Inside Computers

Outside of computers	Inside of computers (Binary-coded decimal systems)			
	For binary computers	For decimal computers		
Number or symbol	(6-bit code) binary	Biquinary	Excess 3	4-bit binary
0	000000	01 00001	0011	0000
1	000001	01 00010	0100	0001
2	000010	01 00100	0101	0010
3	000011	01 01000	0110	0011
4	000100	01 10000	0111	0100
5	000101	10 00001	1000	0101
6	000110	10 00010	1001	0110
7	000111	10 00100	1010	0111
8	001000	10 01000	1011	1000
9	001001	10 10000	1100	1001
A	010001			
B	010010			
C	010011			
D	010100			
E	010101			
⋮	⋮			
X	110111			
Y	111000			
Z	111001			
/	110001			
Blank	110000			
⋮	⋮			

of binary digits according to some known rule. For example, the IBM 1620, a decimal machine, represents a decimal digit 6 internally by four binary digits or bits: 0110 (see Table 2.1). Each of these four digits is treated by the IBM 1620 as a single character. This is the so-called four-bit binary system and is only one of many possible *binary-coded decimal* (BCD) representations. Because of the simplicity of its electronic circuitry and the minimum number of machine components required, the binary system itself is the most widely used system for representing the internal machine code.

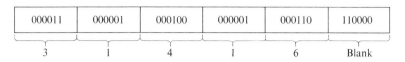

000011	000001	000100	000001	000110	110000
3	1	4	1	6	Blank

Fig. 2.9.   A data word.

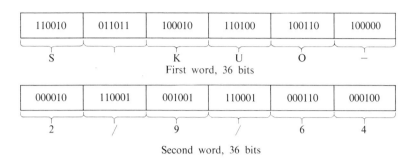

110010	011011	100010	110100	100110	100000
S		K	U	O	—

First word, 36 bits

000010	110001	001001	110001	000110	000100
2	/	9	/	6	4

Second word, 36 bits

Fig. 2.10.   Representation of alphabetic information in computer.

2.5   WORDS

In Section 2.4, we stated that a bit is a single binary digit with a value of either 0 or 1. In many computers, all bits occupying a common storage location make a word. For example, the IBM 7090 and 7094 use words which contain 36 bits each. They are stored in a single vertical row of 36 *magnetic* cores as shown in Fig. 2.4. Specifically, the five-digit information 31416 is represented by 30 of the available 36 bits in a word (Fig. 2.9). The remaining digit is filled with a blank which is considered as a regular symbol.

A word is treated by the computer circuits as a basic unit of information. That is, all bits in one word are generally read, stored, or operated upon simultaneously without disturbing information in any other word.

A word may be either an *instruction* word or a *data* word, and it should be emphasized that both are made up of zeros and ones. An instruction word is used to command the computer to perform a simple operation such as add, subtract, read, punch, or test for minus. However, if, due to an unintentional error, a data word in a program were used as an instruction, the computer would not be able to detect the difference between such a datum and an instruction, and consequently it would perform an illegal operation.

Most computers are also capable of storing alphabetic information, but such information is stored in a binary-coded form and does not look different from any ordinary word. For example, the information, S. Kuo — 2/9/64, can be represented in this code by two words, each 36 bits, as illustrated in Fig. 2.10.

Depending on the particular machine involved, word lengths are either fixed or variable. A computer of the IBM 1620 type is a notable example of computers using such variable word lengths.

BIBLIOGRAPHY

ALT, F. L., *Electronic Digital Computers*. Academic Press, New York, 1958.

ARDEN, B. W., *An Introduction to Digital Computing*. Addison-Wesley, Reading, Mass., 1963.

BUCKHOLZ, W., *Planning a Computer System . . . Project Stretch*. McGraw-Hill, New York, 1962.

ENGINEERING RESEARCH ASSOCIATES, W. W. STIFLER, JR., Ed., *High-Speed Computing Devices*. McGraw-Hill, New York, 1950.

HARTREE, D. R., *Calculating Instruments and Machines*. University of Illinois Press, Urbana, 1949.

HUSKEY, H. D., and G. A. KORN, *Computer Handbook*. McGraw-Hill. New York, 1962.

LIVESLAY, R. K., *An Introduction to Automatic Digital Computers*, 2nd ed. University Press, Cambridge, England, 1960.

McCORMICK, E. M., *Digital Computer Primer*. McGraw-Hill, New York, 1959.

OAKFORD, R. V., *Introduction to Electronic Data Processing Equipment*. McGraw-Hill, New York, 1962.

PHISTER, M., JR., *Logical Design of Digital Computers*. John Wiley and Sons, New York, 1958.

CHAPTER 3

LOGICAL
FLOW CHARTING

3.1 THE SOLUTION OF A SCIENTIFIC OR ENGINEERING PROBLEM ON COMPUTERS

The steps involved in solving a scientific or engineering problem by high-speed digital computers include:

1. Converting the physical system to an idealized mathematical model, and, according to this model, formulating the mathematical equations.

2. Selecting a numerical procedure suitable for a digital computer. (Numerical methods are discussed in PART II.)

3. Drawing a detailed flow chart, i.e., a graphical representation of a sequence of operations, such as "read, compute, compare, write, etc."

4. Based on the flow chart, writing these operations in a language which a specific machine will recognize and accept. The process of writing computer instructions is called "coding."

5. Making a "test run" on the computer. If the machine yields the incorrect answers, or if the machine operates in a manner not planned in the program (such as a permanent loop), the coding should be checked or "debugged."

6. The corrected coding can be used at any time to make a "production run."

If the mathematical model is found to be a poor selection, one should then repeat step 1 after step 5 a few times, until a better model is found.

3.2 FLOW CHART

As mentioned in the previous section, a flow chart is a graphic representation of the course of solution to a given problem. It provides an overall picture of the algebraic and logical processes. The completion of a detailed flow chart is important since coding systems have not yet been standardized, although much effort has been

15

made toward the formulation of a universal algebraic computer language acceptable to all computers. Even if such a language were available, the flow chart would still be a desirable way of representing the procedure for solving a problem. In discussing a complicated program, a flow chart is practically indispensable.

Before presenting a simple example of a flow chart, let us recall that digital computers are at best capable of executing three types of instructions.

The first type is the transfer of data. This type is exemplified by such instructions as "store the content of location 1520 into location 324," "read the constant C_1 into its proper storage location, 1079," and "write out the result which is stored presently in the location 1622."

The second type is arithmetic operations. For example, a machine is capable of performing the following operations: $(A + B \cdot C)/(D - C) \cdot A$.

The third type of machine operation is making logical decisions. For example: Let the answer obtained at a point of computation be A. Then, depending on whether A is positive or negative, the subsequent computations will take one of two entirely different paths.

We shall now illustrate flow charting by a simple example. It is required to evaluate the following polynomial:

$$x = \sum_{i=0}^{8} c_i y^i,$$

where c_i ($i = 0, 1, \ldots, 8$) are known constants. We arbitrarily require that the summation will be made starting from the first term, that is, $c_0 y^0$.

The problem, as solved with a computer, may consist of the following steps:

1. Read in all known values, $c_0, c_1, \ldots, c_8$, and y (transfer of data).
2. Set $x = 0$; that is, store zero in the location for x (transfer of data).
3. Set $i = 0$; that is, store the constant 0 in the location for i (transfer of data).
4. Compute $x_i = c_i y^i$. Note that x_i has its own location (arithmetic operation).
5. Add x and x_i; store the sum in the location for x. This automatically erases the old value of x (arithmetic operation).
6. Increase i by 1 (arithmetic operation).
7. Check whether the present value i is equal to 9 (making a logical decision). If it is not equal to 9, go to step 4 and continue; if i is equal to 9, the required answer, x, has been obtained. The i-value has taken on the ten values $0, 1, \ldots, 9$, but the last one was not used. So we have been through the loop nine times. Print out this answer and then stop the machine.

Figure 3.1 shows the corresponding flow chart for the example. It is seen that a rectangular box is used in connection with an arithmetic operation, while an oval is used to indicate a logical decision or a branch instruction. Furthermore, arrows are used in two different senses; one serves to indicate the direction of computer operation; the other (used *inside* a rectangular box) serves to express "replaced by." For example, in Fig. 3.1,

$$\boxed{x \leftarrow 0}$$

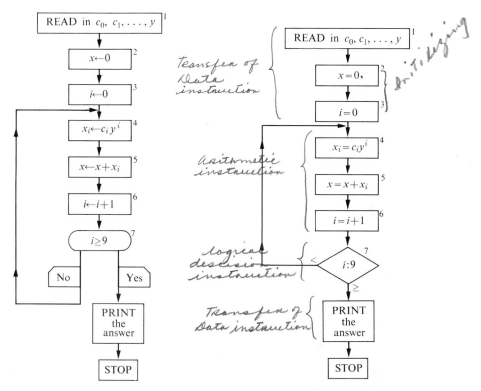

Fig. 3.1. Flow chart for computing
$x = \sum_{i=0}^{8} c_i y^i$.

Fig. 3.2. Another version of a flow
chart for computing $x = \sum_{i=0}^{8} c_i y^i$.

means that the content of x is replaced by zero. Similarly, the step

$$x \leftarrow x + x_i$$

means that the content of x is replaced by the result of the addition of the content of x to that of x_i. It is important to note that this step is often expressed in a flow chart as $x = x + x_i$. The equals sign, as used here, must be interpreted as "replaced by," not as "equal to."

In Fig. 3.1, step 7 is sometimes expressed in the following way:

Step 7 is important in that advantage has been taken of the computer's ability to make a logical decision by comparing one quantity with another. Based on this comparison, there are two possible paths of subsequent operations, and the two arrows coming out of the diamond (or oval) serve to indicate these two possibilities.

Figure 3.2 shows another version of the flow chart given in Fig. 3.1.

3.3 LOOP

In the previous section, a sample flow chart was discussed to evaluate the following polynomial:

$$x = \sum_{i=0}^{8} c_i y^i.$$

Steps 4 through 7 are said to be in a loop since the computation will follow the sequence of steps 4, 5, 6, 7, 4, 5, 6, 7, 4, . . . as long as the condition $i < 9$ is satisfied. (There is a total of 36 steps.) Hence a loop is a repetition of a group of instructions in a program.

A fundamental property of digital computers is their ability to repeat a group of instructions at high speed. A loop in a flow chart serves to reflect this important characteristic. It is very infrequent that a flow chart does not contain one or more loops. Many flow charts even have loops within a loop; this idea will be discussed in the next section.

Returning to Fig. 3.2, we note that we set $x = 0$ and $i = 0$ before executing the loop. This line of reasoning is clear if we examine our procedure closely. In block 6, for example, each i is determined by the one preceding it; however, in the first pass through the loop, the computer needs an initial value of i to work with. It is thus seen that i must be defined (initialized) before the loop is entered, and the equation with which we are working demands that the first value of i be zero. The reasoning here is similar to that used in summations. Thus

$$\sum_{i=0}^{m} x_i \quad \text{and} \quad \sum_{i=1}^{m} x_i$$

have different meanings, and hence the initial value for i must be defined. Similarly, each value for x is defined in terms of the x preceding it, and therefore the initial value of x must be defined as in step 2.

Referring again to Fig. 3.2, we find that step 6 is used to update the quantity i, and hence this step is called updating or incrementing.

So far we have discussed a possible flow chart for evaluating the polynomial

$$x = \sum_{i=0}^{N} c_i y^i,$$

where $N = 8$.

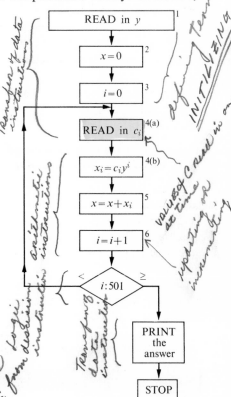

Fig. 3.3. Flow chart for computing $x = \sum_{i=0}^{500} c_i y^i$.

We shall now consider the case for $N = 500$. Making a change in step 7 (Fig. 3.2) of

$$\boxed{i : 9}$$

to

$$\boxed{i : 501}$$

would certainly meet the need. But by doing so, we are required to read in the 501 constants for c_i and the one value for y. This may not be desirable if the storage of a given computer is limited to, say, only 500 locations. To avoid this difficulty, one must not read in all known values $c_0, c_1, \ldots, c_{500}$, and y in the first step. Figure 3.3 shows a possible flow chart for computing the sum of the 501 terms. It is noted that, in the first step, the y-value alone is read in. Furthermore, a new step, 4(a), is inserted at the beginning of the loop to read in the c_i-values. Thus we need only one storage location for the c_i instead of 501.

In the above discussion, the coefficients c_i are assumed to take on random values. If, on the other hand, they follow a certain pattern, it is desirable to *generate* these 501 constants and to avoid reading in a large amount of data. For example, if

$$c_i = i^{1/2}, \qquad i = 0, 1, 2, \ldots, 250,$$

$$c_i = 3i^2, \qquad i = 251, 252, \ldots, 500,$$

then the c_i can be generated as shown in Fig. 3.4. Generating numbers in a computer is an arithmetic operation. It is faster than reading in numbers, which is a data transfer operation.

3.4 LOOP WITHIN A LOOP

In the flow chart shown in Fig. 3.4 it was assumed that the value for y was a single constant. Suppose now that we had to repeat the process for n different values of y. One method of solving the problem is to run the program n times, but an easier solution is given in Fig. 3.5. Here we expand the flow chart shown in Fig. 3.4 so that the necessary steps for the evaluation of the polynomial are executed n times, with different values of y. This illustrates the concept of a loop within a loop. A possible extension to three or more loops is obvious.

As a second example for a loop within a loop we shall consider a problem in the strength of materials. Let us draw a flow chart for computing the deflections of the simply supported beam shown in Fig. 3.6. The beam is divided into eight equal segments. We denote by Δ_{ij} the deflection of the beam at station i due to a concentrated load P applied at point j. Thus the deflection Δ_{53}, shown in Fig. 3.6(b), represents the deflection at station 5 due to a load P acting at station 3. Since both i and j range from 1 to 7, it is clear that a total of 49 deflections are to be computed. The problem is to draw a simple flow chart, using loops, for computing the 49 deflections of the 7 different stations.

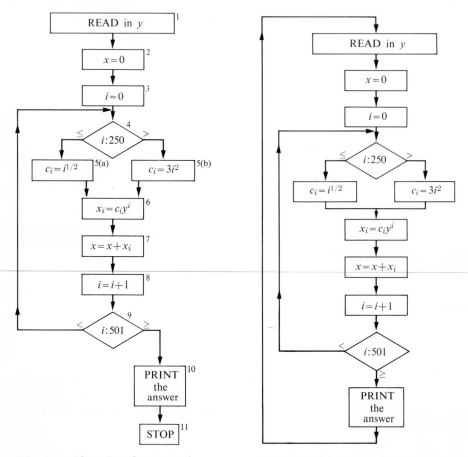

Fig. 3.4. Flow chart for computing $x = \sum_{i=0}^{500} c_i y^i$:

$c_i = \sqrt{i}, \quad 0 \le i \le 250;$
$c_i = 3i^2, \quad 251 \le i \le 500.$

Fig. 3.5. Flow chart for computing $x = \sum_{i=0}^{500} c_i y^i$ for several y-values:

$c_i = \sqrt{i}, \quad 0 \le i \le 250;$
$c_i = 3i^2, \quad 251 \le i \le 500.$

The equations for deflection can be found in standard books on strength of materials.† They are

$$\text{for } x \le a: \quad \Delta = \frac{P}{EI}\frac{bx}{6L}(L^2 - b^2 - x^2), \tag{3.1}$$

$$\text{for } x \ge a: \quad \Delta = \frac{P}{EI}\frac{bx}{6L}(L^2 - b^2 - x^2) + \frac{P(x-a)^3}{6EI}, \tag{3.2}$$

where

$$a = \frac{jL}{8}, \quad b = L - \frac{jL}{8}, \quad x = \frac{iL}{8}.$$

---

† For example, see TIMOSHENKO, S., *Elements of Strength of Materials*, 4th ed. Van Nostrand, Princeton, N. J., 1962, p. 201.

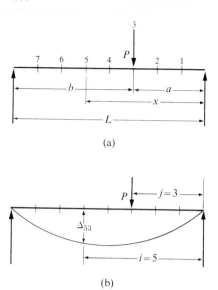

Fig. 3.6. Deflection of a beam due to load P.

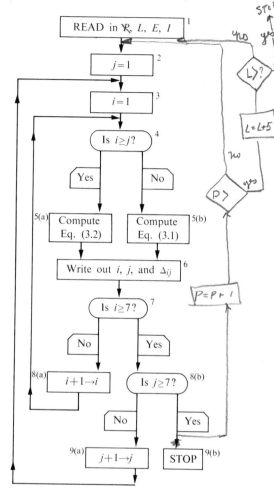

Fig. 3.7. Flow chart for beam deflection.

Figure 3.7 shows a sample flow chart. We observe that it has a loop within a loop; the inner loop principally controls the i's while the outer one controls the j's.

We shall now discuss this flow chart in detail. Step 1 is concerned with the reading in of the four constants (transfer of data). Steps 2 and 3 are for initialization (transfer of data). Step 4 makes a logical decision. If the load is on the right side of the point for which the deflection is sought, $i > j$, then we can go to step 5(a) and compute the deflection based on Eq. (3.2). If the load is on the left side of the point being considered, $i < j$, then we follow step 5(b) and compute the deflection, Eq. (3.1). The third, and last, possibility is that $i = j$, or that the deflection at the loading point is required. The use of either Eq. (3.1) or Eq. (3.2) should yield the same answer. However, the path in a flow chart has to be definite and specific. Hence, we arbitrarily assign Eq. (3.2) for $i=j$. Steps 5(a) and (b) are arithmetic operations. Step 6 causes the answer Δ_{ij} to be written out together with the identifying numbers i and j. It is clear that the first answer is Δ_{11}.

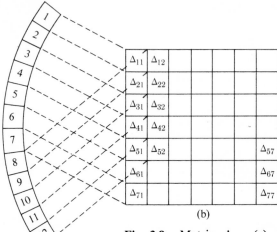

Fig. 3.8. Matrix Δ_{ij}. (a) Order of output. (b) Square matrix.

Steps 4 through 6 are the core of the flow chart. Steps 7 through 9 are concerned with comparing and updating. To complete the discussion, it should be mentioned that the sequence of answers is in the order shown in Fig. 3.8.

An array of numbers such as that shown in Fig. 3.8(b) is called a matrix. For a unit load ($P = 1$), this matrix is called the "flexibility matrix." It plays an important role in analysis of structures.

BIBLIOGRAPHY

GOLDSTINE, H. H., and J. VON NEUMANN, *Planning and Coding of Problems for an Electronic Computing Instrument* (mimeographed reports). Institute for Advanced Study, Princeton, N. J., 1946.

INTERNATIONAL BUSINESS MACHINES CORP. "Flow Charting and Block Diagramming Techniques," *Form* C20–8008–0, IBM, New York, 1961.

PROBLEMS

1. In Fig. 3.1 the sum was obtained from $i = 0$ to $i = 8$. Draw a flow chart to obtain the sum $x = \sum_{i=0}^{8} c_i y^i$, working from $i = 8, 7, 6, \ldots, 0$.

2. The sum $x = \sum_{i=1}^{4} c_i y^i$ can be obtained by the following computer-oriented algorithm:

$$x = y\{c_1 + y[c_2 + y(c_3 + yc_4)]\}.$$

The computation is done from the inside out, or from yc_4. Draw a flow chart for this procedure.

3. Draw a flow chart to compute

$$c = \sum_{k=1}^{62} A_k B_k.$$

It is known that

$$A_k = k \cos k, \qquad k \le 30,$$
$$= k^2 \sin k, \qquad k > 30,$$
$$B_k = e^k.$$

4. Draw a flow chart to compute the number e, using the formula

$$e = \sum_{n=0}^{\infty} (1/n!).$$

Terminate the process when $1/n! < 10^{-8}$.

5. Draw a flow chart to compute the hyperbolic tangent, using the following continued fraction approximation:

For $x < 0$, $\tan hx = - \tan h|x|$;

for $|x| \le 0.00034$, $\tan hx = x$;

for $0.00034 < |x| < 0.17$, $\tan hx = f\{A + f^2[B + C(D + f^2)^{-1}]\}^{-1}$,

where

$$f = 4x \log_2 e, \qquad A = 5.7707801636, \qquad B = 0.0173286795,$$
$$C = 14.1384114018, \qquad D = 349.6699888;$$

for $0.17 \le |x| \le 11.14112$, $\tan hx = \dfrac{e^x - e^{-x}}{e^x + e^{-x}}$;   for $|x| > 11.14112$, $\tan hx = 1$.

6. Draw a flow chart to read in many sets of three unequal positive numbers x, y, and z. If any one of the three numbers in a set is equal to or greater than 77, multiply x by $\tan 16°$ and print it. If all three numbers are less than 77, multiply y by $\cot 16°$ and print the new y. Stop the operation if x is a negative number.

7. Draw a flow chart to obtain the term grade average of K students, each taking N courses, with varying credits $c_1, c_2, \ldots, c_N$. Each course has a positive (nonzero) identification number $I_1, I_2, \ldots, I_m$. Compute also the percentage of students having a final-term grade average higher than 75.

8. Draw a flow chart to obtain factorials 1 through K and their sum.

9. Draw a flow chart to read in a set of x_i, y_i, z_k for $i = 1, 2, \ldots, 7$ and $k = 1, 2, \ldots, 6$, and compute

$$p = \left(\sum_{i=1}^{7} v_i \right) \left(\sum_{k=1}^{6} z_k \right),$$

where

$$v_i = x_i y_i \cos (\pi/8), \qquad \text{if} \qquad |x_i| > |y_i|,$$
$$= x_i y_i \sin (\pi/8), \qquad \text{if} \qquad |x_i| < |y_i|,$$
$$= 0, \qquad \text{if} \qquad |x_i| = |y_i|.$$

Stop the operation when $z_k \ge 10^5$.

10. Write a detailed flow chart to compute the product

continual product. $\longrightarrow$ $\displaystyle\prod_{i=1}^{8} c_i x \cos ix,$

where the values of x and the c_i's are read in as constants.

11. Write a flow chart to evaluate the expression

$$\sum_{j=0}^{5} \left(c_j x \prod_{i=0}^{7} x \cos ix \right).$$

Assume that the values of x and c_j are read in at the beginning of the program.

12. Write a flow chart to evaluate the following double summation:

$$\sum_{i=1}^{10} y_i \left(\sum_{j=1}^{15} c_j x_i^j \right),$$

where $y_i = 4i^3$, $c_j = (-3)^j + 2^j$, and $x_i = 2i$.

$$\prod_{i=1}^{8} c_i x \cos ix = c_1 x \cos 1x \cdot c_2 x \cos 2x \cdot c_9 x \cos 3x \cdots \cdots c_8 x \cos 8x$$

CHAPTER 4

FLOATING-POINT
METHOD

4.1 THE HANDLING OF DECIMALS

While it is not difficult to keep track of the decimal point in a number by using pencil and paper, the handling of decimal points by a computer does not appear to be a simple matter. We recall from Section 2.4 that any number, as stored in a digital computer, is simply a string of either binary or decimal digits. There is no explicit indication as to where a decimal point may be. This chapter deals with the techniques of locating the decimal point of a number in a computer. *Locating decimal pt in a computer*

Two techniques are available: the fixed-point method and the floating-point method. The latter method is a convenience and is widely used in scientific and engineering applications. The principal points vary in magnitude and number of significant places. Before we discuss the floating-point method, we should briefly describe the fixed-point method. In this method the programmer must be concerned *FIXED PT* with two things: (a) when adding or subtracting two numbers, he is responsible for aligning the decimal points, and (b) for multiplication or division, he is responsible for keeping track of the location of the decimal point in the answer.

To fulfill these two requirements, a scale factor is commonly used. We define the scale factor, S, of a fractional number by the expression

$$N = 10^S \cdot n,$$

where N is the fractional number in consideration, n is the integer as it appeared in a storage location, and S is the scale factor, either a positive or a negative integer.

Consider, for example, a number $N = 31.4159$ as it appears in the storage location of a decimal computer, assuming that the fixed word length is 10 digits. There are many possible expressions for n, such as 3141590000, 0314159000, or 0031415900, etc.

25

If we take $n = 3141590000$ and choose to place an imaginary decimal point at the leftmost position, then the scale factor S is equal to 2, as

$$N = 10^S \times n \quad \text{or} \quad 31.4159 = (10)^2 \times 0.3141590000.$$

Although the concept of a scale factor is not difficult, in application it is tedious and conducive to errors. The ideal thing to do is to have the computer keep track of the decimal points. This will be discussed in the following two sections.

4.2   FLOATING-POINT NUMBERS

The computer keeps track of the information on decimal point location.

Engineers and scientists often encounter numbers which vary widely in magnitude. Their literature reveals representative examples such as

(1) Young's modulus of steel $= E = 30 \times 10^6$ pounds per square inch, and

(2) The coefficient of thermal expansion of copper $= \alpha = 9.2 \times 10^{-6}$.

If we rewrite the values E and α in the forms

$$E = 0.3 \times 10^8 \text{ psi}$$

and

$$\alpha = 0.92 \times 10^{-5},$$

then they become floating-point numbers. A floating-point number has two parts: an exponent and a fraction. Although a misnomer, the fractional part is often referred to as "mantissa." In the above example for E, the exponent was 8 and the fractional part was 3. Similarly, for α the exponent was -5 and the fractional part was 92.

In general, a floating-point number N has the following form:

$$N = M \cdot \beta^k,$$

NOTE

where $\beta = 2$ for binary computers,

$\beta = 10$ for decimal computers,

$k =$ the exponent, an integer, and

fractional part of the floating-point number

$M =$ the mantissa, a value which must lie between $+1$ and -1.

Example

Consider the number: $N = -19.2 \times 10^{-8}$.

If this number is rewritten as $N = -0.192 \times 10^{-6}$, then the exponent is equal to -6, an integer, the mantissa is equal to -0.192, and it lies between $+1$ and -1. Thus it meets the requirements of the general form of floating-point numbers.

It should be noted that in its original form, the value -19.2 lay outside the permissible range of M.

In addition to the above range limitation, $-1 < M < 1$, if the value M also satisfies one of the following two conditions:

$$\frac{1}{\beta} \leq |M| < 1 \quad \text{or} \quad M = 0,$$

we can then say that $N = M \cdot \beta^k$ is a *normalized* floating-point number.

Consider, for example, the difference between the following two floating-point numbers:

$$\begin{aligned}
0.27143247 &\times 10^7 \\
-0.27072236 &\times 10^7 \\
\hline
0.00071011 &\times 10^7
\end{aligned}$$

Here, the difference itself is a floating-point number, but not a *normalized* floating-point number due to the presence of the three leading zeros. However, if one shifts the fractional part three places to the left, the resulting 0.71011×10^4 fulfills the requirements of a *normalized* floating-point number.

Having explained the meanings of both a floating-point number and a normalized floating-point number, we ask an important question: what does a floating-point number look like in a memory location?

For the sake of definiteness, let us first take a *decimal* computer with a 10-digit word length and assume that the number in consideration is -0.000031415926. The floating-point notation of this number is $-0.31415926 \times 10^{-4}$. In order to avoid the negative exponent, we *arbitrarily* add 50 to the exponent and the number now becomes $-0.31415926 \times 10^{-4+50}$, or $-0.31415926 \times 10^{46}$. We often call this adjusted exponent, 46, the *characteristic*.

This number can be uniquely represented in a memory location in a form of 10 digits plus a sign, assuming that 8 digits are used for the mantissa.

It should be noted that this method of representation fails for both very large and very small numbers. The characteristic e of a floating-point number is clearly limited by the following expressions: $-50 \leq e \leq 49$. The number in consideration has at best 8-digit accuracy.

The arbitrary number added to avoid a negative exponent may differ according to particular coding systems utilized. The characteristic, always a positive number, may also be placed in front of the mantissa. Coding systems will be discussed later in Chapter 5.

In a similar manner, a floating-point number may also be stored in the memory location of a binary computer. Consider the IBM 7090 computers. A word stored in a computer of this type has a "sign" bit and 35 regular bits. A floating-point number may be represented in the following form:

0	1 2 3 4 5 6 7 8	9 . . . 35
Sign	Binary characteristic	Binary mantissa (binary normalized fraction)

$$\text{Characteristic} = 128 + \text{exponent}$$
$$\text{Sign} \qquad = \text{sign of fraction}$$

The binary characteristics represent powers from 2^{-128} to 2^{+127}. These correspond approximately to 10^{-38} to 10^{+38}. The remaining 27 bits are occupied by the binary normalized fraction, or mantissa. This is equivalent to a little more than 8 decimal digits.

4.3   FLOATING-POINT ARITHMETIC

In the previous section the representation of a floating-point number in a typical decimal computer was discussed. We shall now consider basic arithmetic operations performed with two floating-point numbers, concerning ourselves with a decimal computer having a 10-digit word length. Similar principles are used in a binary computer.

When adding or subtracting two numbers, the computer is instructed first to compare the two adjusted exponents of the given numbers. The four following cases are possible:

(a) When the exponents are equal, mantissa parts are added and the adjusted exponent is kept. For example:

$$\begin{array}{r} 3\ 1\ 4\ 1\ 5\ 9\ 2\ 6\ 5\ 1 \\ +1\ 2\ 3\ 4\ 5\ 6\ 7\ 8\ 5\ 1 \\ \hline 4\ 3\ 7\ 6\ 1\ 6\ 0\ 4\ 5\ 1 \end{array}$$

Adjusted exponent

(b) In the above example, there is neither an overflow, nor a carry from the first digit of the mantissa parts. When overflow appears as shown in the following example,

$$\begin{array}{r} 3\ 1\ 4\ 1\ 5\ 9\ 2\ 6\ 5\ 1 \\ +9\ 8\ 7\ 6\ 5\ 4\ 3\ 2\ 5\ 1 \\ \hline (1)\ 3\ 0\ 1\ 8\ 1\ 3\ 5\ 8\ 5\ 1 \end{array}$$

Overflow   Adjusted exponent (or characteristic)

both given numbers will be shifted one place to the right and then added:

$$\begin{array}{r} 0\ 3\ 1\ 4\ 1\ 5\ 9\ 2\ 5\ 2 \\ +0\ 9\ 8\ 7\ 6\ 5\ 4\ 3\ 5\ 2 \\ \hline 1\ 3\ 0\ 1\ 8\ 1\ 3\ 5\ 5\ 2 \end{array}$$

Adjusted exponent

(c) When the exponents are not equal, the computer is instructed to keep the larger exponent and to convert the smaller exponent. For example:

$$
\begin{array}{r}
3\ 1\ 4\ 1\ 5\ 9\ 2\ 6\ 5\ 1 \longrightarrow \quad 3\ 1\ 4\ 1\ 5\ 9\ 2\ 6\ 5\ 1 \\
+1\ 2\ 3\ 4\ 5\ 6\ 7\ 8\ 5\ 0 \longrightarrow +0\ 1\ 2\ 3\ 4\ 5\ 6\ 7\ 5\ 1 \\
\hline
?\qquad\qquad\quad\ 3\ 2\ 6\ 5\ 0\ 4\ 9\ 3\ 5\ 1
\end{array}
$$

(d) If a leading zero (or zeros) appears in the answer, the computer is instructed to normalize the result.

In multiplication, the exponential part and the mantissa part are considered separately. For example:

$$
\begin{array}{r}
3\ 1\ 4\ 1\ 5\ 9\ 2\ 6\ 5\ 1 \\
\times 1\ 2\ 3\ 4\ 5\ 6\ 7\ 8\ 5\ 4 \\
\hline
?
\end{array}
$$

The mantissa part $= 0.31415926 \times 0.12345678 = 0.0387850906467828$.

The exponential part $= 51 + 54 - 50 = 55$.

After normalization, the answer becomes 3878509054.

We see from the above discussions that floating-point arithmetic, as automatically performed by computers, greatly simplifies the scaling problem. Moreover, in this system all numbers have the same number of significant digits.

It is interesting to note that many computers have built-in components capable of carrying out floating-point arithmetic. By and large, however, most commercial computers are fixed-point for reasons of economy. In this type of computer, a suitable program or subroutine is needed to carry out the floating-point arithmetic. Practically all scientific and engineering problems are solved on computers by using the floating-point system.

BIBLIOGRAPHY

WILKES, M. V., "The Use of a Floating-Address System for Orders in an Automatic Digital Computer," *Proc. Cambridge Phil. Soc.*, **49,** pp. 84–89 (1953).

PROBLEMS

1. Rewrite the following numbers in the general form of floating-point numbers such that the mantissa part lies between 1 and -1.

   (a) 2.7135   (b) -37.214 (c) 12×10^6 (d) 3.1627×10^{-2}

2. What is the value of the exponent in each of the floating-point numbers in Problem 1? What is the adjusted exponent in each case if we arbitrarily add 49 to the original exponent?

3. Using floating-point arithmetic, subtract the following two-number sets:
   (a) 3.141592 and 2.7135   (b) 3.141592 and 12.7135
   (c) 27.14 and 0.374   (d) 3.14×10^{-6} and 2.7×10^{-2}

4. Use floating-point arithmetic to multiply the following two-number sets:
   (a) 6.24×7.28 (b) 16.31×7.15

5. Normalize the following floating-point numbers:
   (a) 0.0214×10^{-6} (b) 12.01×10^{4}

CHAPTER 5

CODING SYSTEMS
FOR DIGITAL COMPUTERS

5.1 INTRODUCTION

Digital computers do not accept or operate from the flow charts discussed in Chapter 3. To convert flow charts into a language which a particular computer will recognize and accept is commonly called "coding."

Basically, each type of computer accepts only one particular language for computation—its own machine language. The general trend is to code in a language (source language) akin to our written language, and then utilize the computer to translate this language into the machine's language (target or object language). The computer then follows the commands in its own machine language and dutifully performs the necessary computations. It should be noted in this connection that computers are used for dual purposes: translation and computation. The human labor previously spent in coding the rather involved machine languages or machinelike languages is actually being saved at the expense of computer processing time.

There are a number of reasons why programming in machine languages or machine-like languages can be both time consuming and expensive: (1) human language has little in common with machine language, yet a programmer must somehow create a perfect set of machine instructions, completely without error; (2) it is often difficult to find and correct errors in a complex program; (3) it may take as much as a year to train a programmer to be really effective; (4) once trained, he will still have to be taught the intimate details of a complex problem; and (5) small changes in the definition of a problem can require extensive changes in the program, and changes in problem definition are quite common, especially in business data processing.

In an attempt to overcome these difficulties, manufacturers and users of computers have devoted much effort in a search for ways to shift the burden of programming from humans to computers. Their work has led to the development of "compilers"; a compiler is essentially a set of computer programs that directs the computer to translate procedure-oriented language into machine-oriented language. Thus, under the guidance of a compiler, a computer will translate a problem described in a simplified version of human language into a set of instructions that can later be executed by the machine. A brief statement in problem-oriented language can usually be translated into a lengthy set of computer instructions.

There are two basic classes of procedure-oriented language for which compilers have been developed: mathematical and nonmathematical (business). Mathematical compilers use mathematical notation to express scientific and engineering problems; a simple statement might look like this:

$$Y = (W + S + T) * (P - Q)/X$$

Mathematical compilers have achieved fairly widespread acceptance and success because mathematical notation is logical and precise. FORTRAN and ALGOL are the most widely accepted; it is probably correct to say that most scientific programs today are being written in these languages.

COBOL is probably the most widely accepted nonmathematical (business) compiler language; a typical COBOL statement looks like this:

```
If MONTHLY FICA less than 16.00 go to SPECIAL FICA:
otherwise add MONTHLY FICA to ANNUAL FICA.
```

In the following section we shall limit our discussion to FORTRAN compiler language. FORTRAN is an abbreviation for *Formula Translation* language.

5.2 FORMULA TRANSLATION LANGUAGE—FORTRAN SYSTEM

The FORTRAN language† is most easily described by presenting some concrete examples.

Example 5.1

Let X_1 and X_2 be the two roots‡ of the quadratic equation $aX^2 + bX + c = 0$, where $X_1 \geq X_2$.

It is desired to compute the unknowns D and E, where $D = X_1 \cos 15°$ and $E = X_2 \sin 15°$ for the four cases listed in the table below.

	Case I	Case II	Case III	Case IV
a	1.0	−22.41	23.12	−3.1415926
b	−3.0	−60.22	−3.14159	11.3232323
c	1.0	1.15	−22.14	0.2134567

---

† In the remainder of this chapter we will be limited to the 1620 FORTRAN II system.
‡ The discussion is limited to the real roots, assuming that $b^2 - 4ac$ is nonnegative.

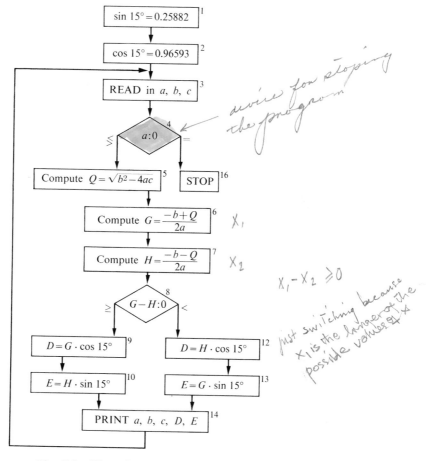

Fig. 5.1. Flow chart for Example 5.1.

We need to draw a detailed flow chart for the machine computation and write a FORTRAN program that will compute D and E, with each answer showing the values of D, E, a, b, and c.

Solution: One possible flow chart is shown in Fig. 5.1; this chart needs little explanation other than some comments on step 4, which is used to determine whether the required computations have been finished by feeding in a fifth set of data a, b, c. In this last set, the value a is deliberately taken as zero. When these data are tested for zero, either step 5 or step 16 will be followed.

Questions may arise as to how the trigonometric functions in steps 1 and 2 are obtained. In this case, where we only have two function values, it is simpler to obtain them from a mathematical table. However, should a great number of the trigonometric functional values be required in a single program, the computer must be instructed to compute them by means of the available subroutines. This will be discussed more fully later.

The commands as written in the FOR-
TRAN languages are commonly known
as "statements." The FORTRAN statements for our example are shown in Fig.
5.2. We shall now give detailed explana-
tions of all statements in our program
except statements 35 and 145, which will be
treated more fully in the next section. Each
statement will be referred to by its statement number.

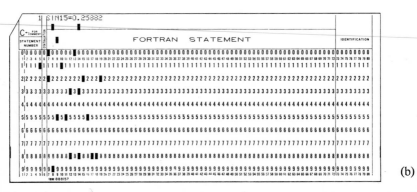

```
 1  SIN15=0.25882
 2  COS15=0.96593
 3  READ 35,A,B,C
35  FORMAT(F10.4,F10.4,F10.4)
 4  IF(A)5,16,5
 5  Q=SQRTF(B*B-4.*A*C)
 6  G=(-B+Q)/(2.*A)
 7  H=(-B-Q)/(2.*A)
 8  IF(G-H) 12,9,9
 9  D=G*COS15
10  E=H*SIN15
11  GO TO 14
12  D=H*COS15
13  E=G*SIN15
14  PRINT145,D,E,A,B,C
145 FORMAT(5F10.4)
15  GO TO 3
16  STOP
17  END
```
                                                                                      (a)

Fig. 5.2. (a) A FORTRAN program for Example 5.1. (b) FORTRAN statement card
showing statement 1.

Statement 1. This statement serves to store the floating-point number in a specific
storage location arbitrarily named SIN15. The automatic conversion of data to a
floating-point number is triggered by the presence of the decimal point in the datum
0.25882. In the FORTRAN system, any number with a decimal point is by necessity
a floating-point number. The naming of a floating-point variable is very flexible, but
it must conform with the following two conditions:

(1) The name must have 6 or less letters or numbers (for example, SIN15, A3, . . .).
(2) The name must begin with alphabetic letters other than I, J, K, L, M, or N.

These six letters are reserved for identifying fixed-point variables. These will be
discussed later since there are no fixed-point variables involved in this particular
program.

Statement 2. This statement transfers a floating-point number into a specific storage
location arbitrarily named COS15.

Statement 3. This is a "read-in" statement asking the computer to read in three floating-point variables from the data card. These three numbers will be stored in three reserved locations for subsequent use. The stored floating-point numbers will be replaced only after the second data card is read in (refer to statement 15 and the related loop). In this program the letters A, B, and C refer to the coefficients a, b, and c in the quadratic equation $aX^2 + bX + c = 0$.

It should be noted that there is always a comma required after the number specifying the format location, which in this statement is the number 35. Any number not already used in the program could have replaced the number 35, so long as the address in front of the format statement would correspond to it.

Statement 4. The computer is asked to make a decision as to whether or not the value of a is zero. This operation is accomplished by use of an IF statement. In this statement, if the value of a is less than zero, then the computer is instructed to go to the first statement number following the parenthesis (in this case, statement 5). If a is zero, the computer is directed to proceed to the second number after the parenthesis, or statement 16. If a is larger than zero, however, the computer is instructed to proceed to the third number or statement 5. Note that there must be *no* comma after the word IF in this statement.

Statement 5. This statement commands the computer to perform the operation of computing the term $\sqrt{b^2 - 4ac}$ and store the quantity in the location Q. The asterisk * indicates that a multiplication operation is to be performed, and the decimal point following the number 4 automatically converts this number into a floating-point form, as already discussed in connection with statement 1. It should be noted that A, B, and C are three floating-point variables, and that it is improper to drop the decimal point after 4. In other words, fixed-point values should never be mixed with floating-point terms in a statement of straight computation.† A square-root subroutine designated by SQRTF is called for in this statement. There are many subroutines available in this system, such as SINF for sine function, COSF for cosine function, EXPF for exponential function, etc. A list of many subroutines for the FORTRAN system is shown in Table 5.1. It is seen that a subroutine is designated

TABLE 5.1. Partial list of library subroutines for the 1620 FORTRAN system

Function name	Usual mathematical notation
COSF (A)	$\cos A$
EXPF (A)	e^A
LOGF (A)	$\ln A$
SINF (A)	$\sin A$
ATANF (A)	$\tan^{-1} A$
SQRTF (A)	$\sqrt{A}$

---

† The only exception is in an operation involving a power, for example a^6. In this situation, the power may be either in fixed-point form as in the expression (A ** 6) or in the floating-point form (A ** 6.).

by a standard word (such as SQRT) always followed by the letter "F." We further note that the term or terms to which the subroutine pertains—the argument—must be enclosed in parentheses. Finally, the designation Q stands for a location in which only a floating-point number is present, since the term does not begin with the letters I, J, K, L, M, N. Should one unintentionally write statement 5 as

$$MQ = SQRTF(B * B - 4. * A * C)$$

an incorrect answer will result. The computer will first perform the operation $\sqrt{b^2 - 4ac}$, in which, for example, the result might turn out as 16.2749. It then drops the digits after the decimal point and the result becomes 16. This would then be stored in a location called MQ. Obviously this is not a correct answer.

Statements 6 and 7. Note the decimal point after 2.

Statement 11. This statement informs the computer to skip the next two statements and proceed directly to statement 14.

Statement 14. This is the "print" instruction which tells the machine what values or answers should be printed out on the typewriter and in what order this should be done. In this case, the product of the larger root and cos 15° is the first answer in the output, the product of the smaller root and sin 15°, the second answer, and the coefficients *a*, *b*, and *c*, the third, fourth, and fifth answers, respectively. Thus a complete record of both the variables read in and the corresponding answers obtained is made available. These values are all in floating-point form. The format statement for the PRINT 145 operates in the same manner as the one for the READ 35, except that it tells the computer where to print the variables instead of where to read them.

Statement 15. After the printing of the answers has been completed for this particular set of *a*, *b*, and *c*, the computer proceeds to statement 3 and reads in a new card with a completely new set of variable coefficients. Calculations are then repeated using the new data.

Statement 16. The STOP statement commands the computer to stop all computations.

Statement 17. The END statement is required at the end of every FORTRAN program.

Additional explanation. We shall now discuss the key punching of statement cards for the source program and of data cards.

The statements are punched one to a card (Fig. 5.2) using the following format: The statement itself is punched in a column field occupying columns 7 to 72. Columns 73 through 80 are either left blank or may contain any information which the programmer may want to use for identification purposes, and columns 1 to 5 are reserved for statement numbers. Column 1 is also used for punching C to indicate a comment card. This card will be ignored by the computer during the subsequent translation. Column 6 of the first card of a statement must be left blank. If the statement is longer than 66 characters including blanks, a second, third, or up to six cards may be used

$35 \ FORMAT \ (F10.4, F10.4, F10.4)$
$(3F10.4)$

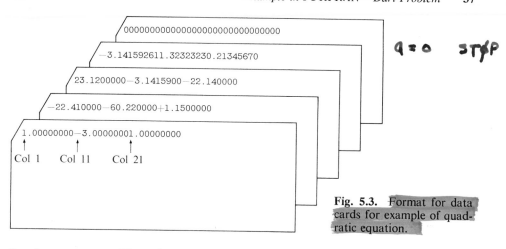

```
000000000000000000000000000000
  -3.141592611.32323230.21345670
 23.1200000-3.1415900-22.140000
-22.410000-60.220000+1.1500000
1.00000000-3.00000001.00000000
  ↑         ↑          ↑
Col 1     Col 11     Col 21
```

$q = 0$ STOP

Fig. 5.3. Format for data cards for example of quadratic equation.

for the statement. These five continuation cards are usually designated by a 1, 2, ..., 5, respectively, punched in column 6.

We now turn to the preparation of data cards. In the above example, the three variables *a*, *b*, and *c* must be punched on the *data card* in the order they will be read in by the READ statement (see Fig. 5.3). In this particular case, statement 35, "FORMAT (F10.4, F10.4, F10.4)," requires that each variable occupy a total of 10 digits. Moreover, 4 digits are expected to be after the decimal point; this is not a rigid requirement, however, since where the decimal point is placed will not affect the input data so long as the number is punched within the first ten columns. Statement 35 can also be written as

$$35 \ FORMAT \ (3F10.4)$$

in FORTRAN II, one of several variations of the FORTRAN language. It is important to note that all 80 columns of cards can be used for data input or output.

5.3 EXAMPLE IN FORTRAN—DART PROBLEM

The purpose of this section is to illustrate the usage of FORMAT and IF statements with a specific example.

A circle in the first quadrant of a coordinate system with axes *x* and *y* has its center at (a, b) and a radius of r: $a = 8.569$, $b = 12.000$, $r = 3.000$. Nine sets of (x, y) are given:

x	y	x	y
2.347	18.176	9.164	13.978
3.291	14.129	11.569	12.000
6.987	11.253	13.875	15.192
7.867	5.967	99999.000	0.000
8.569	9.000		

Use $x \geq 99998.000$ to terminate the problem.

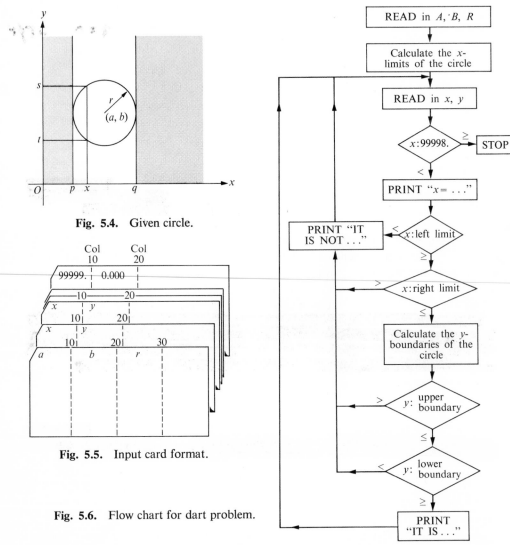

Fig. 5.4. Given circle.

Fig. 5.5. Input card format.

Fig. 5.6. Flow chart for dart problem.

We wish to write a program in FORTRAN to determine which sets of (x, y) will fall within the given circle. If the point falls on the circumference, we assume that it has fallen within the circle.

A possible procedure to solve this problem is (see Fig. 5.4):

(a) Find the left-hand (smallest x) and the right-hand (largest x) limits of the circle. (Note that these are the same in every case.)

(b) Check to see whether the given x falls between or on these two limits, p and q (unshaded region). If not, then it is obvious that the point is not in the circle.

(c) If it falls between or on the two limits p and q, find the two y-values (upper and lower) of the boundary of the circle at the given x. (Note that the two y's are the same if x is equal to either the left-hand or right-hand limits of the circle. Would this cause difficulties?)

```
C                         DART  PROBLEM
      READ  1,  A,  B,  R
    1 FORMAT(F10.3,  F10.3,  F10.3)
      XL = A-R
      XR = A+R
   31 READ  3,  X,  Y
    3 FORMAT(F10.3,  F10.3)
      IF(X-99998.0)4,100,100
    4 PRINT 5,  X,  Y
    5 FORMAT(5H□X□=□,F10.3,10X,5H□Y□=□,F10.3/)
      IF(X-XL)6,8,8
    6 PRINT 7
    7 FORMAT(3X,29H IT   IS   NOT   IN   THE   CIRCLE//)
      GO TO 31
    8 IF(X-XR)9,9,6
    9 YT = B+SQRTF(R*R-(X-A)*(X-A))
      YB = B-SQRTF(R*R-(X-A)*(X-A))
   22 IF(Y-YT)10,10,6
   10 IF(Y-YB)6,11,11
   11 PRINT 12
   12 FORMAT(3X,24H IT   IS   IN   THE   CIRCLE//)
      GO TO 31
  100 STOP
  101 END
  8.569        12.000      3.000
  2.347        18.176
  3.291        14.129
  6.987        11.253
  7.867         5.967
  8.569         9.000
  9.164        13.978
 11.569        12.000
 13.875        15.192
 99999.000  0.000
```

Handwritten annotations: 1 FORMAT (3 F10.3); 3 FORMAT (2 F10.3); indicate blanks.

Fig. 5.7. FORTRAN program for dart problem.

Check to see whether the given y falls between or on the two boundary values s and t. The two y-values, s and t, of the boundary of the circle may be calculated as follows:

The equation of the circle is $(x - a)^2 + (y - b)^2 = r^2$, but we know the value of x. Therefore,

$$(y - b)^2 = r^2 - (x - a)^2, \qquad y = b \pm \sqrt{r^2 - (x - a)^2}$$

or,

$$\overline{os} = b + \sqrt{r^2 - (x - a)^2}, \qquad \overline{ot} = b - \sqrt{r^2 - (x - a)^2}.$$

The required printing format is as follows (a □ indicates that a blank space is to be left):

```
□ □□□ □X□=□000002.347□□□□□□□□□□□□Y□=□000018.176
```

```
        IT IS NOT IN THE CIRCLE
```

or

```
        IT IS IN THE CIRCLE
```

The required input format is F10.3; it is shown in Fig. 5.5. A possible flow chart and a FORTRAN program are presented in Figs. 5.6 and 5.7, respectively.

5.4   EXAMPLE IN FORTRAN—SERIES SUMMATION

In the example of Section 5.2, a loop was accomplished by using the statement GO TO 14 (Fig. 5.2a). We shall present a DO statement and a DIMENSION statement in the following example for a series summation and explain their use in connection with loops.

We desire to obtain the ζ vs. t curve from the expression

$$\zeta = \sum_{N=1}^{M} \frac{(-1)^N}{N} \sin (N\pi X)\left[1 + \frac{A_N}{1 + N^2\psi^2} \cos \left(\frac{2N\pi}{\sqrt{1 + N^2\psi^2}} t\right)\right],$$

where $M \leq 33$.

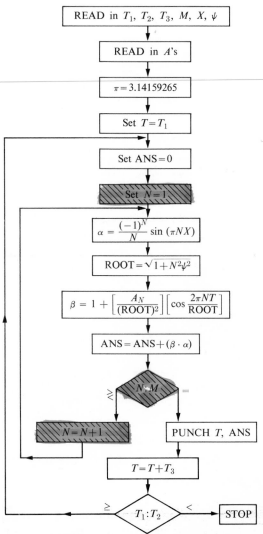

Write a FORTRAN program using $t = T_1$ to $t = T_2$ with interval $\Delta t = T_3$. The values of T_1, T_2, T_3, M, X, and ψ should read in as the first data card. Then read the available values for A_N. The following data should be used for the first production run:

$T_1 = 0.$

$T_2 = 2.$

$T_3 = 0.01$

$M = 30$

$X = 0.500$

$\psi = 1.2051494 \times 10^{-5}$

A_1 through $A_{33} = 1.0$.

Solution: The flow chart and the corresponding FORTRAN program are shown in Figs. 5.8 and 5.9, respectively. The following statements in this program need some explanation:

C   EXAMPLE XI – T CURVE

This is a comment card, indicated by the "C" punched in the first column. The computer will ignore the card throughout the program.

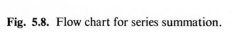
Fig. 5.8. Flow chart for series summation.

```
C        EXAMPLE    XI- T CURVE
         DIMENSION A(33)
         READ 10, T1,T2,T3,M,X,PSI
   10 FORMAT(F10.5,F10.5,F10.5,I10,F10.5,E14.9)
         DO 12 I=1,M
   12 A(I)=1.          reading in values of Aij →A33 ?
         PI=3.14159265
         T=T1                          To get the current value of N into floating point mode.
   17 ANS= 0.
         DO 9 N=1,M
         AN= N        ← To get the current value of N
         ALPHA=(((-1.)**N)/AN)*(SINF(AN*PI*X))
         ROOT= SQRTF(1.+AN*AN*PSI*PSI)
         BETA=1.+(A(N)/ROOT*ROOT)*COSF(2.*PI*AN*T/ROOT)
    9 ANS=ANS+(BETA*ALPHA)
   81 PUNCH 1, T,ANS
         T=T+T3
         IF (T2-T) 15,17,17
    1 FORMAT(3HT= ,F10.5,10X,5HANS= ,F10.5)
   15 STOP
         END
0.00000    2.00000    0.01000           30   0.50000   .12051494E-4
```

Fig. 5.9. FORTRAN program for series summation.

DIMENSION A (33)

This statement instructs the computer to reserve 33 locations in which to store A_1 through A_{33}. This statement is not necessary if there is just a single A-value to be stored. A DIMENSION statement is also required if, in the program, a block of numbers is to be computed and stored.

The DIMENSION statements are also used to reserve a block of locations for an *array* of numbers. For example, if a block of 42 locations is used to store Δ_{ij} (where $i = 1, 2, \ldots, 7$ and $j = 1, 2, \ldots, 6$), then the reservation of these 42 locations is indicated by the statement DIMENSION DELTA (7, 6).

No three-dimensional reservation, for example, DELTA (7, 6, 9), is permitted.

DO 9 N = 1, M

This DO statement is a very powerful one to use for setting up loops. It instructs the computer to follow all the statements down to and including statement 9 for a definite number of times. In this case, it starts with $N = 1$, then $N = 2, 3, \ldots$, and finally, when $N = M$ is completed, the computer will get out of the loop automatically and will execute the next statement, i.e., statement 81. From the flow chart (Fig. 5.8), we see that the three shaded boxes correspond to this single statement. When written in full, this statement is DO 9 N = 1, M, 1. The last number, 1, serves to indicate the increment by which N is increased for each loop. However, if the increment is 1, as in this case, the last number may be left off.

AN = N

The statement serves to convert the fixed-point variable N to a floating-point variable AN. Note that the symbol AN is required in all of the arithmetic statements except as the power of an exponent.

5.5 OUTPUT STATEMENTS FOR A MATRIX PROBLEM

Perhaps one of the most important, yet difficult, topics in FORTRAN programming is handling the class of statements for input and output: READ, PRINT, PUNCH, and FORMAT. This problem becomes more complex when an array of numbers or a matrix is involved. In this section some basic applications of output statements shall be reviewed in order to clarify any difficulties which may have been encountered in Sections 5.2 through 5.4. Then, using the flow chart presented in Fig. 3.7, we shall explain a FORTRAN program to compute the elements in a flexibility matrix. In addition, an improved version of this flow chart will be presented and its related FORTRAN program explained, with emphasis on the matrix output.

Let us review the output statements for single variables by means of the following specific example.

Suppose that a fixed-point variable *I* is equal to 14 and a floating-point variable *A* equals 3.141593. We can write the following two statements to print out *I* and *A*:

```
5   PRINT 6,I, A

6   FORMAT(I3, F10.4)
```

The printout is

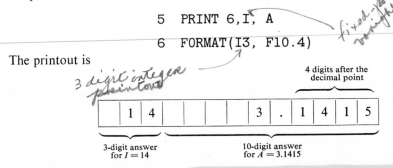

In the above two statements, I in statement 5 stands for a fixed-point variable, while I3 in statement 6 indicates that the answer must be printed out as a three-digit *integer* without a decimal point. The two are completely different in concept.

The FORMAT (statement 6) calls for a total of thirteen spaces for output: three spaces are required by the I3 specification, and the next ten spaces are used for the F10.4 specification. The last digit of I, that is, 4, coincides with the rightmost position in these three spaces. If the value of I were, say, 7, it would be printed out in the rightmost space, preceded by two blank spaces as follows:

The specification F10.4 demands that the next ten spaces will be allotted to the value of A, including the four spaces for the decimal portion of A. Any decimal portion exceeding the FORMAT specification will be discarded and not printed out. Thus, the fifth and sixth decimal digits of A in this example are truncated, since the FORMAT specification allows only the first four digits after the decimal point to be printed.

We now proceed to present a FORTRAN program based on the flow chart shown in Fig. 3.7 to compute the 49 elements in the flexibility matrix. This program (see

```
C     THIS IS THE FORTRAN PROGRAM FOR THE PROBLEM INTRODUCED IN SECTION 3.4
C     FLEXIBILITY MATRIX PROBLEM
C     N = MAXIMUM NUMBER FOR I OR J
      PUNCH 10
10    FORMAT(9X,1HI,9X,1HJ,3X,10HDELTA(I,J)//)
      READ 1,P,ZL,E,AI,N
1     FORMAT(4F10.7,I10)
      ZNP1=N+1
      DIMENSION DELTA(10,10)
      DO 20 I=1,N
      ZI=I
      DO 20 J=1,N
      ZJ=J
      IF(ZI-ZJ)        50,51,51
50    DELTA(I,J)=((P/(E*AI))*(ZL**3)*(1.-ZJ/ZNP1)*ZI/(6.*ZNP1))*(1.-(1.-
     1ZJ/ZNP1)**2-(ZI/ZNP1)**2)
      GO TO 16
51    DELTA(I,J)=((P/(E*AI))*(ZL**3)*(1.-ZJ/ZNP1)*ZI/(6.*ZNP1))*(1.-(1.-
     1ZJ/ZNP1)**2-(ZI/ZNP1)**2)+(P/(E*AI))*ZL*ZL*ZL*(ZI-ZJ)**3/
     2((ZNP1**3)*6.)
16    PUNCH 6,I,J,DELTA(I,J)
6     FORMAT(2I10,F10.4/)
20    CONTINUE
      PUNCH 25
25    FORMAT(8H THE END)
      STOP
      END
```

1.0   1.0   1.0   1.0   7

Fig. 5.10. Flexibility matrix problem.

Fig. 5.10) will read in the given data, namely, P, ZL, E, AI, and N; choose Eqs. (3.1) or (3.2); and finally, print out the values of the 49 elements of the matrix, one value per line. The basic loop in this program is to (a) compute and (b) print out a value of each of the 49 elements in the matrix (see the output in Table 5.2).

We note that a line is left between two consecutive answers. This is accomplished by simply writing a slash in the FORMAT statement (statement 6). In general, k slashes in a FORMAT statement will cause k spaces in the printout if the slashes appear before the first or after the last specification. $N + 1$ consecutive slashes cause N blank lines if the slashes are between two specifications. An example illustrating the use of slashes between the the specifications is given below.

TABLE 5.2. Output from the program of Fig. 5.10

I	J	DELTA(I,J)
1	1	.0039
1	2	.0065
1	3	.0077
1	4	.0076
.	.	.
.	.	.
.	.	.
7	4	.0076
7	5	.0077
7	6	.0065
7	7	.0039

THE END

Example 1

        10   FORMAT(F10.4, F12.4,/F5.2, F12.6)

This FORMAT specification causes the first two variables to be printed on the first line and the second two variables to be printed on the second line.

Example 2

Statements 29 and 30 cause three lines to be skipped:

        29   PRINT 30

        30   FORMAT(///)

Example 3

The following two statements cause the word GOOD to be printed and then three lines to be skipped:

        129   PRINT 130   *Hollerith spec*
                              5H   *skip 3 lines*
        130   FORMAT (5H□GOOD///)

Example 4

The following two statements have the effect that the values of I, J, and the element Δ_{ij} are printed on a single line, and that one line is then skipped:

        16   PRINT 6, I,J,DELTA(I,J)
         6   FORMAT(2I10, F10.4/)

Frequently, the printout of a matrix problem is required to be in matrix form. In other words, the answers are printed out row by row as shown in Fig. 5.11. The

Δ_{11}	Δ_{12}	Δ_{13}	Δ_{14}	Δ_{15}	Δ_{16}	Δ_{17}
Δ_{21}	Δ_{22}	Δ_{23}	Δ_{24}	Δ_{25}	Δ_{26}	Δ_{27}
Δ_{31}	Δ_{32}	Δ_{33}	Δ_{34}	Δ_{35}	Δ_{36}	Δ_{37}
Δ_{41}	Δ_{42}	Δ_{43}	Δ_{44}	Δ_{45}	Δ_{46}	Δ_{47}
Δ_{51}	Δ_{52}	Δ_{53}	Δ_{54}	Δ_{55}	Δ_{56}	Δ_{57}
Δ_{61}	Δ_{62}	Δ_{63}	Δ_{64}	Δ_{65}	Δ_{66}	Δ_{67}
Δ_{71}	Δ_{72}	Δ_{73}	Δ_{74}	Δ_{75}	Δ_{76}	Δ_{77}

Fig. 5.11.   Printout in matrix form.

following two changes in the original program (Fig. 5.10) are therefore necessary:

(a) computation of all elements and printing them out after all of them are computed;

(b) printing the matrix row by row.

In order to compute all 49 elements without immediate printout, we simply move CONTINUE (statement 20) so that it immediately follows statement 51. Printing out the matrix row by row requires the following four statements:†

```
      DO 120 I=1,N
432   PRINT 116, (DELTA(I,J), J=1,N)      implied
                                          do loop.
116   FORMAT(7F10.4/)

120   CONTINUE
```

Perhaps statement 432 needs some explanation. It serves to print out

$$\Delta_{i1}, \Delta_{i2}, \ldots, \Delta_{in}$$

on the ith row. In other words, this statement can be replaced by the following lengthy statement, if we take, for example, $N = 3$:

```
9432   PRINT 116, DELTA(I,1), DELTA(I,2), DELTA(I,3)
```

By means of a DO loop, the answers will be printed out row by row: row 1 ($i = 1$), row 2 ($i = 2$), etc.

It is convenient to print out a heading for each row and use appropriate spacing as illustrated below:

```
                   FLEXIBILITY MATRIX ROW 1
Skip 1 line here  ⟶
                   Δ₁₁  Δ₁₂  Δ₁₃  Δ₁₄  Δ₁₅  Δ₁₆  Δ₁₇
Skip 1 line here  ⟶
                   FLEXIBILITY MATRIX ROW 2
Skip 1 line here  ⟶
                   Δ₂₁  Δ₂₂  Δ₂₃  Δ₂₄  Δ₂₅  Δ₂₆  Δ₂₇
                    ⋮                         ⋮
                   FLEXIBILITY MATRIX ROW 7
Skip 1 line here  ⟶
                   Δ₇₁  Δ₇₂  Δ₇₃  Δ₇₄  Δ₇₅  Δ₇₆  Δ₇₇
```

The matrix rows use subscripts: $\Delta_{11}\ \Delta_{12}\ \Delta_{13}\ \Delta_{14}\ \Delta_{15}\ \Delta_{16}\ \Delta_{17}$ for row 1; $\Delta_{21}\ \Delta_{22}\ \Delta_{23}\ \Delta_{24}\ \Delta_{25}\ \Delta_{26}\ \Delta_{27}$ for row 2; and $\Delta_{71}\ \Delta_{72}\ \Delta_{73}\ \Delta_{74}\ \Delta_{75}\ \Delta_{76}\ \Delta_{77}$ for row 7.

varies most rapidly

varies least rapidly

---

† Or simply use the two statements

```
111   PRINT 116, ((DELTA(I,J), J = 1,N),I = 1,N)
116   FORMAT(7F10.4)
```

to obtain the identical printout for $N \leq 7$.

```
C       THIS IS A MODIFIED FORTRAN PROGRAM FOR A ROW BY ROW MATRIX PRINTOUT
C       N = MAXIMUM NUMBER FOR I OR J
        READ 1,P,ZL,E,AI,N
   1    FORMAT(4F10.7,I10)
        ZNP1=N+1
        DIMENSION DELTA(10,10)
   7    DO 20 I=1,N
        ZI=I
   8    DO 20 J=1,N
        ZJ=J
        IF(ZI-ZJ)50,51,51
  50    DELTA(I,J)=((P/(E*AI))*(ZL**3)*(1.-ZJ/ZNP1)*ZI/(6.*ZNP1))*(1.-(1.-
       1ZJ/ZNP1)**2-(ZI/ZNP1)**2)
        GO TO 20
  51    DELTA(I,J)=((P/(E*AI))*(ZL**3)*(1.-ZJ/ZNP1)*ZI/(6.*ZNP1))*(1.-(1.-
       1ZJ/ZNP1)**2-(ZI/ZNP1)**2)+(P/(E*AI))*ZL*ZL*ZL*(ZI-ZJ)**3/
       2((ZNP1**3)*6.)
  20    CONTINUE
        DO 120 I=1,N
        PUNCH 100,I
  16    PUNCH 6,(DELTA(I,J),J=1,N)
   6    FORMAT(7F10.4/)
 100    FORMAT(23X,23H FLEXIBILITY MATRIX ROW,I2/)
 120    CONTINUE
        PUNCH 25
  25    FORMAT(8H THE END)
        STOP
        END
1.0        1.0        1.0        1.0              7
```

Fig. 5.12. Program for row-by-row printing.

This elegant printout can readily be accomplished by using the following five statements:

```
        DO 432 I=1,N
        PRINT 108, I
 108    FORMAT(23X,23H FLEXIBILITY MATRIX ROW, I2/)
 432    PRINT 116, (DELTA(I,J),J=1,N)
 116    FORMAT(7F10.4/)
```

The statement 116 means "print out a maximum of seven numbers per line, each number having ten digits of which four digits are behind the decimal point and after printing this complete row, skip one line."

Table 5.3 is the printout for the improved version of the FORTRAN program, which is shown in Fig. 5.12.

We note that in Table 5.3 the computed values of all elements are symmetrical about the main diagonal, for example,

$$DELTA(1,4) = DELTA(4,1),$$

$$DELTA(2,3) = DELTA(3,2), \text{ etc.}$$

TABLE 5.3.   Row-by-row output of a matrix

FLEXIBILITY MATRIX ROW 1

| .0039 | .0065 | .0077 | .0076 | .0065 | .0048 | .0025 |

FLEXIBILITY MATRIX ROW 2

| .0065 | .0117 | .0142 | .0143 | .0124 | .0091 | .0048 |

FLEXIBILITY MATRIX ROW 3

| .0077 | .0142 | .0183 | .0190 | .0168 | .0124 | .0065 |

FLEXIBILITY MATRIX ROW 4

| .0076 | .0143 | .0190 | .0208 | .0190 | .0143 | .0076 |

FLEXIBILITY MATRIX ROW 5

| .0065 | .0124 | .0168 | .0190 | .0183 | .0142 | .0077 |

FLEXIBILITY MATRIX ROW 6

| .0048 | .0091 | .0124 | .0143 | .0142 | .0117 | .0065 |

FLEXIBILITY MATRIX ROW 7

| .0025 | .0048 | .0065 | .0076 | .0077 | .0065 | .0039 |

THE END

Therefore it is possible to print out either the lower or upper triangular matrix for the output. A lower triangular matrix has the following appearance:

$$
\begin{array}{llllllll}
\Delta_{11} & \Delta_{12} & \Delta_{13} & \Delta_{14} & \Delta_{15} \\
\Delta_{21} & \Delta_{22} & \Delta_{23} & \Delta_{24} \\
\Delta_{31} & \Delta_{32} & \Delta_{33} & \Delta_{34} \\
\Delta_{41} & \Delta_{42} & \Delta_{43} & \Delta_{44} \\
\Delta_{51} & \Delta_{52} & \Delta_{53} & \Delta_{54} & \Delta_{55} \\
\Delta_{61} & \Delta_{62} & \Delta_{63} & \Delta_{64} & \Delta_{65} & \Delta_{66} \\
\Delta_{71} & \Delta_{72} & \Delta_{73} & \Delta_{74} & \Delta_{75} & \Delta_{76} & \Delta_{77}
\end{array}
$$

$J = I+1$

$NA = I+1$

This matrix excludes any element to the right of the main diagonal line. To print out the elements for a lower triangular matrix, we can use the following three statements:

```
C       PROGRAM ADDITIONS FOR A LOWER TRIANGULAR MATRIX OUTPUT
        DO 220 I=1,N
220     PUNCH 221,(DELTA(I,J),J=1,I)
221     FORMAT(7F10.4/)
```

We note that the limiting value for J in statement 220 is I *rather than N*. Thus, when I=1, J will be incremented to a limiting value of 1. Hence DELTA(1,1) is printed on the first line. Similarly, when I=2, J will be equal to 1 and 2, respectively. This will cause the printout of DELTA(2,1) and DELTA(2,2) on the second line, etc.

Similarly, an upper triangular matrix may be printed out by using the following three statements:

```
C      PROGRAM ADDITIONS FOR AN UPPER TRIANGULAR MATRIX OUTPUT
       DO 222 I=1,N
222    PUNCH 223, (DELTA(I,J),J=I,N)
223    FORMAT(7F10.4/)
```

must include the diagonal

In this discussion of input-output statements, the difference between a print and a punch statement must be mentioned. Both statements are instructions to the computer which determine the form in which the answer should be given. When the computer reads a print statement, it prints out the answers directly on its typewriter. When it reads a punch statement, it punches out the answers on the eighty-column cards, which must be printed out on a high-speed printer. Both statements have their advantages. The punch statement often is much faster than the print statement. On the other hand, the latter might be necessary because a high-speed printer is not available. Some computers have been arranged so that they read both print and punch statements and always punch all their answers, while other machines will not accept either one or the other.

Before turning to the next section, we remark on a new format for output, the E format. This format is most suitable when the order of magnitude of the answers to be printed is not clearly known ahead of time. For example, the following two statements may be used advantageously to print, on the same line, both the value of I, for example 17, and the variable ANS, say, having a value of -0.031415926:

```
          PRINT 12, I, ANS
      12  FORMAT(I3, E15.8)
```

The output will look like

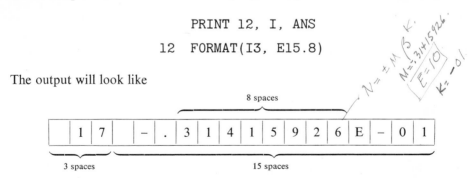

The format E15.8 needs some explanation. Fifteen spaces are required for this answer in which 8 places, or 31415926, are used for the mantissa (see Section 4.2), and the four rightmost places are used for, respectively, the letter E, the sign of the exponent, and the two-digit true exponent XX.

5.6 INPUT STATEMENTS FOR A MATRIX PROBLEM

We shall proceed, by means of specific examples, to discuss how to READ IN a matrix. Essentially, the line of reasoning for matrix input is the same as that for matrix output. Suppose, for example, that an array of numbers in six rows and eight columns is to be read in. This can be accomplished by the following four statements:

```
C       READ IN A 6 X 8 MATRIX
        DIMENSION A(6,8)
        DO 128 I=1,6
  128   READ 129,(A(I,J),J=1,8)
  129   FORMAT(7F10.4)
```

In this case, we need two data cards for each row. The first card has seven elements, namely, A(1,1), A(1,2), ... , A(1,7); and the second card is punched only A(1,8) in the first 10 columns. The remaining 70 columns are left blank.

Frequently, we wish to read in a lower triangular matrix, say, of five rows and five columns. We can use the following four statements:

```
C       READ IN A LOWER TRIANGULAR MATRIX
        DIMENSION A(5,5)
        DO 226 I=1,5
  226   READ 227, (A(I,J),J=1,I)
  227   FORMAT(7F10.4)
```

It is important to note that we need five data cards in this example. The first card has one element only, namely A(1,1), in the first 10 columns. The second has two elements, A(2,1) and A(2,2), in the first 20 columns. The third card has three elements, A(3,1), A(3,2), and A(3,3), in the first 30 columns. The fourth data card has four elements. Finally, the fifth card has five elements of the last row in the matrix. The last card is punched only in the first 50 columns as per FORMAT Statement 227.

Alternatively, we can simply use the following three statements to read in the same lower triangular matrix:

```
        DIMENSION A(5,5)
        READ 227, ((A(I,J),J=1,I),I=1,5)
  227   FORMAT(7F10.4)
```

Here only three data cards are needed. The first card has seven elements, namely, A(1,1), A(2,1,), A(2,2), A(3,1), A(3,2), A(3,3), and A(4,1), each having the F10.4 format. The second card has seven elements. They are A(4,2), A(4,3), A(4,4), A(5,1), A(5,2), A(5,3), and A(5,4). The remaining element, A(5,5), is punched in the first 10 columns of the third card.

One can readily see the similarity between the preceding group of statements and the output statements for a lower triangular matrix discussed in the previous section.

There are occasions when data cards are punched prior to the writing of a computer program. Thus, if we wish the computer not to read the even-numbered cards, i.e., the second, the fourth, etc., then we use the *slash* introduced in the previous section.

```
C      READ IN A 6 X 6 MATRIX
       DIMENSION A(6,6)
       DO 128 I=1,6
128    READ 129, (A(I,J),J=1,6)
129    FORMAT(7F10.4/)
```

A total of twelve data cards are required here. The six odd-numbered cards are read in, and the other six cards are skipped.

Before concluding this section, we digress to remark on an elegant echo print statement. We utilize an echo print when we wish to read in a card and print out the same information. This can be accomplished by the following five statements and one data card, which together form a *complete* program.

```
       READ 20
20     FORMAT (49H □□□□□□□□□□□□□□□□□□□□□□□□□□□□□□□□□□□□□□□□□□□□□□□□□□□)
       PRINT 20
       STOP
       END
```

It is important to note the flexibility of this program in that the information on the data cards may be changed at ease without affecting the program. In this particular example, the format specification is a Hollerith field for which a maximum of 49 spaces may be used per FORMAT statement.

5.7   FORTRAN SUBROUTINE SUBPROGRAMS

In writing a computer program, we find that it is often necessary to repeat the same group of statements many times within the same program. For example, suppose that we wish to write a FORTRAN program to perform a 90-degree clockwise rotation of the elements in the following array of numbers:

2	7	6
9	5	1
4	3	8

```
C        PROGRAM FOR MATRIX ROTATION
C        N=NUMBER OF ROWS AND COLUMNS OF THE GIVEN MATRIX
C
         READ 2,N
       2 FORMAT(I2)
         DIMENSION A(10,10),SWAP(10,10)
         DO 5 I=1,N
       5 READ 6,(A(I,J),J=1,N)
       6 FORMAT(10F5.2)
       7 DO 9 I=1,N
         DO 9 J=1,N
       9 SWAP(I,J)=A(I,J)
         DO 13 I=1,N
         DO 13 K=1,N
         J=N-K+1
      13 A(I,K)=SWAP(J,I)
         DO 15 I=1,N
      15 PUNCH 16,(A(I,J),J=1,N)
      16 FORMAT(26X,10F5.2)
      17 STOP
         END
03
 2.0   7.0   6.0
 9.0   5.0   1.0
 4.0   3.0   8.0
```

Fig. 5.13. FORTRAN program for matrix rotation.

This operation is carried out by interchanging the first row with the third column, the second row with the second column, etc. Thus we have the new array of numbers

4	9	2
3	5	7
8	1	6

A FORTRAN program related to this operation and also to the printout is shown in Fig. 5.13, where the array SWAP indicates the temporary storages, and A, the given array of numbers.

If we now wish to make two or more successive 90-degree clockwise rotations of the given square matrix with a printout after each rotation, we would have to repeat statements 7 through 16 two or more times. Figure 5.14 shows a long, repetitious, and therefore undesirable, FORTRAN program for successive rotations. Imagine how much worse the repetition can become when the group of statements to be repeated is very long to begin with!

To avoid this undesirable repetition we often use a SUBROUTINE subprogram, sometimes called a *subroutine*. A subroutine is a collection of statements, or "packaged statements," for the purpose of achieving some specific objectives, such as rotating a given matrix and punching out the results. Figure 5.15 is such a subroutine. Called SUBROUTINE ROTATE, its statements 7 through 16 are taken directly

```
C       PROGRAM FOR SEVERAL ROTATIONS
C       N=NUMBER OF ROWS AND OF COLUMNS OF THE GIVEN MATRIX
C
        READ 3, N
      3 FORMAT(I2)
        DIMENSION A(10,10), SWAP(10,10)
        DO 5 I=1,N
      5 READ 8, (A(I,J), J=1,N)
      8 FORMAT(10F5.2)
C
C       FIRST ROTATION AND PRINTING OUT
C
     12 DO 15 I=1,N
        DO 15 J=1,N
     15 SWAP(I,J)= A(I,J)
        DO 16 I=1,N
        DO 16 K=1,N
        J=N-K+1
     16 A(I,K)=SWAP(J,I)
        DO 19 I=1,N
     19 PUNCH 20, (A(I,J), J=1,N)
     20 FORMAT(26X,10F5.2)
C
C       SECOND ROTATION AND PRINTING OUT
C
        DO 115 I=1,N
        DO 115 J=1,N
    115 SWAP(I,J)=A(I,J)
        DO 116 I=1,N
        DO 116 K=1,N
        J=N-K+1
    116 A(I,K)=SWAP(J,I)
        DO 119 I=1,N
    119 PUNCH 20, (A(I,J), J=1,N)
C
C       THIRD ROTATION AND PRINTING
C
        DO 215 I=1,N
        DO 215 J=1,N
    215 SWAP(I,J)=A(I,J)
        DO 216 I=1,N
        DO 216 K=1,N
        J=N-K+1
    216 A(I,K)=SWAP(J,I)
        DO 219 I=1,N
    219 PUNCH 20, (A(I,J), J=1,N)
        STOP
        END
 03
  2.0   7.0   6.0
  9.0   5.0   1.0
  4.0   3.0   8.0
```

Fig. 5.14.   FORTRAN program for three matrix rotations.

as a "package" from Fig. 5.13 (see the shaded portion). To complete this subroutine it is necessary to add (1) the NAME statement, (2) the DIMENSION statement, (3) the RETURN statement, and (4) the END statement to the above-mentioned package. We shall now discuss these statements in detail.

The first statement in a subroutine, the NAME statement, serves two purposes, namely, to identify and to present the arguments involved. The name required for identification has several limitations:

(a) It must not be more than six characters in length.

Example

Correct:	SUBROUTINE ROTATE
Incorrect:	SUBROUTINE REVOLVE

(b) It must begin with an alphabetic character.

Example

Correct:	SUBROUTINE SEA7
Incorrect:	SUBROUTINE 7SEA

(c) It must not end in F if it is longer than three characters.

Example

Correct:	SUBROUTINE JEF
Incorrect:	SUBROUTINE CALF

The parentheses following the name of the subroutine enclose the arguments which specify the variables in the subprogram. The arguments may be (1) floating-point variables, for example ANS; (2) fixed-point variables, for example N; or (3) subscripted variables, for example A, but not A(I,J), which represents the entire array.

```
      SUBROUTINE ROTATE(A,N)
      DIMENSION A(10,10),SWAP(10,10)
    7 DO 9 I=1,N
      DO 9 J=1,N
    9 SWAP(I,J)=A(I,J)
      DO 13 I=1,N
      DO 13 K=1,N
      JJ=N-K+1
   13 A(I,K)=SWAP(JJ,I)
      DO 15 I=1,N
   15 PUNCH 16,(A(I,J),J=1,N)
   16 FORMAT(26X,10F5.2)
      RETURN
      END
```

Fig. 5.15. SUBROUTINE ROTATE.

It may be well to note that in the first statement of Fig. 5.15 there are only two arguments, A and N. An inspection of the complete listing shows, however, that five more variables, SWAP, I, J, K, and JJ, are also used in this subroutine. These variables are omitted from the parentheses because they are not independent variables. The array SWAP, for example, is defined in statement 9 of the subroutine by the current values of the array A. In other words, the array SWAP is completely defined once the array A is known. Hence, using SWAP as an argument is a superfluous step; however, it will not cause any difficulties during compilation. Consider now I, J, and K in the subroutine. These are used exclusively as indices of DO loops, and hence are not counted as arguments. The variable JJ is defined by the two variables N and K and therefore is not required as an argument either. We now see that the only arguments required for the NAME statement in SUBROUTINE ROTATE are A and N.

The next statement in this subroutine is a DIMENSION statement. This statement is required in a subroutine in two situations:

1. When an argument representing an array already appears in the NAME statement of the subroutine; for example, A(10,10) represents a two-dimensional array.

2. When *new* subscripted variables are introduced in the subroutine; for example, The array SWAP, a new subscripted variable in the rotation subroutine, is dimensioned SWAP(10,10).

The arrays mentioned here may be both one-dimensional, for example X(20), Y(16); and two-dimensional, for example, A(10,10), SWAP(10,10), Z(10,10). However, since SUBROUTINE ROTATE involves only two-dimensional arrays, its dimension statement is

$$\text{DIMENSION A(10,10), SWAP(10,10)}$$

or

$$\text{DIMENSION SWAP(10,10), A(10,10)}$$

The RETURN statement signifies an exit from the subroutine. In our example, SUBROUTINE ROTATE, it serves to pass the control to the first statement immediately following the shaded portion of Fig. 5.13. This is statement 17, which is STOP. Every subroutine requires at least one† RETURN statement. The last statement of any subroutine must be the END statement. It may not be omitted.

5.8 MAIN PROGRAM

We now proceed to introduce the concept of a main program, using the specific example of matrix rotation. Consider the program in Fig. 5.13. We recall that the shaded portion was removed to form the subroutine ROTATE. If we insert a single CALL STATEMENT in place of this missing portion,

$$\text{CALL ROTATE (A, N)}$$

then the resulting program (Fig. 5.16) is designated as the main program. Digressing momentarily, we observe that SWAP has been omitted from the DIMENSION statement in the main program since it does not appear explicitly in any of the nine statements of the main program.

We now see that the original program (Fig. 5.13) has been replaced by a main program and its accompanying subprogram, SUBROUTINE ROTATE. The state-

---

† See, for example, Fig. 12.2, where three RETURN statements are used in one subroutine.

ment CALL ROTATE in the main program transfers the control of execution to SUBROUTINE ROTATE; that is, the computer proceeds to SUBROUTINE ROTATE and performs whatever operations are indicated by the package of statements. The RETURN statement then turns the control of execution back to the statement succeeding the CALL statement, i.e., statement 17 in the main program.

```
      READ 2,N
   2  FORMAT(I2)
      DIMENSION A(10,10)
      DO 5 I=1,N
   5  READ 6,(A(I,J), J=1,N)
   6  FORMAT(10F5.2)
      CALL ROTATE(A,N)
  17  STOP
      END
      SUBROUTINE ROTATE(A,N)
      DIMENSION A(10,10),SWAP(10,10)
   7  DO 9 I=1,N
      DO 9 J=1,N
   9  SWAP(I,J)   =   A(I,J)
      DO 13 I=1,N
      DO 13 K=1,N
      J=N-K+1
  13  A(I,K)   =   SWAP(J,I)
      DO 15 I=1,N
  15  PUNCH 16,(A(I,J),J=1,N)
  16  FORMAT(26X,10F5.2)
      RETURN
      END
  03
   2.0   7.0   6.0
   9.0   5.0   1.0
   4.0   3.0   8.0
```

Fig. 5.16. A complete program consisting of the main program, one subroutine, and the required data.

At first glance, the concept of partitioning a main program and its subroutine seems unwarranted; the partitioned program appears more complex than the original (Fig. 5.13). The usefulness of this concept can be illustrated, however, by making, say, three successive rotations of a given matrix with a printout after each rotation. We remember that the FORTRAN program previously prepared for this problem (Fig. 5.14) was long, repetitious, and undesirable. However, as shown in Fig. 5.16, our task is simplified when we employ subroutines; we just place three CALL ROTATE statements in the main program. If we now compare the total number of statements in the two schemes mentioned above, that is,

(1) the single program shown in Fig. 5.13, and

(2) the main program plus SUBROUTINE ROTATE (Fig. 5.16),

then we can readily conclude that scheme 2 is far shorter than scheme 1 principally because it avoids repeating a large group of statements.

```
C         M=THE SIZE OF THE GIVEN (M*M) MATRIX B
C         MAIN PROGRAM FOR THREE ROTATIONS USING SUBROUTINE
C
          READ 2,M
     2 FORMAT(I2)
          DIMENSION B(10,10;
          DO 5 ICOL=1,M
          READ 9,(B(ICOL,JROW),JROW=1,M)
     5 PUNCH 9,(B(ICOL,JROW),JROW=1,M)
     9 FORMAT(26X,10F5.2)
          CALL ROTATE(B,M)
          CALL ROTATE(B,M)
          CALL ROTATE(B,M)
          STOP
          END
```

Fig. 5.17.   Main program for three rotations using subroutine.

In the main program shown in Fig. 5.17, each variable (both single and subscripted) has been deliberately renamed (for example, B,M) and therefore differs from its counterpart (for example, A,N) in the accompanying subroutine ROTATE.

In order to link the main program with the required subroutine, we note the following rule:

> The arguments in the calling statement of a main program must agree in number, order, and mode with the arguments in the first statement (NAME) of a subroutine.

Examples

Correct:	`CALL ROTATE(B,M)`	in main program
	`SUBROUTINE ROTATE(A,N)`	in subroutine
Correct:	`CALL ROTATE(M,B)`	in main program
	`SUBROUTINE ROTATE(N,A)`	in subroutine
Correct:	`CALL ROTATE(3,B)`	in main program (if M = 3 in the main program)
	`SUBROUTINE ROTATE(N,A)`	in subroutine
Incorrect:	`CALL ROTATE (B,M)`	in main program
	`SUBROUTINE ROTATE(N,A)`	in subroutine
Incorrect:	`CALL ROTATE(B,M)`	in main program
	`SUBROUTINE ROTATE(A,AN)`	in subroutine
Incorrect:	`CALL ROTATE(B,M)`	in main program
	`SUBROUTINE ROTATE(A,N,SWAP)`	in subroutine

Before concluding this section, let us emphasize a few of the advantages of using subroutines.

First, a subroutine can be summoned any number of times by the main program (or by another subroutine). This procedure allows the repeated use of a package of statements without actually writing them out in the main program or the calling program each time they are needed. Second, many useful subroutines are available through various computer user's organizations or at computer centers. Finally, main programs and subroutines can be compiled individually, even at different times; thus it is possible to significantly reduce the debugging time spent by programmers.

5.9   FUNCTION SUBPROGRAM AND FUNCTION STATEMENT

A FUNCTION subprogram may be considered as a smaller version of the SUBROUTINE subprogram discussed in Section 5.7. A SUBROUTINE may have more than one result, while a FUNCTION is limited to computing only one value. Just as in a SUBROUTINE, in each FUNCTION subprogram many arguments may be enclosed in the parentheses. The essential features will be illustrated with an example. Let us compute

$$DOT(A,B,K) = \sum_{i=1}^{K} A_i B_i, \qquad (5.1)$$

where both A and B are one-dimensional arrays of 25 elements each ($K \leq 25$). It is assumed that Eq. (5.1) is used frequently in a given program.

A possible FUNCTION DOT program is shown in Fig. 5.18. It may be noted that, like a SUBROUTINE, a FUNCTION subprogram invariably contains the following four types of statements:

(1) FUNCTION name statement

(2) DIMENSION, if one or more arrays are involved

(3) RETURN

(4) END

To obtain the numerical value of the expression

$$\alpha = \sqrt{\left(\sum_{i=1}^{17} C_i D_i\right) + 1} + \sum_{i=1}^{5} C_i D_i,$$

```
FUNCTION DOT(A,B,K)

DIMENSION A(25),B(25)

DOT = 0.

DO 90 I = 1,K

SAK = A(I)*B(I)

90   DOT = DOT + SAK

RETURN

END
```

Fig. 5.18.   FUNCTION subprogram.

where C and D are one-dimensional arrays, we may write

ALPHA = SQRTF $\left(1. + DOT(C,D,17)\right)$ + DOT(C,D,5)

The above statement will bring the FUNCTION subprogram into operation without a CALL statement.

The essential differences between a SUBROUTINE and a FUNCTION subprogram are tabulated below:

SUBROUTINE subprogram	FUNCTION subprogram
Name: One to six letters or digits. The first character must be a letter and the last must not be F if the name contains more than three characters.	*Name:* One to six letters or digits, the first of which must be I, J, K, L, M, or N if and only if the value of the function is a fixed point, The last character must not be F if the name contains more than three characters.
Calling into operation: By a CALL statement.	*Calling into operation:* By writing the name of the function in an expression where numerical value is to be determined.
Number of arguments: From *none* to some maximum.	*Number of arguments:* From *one* to some maximum.

Both SUBROUTINE and FUNCTION subprogram can be compiled independently from their main programs and both can consist of many statements.

We now proceed to describe a third type of function, the function statement, which has only one arithmetic statement and therefore *cannot* be compiled independently.

Example

It is known that

$$\phi(x) = x^2 - 2x + 7, \qquad \theta(y) = 3y^2 - 14,$$
$$Q(x, y, z) = 3\phi(x)\sqrt{\theta(y)} - 2.4z^2.$$

We wish to compute T = Q(A, B, C), where A = 1.46, B = 28.3, and C = 31.5. A program to compute T consists of the following statements:

```
PHIF(X) = X * X - 2. * X + 7.
THETAF(Y) = 3. * Y * Y - 14.
QF(X,Y,Z) = 3. * PHIF(X) * SQRTF(THETAF(Y)) - 2.4 * Z * Z
T = QF(1.46, 28.3, 31.5)
```

The use of a function statement is subject to the following four restrictions:

(1) The name may have one to six characters. The first character must be alphabetic. Those functions beginning with I, J, K, L, M, or N will be computed as fixed-point numbers; all others will be computed as floating-point numbers.

(2) The function statement must be placed at the beginning of the program before the first executable statement.

(3) Each function is defined as a *single arithmetic* statement.

(4) The arguments in parentheses may not be subscripted.

In summary, we see that there are four types of functions in FORTRAN compiler language, namely, SUBROUTINE subprograms (Sections 5.7 and 5.8), FUNCTION subprograms (Section 5.9), arithmetic function statements (Section 5.9), and library functions (Table 5.1).

FUNCTION subprograms are, in a sense, smaller versions of SUBROUTINE subprograms. The output from a FUNCTION subprogram is limited to a single variable, whereas that from a SUBROUTINE subprogram may yield many variables. Thus it is impossible for a FUNCTION subprogram to handle a matrix output.

An arithmetic function statement is quite similar to a library function. The latter, often referred to as the built-in routine or library subroutine, is supplied by the FORTRAN system; the arithmetic function statement is written by the user.

5.10 SUMMARY OF THE FORTRAN COMPILER LANGUAGE

As mentioned before, FORTRAN compiler language comprises a number of types of statements that a programmer may write to code a particular problem. This compiler language was initially prepared for the IBM 704 computer and has subsequently been extended to many other types. The essential portion of the FORTRAN language available on the 1620 and many other medium-size computers is summarized in this section.

The IBM 1620 uses several variations of the FORTRAN language; among them are FORTRAN II, FORGO, and FORTRAN I. The following is a description of FORTRAN II. We also list the differences, if any, for FORGO and FORTRAN I,† respectively.

A. Types of Numbers and Variables

1. *Fixed-point constants.* Unless otherwise specified, fixed-point constants are limited to one to five digits. In other words, the absolute value of an integer is less than 99999. These numbers are used primarily for counting and similar processes. Integral (fixed-point) constants are written in decimal notation without a decimal point (for example, -256, 95473, -1, 1, and -98675). The plus sign may not be required. If a fixed-point computation greater than 99999 occurs, only the five rightmost digits are retained (for example, 31415926 is retained as 15926).

2. *Fixed-point variables.* Names of variables which take on fixed-point values have from one to six alphabetic or numerical characters, starting with I, J, K, L, M, or N (for example, I, KAT, L90, and NIM). The value of fixed-point variables must not exceed five digits.

FORGO. Variable names have from one to five characters.

FORTRAN I. The magnitude of an integer is less than or equal to 9999. Variable names have from one to five characters.

---

† In IBM literature this processor is also called "1620 FORTRAN (with FORMAT)."

3. *Floating-point constants.* The absolute value of a floating-point constant may be from 10^{-99} to 10^{99}, including zero. Unless otherwise specified, the machine computes with only eight significant digits. These numbers are primarily used for data involved in arithmetic operations. Floating-point constants are written in one of the following two ways:

(a) in decimal form with a sign and a decimal point, for example, 22.976, $-.0003$, or
(b) in decimal exponent form (a one- or two-digit fixed-point constant) preceded by an E, for example,

5.1E3	means	5.1×10^3,
5.1E+3	means	5.1×10^3,
5.12E−91	means	5.12×10^{-91}.

4. *Floating-point variables.* Names of variables which take on floating-point values have from one to six alphabetic and numerical characters beginning with a character *not* I, J, K, L, M, or N, for example, EQ76A, A, BATE, TIME, DELT, and DXDT.

FORGO. The magnitude is zero, or from 10^{-51} to 10^{49}. The machine works with eight significant digits. Variable names have from one to five characters.

FORTRAN I. The machine works with eight significant digits. Variable names have from one to five characters.

B. Arrays

Arrays may be either one- or two-dimensional and may contain as elements either fixed- or floating-point numbers. (The same name rules mentioned above for naming variables apply also to fixed- and floating-point arrays.) A particular element in an array is designated by subscripts, which must be in the form of one or more of the following forms:

$$c, \quad v, \quad v \pm c, \quad c' * v \pm c,$$

where c and c' are fixed-point constants, v is a fixed-point variable, and the signs *, +, and − are interpreted as multiplication, addition, and subtraction, respectively. For notational purposes, subscripts are enclosed in parentheses and separated by commas, for example,

```
A(2,I−5),    B(5*KMAX−2,9*J),    IC(I,J),    BATE(10).
```

C. Expressions

Arithmetic expressions may be formed by using parentheses and the five connectives +, −, *, **, and / for addition, subtraction, multiplication, exponentiation, and division, respectively. The allowable constituents of expressions are variables, elements of arrays, constants, and functions. All the constituents of an expression must be in either fixed-point or floating-point mode. An exception to this rule is made for subscripts, which must be fixed-point, even though they may be in a floating-point expression. A fixed-point quantity may also appear as an exponent in a floating-point expression. The following examples show the correct usage of notation.

FORTRAN	Mathematical notation
A*B	AB
A*(−B)	$-AB$
−A*B	$-AB$
A+2	$A + 2$
A**(B+2.)*C	$A^{B+2}(C)$
A**(I−2)	A^{I-2}
A*B/(C*D)	AB/CD
A*(X−B*(X+C))	$A(X - B(X + C))$
((A−B)/C)**2.5	$(A - B)^{2.5}/(C)^{2.5}$

Two operation symbols may not appear together, but must be separated by parentheses such as was done in the second example above. The use of parentheses also helps to determine the hierarchy of operations in an expression. When the expression is explicitly written, the rank of the hierarchy is assumed to be as follows:

Rank	Symbol	Operation
First	**	Exponentiation
Second	/ and *	Division and multiplication
Third	+ and −	Addition and subtraction

FORGO. When raising a floating-point quantity to a fixed-point power, the exponent may be either a single variable or a constant, but may not involve fixed-point operations. For example, (A−B)**I is permissible, but A**(I−J) is not.

D. Library Functions

Library functions are prewritten subroutines. They are single-valued, and have only one argument; that is, they use one value to compute a function of that value; for example, Y = SINF(X). The names have from one to six characters and the last character is F. The arguments of functions may be arithmetic functions. The following internal functions are available:

FUNCTION name	Explanation
SINF(X)	Sine of x in radians
COSF(X)	Cosine of x in radians
SQRTF(X)	Square root of x
ATANF(X)	Arctangent of x (angle is in radians)
LOGF(X)	Natural logarithm of x
EXPF(X)	Exponential of x (meaning e^x)
ABSF(X)	Absolute value of x

These functions are used in the same manner as constants and variables. They compute floating-point values, for example,

$$Y = \mathrm{SQRTF}(B * FAT) - \mathrm{EXPF}(\mathrm{SINF}(G(10)))$$

FORGO. The last character is not required to be F; hence SIN(X) is permissible. The functions SQR(X) and ATN(X) are also available.

FORTRAN I. The function ABSF(X) is not available.

E. Statements

A complete program consists of a main program and possibly one or more subprograms, each of which is comprised of a sequence of FORTRAN statements. These statements fall into five main types.

1. *Arithmetic statements.* These statements have the form

$$a = b,$$

where the variable or array element *a* is replaced by the value of the expression *b*. The area elements *a* and *b* may be of the same mode (fixed- or floating-point), or they may be in opposite modes. It is thus possible to change from fixed- to floating-point, and vice versa.

FORTRAN	Mathematical expression
R=(A-B*X)/(C-D*X)	$R = (A - BX)/(C - DX)$
FY=X*(X**2-Y**2)/(X**2+Y**2)	$FY = X(X^2 - Y^2)/(X^2 + Y^2)$
PI=3.1415926	$\pi = 3.1415926$
M=2*M-10*J	$M_{\mathrm{new}} = 2M_{\mathrm{old}} - 10J$

2. *Control statements.* This type of statement is used to govern the flow of control in the program.

(a) The GO TO statement when executed causes the computer to transfer control to the statement numbered *N*. (In columns 1 to 5, statements are numbered arbitrarily from 1 to 99999. They do not have to be in sequence and not every card need be numbered.) For example,

$$\mathrm{GO\ TO\ 3}$$

(b) The computed GO TO statement, GO TO $(n_1, n_2, \ldots, n_m)$, *i* is such that when executed, control is transferred to statement n_j, where *j* is the value of the fixed-point variable *i* $(1 \leq j \leq m)$. For example,

$$\mathrm{GO\ TO\ (12,\ 957,\ 34,\ 21,\ 16),\ L}$$

when $L = 1$ applies, GO TO statement 12; when $L = 2$, then GO TO statement 957, ... ; and finally, when $L = 5$, then GO TO statement 16.

(c) If (A)n_1, n_2, n_3 is a conditional statement causing transfer to statement n_1, n_2, or n_3 depending on whether the value of the expression A is negative, zero, or positive. Some examples are

```
IF (C(J,K)-B) 10,4,30
IF (I) 5,5,2
IF (D**2-SINF(X**2)) 2,3,3
IF (I-5*J-6) 998, 678, 678
```

(d) IF (SENSE SWITCH i) n_1, n_2, where n_1 and n_2 are statement numbers and i is 1, 2, 3 or 4. This statement causes control transferred to statement n_1 or n_2 depending on whether the console program switch i is on or off. For example,

```
IF(SENSE SWITCH 3) 65, 23
                   on  off
```

FORGO. This statement is not permissible.

(e) The PAUSE statement stops the computer from going to the next sequential FORTRAN statement until the START button on the 1620 console is pressed. It is most often used before an IF(SENSE SWITCH i) statement to provide time for setting the desired switch. The statement appears in a program as follows:

```
PAUSE
```

FORGO. This statement is not permissible.

(f) The STOP statement is similar to a PAUSE, except that the computer cannot be made to continue by pressing the "START" button. It is equivalent to the following two statements:

```
100    PAUSE
       GO TO 100
```

(g) The DO statement may be in one of two forms:

$$\text{DO } n \quad i = m_1, m_2$$
$$\text{DO } n \quad i = m_1, m_2, m_3$$

where n is a statement number, i is a fixed point variable, and m_1, m_2, and m_3 are fixed-point variables or constants, but not expressions. When m_3, is not stated, as in the first form above, it is assumed to be 1. All statements between the DO statement and n are first executed with the variable i set equal to m_1. The quantity i is then incremented by m_3 and the same procedure is repeated until i is greater than m_2.

When this occurs, control is transferred to the statement following *n*. For example,

```
    L(1) = 1
    DO 26 I = 1, 5                          DO 17 LITE = K, J, 20
                          or
    K(I) = L(I) + 2                         DO 89 I = 4, 299
 26 L(I + 1) = L(I) + 1
```

The restrictions on a DO loop are:

(1) The first statement after the DO statement must not be an END, CONTINUE, DIMENSION, or FORMAT.

(2) Statement *n* must not be a control statement.

(3) Entrance into a DO loop must be through the DO statement.

(4) If there is a DO within a DO, all statements in the inner DO must be within the outer DO loop. This is called a nest of DO's.

In a nest of DO's the innermost loop must be satisfied first. The following example of a nest of DO's might be helpful:

$$\sigma = \sum_{i=0}^{5} \sum_{j=0}^{N} \sum_{k=1}^{N} [kC + (B - i) + A^j],$$

where *A*, *B*, *C* are given constants. A FORTRAN program for this is shown in Fig. 5.19. In this example, the innermost loop is satisfied first and the outermost last. It is important to note that a nest of DO loops may have a common ending point, but that the inner loop cannot end after the outer loops. The following example shows loops incorrectly ended:

Incorrect loops: ┌Outer loop
                    └┌Inner loop

(h) The CONTINUE statement is a dummy statement made to ensure that the last statement in a DO loop is not a transfer of control.

(i) END is the last card, physically, of all programs, both main and subprogram. It tells the compiler that this is the last card in the program. The object program will not be compiled if an END statement does not appear as the *last* statement in the program.

3. *Functions and Subprogram Statements.*

SUBPROGRAMS

(a) CALL NAME (argument list) is a main program statement which generates a calling sequence to the named subprogram with the listed arguments as input. These arguments may be expressions; for example, CALL LULU (.5, X+Y, Z**5) creates a calling sequence to the subprogram LULU with the values of the three expressions

```
        READ 2,A,B,C,N

      2 FORMAT(3F10.4,I2)

        SIGMA = 0.

        NP1 = N + 1

        DO 10 I = 1,6

        ZI = I - 1

        BMI = B-ZI

        DO 10 JP1 = 1,NP1

        AJ= A * * (JP1-1)

        DO 10 K = 1, N

        ZK = K

     10 SIGMA = SIGMA + ZK * C+BMI+AJ

     20 PRINT 4,A,B,C,SIGMA,N

      4 FORMAT(4(F10.4,2X),I2)

        STOP

        END
```

Figure 5.19

as input arguments. Other examples include

```
        CALL MAT (X, A, I, .000982)
        CALL MULT (I, 16.3)
        CALL ADDER (X, Y, C)
```

FORGO. The arguments may not be specified in the CALL statement.

FORTRAN I. No subprograms are permitted.

(b) SUBROUTINE NAME $(a_1, a_2, \ldots, a_n)$, where NAME is the symbolic name of the subroutine and the arguments $a_1, \ldots, a_n$ are nonsubscripted variables. The name of the subroutine contains from one to six alphabetic and numerical characters, the first of which must be alphabetic.

The SUBROUTINE statement always comes first in a subprogram and defines it as a subroutine subprogram. A subroutine is brought into use by a CALL statement. At the time of execution of the subroutine, the variables in the definition are replaced by the constants, variables, and expressions in the CALL statement. (The arguments may be arrays.) Some examples are:

```
SUBROUTINE LULU (A, B, C)

SUBROUTINE MAT (A, D, G, K)

SUBROUTINE ANS77
```

The name must not end in F if it contains more than three characters.

FORGO. The arguments must not be specified in the definition. The name has from one to five characters.

FORTRAN I. Subprograms are not permitted.

FUNCTIONS

(c) The FUNCTION statement, always first in the subprogram, defines it as a FUNCTION subprogram. The general form is

$$\text{FUNCTION NAME } (a_1, a_2, \ldots, a_n),$$

where NAME is the symbolic name of the subprogram and the arguments are non-subscripted variables. The name consists of one to six alphabetic and numerical characters, the first being alphabetic. The name must appear either in the input statement list or at least once on the left-hand side of an arithmetic statement. The name of the function must start with I, J, K, L, M, or N if and only if the value of the function is fixed point. The function subprograms are used in the same manner as the internal functions described previously. Their names are used as though the internal functions were variables. The desired arguments are enclosed in parentheses. Some examples are:

```
FUNCTION ARCSN(RADS)

FUNCTION ROOT (B,A,C)

FUNCTION INTRT(RATE,YEARS)

FUNCTION H2Q (K,A)
```

The name must not end in F if it is longer than three characters.

FORGO and FORTRAN I. The FUNCTION statement is not permitted.

(d) The RETURN statement returns control from the subprogram to the main program. It stops further computation by the subprogram and returns the values calculated for use in the main program. It is the last executed statement in the SUBROUTINE and FUNCTION subprograms. The statement appears in the program as follows:

```
RETURN
```

FORTRAN I. The RETURN statement is not permitted.

4. *Input-Output Statements.*

(a) FORMAT (specification) is a statement which tells the computer how information is to be read in, printed, or punched out. The data may be either numerical or alphabetical.

The Hollerith FORMAT is used for reading, printing, or punching out alphabetic information such as column headings, etc. An example is

FORMAT (5HA☐DOG)

The H signifies that a Hollerith specification follows. Every character following the H (including blanks) is printed or punched out exactly as it is written, and the total number of spaces to be used is placed before the H.

FORMAT (30H☐JOHN☐JONES☐☐DECEMBER☐31,☐1968)

FORMAT (24H☐THIS☐IS☐ALPHAMERIC☐DATA//)

The symbol ☐ in the above examples indicates a blank. For numerical quantities the mode (fixed or floating) and the number of spaces to be allotted to the number must be specified by the FORMAT statement, for example,

FORMAT (I5,F9.2,E15.8)

This statement tells the computer how to read, print, or punch three numbers. The first would be in the fixed-point mode and would be allowed five spaces at most. The second is without a power of 10, for example, -27561.09, for which there are, at most, nine spaces allowed, and two places are to the right of the decimal point. The third has a power of 10, for example, $-.95629371E-21$. There are 15 spaces allowed for this number, and eight places are to the right of the decimal point. A comma separates each FORMAT specification:

FORMAT (12,10H☐DEGREE☐=☐,F10.7)

FORMAT (F18.9,I10,E22.9)

However, a comma may not be needed after a Hollerith or X-specification. A variation of the numerical FORMAT is

FORMAT (5I3,2E9.2,3F7.2)

This means that there are five numbers read (printed) according to I3, two according to E9.2, and three according to F7.2. Another example is

FORMAT(7H☐RESULT,3F9.6)

FORTRAN I. No multiple FORMAT specifications such as 5I8 etc. are allowed. The maximum Hollerith specification is 49H.

The final type of FORMAT specification is the X-notation. For example:

FORMAT(I5,22X,F12.7)

The 22X means that 22 spaces will be skipped between the number read (printed) as I5 and the number read (printed) as F12.7.

FORTRAN I. The maximum X-notation is 49X.

(b) The READ *n*, LIST statement will instruct the computer to read, according to FORMAT statement *n*, the list of fixed- and/or floating-point variables. Each READ statement causes one data card to be read. For example,

$$\text{READ 5, A, B, K, L(1)}$$

$$\text{READ 987, EPS, X, Y}$$

(c) The PRINT *n*, LIST or PUNCH *n*, LIST statement causes the list variables to be printed (punched) according to FORMAT statement *n*.

FORGO. The PRINT statement is not permitted unless otherwise specified.

5. *Specification Statements.*

(a) Comment. Any card with a C in column 1 is called a *comment card* and is ignored by the compiler. These cards may contain arbitrary comments giving the programmer's name, the name of the program, or any other useful information, for example,

                    C   JOHN JONES

FORGO. The first card of a program must be a card called a *control card*. It has a C in columns 1 and 4. Each program has one and only one control card, but there may be as many comment cards as desired.

(b) DIMENSION A(20, 40), B(15, 2), C(109), I(98) is a sample of a dimension statement giving the amount of storage space to be reserved for the two-dimensional array A, the two-dimensional array B, the one-dimensional array C, and the one-dimensional array I. An array must be dimensioned before it is first used in the program. When a main program and subprograms are used jointly, corresponding arrays must have the same dimensions.

(c) COMMON and EQUIVALENCE statements will be discussed in Section 8.9.

6. *Execution of the Program.* The FORTRAN statements prepared for a problem make a source program, and when punched on IBM cards, a source deck. The 1620 does not understand the FORTRAN language; it understands only machine language. This means that FORTRAN has to be translated into machine language before computation can begin, a feat the 1620 can do automatically. When FORTRAN I and II are used, the computer produces a machine language deck from the source deck. This former is then fed back into the computer and computation begins. Using FORGO, however, no machine language deck is produced. The source deck is fed into the computer; the source statements are translated into machine language internally, and if there are no FORTRAN errors, computation begins. It should be noted that the computer storages available to a user are much reduced when FORGO is used.

5.11 COMMON ERRORS IN FORTRAN

Despite the fact that the FORTRAN compiler language uses mathematical notation and the English language, there are many pitfalls which trouble both new and
experienced programmers. In this section, some common errors will be presented
along with examples of incorrect programming taken from actual runs. It must be
emphasized that logical errors are not discussed here. These consist principally of
incorrect original equations or an incorrect sequence of statements. Furthermore,
errors in key punching are rather commonplace. In particular, the letter O is often
mistaken for the number 0; or an I for a 1.

In this section, we shall consider only the most frequent errors occurring in the
following three general areas:

A. Errors associated with arithmetic and control statements
B. Errors associated with input and output statements
C. Errors associated with subprograms

A. Rules to Follow with Arithmetic and Control Statements

1. The number of left parentheses must equal the number of right parentheses.

   Examples

   ```
   EULER = ((SINF(X)*H/EULER) + EULER        Incorrect

   EULER = (SINF(X)*H/EULER) + EULER         Correct
   ```

2. Once a statement number is used, it may not be used again.

   Examples

   ```
   30 IF(Y - Z) 36, 36, 34
                                             Incorrect
   30 X(I + 101) = X(I + 100) + 0.2


   30 IF(Y - Z) 36, 36, 34
                                             Correct
   29 X(I + 101) = X(I + 100) + 0.2
   ```

3. Subscripts must be in fixed-point mode.

   Examples

   ```
   X(I + 100) = X(I + 99.) + .2        Incorrect

   X(I + 100) = X(I + 99) + .2         Correct
   ```

4. If a statement number is mentioned, there must be a corresponding statement
in the program.

   Example (Incorrect)

   ```
   28 IF(Y - YSTOP) 36, 36, 34
      ⋮
   ```
   No statement 36.

5. When a variable is raised to a *negative* power, using the ** notation, the exponent preceded by a minus sign must be enclosed in parentheses.

Examples

Y = A + B** −2	Incorrect
Y = A + B**(−2)	Correct

6. No two operation symbols should appear in sequence.

Examples

AREA = RH/−B	Incorrect
AREA = RH/(−B)	Correct

7. The indices of a DO loop must never be reset by one of the statements within the DO.

Example

```
        DO 12 I = 1, 5
        DO 11 I = 1, 15
          ⋮
    11  CONTINUE                    Incorrect
          ⋮
    12  CONTINUE
```

8. If a computed GO TO statement is used, the value of the index (K in the example below) must be no greater than the total number of statements referred to.

Examples

```
        K = 5
                                    Incorrect
        GO TO (15, 16), K
```

9. The * cannot be omitted in a multiplication.

Examples

Y = 2.PI*X	Incorrect
Y = 2.*PI*X	Correct

10. If a variable is to be used, it must be defined previously either in a READ statement or on the left-hand side of an equal sign.

Examples

```
    C       START
                                    Incorrect
            Z = 2.*PI


    C       START

            PI = 3.141519           Correct

            Z = 2.*PI
```

B. Rules to Follow with Input and Output Statements

1. A comma must be present in PRINT, READ, and PUNCH statements.

   Examples

PRINT 48 I	Incorrect
PRINT 48, I	Correct

2. Dimensions must be large enough for the intended computation.

   Example

   ```
   DIMENSION A(3, 3)
   DO 5 I = 1, 5                    Incorrect
   5 READ 6, (A(I,J), J = 1, 3)
   ```

3. *Data* should begin in column 1, not 7.

4. The required data cards must agree *exactly* with the supplied data cards in total number and in sequence.

5. Integers must be punched in the rightmost position of the field.

   Example

   If we wish to read N = 3, we write

   ```
   READ 4, N

   4 FORMAT (I4)
   ```

   If the number 3 is punched in column 4, N will be read as   3
   If the number 3 is punched in column 3, N will be read as   30
   If the number 3 is punched in column 2, N will be read as 300
   If the number 3 is punched in column 1, N will be read as 3000

6. No comment cards are allowed among the data cards.

   Examples

C DATA	
.0471 .591	Incorrect
.4198 .724	
C NEXT TRIAL	
.0125 .781	Incorrect
.6324 .992	
C END OF DATA	

7. Floating-point variables should not be read in with an I-format.

8. Hollerith characters in a format statement should be counted carefully.

Example (Correct)

$$\text{FORMAT}(6X,3HA\square=,F9.5,5HFAB\square=,F9.5)$$

(The symbol $\square$ denotes a blank.)

9. When using the X-specification for blank fields, place the number denoting the number of blanks before the X. Also, 1X must be written (not just X) to obtain one blank.

Example

```
FORMAT(X6,F10.5,  X,  F3.2)         Incorrect
```

10. Column 1 of the output on certain off-line printers is used for carriage controls and not for general output.

Example

```
    PRINT 6,X
                                    Incorrect
6   FORMAT (7HANSWER=,F10.5)
```

Note: The corrected statement 6 should read:

```
6   FORMAT (8H□ANSWER=,F10.5)
```
or
```
6   FORMAT (5X,7HANSWER=,F10.5)
```

C. Rules to Follow with Subprograms

1. The required subprogram must be provided by the programmer.
2. There must be an END card for each subprogram.
3. When separately compiled main program and subprograms are used jointly, they must have the same numerical dimensions for corresponding arrays.

Example   (Incorrect)

```
C   MAIN PROGRAM             SUBROUTINE ROTATE(A,N)

    DIMENSION A(12, 12)      DIMENSION A(24, 24)
```

4. The arguments in CALL statements must agree exactly in number, order, and mode with those in the subroutines.

Example   (Incorrect)

```
C   MAIN PROGRAM             SUBROUTINE ROTATE(A,N)
    ⋮
    CALL ROTATE(A,.6,B)
```

5. The name of a function subprogram cannot end in **F** if it has more than three letters.

Example   (Incorrect)

```
FUNCTION GULF(X)
GULF(X) = X + 3. - 16*SINF(X)
RETURN
END
```

5.12 COMMUNICATION WITH A COMPUTATION CENTER

Due to the recent rapidly expanding role of computation in education, research, and development, the number of computation centers is ever increasing.

As computer operating procedures have become increasingly sophisticated, the knowledge required to use a *computation center*, rather than *computers*, varies from one installation to another, depending on the set up in the individual center. In addition, this knowledge is in many cases either gained by personal trial-and-error procedure or passed on by word of mouth. The purpose of this section is to provide the reader with a detailed check list (Table 5.4) for the hardware, software, and operating procedures of his own computation center.

TABLE 5–4

I. Hardware

A. Digital Computer

1. Type of digital computer to be used ☐

        decimal computer ☐

        binary computer ☐

                in words ☐

2. Memory size _____

                in bits ☐

                in bytes ☐

3. Internal memory cycle

    Less than 2 microseconds (μsec) ☐

    2–10 μsec ☐

    Above 10 μsec ☐

4. Time to add two numbers

    Less than 25 μsec ☐

    25–100 μsec ☐

    Above 100 μsec ☐

B. Peripheral Equipment

1. Punched Card equipment
   (a) Key punch   Type _____

   (b) Reproducer   Type _____

   (c) Sorter   Type _____

   (d) Verifier   Type _____

2. High-speed printer

   _____ lines per minute

3. Input-output typewriter
   User is permitted ☐
                                          to use the typewriter.
        not permitted ☐

4. Additional Memory Units
   (a) Tape transport   yes ☐   no ☐
        Recommended tape density is _____ bits per inch

   (b) Magnetic drum   yes ☐   no ☐
        additional words _____
                or bits _____

   (c) Disk   yes ☐   no ☐
        additional words _____
                or bits _____

   (d) Core   yes ☐   no ☐
        additional words _____
                or bits _____

5. Readers
        Optical characters   yes ☐   no ☐
        Magnetic characters   yes ☐   no ☐

6. Plotter   yes ☐
                                    Type _____
                       no ☐

7. Oscilloscope unit   yes ☐
                                     Type _____
                       no ☐

8. Data transmission devices   Yes ☐
                                          Type
                               no ☐

9. Converters
   (a) Card to magnetic tape   yes ☐   no ☐
   (b) Card to paper tape   yes ☐   no ☐
   (c) Magnetic tape to card   yes ☐   no ☐
   (d) Paper tape to card   yes ☐   no ☐

II. Software

A. Compilers available

FORTRAN I	☐	FORTRAN II	☐	FORTRAN IV	☐
MAD	☐	SPS	☐	GOTRAN	☐
ALGOL	☐	FORGO	☐	Others	☐

B. Input Cards ☐   Typewriter ☐   Tape ☐

C. Output format permitted

	Print	Punch	Write on tape
FORTRAN I			
FORTRAN II			
FORTRAN IV			
MAD			
SPS			
FORGO			
GOTRAN			
ALGOL			
Other compiler languages			

D. Library subroutines available

SINF   _____   LOGF   _____

COSF   _____   ATANF _____

ABSF   _____   EXPF   _____

SQRTF _____   Others   _____

E. The following FORTRAN statements are not permitted

PRINT _____

STOP   _____

PAUSE _____

F. Monitor system used   yes ☐   no ☐

III. Routine Operation of Computation Center

A. Type of Operation

Open shop ☐   Closed shop ☐   Partially closed and partially open ☐

B. Consulting supervisor at the center _____

C. My identification number, if required, for using the computer _____

D. Maximum allowable running time for each program _____ min

E. Normal turn-around time _____ hours

F. Trace feature available   yes ☐   no ☐

G. An object deck has to be made   yes ☐   no ☐

H. Submitting decks for running with emphasis on the format of the identification card (Simulate a typical run deck by labeling the cards below.)

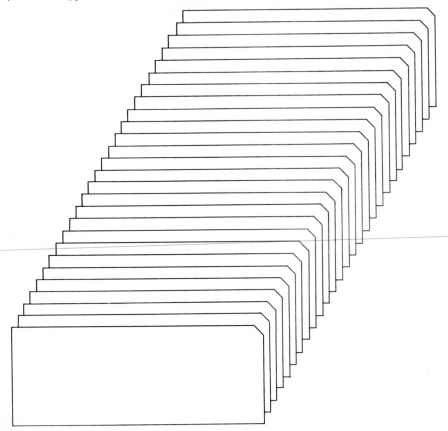

BIBLIOGRAPHY

BACKUS, J. W., *et al.*, "Report on the Algorithmic Language ALGOL 60," *Numer. Math.*, **2**, pp. 106–136 (1960), or *Comm. Assoc. Comput. Mach.*, **3**, pp. 299–314 (1960).

CARR, J. W., III, "Digital Computer Programming," *Handbook of Automation, Computation and Control*, E. M. GRABB, S. RAMO, and D. E. WOOLDRIDGE, EDS., **2**, Chap 2. John Wiley and Sons, New York, 1959.

CHORAFAS, D. N., *Programming Systems for Electronic Computers*. Butterworths, London, 1962.

COLMAN, H. L., and C. SMALLWOOD, *Computer Language . . . an Autoinstructional Introduction to FORTRAN*. McGraw-Hill, New York, 1962.

DIJKSTRA, E. W., *A Primer of ALGOL 60 Programming*. Academic Press, New York, 1962.

GERMAIN, C. B., *Programming the IBM 1620*. Prentice-Hall, Englewood Cliffs, N. J., 1962.

GILL, S., "Current Theory and Practice of Automatic Programming," *Comput. J.*, **2**, pp. 110–114 (1959).

HALSTEAD, M. H., *Machine-Independent Computer Programming.* Spartan Books, Washington, D. C., 1962.

INTERNATIONAL BUSINESS MACHINES CORP., *General Information Manual . . . FORTRAN.* IBM, New York, 1961.

JEENEL, J., *Programming for Digital Computers.* McGraw-Hill, New York, 1959.

LEDLEY, R. S., *Programming and Utilizing Digital Computers.* McGraw-Hill, New York, 1962.

LEEDS, H. D., and G. M. WEINBERG, *Computer Programming Fundamentals.* McGraw-Hill, New York, 1961.

LEESON, D. N., and D. L. DIMITRY, *Basic Programming Concepts and the 1620 Computer.* Holt, Rinehart & Winston, New York, 1962.

MCCRACKEN, D. D., *A Guide to ALGOL Programming.* John Wiley and Sons, New York, 1962.

MCCRACKEN, D. D., *A Guide to COBOL Programming.* John Wiley and Sons, New York, 1963.

MCCRACKEN, D. D., *A Guide to FORTRAN Programming.* John Wiley and Sons, New York, 1961.

MCCRACKEN, D. D., *A Guide to IBM 1401 Programming.* John Wiley and Sons, New York, 1961.

MCCRACKEN, D. D., *Digital Computer Programming.* John Wiley and Sons, New York, 1957.

MCCRACKEN, D. D., H. WEISS, and T. H. LEE, *Programming Business Computers.* John Wiley and Sons, New York, 1959.

NATHAN, R., and E. HANES, *Computer Programming Handbook, A Guide for Beginners.* Prentice-Hall, Englewood Cliffs, N. J., 1961.

ORGANICK, E. I., *A FORTRAN Primer.* Addison-Wesley, Reading, Mass., 1963.

SAXON, J. A., *Programming the IBM 7090 . . . A Self-Instructional Programmed Manual.* Prentice-Hall, Englewood Cliffs, N. J., 1963.

SAXON, J. A., and W. S. PLETTE, *Programming the IBM 1401.* Prentice-Hall, Englewood Cliffs, N. J., 1962.

SCOTT, T. G., *Basic Computer Programming.* Doubleday, Garden City, N. Y., 1962.

SHERMAN, P. M., and B. A. STEVENS, *Bibliography on Digital Computer Programming, 1955–1961.* Bell Telephone Laboratories, Technical Information Libraries, 1963.

SMITH, R. E., and D. E. JOHNSON, *FORTRAN Autotester.* John Wiley and Sons, New York, 1962.

PROBLEMS

1. Identify each of the following as a permissible (a) fixed-point constant, (b) fixed-point variable, (c) floating-point constant, (d) floating-point variable, or none of the four:

   (a) -86 (b) 3.1416   (c) $-8 . E - 17$ (d) $8 . E + 92$ (e) 82,189

   (f) UNH   (g) 2PI   (h) N/H   (i) N33   (j) 34,513

E X P

2. Translate the following mathematical expressions into FORTRAN expressions

   (a) $X + (Y - C)$ (b) $\dfrac{\pi}{e - 7.24}$ (c) x^{b-2}

   (d) $\sqrt{b^2 - 4ac}$ (e) $\dfrac{\pi}{6} h(3r^2 + h^2)$

3. Debug each of the following unrelated FORTRAN statements (write the corrected statement under each given statement).

   Col 6

   ```
   A = B + (ZM - 3)/C          (This must be one?)   needs decimal

   DO 17, JACK = 0, 100, 5      To many decimal / must be an integer

   A   SACKSON(5) = 6./(2 + ZM)   only not 9999 max

   2   IF (3.14159 - X) 3, 0.75, 6    E! not F

   42345   PI = 3.1416F3.5     needs a statement number.
                               (not enough) need one more
                               should be decimal

   CONTINUE

   PI = (3.14 * (2/ZA) = 2.    illegal

   2 = 8. * ZN    ZN = 8./2. = 4.   must rewrite since variable must be to left

   ROOT + SQRTF(1. + AN * AN * PSI * PSI).   Something must equal this PT =

   GO TO END    must be a statement number
   ```

4. The rectangular coordinates x, y of a set of points are:

x	1	2	3	4 ... 25
y	1	4	9	16 ... 625

   Write a FORTRAN program to calculate the corresponding polar coordinates for each point. The following equations are given:

   $$\rho = \sqrt{x^2 + y^2}, \qquad \theta = \tan^{-1}(y/x).$$

5. Write a program to calculate

   $$y = 1/\sqrt{1 + x^2}$$

   for $x = 0(0.1)10$. (*Note:* This means that x starts at zero and ends at 10 with interval 0.1.)

6. Suppose that we have a set of 100 values x_k ($k = 0, 1, \ldots, 99$), where

   $$x_k = k^{2/3} \sin(1/k).$$

   Write a program to calculate

   $$y_m = \sum_{k=0}^{99-m} x_k x_{99-m-k},$$

   for $m = 0, 1, \ldots, 15$.

7. Convert Fig. 3.1 into a complete FORTRAN program.

8. An array A of N numbers is given. Sort the numbers in descending order so that the largest number is in A(1), the next smaller number in A(2), . . ., the smallest number in A(N). Write a FORTRAN program for this task.

9. Write a FORTRAN program to compute 100 elements in a single-dimensioned fixed-point array I in the following manner:

   (a) Place 1 in each element of the array,

   (b) Add 2 to the elements 2, 4, 6, . . ., 100,

   (c) Add 3 to the elements 3, 6, 9, . . ., 99,

   $\vdots$

   (k) Add k to the elements $k, 2k, 3k, \ldots$

   Print the 100 answers in 10 rows of 10 numbers each.

10. Write a detailed flow chart and a FORTRAN program to check whether a set of three given points is on a straight line. The program should accomplish the following:

    (a) Read in the coordinates of a set of three points.

    (b) Compute and print the shortest distance, d, between the second point and the straight line joining the first and third points.

    (d) (i) If d is less than the given tolerance, print out a message (e.g., COLINEAR).
    (ii) If d is larger than the given tolerance, print out (e.g., NOT COLINEAR).

    (e) Read in another set of data.

    How would you terminate the process?

11. Matrix A:

$$a_{ij} = m \sin{(i^2 j^2 \pi/p)} + n \cos{(q i^3 j^3)}, \qquad i \le j,$$
$$a_{ij} = \sqrt{m} \cos{(i^2 j^2 \pi/p)}, \qquad i > j,$$

    where

$$i = 1, 2, 3, \qquad m = 8.2913, \qquad p = 6.21,$$
$$j = 1, 2, 3, \qquad n = 0.528, \qquad q = 3.142.$$

    Symmetric matrix B:

$$b_{11} = 1.342, \qquad b_{22} = 7.293,$$
$$b_{12} = 6.87, \qquad b_{23} = 1,$$
$$b_{13} = 0, \qquad b_{33} = 3,$$
$$c_{ij} = a_{ij} + b_{ij}, \qquad i = 1, 2, 3; \quad j = 1, 2, 3.$$

    Write a program in FORTRAN which, if necessary, will handle a 10 × 10 matrix and will do the following:

    (a) Compute and print all elements of matrix A row by row (see Table 5.3).

    (b) Print the *complete* matrix B row by row.

    (c) Compute and print matrix C row by row.

    (d) Print the lower triangular matrix B.

    Matrix B information: The input format will be 7F10.4. The first data card will contain three numbers, namely b_{11}, b_{12}, and b_{13}. The second data card will contain two numbers, b_{22} and b_{23}, and the last card will contain only one number, b_{33}.

12. Given an $N \times N$ square matrix A. Find those off-diagonal elements which are symmetric, or

$$|a_{ij} - a_{ji}| \leq \epsilon,$$

where ϵ is an assigned small number. Print them out in the following format:

$$I = xx \qquad J = xx \qquad A(I,J) = xx.xxx$$
$$\vdots$$

13. Write a subroutine to compute N-factorial by using the following calling statement:

$$CALL \ FAC(N, \ IANS)$$

where N is the number and IANS is the result. Assume that $N > 0$ and $N_{max} = 25$.

14. The number of combinations of N things taken K at a time is

$$C_K^N = \frac{N!}{K!(N - K)!} .$$

Using the *SUBROUTINE* FAC of Problem 13, write a main program to compute C.

15. Write a subroutine FLIP to perform a "flipping" of the following array of numbers and to print the results row by row.

2	7	6
9	5	1
4	3	8

This operation can be readily carried out by interchanging the first and third columns.

16. Write a main program to flip the array of Problem 15 consecutively five times.

PART **II**

COMPUTER-ORIENTED
NUMERICAL METHODS

Part II deals principally with selected mathematical methods which are either extensively used on, or particularly suitable for, digital computers. Many problems in science and engineering frequently reduce to one or two standard mathematical problems. Subroutines for these standard problems are usually available in program libraries commonly affiliated with computer centers. However, it is dangerous, and therefore not recommended, to use a subroutine without understanding the related numerical method.

In this book, methods which can be regarded as essential tools only for desk computers or slide rules are not discussed. Only those methods suitable for digital computers are set forth in detail.

Transcendental equations. These are all functions that are not algebraic, they yield a transcendental curve.
expression of the following nature are transcendental:

(1) exponential $y = a^x, e^x$

(2) logarithmic $y = \log x$, $\ln x$, $\log(x^2 - 1)$

(3) Trigonometric $y = \sin x, \cos x, \tan x, \cot x, \sec x, \csc x$

(4) inverse Trigonometric $y = \sin^{-1} x$. - - -

(5) hyperbolic functions $y = \sinh x, \cosh x, \tanh x, \coth x$
$$\operatorname{sech} x, \operatorname{cosech} x$$

(6) Inverse hyperbolic $y = \sinh^{-1} x$ - - -

Transcendental numbers: (J Liouville 1851) all non-algebraic real numbers (an algebraic number is the solution (x) of an algebraic equation of the form $a_0 x^n + a_1 x^{n-1} \cdots a_n = 0$ $a_{0n} = $ Rational coefficients

Polynomial This is an algebraic expression of the type $a_0 x^n + a_1 x^{n-1} \cdots a_n = 0$, it has only one unknown x.

Binomials have two unknowns $f(x, y) = 0$

CHAPTER 6

COMPUTER SOLUTION OF POLYNOMIAL AND TRANSCENDENTAL EQUATIONS

6.1 INTRODUCTION

In scientific and engineering analysis it is often necessary to solve transcendental or higher-degree polynomial equations. Two typical examples are:

$$e^{-x} - \sin(\pi x/2) = 0 \tag{6.1}$$

and

$$x^4 - x^3 - 10x^2 - x + 1 = 0. \tag{6.2}$$

Equation (6.1) represents a transcendental equation since sine and exponential functions are involved. Equation (6.2) is a fourth-order polynomial equation.

The problem may be stated in two ways: first, to obtain a more accurate value for a real root whose approximate location is already known by other means, including graphical determination; and second, to find *all* roots, both real and complex, of the given equation without any prior information about their approximate locations. The second type of problem is obviously more difficult.

This chapter is concerned with a discussion of the possible methods of numerical solution of transcendental or higher-degree polynomial equations.

6.2 HALF-INTERVAL SEARCH   *for equations of form* $f(x) = 0$

As an example, let us solve the transcendental equation

$$e^{-x} - \sin(\pi x/2) = 0. \tag{6.1}$$

This equation has a single solution between 0 and 1, as may be seen from the intersection of the two curves shown in Fig. 6.1. The basic problem is to find the root according to a specified tolerance. We shall employ the notation $f(x)$ to represent the function appearing on the left-hand side of the equation. Thus in Eq. (6.1), $f(x)$ is equal to $e^{-x} - \sin(\pi x/2)$.

Using this method, one must compute the left-hand side of Eq. (6.1), or $f(x)$, at $x = 0.5$ and determine whether the solution is to the right or to the left of $x = \frac{1}{2}$. The location of the root is then known to be in an interval of length $\frac{1}{2}$ instead of 1. By computing the given expression $f(x)$ at the midpoint of this interval, the solution can further be localized to an interval of length $\frac{1}{4}$. This procedure can then be repeated to locate the root to an accuracy of any reasonable number of significant digits. What we are trying to determine in each step is whether the required root lies in the right or left half of the previous interval. Some representative computations are shown in Table 6.1.

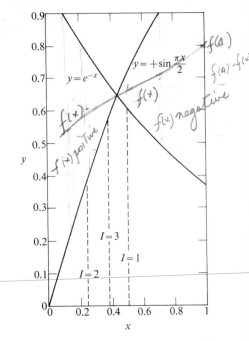

Fig. 6.1. Half-interval search for the root of $e^{-x} - \sin(\pi x/2) = 0$.

Figure 6.2 shows a possible flow chart for the half-interval search procedure. Data A and B are the initial left- and right-hand limits, respectively, in which the root lies. Data ϵ represents the tolerance of $f(x)$. In other words, the search is continued until the condition $|f(x_i)| \leq \epsilon$ is satisfied, where ϵ is some arbitrarily chosen small number.

As a practical programming detail, it is worth while to note that the product of $f(A)$ and $f(x)$ is used to compare the sign of two quantities. This is shown in block

TABLE 6.1.   Example of Half-Interval Search

(1)	(2)	(3)	(4)	(5)	
Step number i	x_i	e^{-x}	$\sin(\pi x/2)$	(3) − (4)	
				(+)	(−)
1	0.50	0.6065	0.7071		✓
2	0.25	0.7788	0.3827	✓	
3	0.375	0.6873	0.5556	✓	
4	0.4375	0.6456	0.6344	✓	
5	0.46875	0.6258	0.6716		✓
⋮					

$$f(x) = e^{-Y} - \sin\left(\frac{\pi x}{2}\right) = 0$$

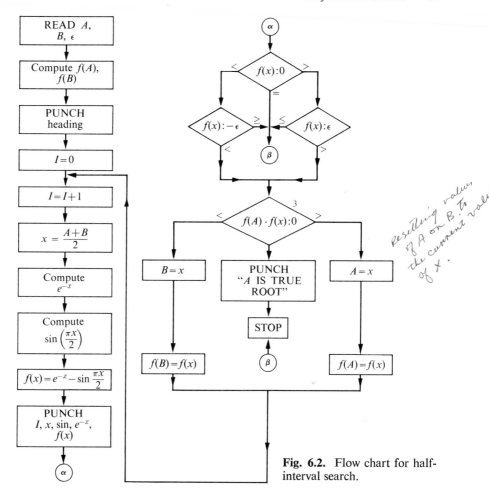

Resulting values of A or B to the current value of x.

Fig. 6.2. Flow chart for half-interval search.

3 in Fig. 6.2. Here $f(A)$ stands for the value of $f(x)$ when $x = A$. Similarly $f(B)$ represents the value of $f(x)$ for $x = B$. When the product has a positive value, $f(A)$ and $f(x)$ must have the same sign. Conversely, if the product is negative, $f(A)$ and $f(x)$ are of different signs. If the product happens to be equal to zero, $f(A)$ must be equal to zero. Therefore, A is the true root.

In Fig. 6.2, the graphical device α should be noted. This device is often used when the flow chart is too long to finish in the same column.

It is required that the results be printed out in this format:

I	X(I)	SIN	EXP	F(X)
———	———	———	———	———
———	———	———	———	———
———	———	———	———	———
(I6)	(F15.8)	(F15.8)	(F15.8)	(F20.8)

```
C                        HALF      INTERVAL      SEARCH
       READ 22,A,B,EPS
    22 FORMAT(F10.4,F10.4,F10.4)
       PI=3.14159265
       FA=EXPF(-A)-SINF(PI*A/2.)
       FB=EXPF(-B)-SINF(PI*B/2.)
       PUNCH 81
    81 FORMAT(5X,1HI,9X,4HX(I),11X,3HSIN,12X,3HEXP,17X,4HF(X)//)
       I=0
     7 I=I+1
       X=(A+B)/2.
       EX=EXPF(-X)
       SI=SINF(PI*X/2.)
       F=EX-SI
       PUNCH 99, I,X,SI,EX,F
    99 FORMAT(I6,F15.8,F15.8,F15.8,F20.8//)
       IF(F) 12,10,11
    12 IF(F+EPS)3,10,10
    11 IF(F-EPS)10,10,3
     3 IF(F*FA)5,8,6
     5 B=X
       FB=F
       GO TO 7
     6 A=X
       FA=F
       GO TO 7
     8 PUNCH 9
     9 FORMAT(14HA IS TRUE ROOT)
    10 STOP
       END
       .0          1.0          .0001
```

Fig. 6.3. FORTRAN program for half-interval search.

TABLE 6.2. Answers for Half-Interval Search

I	X(I)	SIN	EXP	F(X)
1	.50000000	.70710681	.60653069	-.10057612
2	.25000000	.38268344	.77880079	.39611735
3	.37500000	.55557026	.68728929	.13171903
4	.43750000	.63439329	.64564857	.01125528
5	.46875000	.67155898	.62578403	-.04577495
6	.45312500	.65317286	.63563873	-.01753413
7	.44531250	.64383156	.64062406	-.00320750
8	.44140625	.63912448	.64313140	.00400692
9	.44335938	.64148104	.64187650	.00039546
10	.44433594	.64265703	.64125000	-.00140703
11	.44384766	.64206924	.64156320	-.00050604
12	.44360352	.64177518	.64171981	-.00005537

Here "I" represents the number of iterations and the figures in parentheses represent the format to be used in the FORTRAN program. Figure 6.3 shows the corresponding 1620 FORTRAN program, together with the required data. From the answer sheet (Table 6.2), we see that the value of the required root is approximately equal to 0.4436. In this computation we used $\epsilon = 0.0001$.

6.3 METHOD OF FALSE POSITION (*REGULA FALSI*)

The half-interval search procedure discussed in the last section is one of several computer methods available for obtaining an approximate solution to an equation $f(x) = 0$. All the methods are iterative, since an initial approximation, $x = x_0$, to the root is usually made and a sequence of approximations, $x_1, x_2, \ldots, x_n$, is generated to get closer to the true root. A second iterative procedure is the method of *false position*. With this method we seek to find an interval $x_L < x < x_R$ in which $f(x)$ changes its sign (Fig. 6.4). The linear interpolation is then used to find the next iterated value x_{app} of the true root x_{root}, where x_{app}, the approximate value, lies between x_L and x_R. First, by the similar triangles shaded in Fig. 6.4, we have

$$\frac{f(x_L)}{x_{app} - x_L} = \frac{f(x_L) - f(x_R)}{x_R - x_L}$$

or

$$x_{app} = x_L + \frac{f(x_L)(x_R - x_L)}{f(x_L) - f(x_R)}. \quad (6.3)$$

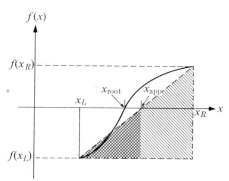

Fig. 6.4. Method of false position.

We now seek to determine which of the two subintervals, $x_L < x < x_{app}$ or $x_{app} < x < x_R$, contains the true root x_{root}. This can be done by checking the sign of $f(x_{app})$. If $f(x_R) \cdot f(x_{app}) < 0$, then the right-hand interval contains the root, and x_{app} becomes the new x_L for the next iteration. On the other hand, if $f(x_L) \cdot f(x_{app}) < 0$, then $x_L < x_{root} < x_{app}$, and x_{app} becomes the new x_R for the next iteration.

The iteration is continued until the following relation is established:

$$|f(x_{app})| < \epsilon,$$

where ϵ is a preassigned, small positive member, say 10^{-5}. The iteration may also be terminated by narrowing down the interval, that is,

$$(x_R - x_L) < \epsilon',$$

where ϵ' is some arbitrarily chosen small number.

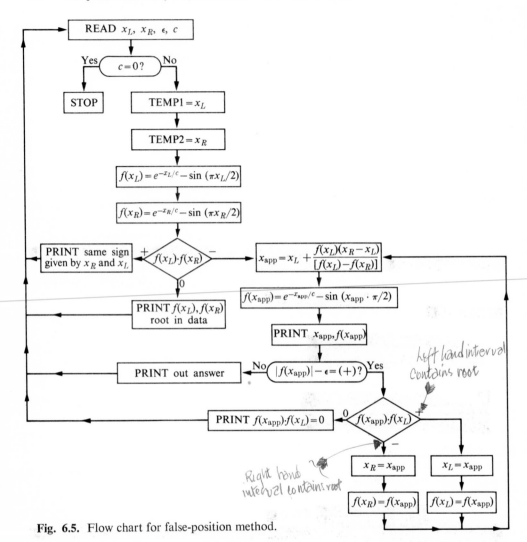

Fig. 6.5. Flow chart for false-position method.

Example

Solve $e^{-x/c} - \sin(\pi x/2) = 0$, using the method of false position. Since there is a root between 0 and 1, we take

$$x_{\mathrm{L}} = 0,$$

$$x_{\mathrm{R}} = 1,$$

and

$$\epsilon = 0.0001.$$

A sample flow chart is presented in Fig. 6.5, and the related **FORTRAN** program and its results are shown in Fig. 6.6 and Table 6.3, respectively.

Note that $c = 1$ is used in Fig. 6.6. (Question: how should the data be prepared so that $c = 1, 2, 3, \ldots, 9$, respectively, for nine different cases?)

```
C                           METHOD OF FALSE POSITION
      PI = 3.14159265
   25 READ 10, XL, XR, EPS, C
   10 FORMAT(F10.4,F10.4,F10.4,F10.4)
      IF(C) 20,21,20
   20 TEMP1=XL
      TEMP2=XR
      FXL = EXPF(-XL/C) - SINF(PI*XL/2.)
      FXR = EXPF(-XR/C) - SINF(PI*XR/2.)
      IF(FXL*FXR) 22,23,24
   24 PUNCH 11
   11 FORMAT(5X,30H SAME SIGN  GIVEN BY XR AND XL)
      GO TO 25
   23 PUNCH 12, FXL, FXR
   12 FORMAT(E14.8,E14.8,13H ROOT IN DATA)
      GO TO 25
   22 PUNCH 13
   13 FORMAT(7X,5H XAPP,9X, 6H FXAPP)
   31 XAPP = XL + FXL*(XR-XL)/(FXL-FXR)
      FXAPP = EXPF(-XAPP/C) - SINF(XAPP*PI/2.)
      PUNCH 14, XAPP, FXAPP
   14 FORMAT(F15.8,F15.8)
      IF(SQRTF(FXAPP*FXAPP) - EPS) 26,26,27
   26 PUNCH 18
   18 FORMAT(//)
      PUNCH 15, C,TEMP2, TEMP1
   15 FORMAT(5X,2HC=,F5.2,2X,3HXR=F6.2,2X,3HXL=F6.2/)
      PUNCH 16, XAPP, EPS
   16 FORMAT(9H ROOT IS F8.4,2X,19HBASED ON EPSILON = F7.4)
      GO TO 25
   27 IF(FXAPP*FXL) 28,29,30
   28 XR = XAPP
      FXR = FXAPP
      GO TO 31
   29 PUNCH 17
   17 FORMAT(14H FXAPP*FXL = 0)
      GO TO 25
   30 XL = XAPP
      FXL = FXAPP
      GO TO 31
   21 STOP
      END
      0.0        1.0        0.0001        1.0
      0.0        0.0        0.0           0.0
```

Fig. 6.6. FORTRAN program.

TABLE 6.3.   Answers by Method of False Position

XAPP	FXAPP
.61269986	-.27869499
.47916032	-.06428183
.45021941	-.01222181
.44478336	-.00223222
.44379273	-.00040465
.44361324	-.00007329

```
      C= 1.00   XR=  1.00   XL=  0.00
   ROOT IS      .4436  BASED ON EPSILON =    .0001
```

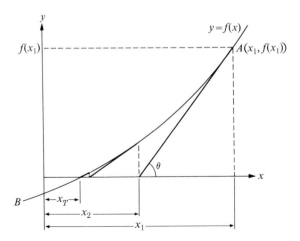

Fig. 6.7. Newton-Raphson method.

6.4 NEWTON-RAPHSON METHOD

The solution to an equation $f(x) = 0$ may often be found by a simple procedure known as the Newton-Raphson method. This method consists of drawing the tangent to the curve at the point A, as shown in Fig. 6.7. The x-intercept of the tangent, or x_2, is then used as the first approximation. Figure 6.7 shows the use of the Newton-Raphson method to solve $f(x) = 0$ to the root x_T. From the figure, we have

$$f'(x_1) = \tan \theta = \frac{f(x_1)}{x_1 - x_2}, \tag{6.4}$$

where $f'(x_1)$ denotes the derivative of $f(x)$ evaluated at $x = x_1$. Hence

$$x_2 = x_1 - \frac{f(x_1)}{f'(x_1)}. \tag{6.5}$$

An iterative sequence can now be set up as follows:

$$x_{n+1} = x_n - \frac{f(x_n)}{f'(x_n)}. \tag{6.6}$$

This formula can be repeatedly used to find improved approximations to the real root x_T. It should be noted that this process does not work well when the slope of the curve becomes very small; it will not work at all if the slope of the curve becomes zero along the arc AB. It is further assumed in this method that there is no inflection point along the arc AB.

The recurrence relation, as expressed in Eq. (6.6), may also be derived from the Taylor-series expansion for $f(x_T)$ about x:

$$f(x_T) = f(x) + (x_T - x)f'(x) + \cdots + \frac{f^{(k)}(x)}{k!}(x_T - x)^k + R. \tag{6.7}$$

Taylor's series
in general form $f(x) = f(x_1) + \dfrac{f'(x)}{1!} x + \dfrac{f''(x)(x^2)}{2!} + \cdots - + f^{n-1}$

Taking only the first two terms, we obtain

$$f(x_T) \doteq f(x) + (x_T - x)f'(x),$$
$$0 \doteq f(x) + (x_T - x)f'(x),$$

and from this, Eq. (6.6) follows.

Example

The iterative equation (6.6) can be readily used to approximate the square root of C by solving $x^2 - C = 0$. Here we take

$$f(x) = x^2 - C,$$
$$f'(x) = 2x.$$

The iterative sequence then becomes

$$x_{n+1} = x_n - \frac{x_n^2 - C}{2x_n},$$

or

$$x_{n+1} = \tfrac{1}{2}\left(x_n + \frac{C}{x_n}\right). \quad (6.8)$$

Let us carry this process through to compute $\sqrt{24}$. First we take

$$x_1 = 1 \text{ (arbitrarily)}.$$

Then

$$x_2 = \tfrac{1}{2}(1 + 24) = 12.5,$$
$$x_3 = \tfrac{1}{2}(12.5 + 24/12.5) = 7.21,$$
$$x_4 = \tfrac{1}{2}(7.21 + 24/7.21) = 5.2693,$$
$$x_5 = \tfrac{1}{2}(5.2693 + 24/5.2693) = 4.9119,$$
$$x_6 = \tfrac{1}{2}(4.9119 + 24/4.9119) = 4.8989,$$
$$\vdots$$

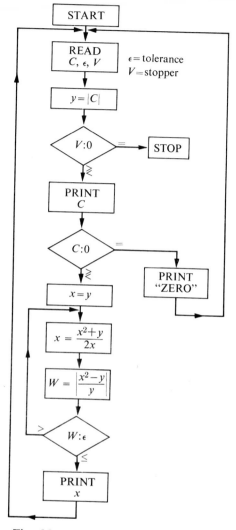

Fig. 6.8. Flow chart for computing square root.

Figure 6.8 shows the flow chart for this method of solving $x^2 - C = 0$. A FORTRAN program is presented in Fig. 6.9. It should be noted that the iteration continues until the following relation is established:

$$\left|\frac{x^2 - C}{C}\right| \leq \epsilon,$$

where ϵ is a preassigned, small positive number. In this example, we take

$$\epsilon = 10^{-5}.$$

The Newton-Raphson formula can readily be extended to obtain the rth root of the number C. Making use of Eq. (6.6), we have

$$x_{n+1} = x_n - \frac{x_n^r - C}{r x_n^{r-1}},$$

or

$$x_{n+1} = \frac{1}{r}\left[(r-1)x_n + \frac{C}{x_n^{r-1}}\right]. \tag{6.9}$$

It can be seen that when $r = 2$, Eq. (6.9) becomes Eq. (6.8). Equation (6.9) is the basic iterative formula used to obtain the rth root of a given number C. It should be noted that only real roots will be obtained from Eq. (6.9).

```
C       NEWTON-RAPHSON METHOD FOR FINDING SQUARE ROOT
 31 READ 2, C, E, V
  2 FORMAT (F10.5,F10.5,F10.5)
    Y=ABSF(C)
    IF (V) 10,40,10
 10 PRINT 7,C
  7 FORMAT (10X,4H C= ,F12.5)
    IF (C) 11,12,11
 12 PRINT 17
 17 FORMAT (8H X= ZERO//)
    GO TO 31
 11 X=Y
 14 X=(X*X+Y)/(2.*X)
    W=ABSF((X*X-Y)/Y)
    IF (W-E)30,30,14
 30 PRINT 50, X
 50 FORMAT(10X,4H X= ,F12.5//)
    GO TO 31
 40 STOP
    END
```

Fig. 6.9. FORTRAN program for Newton-Raphson method.

As a second example, let us consider a circle of radius R ($R = 3.00$) and six different values of A, the shaded area as shown in Fig. 6.10.

$A = 28.274333$

$\quad = 30.000000$

$\quad = 14.137166$

$\quad = 7.100000$

$\quad = 4.999999$

$\quad = 0.000000$

Figure 6.10

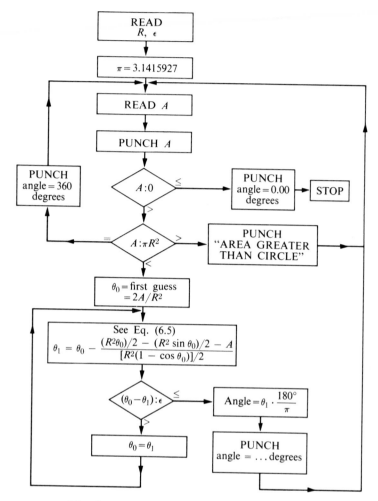

Fig. 6.11.   Flow chart to find angle at center.

Using the Newton-Raphson method, write a FORTRAN program to find θ in degrees for the corresponding value of A. As shown in the flow chart (Fig. 6.11), the program is terminated when A equals zero. Figure 6.12 shows the FORTRAN program for this example.

The computer carries out all mathematical operations with a finite number of significant digits. All excess digits are generally truncated (chopped off). Therefore, the equation

$$\theta_n - \theta_{n+1} = 0$$

may never be satisfied. We will introduce a tolerance ϵ and substitute the equation

$$|\theta_n - \theta_{n+1}| - \epsilon \le 0.$$

```
C        ANGLE   AT CENTER FROM GIVEN AREA OF THE CIRCLE
C
         READ 101, R, EPS
 101 FORMAT(F4.2,F6.3)
         PUNCH  100
 100 FORMAT(15X,1HA,30X,5HANGLE//)
         PI = 3.14159265
   1 READ 102,A
 102 FORMAT(F9.6)
         IF(A)99,99,2
   2 ARCLE = PI*R*R
         IF(A-ARCLE)7,5,6
   5 ANGLE = 360.0
  21 PUNCH  111,A,ANGLE
         GO TO 1
 111 FORMAT(10X,F10.6,10X,10HDEGREES = ,F13.5//)
   6 PUNCH 112,A
 112 FORMAT(10X,F10.6,10X,27HAREA   GREATER   THAN   CIRCLE//)
         GO TO 1
   7 THETO = 2. *A/(R*R)
   3 THET1 = THETO-(THETO-SIN(THETO)-2.0*A/(R*R))/(1.0-COS(THETO))
         Z = THETO-THET1
         IF(Z)8,10,9
  10 ANGLE = THET1*180.0/PI
         GO TO 21
   8 IF(Z+EPS)11,10,10
   9 IF(Z-EPS)10,10,11
  11 THETO = THET1
         GO TO 3
  99 ANGLE = 0.
         PUNCH 111,A, ANGLE
         STOP
         END
3.0000.001
28.274333
30.000000
14.137166
07.100000
04.999999
00.000000
```

Fig. 6.12. FORTRAN program for angles at center.

For this problem we will use $\epsilon = 0.001$. Data cards for this example require the following format:

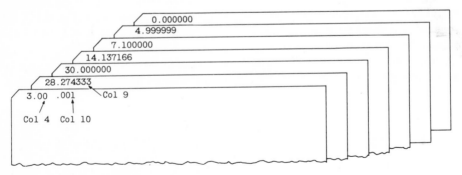

Table 6.4 shows a sample answer sheet.

TABLE 6.4.   Answers for Angles at Center

A		ANGLE
28.274333	DEGREES =	359.46544
30.000000	AREA GREATER THAN CIRCLE	
14.137166	DEGREES =	179.99999
7.100000	DEGREES =	132.58525
4.999999	DEGREES =	115.41348
0.000000	DEGREES =	0.00000

[handwritten margin note:] DESCARTS RULE OF SIGN
$f(x)=0$ the number of sign variations (changes) is the maximum number of roots — may be reduced by an even integer

$f(-x)=0$ the number of successive sign variations gives the maximum number of negative roots.

Brust - Fourier Theorem of which above is a special case.

6.5   BAIRSTOW'S METHOD FOR POLYNOMIAL EQUATIONS WITH REAL COEFFICIENTS

In the last section we considered some examples for the solutions of transcendental equations. We shall now discuss a method for the solution of a polynomial equation of any degree with real coefficients:

$$y^n + a_1 y^{n-1} + a_2 y^{n-2} + \cdots + a_n = 0. \tag{6.10}$$

This equation has the following properties:

(a) It has n roots, single or repeated.
(b) It always contains a single real root if n is a positive odd integer.
(c) The complex roots present themselves in conjugate complex pairs, say, $D + Ej$ and $D - Ej$, where D and E are real and $j = \sqrt{-1}$.
(d) Descartes' rule of signs applies to this equation. ⌐

The method we shall discuss was suggested by Bairstow† in 1914 and modified by Hitchcock‡ in 1944. The fundamental principle of the method may best be indicated by an example. Consider the polynomial equation

$$y^5 - 17y^4 + 124y^3 - 508y^2 + 1035y - 875 = 0. \tag{6.11}$$

[handwritten margin note: Synthetic division?]

Dividing the left-hand side of Eq. (6.11) by a quadratic factor $(y^2 + py + q)$ leads to the identity

$$y^5 - 17y^4 + 124y^3 - 508y^2 + 1035y - 875$$
$$= (y^2 + py + q)(y^3 + B_1 y^2 + B_2 y + B_3) + Ry + S. \tag{6.12}$$

[handwritten margin note:] $\left. \begin{array}{l} p+qj \\ p-qj \end{array} \right\}$ factoring out of nth degree polynomial

---

† Bairstow, L., "Investigations Relating to the Stability of the Aeroplane," *Reports and Memoranda No. 154*, Advisory Committee of Aeronautics, 1914.
‡ Hitchcock, F. L. "An Improvement on the G.C.D. Method for Complex Roots," J. Math. Phys., **23**, pp. 69–74 (1944).

Equating the coefficients, we get

$$p + B_1 = -17,$$
$$B_2 + B_1 p + q = 124,$$
$$B_3 + B_2 p + B_1 q = -508,$$
$$R + B_3 p + B_2 q = 1035,$$
$$S + B_3 q = -875.$$

(6.13)

From the first three equations in (6.13) we find

$$B_1 = -17 - p,$$
$$B_2 = 124 + 17p + p^2 - q,$$
$$B_3 = -508 - 124p - 17p^2 - p^3 + 2pq + 17q.$$

Substituting into the last two equations of Eq. (6.13), we have

$$p^4 + 17p^3 + 124p^2 + 508p + 1035 - 3qp^2 - 3468 - 124q - q^2 = R, \quad (6.14)$$
$$p^3 q + 17p^2 q + 124pq - 2pq^2 - 17q^2 + 508q - 875 = S. \quad (6.15)$$

The fundamental problem is to find p and q such that both R and S in Eqs. (6.14) and (6.15) become zero. Once p and q are known, we can then obtain two roots of the original equation (6.11) by solving the quadratic equation. In this example, p and q are found, by an iterative procedure to be described below, to be -4.0 and 5.0, respectively. Thus the quadratic factor is $(y^2 - 4y + 5)$, and the two roots are $2 \pm j$.

We shall now describe the step-by-step procedure for obtaining p and q, and cite some numerical examples. The detailed derivations will be discussed in Appendix C. The steps in the computation of p and q are as follows:

(1) Select the initial values for p and q. ($A_1, \ldots, A_n$ are n given coefficients.)
(2) Compute all B_k's from $B_1, \ldots, B_n$ from

$$B_k = A_k - pB_{k-1} - qB_{k-2}, \quad (6.16)$$

where $B_{-1} = 0$, and $B_0 = 1$.

(3) Compute all C_k's from $C_1, \ldots, C_{n-1}$ from

$$C_k = B_k - pC_{k-1} - qC_{k-2}, \quad (6.17)$$

where $C_{-1} = 0$, and $C_0 = 1$.

(4) Compute $\overline{C}_{n-1} = C_{n-1} - B_{n-1}$.

(5) Using the values of C_{n-3}, C_{n-2}, $\overline{C}_{n-1}$, B_n and B_{n-1} obtained in steps 2, 3, and 4, compute Δp and Δq:

$$\Delta p = \frac{B_{n-1}C_{n-2} - B_n C_{n-3}}{(C_{n-2}^2 - \overline{C}_{n-1}C_{n-3})}, \quad (6.18)$$

$$\Delta q = \frac{B_n C_{n-2} - B_{n-1}\overline{C}_{n-1}}{(C_{n-2}^2 - \overline{C}_{n-1}C_{n-3})}. \quad (6.19)$$

(6) Increment p and q by the amounts Δp and Δq:

$$p_{i+1} = p_i + \Delta p, \qquad (6.20)$$

$$q_{i+1} = q_i + \Delta q, \qquad (6.21)$$

where i is the number of iterations.

(7) Test for convergence:

$$M = |\Delta p| + |\Delta q| < \epsilon.$$

If $M > \epsilon$, return to step 2 and repeat the process (an upper limit on i is imposed for possible nonconvergent cases). If $M \leq \epsilon$, then p and q are satisfactory values of the coefficients in the desired quadratic factor $(y^2 + py + q)$.

In order to compute the two roots $D + Ej$ and $D - Ej$, the following expressions are used:

$$D = -p/2, \qquad (6.22)$$

$$E = \sqrt{q - p^2/4}. \qquad (6.23)$$

Example

Consider the polynomial

$$y^5 - 17y^4 + 124y^3 - 508y^2 + 1035y - 875 = 0,$$

which may be factored as

$$(y^2 - 4y + 5)(y^3 - 13y^2 + 67y - 175)$$
$$= (y^2 - 4y + 5)(y^2 - 6y + 25)(y - 7) = 0.$$

We assume that the initial values of both p and q are zero. The procedure to be followed, i.e., the five iterations, are illustrated in Table 6.5. We find that the quadratic factor is $(y^2 - 4y + 5)$, and the two roots are $2 + j$ and $2 - j$.

We next solve the polynomial

$$y^3 - 13.029y^2 + 67.311y - 176.196 = 0,$$

where the coefficients are B_k's $(k = 1, 2, \ldots, 3)$, obtained in the fifth iteration. Using the same procedure, one obtains the following quadratic factor after four iterations:

$$(y^2 - 6.0y + 25.2).$$

The two roots corresponding to this quadratic factor are $3 + 4j$ and $3 - 4j$.

Figures 6.13 and 6.14 show a flow chart and FORTRAN program for computing all the roots of a given polynomial with real coefficients. Table 6.6 shows the answer for the five roots of Eq. (6.11).

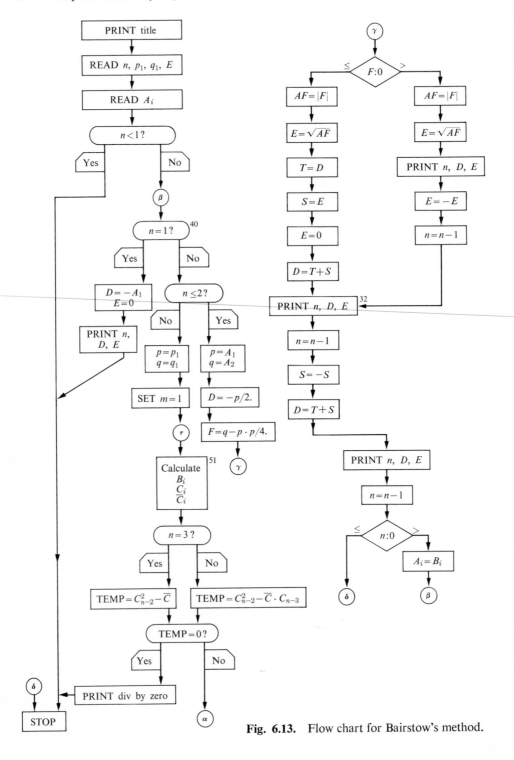

Fig. 6.13. Flow chart for Bairstow's method.

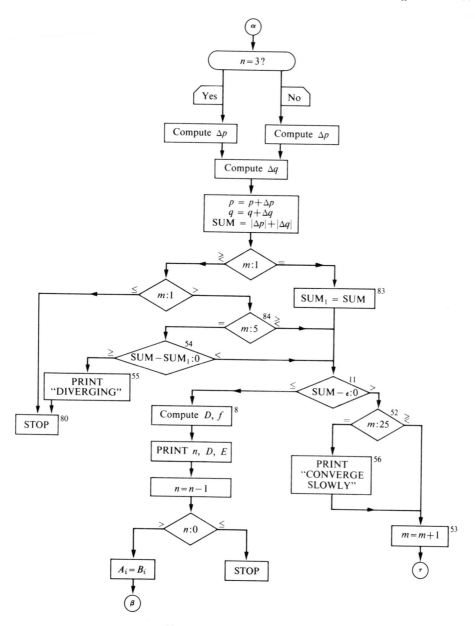

Fig. 6.13. (*cont.*)

```
C         BAIRSTOW'S METHOD FOR FINDING QUADRATIC FACTORS OF POLYNOMIALS
C         SOLUTION OF POLYNOMIAL UP TO X**99 WITH REAL COEFFICIENTS
C          FORTRAN II MUST BE USED
C         N IS THE HIGHEST POWER OF THE POLYNOMIAL
C         THE ORIGINAL EQUATION MUST BE OF THE FORM
C         X**N + A(1)X**(N-1) + A(2)X**(N-2) + ... + A(N-1)X**(1) + A(N)
C         P1 AND Q1 INITIALLY ARE GUESSES AT THE QUADRATIC COEFFICIENTS
C         EPSILON IS THE DESIRED ACCURACY OF P AND Q
          PUNCH 12
   12 FORMAT(20X,4HREAL,20X,9HIMAGINARY//)
          DIMENSION A(100),B(100),C(100)
          READ 10,P1,Q1,EPSON,N
   10 FORMAT(F10.4,F10.4,F10.4,I2)
          READ 20, (A(I),I=1,N)
   20 FORMAT(F8.4,F8.4,F8.4,F8.4,F8.4,F8.4,F8.4,F8.4,F8.4)
   40 IF(N-1) 80,42,43
   42 D=(-1.)*A(1)
          E=0.
          PUNCH 13,N,D,E
          PRINT 13,N,D,E
   13 FORMAT(7X,2HX(,I2,3H) =,3X,F8.4,19X,F8.4)
          GO TO 80
   43 IF(N-2) 45,45,46
   45 P=A(1)
          Q=A(2)
          GO TO 8
   46 P=P1
          Q=Q1
          M=1
   51 B(1)=A(1)-P
          B(2)=A(2)-P*B(1)-Q
          DO 6 K=3,N
    6 B(K)=A(K)-P*B(K-1)-Q*B(K-2)
          L=N-1
          C(1)=B(1)-P
          C(2)=B(2)-P*C(1)-Q
          DO 7 J=3,L
    7 C(J)=B(J)-P*C(J-1)-Q*C(J-2)
          CBARL=C(L)-B(L)
          IF(N-3) 70,71,70
   71 DEN=C(N-2)*C(N-2)-CBARL
          GO TO 72
   70 DEN=C(N-2)*C(N-2)-CBARL*C(N-3)
   72 IF(DEN) 75,48,75
   75 IF(N-3) 47,73,47
   73 DELTP=(B(N-1)*C(N-2)-B(N))/DEN
          GO TO 74
   47 DELTP=(B(N-1)*C(N-2)-B(N)*C(N-3))/DEN
   74 DELTQ=(B(N)*C(N-2)-B(N-1)*CBARL)/DEN
          P=P+DELTP
          Q=Q+DELTQ
          ABSDP=ABSF(DELTP)
          ABSDQ=ABSF(DELTQ)
          SUM=ABSDP+ABSDQ
          IF(M-1) 80,83,84
   83 SUM1=SUM
          GO TO 11
```

Fig. 6.14. FORTRAN program for Bairstow's method.

```
84 IF(M-5) 11,54,11
54 IF(SUM-SUM1) 11,55,55
11 IF(SUM-EPSON) 8,8,52
52 IF(M-25) 53,56,53
53 M=M+1
   GO TO 51
55 PUNCH57
57 FORMAT(9X32HFUNCTIONS DIVERGING FOR ASSUMED ,17HVALUES OF P AND Q)
   GO TO 80
56 PUNCH 59
59 FORMAT(20X,35HTHE FUNCTIONS ARE CONVERGING SLOWLY/)
   PUNCH 60,P,Q
60 FORMAT(20X,2HP=,E14.8,3X,2HQ=,E14.8)
   GO TO 53
 8 D=-P/2.
   F=Q-P*P/4.
   IF(F) 30,30,31
30 AF=ABSF(F)
   E=SQRTF(AF)
   T = D
   S = E
   E = 0.0
   D = T + S
   PUNCH 13,N,D,E
   N=N-1
   S=(-1.)*S
   D= T + S
32 PUNCH 13,N,D,E
   N=N-1
   IF(N)80,80,81
31 AF= ABSF(F)
   E = SQRTF(AF)
   PUNCH 13,N,D,E
   E=(-1.)*E
   N = N-1
   GO TO 32
81 DO 82 I=1,N
82 A(I)=B(I)
   GO TO 40
48 PUNCH 49
49 FORMAT(41HDIVIDED BY ZERO TRY NEW VALUES OF P AND Q)
80 STOP
   END
 0.        0.        .0001      5
  -17.     +124.    -508.   +1035.   -875.
```

Fig. 6.14. (*cont.*)

TABLE 6.5

FIRST ITERATION

k	A_k	B_k	C_k
0	1	1	1
1	−17	−17	−17
2	124	124	124
3	−508	−508	−508
4	1035	1035	1035
$n = 5$	−875	−875	

$p = 0,$ $q = 0,$ $n = 5$ (fifth-order equation)

A_k = given coefficients, $k = 0, 1, \ldots, 5$

B_k and C_k can be computed from Eqs. (6.16) and (6.17)

$\overline{C}_4 = C_4 - B_4 = 0$

$$\Delta p = \frac{(1035)(-508) - (-875)(124)}{(-508)^2 - (0)(124)} = -1.617$$

$$\Delta q = \frac{(-875)(-508) - (1035)(0)}{(-508)^2 - (0)(124)} = 1.722$$

$p + \Delta p = -1.617,$ $q + \Delta q = +1.722$

SECOND ITERATION

k	A_k	B_k	C_k
0	1	1	1
1	−17	−15.383	−13.766
2	124	97.404	73.422
3	−508	−324.005	−181.573
4	1035	343.323	−76.739
5	−875	238.221	

$p = -1.617,$ $q = 1.722$

$\overline{C}_4 = -76.739 - 343.323 = -420.063$

$$\Delta p = \frac{(343.323)(-181.573) - (238.221)(73.422)}{(-181.573)^2 - (-420.063)(73.422)} = -1.251$$

$$\Delta q = \frac{(238.221)(-181.573) - (343.323)(-420.063)}{(-181.573)^2 - (-420.063)(73.422)} = 1.582$$

$p + \Delta p = -2.868,$ $q + \Delta q = 3.305$

THIRD ITERATION

k	A_k	B_k	C_k
0	1	1	1
1	−17	−14.132	−11.264
2	124	80.165	44.555
3	−508	−231.386	−66.379
4	1035	106.468	−231.146
5	−875	195.004	

$p = -2.868,$ $q = 3.305$

$\overline{C}_4 = -337.614$

$$\Delta p = \frac{(106.5)(-66.4) - (195)(44.6)}{(-66.4)^2 - (-337.6)(44.6)} = -0.810$$

$$\Delta q = \frac{(195)(-66.4) - (106.5)(-337.6)}{(-66.4)^2 - (-337.6)(44.6)} = 1.183$$

$p + \Delta p = -3.678,$ $q + \Delta q = 4.487$

FOURTH ITERATION

k	A_k	B_k	C_k
0	1	1	1
1	−17	−13.322	−9.644
2	124	70.513	30.555
3	−508	−188.865	−33.205
4	1035	23.919	−235.323
5	−875	60.473	

$p = -3.678,$ $q = 4.487$

$\overline{C}_4 = -235.323 - 23.919 = -259.242$

$$\Delta p = \frac{(23.9)(-33.2) - (60.5)(30.6)}{(-33.2)^2 - (-259.2)(30.6)} = -0.293$$

$$\Delta q = \frac{(60.5)(-33.2) - (23.9)(-259.2)}{(-33.2)^2 - (-259.2)(30.6)} = 0.465$$

$p + \Delta p = -3.971,$ $q + \Delta q = 4.952$

FIFTH ITERATION

k	A_k	B_k	C_k
0	1	1	1
1	−17	−13.029	−9.058
2	124	67.311	26.390
3	−508	−176.196	−26.550
4	1035	2.023	−234.083
5	−875	5.550	

$p = -3.971,$ $q = 4.952$

$\overline{C}_4 = -234.083 - 2.023 = -236.107$

$$\Delta p = \frac{(2)(-26.6) - (5.6)(26.4)}{(-26.6)^2 - (-236.1)(26.4)} = -0.029$$

$$\Delta q = \frac{(5.6)(-26.6) - (-234.1)(-236.1)}{(-26.6)^2 - (-236.1)(26.4)} = 0.048$$

$p + \Delta p = -4.000,$ $q + \Delta q = 5.000$

TABLE 6.6. Solution of $x^5 - 17x^4 + 124x^2 - 508x + 1035x - 876 = 0$

	REAL	IMAGINARY
X(5) =	2.0000	1.0000
X(4) =	2.0000	−1.0000
X(3) =	3.0000	4.0000
X(2) =	3.0000	−4.0000
X(1) =	7.0000	0.0000

103

BIBLIOGRAPHY

General References

FRANK, E., "On the Calculation of the Roots of Equations," *J. Math. Phys.*, pp. 187–197 (1955).

HILDEBRAND, F. B., *Introduction to Numerical Analysis*. McGraw-Hill, New York, 1956.

HOUSEHOLDER, A. S., *Principles of Numerical Analysis*. McGraw-Hill, New York, 1953.

MASAITIS, C., "Numerical Location of Zeros," *Aberdeen Proving Ground Ordn. Comput. Res. Rep.*, **4**, pp. 26–28 (1957).

OSTROWSKI, A. M., *Theory of the Solution of Equations and Systems of Equations*. Academic Press, New York, 1960.

Polynomials

DERR, J. J., "A Unified Process for the Evaluation of the Zeros of Polynomials Over the Complex Number Field," *Math. Tables Aids Comput.*, **13**, pp. 29–36 (1959).

FLANAGAN, C., and J. E. MAXFIELD, "Estimates of the Roots of Certain Polynomials," *J. Soc. Ind. Appl. Math.*, **7**, pp. 367–373 (1959).

GREENSPAN, D. D., "On Popular Methods and Extant Problems in the Solution of Polynomial Equations," *Math. Mag.*, **31**, pp. 239–253 (1957–58).

LEHMER, D. H., "A Machine Method for Solving Polynomial Equations," *J. Assoc. Comput. Mach.*, **8**, pp. 15–162 (1961).

MACK, C., "Routh Test Function Methods for the Numerical Solution of Polynomial Equations," *Quart. J. Mech. Appl. Math.*, **12**, pp. 365–378 (1959).

SALZER, H. E., C. H. RICHARDS, and I. ARSHAM. *Table for the Solution of Cubic Equations*. McGraw-Hill, New York, 1958.

WILKINSON, J. H., "The Evaluation of the Zeros of Ill-conditioned Polynomials," *Numer. Math.*, **1**, pp. 150–180 (1959).

Transcendental Functions

ERDELYI, A., W. MAGNUS, F. OBERHETTINGER, and F. G. TRICOMI, *Higher Transcendental Functions*, Vol. 2. McGraw-Hill, New York, 1953.

LANCE, G. N., "Solutions of Algebraic and Transcendental Equations on an Automatic Digital Computer," *J. Assoc. Comput. Mach.*, **6**, pp. 97–101 (1959).

Algebraic Equations

AITKIN, A. C., "On Bernoulli's Numerical Solution of Algebraic Equations," *Proc. Roy. Soc. Edinburgh*, **46**, pp. 289–305 (1926).

BROOKER, R. A., "The Solution of Algebraic Equations on the EDSAC," *Proc. Cambridge Phil. Soc.*, **48**, pp. 255–270 (1952).

FRANK, W. L., "Finding Zeros of Arbitrary Functions," *J. Assoc. Comput. Mach.*, **5**, pp. 154–165 (1958).

HEINRICH, H. "Zur Vorbehandlung algebraischer Gleichungen," *Z. Angew. Math. Mech.*, **36**, pp. 145–148 (1956).

MULLER, D., "A Method for Solving Algebraic Equations Using an Automatic Computer," *Math. Tables Aids Comput.*, **10**, pp. 208–215 (1956).

PELTIER, J., *Résolution numérique des équations algébriques.* Gauthier-Villars, Paris, 1957.

PORTER, A., and C. MACK, "New Methods for the Numerical Solution of Algebraic Equations," *Phil. Mag.*, **40**, pp. 578–585 (1949).

Graeffe Method

BAREISS, E. H., "Resultant Procedure and the Mechanization of the Graeffe Process," *J. Assoc. Comput. Mach.*, **7**, pp. 346–386 (1960).

Miscellaneous Methods

CALDWELL, G., "A Note on the Downhill Method," *J. Assoc. Comput. Mach.*, **6**, pp. 223–225 (1959).

EVERLING, W., "Eine Verallgemeinerung des Hornerschen Schemas," *Z. Angew. Math. Mech.*, **37**, p. 74 (1957).

GROSS, O., and S. M. JOHNSON, "Sequential Minimax Search for a Zero or a Convex Function," *Math. Tables Aids Comput.*, **13**, pp. 44–51 (1959).

KULIK, S., "A Method of Approximating the Complex Roots of Equations," *Pacific J. Math.*, **8**, pp. 277–281 (1958). "On the Solution of Algebraic Equations," *Proc. Am. Math. Soc.*, **10**, pp. 185–192 (1959).

MUNRO, W. D., "Some Iterative Methods for Determining Zeros of Functions of a Complex Variable," *Pacific J. Math.*, **9**, pp. 555–566 (1959).

WYNN, P., "Cubically Convergent Process for Zeros," *Math. Tables Aids Comput.*, **10**, pp. 164–169 (1956).

PROBLEMS

1. In the study of Fraunhofer diffraction, we encounter the equation

$$\left(\frac{\sin \alpha}{\alpha}\right)^2 = \frac{1}{2}.$$

   Solve for α in radians.

2. The following equation describes the motion of a system of helical gears:

$$\tan \phi - \phi = c.$$

   Find the angle ϕ for the two different cases: (a) $c = 0.01$ and (b) $c = 0.001$.

3. The following equation describes the motion of a planetary gear system used in an automatic transmission:

$$\sin \omega t - e^{-at} = 0.$$

   Determine the smallest positive root for

$$\text{Case 1:} \quad \omega = 0.573, \qquad \text{Case 2:} \quad \omega = 0.01,$$
$$a = 0.01. \qquad\qquad\qquad a = 0.1.$$

4. Find the smallest positive root of the following equation used in the study of vibrations:

$$\tanh x + \tan x = 0.$$

5. Find the smallest positive value of kL which satisfies the following equation derived in a column-buckling problem:

$$\tan kL - kL = 0.$$

6. In many circumstances tubular insulators are used for high-potential conducting through-walls (see Fig. 6.15). What must the ratio x of the external diameter $2R$ be to the bore width $2r$, to produce a minimum cross section Q? The cross section is defined as follows:

$$Q = \pi q^2 (x^2 - 1)/(\ln x)^2,$$

where q is the ratio of the line voltage to the maximum admissible field strength and is considered a constant in the problem.

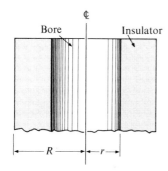

Figure 6.15

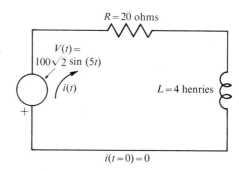

Figure 6.16

7. The circuit shown in Fig. 6.16 has a current given by

$$i = 5e^{-5t} \sin (\pi/4) + 5 \sin (5t - \pi/4).$$

Find the time between 0.5 and 1.4 sec, at which the current is zero ($e = 2.71828$).

8. Find the real root of $xe^x = 1$ using Newton's method. Use $x = 1$ for the first approximation and repeat until

$$|(e^{-x} - x)/(x + 1)| < 10^{-6}.$$

9. Find the root between 0 and -1 of the equation

$$e^{ct} + \sqrt{2/\pi}\, t/c^2 - t^2 = 0,$$

where $e = 2.71828$, for $c = 0.8$; $c = 0.9$.

10. Find the smallest positive root of the equation $2 - te^{2t} + 4t = 0$.

11. Find the root between 0 and 1 of the equation $1 + \cos t - 4t = 0$.

12. Find the smallest root of the equation $e^{2t} \tan t = e^{-3\pi/2}$. [Hint: the smallest root is close to the value $e^{-3\pi/2}$.]

13. Find the real root between 0 and 1 of $2x - 1 - \cos x = 0$.

Use Bairstow's method to find the roots of each of the following polynomial equations.

14. $y^5 - 5y^3 + 4y = 0$.

15. $x^4 - 6x^3 + 23x^2 - 34x + 26 = 0$.   } use library function and subroutine Lin' method

16. $x^4 - x^3 - 2x^2 - 6x - 4 = 0$.

17. In pipe-flow problems one frequently encounters the equation

$$C_5 D^5 + C_1 D + C_0 F = 0.$$

Solve for D in feet, given that $C_5 = 8820$, $C_1 = -2.31$, $C_0 = -431$, and $F = 0.015$.

CHAPTER 7

ORDINARY DIFFERENTIAL EQUATIONS WITH INITIAL CONDITIONS

7.1 INTRODUCTION

The formulation of a large class of engineering and scientific problems in mathematical form leads to either ordinary or partial differential equations. In a great many cases, it is found that the resultant equations do not possess closed-form solutions; that is, specific expressions for the dependent variables cannot be found.

In this chapter, we shall discuss some useful numerical methods for solving ordinary differential equations on a digital computer. These methods are so well developed† that only a suitable program is necessary to obtain the required answers in tabulated form.

Depending upon the given conditions, ordinary differential equations derived from scientific and engineering problems may customarily be classified into two distinct types. The first type is called an initial-value problem and the second, a boundary-value problem.

An initial-value problem is characterized by the fact that the information given concerns all the conditions at a given point. Thus a differential equation of the nth order, together with the known values of $x, x', x'', \ldots, x^{n-1}$ at a specific point $t = t_0$, may be described as an initial-value problem. For example, the basic differential equation describing the motion of a spring-mass system (Fig. 7.1) is

$$m \frac{d^2x}{dt^2} + c \frac{dx}{dt} + R(x) = F(t), \tag{7.1}$$

---

† Except for some questions concerning the singular points of the solutions.

where

  x = displacement of mass m,

  t = time,

  c = damping coefficient,

  $R(x)$ = resistance of spring, function of x,

  $F(t)$ = applied forcing function,

and a given set of initial conditions is

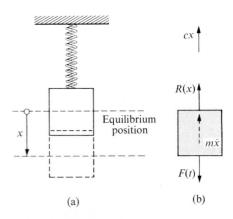

$$t = 0, \qquad x = 1; \qquad (7.2)$$

$$t = 0, \qquad \frac{dx}{dt} = 0. \qquad (7.3)$$

Fig. 7.1. Motion of a spring-mass system. (a) System. (b) Free body.

Note that the two initial conditions in Eqs. (7.2) and (7.3) refer to $t = 0$. The fundamental problem is to find the x-t and $\dot{x}$-t relations as t increases with a given increment. Hence, the initial-value problem is sometimes referred to as a "marching problem." The solutions of Eq. (7.1) will be discussed in detail in Section 7.6.

In contrast to initial-value problems, a boundary-value problem is one in which the conditions are given at two or more distinct points. For example, a second-order differential equation

$$\frac{d^2y}{dx^2} - 2y = 7, \qquad (7.4)$$

together with the boundary conditions

$$x = 0, \qquad y = 6; \qquad (7.5)$$
$$x = 6, \qquad y = 17, \qquad (7.6)$$

forms a boundary-value problem. Here we are seeking the y-x relation to satisfy Eqs. (7.4) through (7.6). This type of problem is often called a "jury problem."

Because a first-order differential equation can have only one given condition, it is always an initial-value, rather than a boundary-value, problem.

Since numerical solutions of the marching problems are generally much simpler than those of jury problems, we shall limit our discussion in this book to computer methods for solving initial-value problems.

7.2 RUNGE-KUTTA METHOD WITH RUNGE'S COEFFICIENTS

Among the vast number of numerical methods available for solving initial-value problems, the Runge-Kutta method is probably the one most frequently used on computers because it simplifies programming. Detailed derivations are given in the next section. Here we shall be primarily concerned with the procedures and some typical examples.

Take a differential equation of the first order, $y' = f(t, y)$. The initial condition is given as (t_0, y_0). Our problem is to find the y_1 corresponding to a new $t = t_0 + \Delta t$ (Fig. 7.2). Once y_1 is found, a new y-value, y_2, can then be obtained that corresponds to a second t-value, say, $t_0 + 2\Delta t$. In this step-by-step manner, the required y-t relation can then be obtained and tabulated.

In the Runge-Kutta method, the basic formula with Runge's coefficients is

$$y_{n+1} = y_n + \Delta y_n, \qquad (7.7)$$

where

$$\Delta y_n = \frac{\Delta t}{6} (k_0 + 2k_1 + 2k_2 + k_3)$$

and

$$k_0 = f(t_n, y_n),$$

$$k_1 = f\left(t_n + \frac{\Delta t}{2}, \; y_n + \frac{k_0}{2}\Delta t\right),$$

$$k_2 = f\left(t_n + \frac{\Delta t}{2}, \; y_n + \frac{k_1}{2}\Delta t\right),$$

$$k_3 = f(t_n + \Delta t, \; y_n + k_2\Delta t).$$

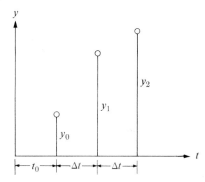

Fig. 7.2. Step-by-step solution of $y' = f(y, t)$.

The geometrical interpretation of the values k_0 through k_3 is shown in Fig. 7.3(a). All four k-values represent the slopes at various points: the value k_0 is the slope at the starting point; k_3 is the slope at the right-hand point whose ordinate is $y_n + k_2\Delta t$; k_2 is one of the two slopes considered at the midpoint with the ordinate $y_n + \frac{1}{2}k_1\Delta t$; and finally, k_1 is the second slope at the midpoint whose ordinate is $y_n + \frac{1}{2}k_0\Delta t$.

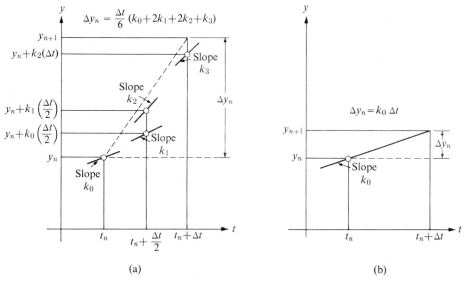

(a)   (b)

Fig. 7.3. Comparison of slopes used. (a) Four slopes used in Runge-Kutta method. (b) The slope k_0 used in Euler's method.

It is interesting to compare the Runge-Kutta method with Euler's method, which is usually discussed in basic calculus courses. In the latter, the basic formula is simply

$$y_{n+1} = y_n + k_0 \, \Delta t, \tag{7.8}$$

where $k_0 = y_n' = f'(t_n, y_n)$. Thus in the Euler method the approximate solution y_{n+1} (Fig. 7.3b) depends on y_n and a slope k_0 at a point (t_n, y_n), whereas in the Runge-Kutta method, it depends not only on y_n and k_0, but also on three additional slopes at points other than (t_n, y_n). In this way, the Runge-Kutta procedure uses a weighted average of slopes, with those in the center receiving twice as much weight as those on the ends.

We shall illustrate the Runge-Kutta method with Runge's coefficients by the following example.

Example 7.1

It is known that the motion of a simple pendulum, as shown in Fig. 7.4, may be expressed by the following first-order differential equation:

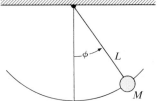

$$\frac{d\omega}{d\phi} = \frac{-g}{L} \frac{\sin \phi}{\omega}, \tag{7.9}$$

where

ω = angular velocity in rad/sec,

ϕ = angle (see Fig. 7.4),

g = 32.2014 ft/sec^2,

L = 2.5 ft.

Fig. 7.4. Simple pendulum.

The initial condition is $\phi = 79°$, $\omega = 0.66488546$. Tabulate the solution at the interval of

$$\Delta\phi = -0.5°.$$

Solution by Runge-Kutta Method with Runge's Coefficients. With the given initial condition, we find that

$$k_0 = f(\phi_0, \omega_0) = \frac{-g}{L} \frac{\sin \phi}{\omega}$$

$$= \frac{-32.2014}{2.5} \frac{\sin 79°}{0.66488546} = -19.016673,$$

$$k_1 = f\left[\phi_0 + \frac{\Delta\phi}{2}, \omega_0 + \tfrac{1}{2}k_0 \, \Delta\phi\right]$$

$$= \frac{-32.2014}{2.5} \frac{\sin 78.75°}{0.66488546 + (-19.016673) \times (-0.25) \times (3.141593/180)}$$

$$= -16.892255,$$

$$k_2 = f\left[\phi_0 + \frac{\Delta\phi}{2}, \omega_0 + \tfrac{1}{2}k_1\,\Delta\phi\right]$$

$$= \frac{-32.2014}{2.5}\ \frac{\sin 78.75°}{0.66488546 + (-16.892255) \times (-0.25) \times (3.1415926/180)}$$

$$= -17.104257,$$

$$k_3 = f(\phi_0 + \Delta\phi, \omega_0 + k_2\,\Delta\phi)$$

$$= \frac{-32.2014}{2.5}\ \frac{\sin 78.5°}{0.66488546 + (-17.104257) \times (-0.5) \times (3.1415926/180)}$$

$$= -15.503294,$$

and

$$\Delta\omega = \frac{1}{6}\left(\frac{-0.5 \times 3.14159265}{180}\right) \times (k_0 + 2k_1 + 2k_2 + k_3)$$

$$= 0.14909917.$$

Therefore for $\phi = 78.5°$,

$$\omega = 0.66488546 + 0.14909917 = 0.81398463.$$

The computation may be conveniently arranged as follows:

ϕ	ω	k_0	k_1	k_2	k_3	$\Delta\omega$
79°	0.66488546	−19.016673	−16.892255	−17.104257	−15.503294	0.14909917
78.5°	0.81398463	−15.506411	−14.303566	−14.389225	−13.409645	0.12552070
78°	0.93950533					

Solution by Euler's Method. Let $\phi_i = 79° - i(\Delta\phi)$ and $\omega_i = \omega(\phi_i)$, where $i = 0, 1, 2, \ldots$ and approximate $d\omega/d\phi$ at ϕ_i by $(\omega_{i+1} - \omega_i)/\Delta\phi$. This yields the difference equation

$$\omega_{i+1} = \frac{-g}{L}\ \frac{\sin \phi_i}{\omega_i}\ \Delta\phi + \omega_i,$$

which is used to determine all values of ω_i. The initial value of ω is given as 0.66488546.

The Exact Solution. It should be noted that Eq. (7.9) does have an exact solution:

$$\omega = \sqrt{(2g/L)(\cos \phi - \cos 79°) + \omega_{79}^2}\ . \tag{7.10}$$

For the sake of comparison, the solutions based on both the Euler and the Runge-Kutta methods, as well as exact solutions are tabulated in Table 7.2. All these solutions were carried out on a high-speed digital computer. A sample flow chart and a FORTRAN program are given in Figs. 7.5 and 7.6, respectively. In the program it is required to read in g and L from the first data card and ϕ_{79}, ω_{79}, $\Delta\phi$, $\phi_{\max}$ from the second card. It is also required to print the five results per line immediately after the related computations. This required printing format is as shown in Table 7.1 and the actual printout is as shown in Table 7.2.

TABLE 7.1.

(1)	(2)	(3)	(4)	(5)	(6)
Angle	Closed	Euler	(2)-(3)	Runge	(2)-(5)
79.0	——	——	——	——	——
78.5	——	——	——	——	——
78.0	——	——	——	——	——
——	——	——	——		
——	——	——			
——	——				
——					
ϕ_{max}					
(F6.2)	(F12.8)	(F12.8)	(F12.8)	(F12.8)	(F12.8)

Column 1 is the angle in degrees. Column 2 is the exact solution. Column 3 is Euler's solution. Column 5 is the Runge-Kutta solution (Runge's coefficients).

TABLE 7.2. Simple Pendulum Problem

(1) ANGLE	(2) CLOSED	(3) EULER	(4) (2)-(3)	(5) RUNGE	(6) (2)-(5)
79.00	.66488546	.66488546	0.00000000	.66488546	0.00000000
78.50	.81397756	.83083723	-.01685967	.81398457	-.00000701
78.00	.93949705	.96341139	-.02391434	.93950522	-.00000817
77.50	1.04992610	1.07753480	-.02760870	1.04993320	-.00000710
77.00	1.14961220	1.17937800	-.02976580	1.14961920	-.00000700
76.50	1.24114130	1.27224320	-.03110190	1.24114760	-.00000630
76.00	1.32619610	1.35815310	-.03195700	1.32620220	-.00000610
75.50	1.40594740	1.43845710	-.03250970	1.40595250	-.00000510
75.00	1.48124480	1.51411020	-.03286540	1.48125000	-.00000520
74.50	1.55273250	1.58581830	-.03308580	1.55273720	-.00000470
74.00	1.62090830	1.65412120	-.03321290	1.62091330	-.00000500
73.50	1.68617060	1.71944270	-.03327210	1.68617500	-.00000440
73.00	1.74883960	1.78212300	-.03328340	1.74884400	-.00000440
72.50	1.80918130	1.84244010	-.03325880	1.80918510	-.00000380
72.00	1.86741590	1.90062470	-.03320880	1.86741970	-.00000380
71.50	1.92373160	1.95687070	-.03313910	1.92373480	-.00000320
71.00	1.97828680	2.01134310	-.03305630	1.97829030	-.00000350
70.50	2.03122010	2.06418340	-.03296330	2.03122390	-.00000380
70.00	2.08265200	2.11551440	-.03286240	2.08265550	-.00000350
69.50	2.13268610	2.16544320	-.03275710	2.13268990	-.00000380
69.00	2.18141600	2.21406400	-.03264800	2.18141960	-.00000360
68.50	2.22892280	2.26146020	-.03253740	2.22892660	-.00000380
68.00	2.27528060	2.30770580	-.03242520	2.27528390	-.00000330
67.50	2.32055370	2.35286720	-.03231350	2.32055700	-.00000330
67.00	2.36480210	2.39700390	-.03220180	2.36480490	-.00000280
66.50	2.40807800	2.44016960	-.03209160	2.40808080	-.00000280
66.00	2.45043070	2.48241300	-.03198230	2.45043300	-.00000230
65.50	2.49190310	2.52377840	-.03187530	2.49190540	-.00000230
65.00	2.53253620	2.56430620	-.03177000	2.53253820	-.00000200

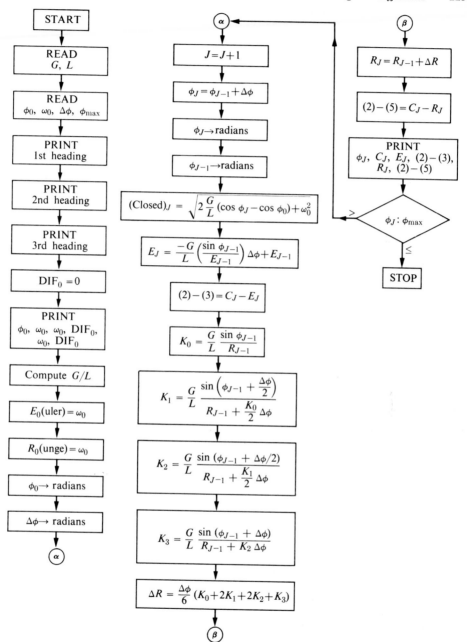

Fig. 7.5. Flow chart for simple pendulum problem.

```
C        EXAMPLE 7.1          ANGULAR VELOCITIES
         READ 10,G,ZL
      10 FORMAT(F10.4,F6.2)
         READ 12, PHI,W,H,PHMAX
      12 FORMAT(F6.2,F10.8,F8.2,F6.2)
         PUNCH 66
      66 FORMAT(2X,3H(1),8X,3H(2),10X,3H(3),10X,3H(4),10X,3H(5),10X,3H(6)/)
         PUNCH 31
      31 FORMAT(6H ANGLE,5X,6HCLOSED,8X,5HEULER,21X,5HRUNGE)
         PUNCH 33
      33 FORMAT(37X,7H(2)-(3),19X,7H(2)-(5)////)
         DIF=0.
         PUNCH 51,PHI,W,W,DIF,W,DIF
      51 FORMAT(F6.2,F13.8,F13.8,F13.8,F13.8,F13.8)
         GOL=G/ZL
         EULER = W
         RUNGE = W
         CONV= 3.14159265/180.
         PCONV = PHI*CONV
         HCONV = H*CONV
       9 PHI = PHI+H
         PP = PHI*CONV
         PPP = (PHI-H)*CONV
         CLOSE=SQRTF((-2.*GOL)*(COSF(PP)-COSF(PCONV))+W*W)
         EULER=(GOL*SINF(PPP)*HCONV/EULER)+EULER
         ANS4= CLOSE - EULER
         ZK0=GOL*SINF(PPP)/RUNGE
         ZK1=GOL*(SINF(PPP+0.5*HCONV)/(RUNGE+0.5*ZK0*HCONV))
         ZK2=GOL*(SINF(PPP+0.5*HCONV)/(RUNGE+0.5*ZK1*HCONV))
         ZK3=GOL*(SINF(PPP+HCONV)/(RUNGE+ZK2*HCONV))
         TEMP=(HCONV/6.)*(ZK0+2.*(ZK1+ZK2)+ZK3)
         RUNGE=RUNGE+TEMP
         ANS6= CLOSE- RUNGE
         PUNCH 51,PHI,CLOSE,EULER,ANS4,RUNGE,ANS6
         IF (PHI-PHMAX) 8,8,9
       8 STOP
         END
  -32.2014   2.5
  79.    .66488546  -.5      65.
```

Fig. 7.6. FORTRAN program for simple pendulum problem.

7.3 DERIVATION OF THE RUNGE-KUTTA FORMULA

In the last section, the procedure of the Runge-Kutta method was described. We turn now to the derivation of Eq. (7.7), the basic Runge-Kutta formula with Runge's coefficients. It should be noted that Eq. (7.7) is only one of many possible forms of the Runge-Kutta equations. All of them may be obtained from the following Taylor-series expansion:

$$y_{n+1} = y_n + y_n'(t_{n+1} - t_n) + \frac{y_n''}{2!}(t_{n+1} - t_n)^2$$

$$+ \frac{y_n'''}{3!}(t_{n+1} - t_n)^3 + \frac{y_n^{\text{iv}}}{4!}(t_{n+1} - t_n)^4 + \cdots \quad (7.11)$$

$$\frac{dz}{d(\ )} = \frac{\partial z}{\partial x}\frac{dx}{d(\ )} + \frac{\partial z}{\partial y}\frac{dy}{d(\ )}$$

$$z = f(x,y)$$

Assuming that $t = t_{n+1} = t_n + \Delta t$, we find that Eq. (7.11) becomes

$$y_{n+1} = y_n + y_n'(\Delta t) + \frac{y_n''}{2!}(\Delta t)^2 + \frac{y_n'''}{3!}(\Delta t)^3 + \frac{y_n^{iv}}{4!}(\Delta t)^4 + \cdots \quad (7.12)$$

If we call

$$\Delta y_n = y_{n+1} - y_n, \qquad y_{n+1} = \Delta y_n + y_n \quad (7.13)$$

then

$$\Delta y_n = y_n'(\Delta t) + \frac{y_n''}{2!}(\Delta t)^2 + \frac{y_n'''}{3!}(\Delta t)^3 + \frac{y_n^{iv}}{4!}(\Delta t)^4 + \cdots, \quad (7.14)$$

and we note that

$$y' = f(t, y), = f \qquad \frac{dy}{dx} = \frac{\partial f}{\partial x}\frac{dx}{dx} + \frac{\partial f}{\partial y}\frac{dy}{dx} \quad (7.15)$$

$$y'' = f' = \frac{\partial f}{\partial t} + \frac{\partial f}{\partial y}\frac{dy}{dt} = f_t + f_y f, \quad (7.16)$$

OK.

$$y''' = f'' = \frac{\partial f'}{\partial t} + \frac{\partial f'}{\partial y} f$$

$$= [f_{tt} + (f_{yt}f + f_y f_t)] + [f_{ty} + (f_{yy}f + f_y^2)]f, \quad (7.17)$$

$$y^{iv} = f_{ttt} + \cdots, \quad (7.18)$$

where the subscripts t and y designate the differentiation with respect to t and y.
Substituting Eqs. (7.15) through (7.18) into Eq. (7.14), we have

$$\Delta y_n = f_n(\Delta t) + (1/2!)(f_t + f_y f)_n(\Delta t)^2$$
$$+ (1/3!)[f_{tt} + 2f_{ty}f + f_{yy}f^2 + (f_t + f_y f)f_y]_n(\Delta t)^3$$
$$+ (1/4!)[f_{ttt} + \cdots]_n(\Delta t)^4, \quad (7.19)$$

where the subscript n denotes that the functions are to be evaluated at the point (t_n, y_n).

Because there are many derivatives to be evaluated, it is far from practical to use Eq. (7.19) in computing the value Δy_n. To avoid this difficulty, we arbitrarily take

$$\Delta y_n = (\mu_0 z_0 + \mu_1 z_1 + \mu_2 z_2 + \cdots + \mu_m z_m), \quad (7.20)$$

where

$$z_0 = f(t_n, y_n)\,\Delta t,$$

$$z_1 = f(t_n + \alpha_1\,\Delta t, y_n + \beta_{10}z_0)\,\Delta t, \qquad \mu \ \alpha \ \beta \ \text{constants}$$

$$z_2 = f(t_n + \alpha_2\,\Delta t, y_n + \beta_{20}z_0 + \beta_{21}z_1)\,\Delta t,$$

$$\vdots$$

$$z_m = f(t_n + \alpha_n\,\Delta t, y_n + \beta_{m0}z_0 + \beta_{m1}z_1 + \cdots)\,\Delta t,$$

and seek to determine all three sets of the constants μ and α, and the β. In Eq. (7.20) the subscript m is used to indicate that the Δy_n-value thus obtained coincides with Eq. (7.19) up to the term involving $(\Delta t)^{m-1}$.

If we take $m = 3$, then Eq. (7.20) becomes

$$\Delta y_n = \mu_0 z_0 + \mu_1 z_1 + \mu_2 z_2 + \mu_3 z_3, \tag{7.21}$$

where

$$z_0 = f(t_n, y_n)\,\Delta t,$$
$$z_1 = f(t_n + \alpha_1\,\Delta t, y_n + \beta_{10}z_0)\,\Delta t,$$
$$z_2 = f(t_n + \alpha_2\,\Delta t, y_n + \beta_{20}z_0 + \beta_{21}z_1)\,\Delta t,$$
$$z_3 = f(t_n + \alpha_3\,\Delta t, y_n + \beta_{30}z_0 + \beta_{31}z_1 + \beta_{32}z_2)\,\Delta t.$$

Since Eq. (7.21) consists of four terms, it is often referred to as a fourth-order formula. We now seek to determine the following thirteen constants:

$$\mu_0, \ \mu_1, \ \mu_2, \ \mu_3;$$
$$\alpha_1, \ \alpha_2, \ \alpha_3;$$
$$\beta_{10}, \ \beta_{20}, \ \beta_{30}, \ \beta_{21}, \ \beta_{31}, \ \text{and} \ \beta_{32}.$$

We recall† that the Taylor series for two independent variables about the point (a, b) is

$$f(a + h, b + k) = f(a, b) + \left[f_x(a, b)h + f_y(a, b)k \right.$$
$$+ \frac{1}{2!}\left[f_{xx}(a, b)h^2 + 2f_{xy}(a, b)hk \right.$$
$$\left. + f_{yy}(a, b)k^2 \right] + \cdots, \tag{7.22}$$

which is frequently written symbolically as

$$f(a + h, b + k) = f(a, b) + \left(h\frac{\partial}{\partial x} + k\frac{\partial}{\partial y} \right) f(a, b)$$
$$+ \frac{1}{2!}\left(h\frac{\partial}{\partial x} + k\frac{\partial}{\partial y} \right)^2 f(a, b)$$
$$+ \frac{1}{3!}\left(h\frac{\partial}{\partial x} + k\frac{\partial}{\partial y} \right)^3 f(a, b) + \cdots \tag{7.23}$$

Substituting z_0 through z_3 into Eq. (7.23), we have, in the following symbolic form,

$$z_0 = f_n\,\Delta t, \tag{7.24}$$

$$z_1 = \left[f_n + \left(\alpha_1\,\Delta t\,\frac{\partial}{\partial t} + \beta_{10}z_0\,\frac{\partial}{\partial y} \right) f_n \right.$$
$$+ \frac{1}{2!}\left(\alpha_1\,\Delta t\,\frac{\partial}{\partial t} + \beta_{10}z_0\,\frac{\partial}{\partial y} \right)^2 f_n$$
$$\left. + \frac{1}{3!}\left(\alpha_1\,\Delta t\,\frac{\partial}{\partial t} + \beta_{10}z_0\,\frac{\partial}{\partial y} \right)^3 f_n + \cdots \right]\Delta t, \tag{7.25}$$

---

† For example, see Kaplan, W., *Advanced Calculus*. Addison-Wesley, Reading, Mass., p. 370 (1952).

$$z_2 = \left\{ f_n + \left[\alpha_2 \, \Delta t \, \frac{\partial}{\partial t} + (\beta_{20} z_0 + \beta_{21} z_1) \frac{\partial}{\partial y} \right] f_n \right.$$
$$+ \frac{1}{2!} \left[\alpha_2 \, \Delta t \, \frac{\partial}{\partial t} + (\beta_{20} z_0 + \beta_{21} z_1) \frac{\partial}{\partial y} \right]^2 f_n$$
$$\left. + \frac{1}{3!} \left[\alpha_2 \, \Delta t \, \frac{\partial}{\partial t} + (\beta_{20} z_0 + \beta_{21} z_1) \frac{\partial}{\partial y} \right]^3 f_n + \cdots \right\} \Delta t, \tag{7.26}$$

$$z_3 = \left\{ f_n + \left[\alpha_3 \, \Delta t \, \frac{\partial}{\partial t} + (\beta_{30} z_0 + \beta_{31} z_1 + \beta_{32} z_2) \frac{\partial}{\partial y} \right] f_n \right.$$
$$+ \frac{1}{2!} \left[\alpha_3 \, \Delta t \, \frac{\partial}{\partial t} + (\beta_{30} z_0 + \beta_{31} z_1 + \beta_{32} z_2 \frac{\partial}{\partial y} \right]^2 f_n$$
$$\left. + \frac{1}{3!} \left[\alpha_3 \, \Delta t \, \frac{\partial}{\partial t} + (\beta_{30} z_0 + \beta_{31} z_1 + \beta_{32} z_2 \frac{\partial}{\partial y} \right]^3 f_n + \cdots \right\} \Delta t. \tag{7.27}$$

So far, we have obtained two expressions for Δy_n: one from Eqs. (7.21) and (7.23) through (7.27); the other from Eq. (7.19). Equating all of the coefficients of corresponding terms in these two expressions, we have

$$\alpha_1 = \beta_{10},$$
$$\alpha_2 = \beta_{20} + \beta_{21},$$
$$\alpha_3 = \beta_{30} + \beta_{31} + \beta_{32};$$
$$\mu_0 + \mu_1 + \mu_2 + \mu_3 = 1,$$
$$\mu_1 \alpha_1 + \mu_2 \alpha_2 + \mu_3 \alpha_3 = \tfrac{1}{2},$$
$$\mu_1 \alpha_1^2 + \mu_2 \alpha_2^2 + \mu_3 \alpha_3^2 = \tfrac{1}{3},$$
$$\mu_1 \alpha_1^3 + \mu_2 \alpha_2^3 + \mu_3 \alpha_3^3 = \tfrac{1}{4}, \tag{7.28}$$
$$\mu_2 \alpha_1 \beta_{21} + \mu_3 (\alpha_1 \beta_{31} + \alpha_2 \beta_{32}) = \tfrac{1}{6},$$
$$\mu_2 \alpha_1^2 \beta_{21} + \mu_3 (\alpha_1^2 \beta_{31} + \alpha_2^2 \beta_{32}) = \tfrac{1}{12},$$
$$\mu_2 \alpha_1 \alpha_2 \beta_{21} + \mu_3 (\alpha_1 \beta_{31} + \alpha_2 \beta_{32}) \alpha_3 = \tfrac{1}{8},$$
$$\mu_3 \alpha_1 \beta_{21} \beta_{32} = \tfrac{1}{24}.$$

With eleven equations and thirteen unknowns, we arbitrarily take $\mu_1 = \mu_2 = \tfrac{1}{3}$.

It can be shown by simple substitution that Eqs. (7.28) are satisfied by the values shown in the following table:

μ_0	μ_1	μ_2	μ_3	α_1	α_2	α_3	β_{10}	β_{20}	β_{30}	β_{21}	β_{31}	β_{32}
$\tfrac{1}{6}$	$\tfrac{1}{3}$	$\tfrac{1}{3}$	$\tfrac{1}{6}$	$\tfrac{1}{2}$	$\tfrac{1}{2}$	1	$\tfrac{1}{2}$	0	0	$\tfrac{1}{2}$	0	1

Substituting these values into Eq. (7.20), we obtain Eq. (7.7), the Runge-Kutta formula with Runge's coefficients. If, however, a choice is made from

μ_0	μ_1	μ_2	μ_3	α_1	α_2	α_3	β_{10}	β_{20}	β_{30}	β_{21}	β_{31}	β_{32}
$\tfrac{1}{8}$	$\tfrac{3}{8}$	$\tfrac{3}{8}$	$\tfrac{1}{8}$	$\tfrac{1}{3}$	$\tfrac{2}{3}$	1	$\tfrac{1}{3}$	$-\tfrac{1}{3}$	1	1	-1	1

it can readily be shown that these values also satisfy Eqs. (7.28). Substituting them into Eq. (7.20), we have the following Runge-Kutta formula with coefficients due to Kutta:

$$y_{n+1} = y_n + \Delta y_n, \tag{7.29}$$

where

$$\Delta y_n = \frac{\Delta t}{8} (k_0 + 3k_1 + 3k_2 + k_3),$$

and

$$k_0 = f(t_n, y_n),$$

$$k_1 = f\left(t_n + \frac{\Delta t}{3}, y_n + \frac{k_0}{3}\Delta t\right),$$

$$k_2 = f\left[t_n + \frac{2\Delta t}{3}, y_n + \left(\frac{-k_0 + k_1}{3}\right)\Delta t\right],$$

$$k_3 = f[t_n + \Delta t, y_n + (k_0 - k_1 + k_2)\Delta t].$$

Before we turn to the next section, it is interesting to note that the Runge-Kutta equation with Runge coefficients (Eq. 7.7), has an important special case: when $y' = f(t, y)$ is independent of y, Eq. (7.7) becomes

$$y_{n+1} = y_n + \Delta y_n, \tag{7.7a}$$

where

$$\Delta y_n = \frac{\Delta t}{6} (k_0 + 2k_1 + 2k_2 + k_3)$$

and

$$k_0 = f(t_n),$$

$$k_1 = f\left(t_n + \frac{\Delta t}{2}\right),$$

$$k_2 = f\left(t_n + \frac{\Delta t}{2}\right),$$

$$k_3 = f(t_n + \Delta t),$$

or

$$\Delta y_n = \frac{\Delta t}{6}\left[f(t_n) + 4f\left(t_n + \frac{\Delta t}{2}\right) + f(t_n + \Delta t)\right].$$

This is the well-known Simpson rule.

7.4 RUNGE-KUTTA METHOD WITH GILL'S COEFFICIENTS

In the last section, it was mentioned that in Eqs. (7.28) there are eleven equations but thirteen unknowns; there are, therefore, two degrees of freedom in the choice of these thirteen unknowns. In the formula using Runge's coefficients, we arbitrarily take $\mu_1 = \mu_2 = \frac{1}{3}$. This choice leads to Eq. (7.7). In the formula using Kutta's coefficients, μ_1 and μ_2 are taken as $\frac{3}{8}$, and this second choice leads to Eq. (7.29).

A third, and different, choice of two out of the thirteen unknowns in Eqs. (7.28) was suggested by Gill. Here we arbitrarily take

$$\mu_1 = \frac{1}{3}\left(1 - \frac{1}{\sqrt{2}}\right) \quad \text{and} \quad \mu_2 = \frac{1}{3}\left(1 + \frac{1}{\sqrt{2}}\right).$$

By direct substitution it can be shown that Eqs. (7.28) are satisfied by the following values:

						β_{10}	$\frac{1}{2}$
μ_0	$\frac{1}{6}$					β_{20}	$-\frac{1}{2} + \frac{1}{\sqrt{2}}$
μ_1	$\frac{1}{3}\left(1 - \frac{1}{\sqrt{2}}\right)$		α_1	$\frac{1}{2}$		β_{30}	0
μ_2	$\frac{1}{3}\left(1 + \frac{1}{\sqrt{2}}\right)$		α_2	$\frac{1}{2}$		β_{21}	$1 - \frac{1}{\sqrt{2}}$
μ_3	$\frac{1}{6}$		α_3	1		β_{31}	$\frac{-1}{\sqrt{2}}$
						β_{32}	$1 + \frac{1}{\sqrt{2}}$

Substituting the above values into Eq. (7.21), we have

$$\Delta y_n = y_{n+1} - y_n$$
$$= \tfrac{1}{6}[z_0 + (2 - \sqrt{2})z_1 + (2 + \sqrt{2})z_2 + z_3], \qquad (7.30)$$

where

$$z_0 = f(t_n, y_n)\,\Delta t,$$
$$z_1 = f(t_n + \tfrac{1}{2}\Delta t, y_n + \tfrac{1}{2}z_0)\,\Delta t,$$
$$z_2 = f\left[t_n + \frac{1}{2}\Delta t,\, y_n + \left(-\frac{1}{2} + \frac{1}{\sqrt{2}}\right)z_0 + \left(1 - \frac{1}{\sqrt{2}}\right)z_1\right]\Delta t,$$
$$z_3 = f\left[t_n + \Delta t,\, y_n - \frac{1}{\sqrt{2}}z_1 + \left(1 + \frac{1}{\sqrt{2}}\right)z_2\right]\Delta t.$$

The chief advantage of Gill's procedure lies in the requirement of a minimum amount of storage locations. This is important when the digital computer available has limited memory locations. To accomplish this minimization of storage, one may introduce the following three new quantities:

$$q_1 = z_0,$$
$$q_2 = (-2 + 3/\sqrt{2})z_0 + (2 - \sqrt{2})z_1, \qquad (7.31)$$
$$q_3 = -\tfrac{1}{2}z_0 - (1 + \sqrt{2})z_1 + (2 + \sqrt{2})z_2.$$

For ordinary differential equations of first order, the algorithm we use to compute y_{n+1}, when we know t_n, y_n, and t, is:

Step 1

$$z_0 = f(t_n, y_n)\, \Delta t,$$
$$y_{n+1}^{(1)} = y_n + \tfrac{1}{2}z_0,$$
$$q_1 = z_0.$$

Step 2

$$z_1 = f(t_n + \tfrac{1}{2}\Delta t, y_{n+1}^{(1)})\, \Delta t,$$
$$y_{n+1}^{(2)} = y_{n+1}^{(1)} + (1 - \sqrt{2}/2)(z_1 - q_1),$$
$$q_2 = (-2 + 3/\sqrt{2})q_1 + (2 - \sqrt{2})z_1.$$

Step 3

$$z_2 = f(t_n + \tfrac{1}{2}\Delta t, y_{n+1}^{(2)})\, \Delta t,$$
$$y_{n+1}^{(3)} = y_{n+1}^{(2)} + (1 + 1/\sqrt{2})(z_2 - q_2),$$
$$q_3 = -(2 + 3/\sqrt{2})q_2 + (2 + \sqrt{2})z_2.$$

Step 4

$$z_3 = f(t_n + \Delta t, y_{n+1}^{(3)})\, \Delta t,$$
$$y_{n+1}^{(4)} = y_{n+1}^{(3)} + \tfrac{1}{6}z_3 - \tfrac{1}{3}q_3.$$

Here $y_{n+1}^{(4)}$ is the final answer at any stage. It should be noted from the above algorithm that four temporary storage spaces are required throughout the computation, namely, memory for one z-value, one y_{n+1}-value, one q-value, and one Δt-value. One memory space for the initial value t_0 should also be provided.

Steps 1 through 3 may be conveniently written in a shorthand form as follows:

$$y^{(j)} = y^{(j-1)} + a_j[f_{j-1}\,\Delta t - q_{j-1}],$$
$$q_j = (1 - 3a_j)q_{j-1} + 2a_j f_{j-1}\,\Delta t,$$

$$(7.32)$$

where

$j = 1, 2, 3$ (indicating the three different computational steps for a new Δy-value),

$t^{(0)}, y^{(0)}$ = values of t and y, respectively, at the beginning of an increment in which y is to be computed,

$f_0 = f(t^{(0)}, y^{(0)}),\qquad f_1 = f(t^{(0)} + \tfrac{1}{2}\Delta t, y^{(1)}),\qquad f_2 = f(t^{(0)} + \tfrac{1}{2}\Delta t, y^{(2)}),$

$q_0 = 0,$

$a_1 = \tfrac{1}{2},\qquad a_2 = 1 - (\sqrt{2}/2) = 0.2928,\qquad a_3 = 1 + (\sqrt{2}/2) = 1.707,$

$y^{(1)}, y^{(2)}$ = values of y obtained in the first and second steps, respectively.

Example 7.2

The differential equation associated with the motion of a simple pendulum is

$$\frac{d\omega}{d\phi} = -\frac{g}{L}\frac{\sin \phi}{\omega},$$

$$(7.9)$$

and the given initial conditions are

$$\phi = 79°, \qquad \omega = 0.66488546 \text{ rad/sec}, \qquad L = 2.5', \qquad g = 32.2014 \text{ ft/sec}$$

Integrate to $\phi = 0°$; the interval of $\phi = -0.5°$.

Using the Runge-Kutta method with Gill's coefficients, we proceed as follows.

Solution: We shall show the detailed calculation to obtain ω at $\phi = 78.5$. Let f be the derivative of ω. We then have

$$f = \frac{d\omega}{d\phi} = \frac{-g}{L} \frac{\sin \phi}{\omega}.$$

Using Eq. (7.32) with $y^{(j)} = \omega_j$ and $t = \phi$, we obtain

$$\omega_1 = \omega_0 + a_1(f_0 \, \Delta\phi - q_0)$$

$$= 0.66488546 + \frac{1}{2}\left(\frac{-32.2014}{2.5} \frac{\sin 79°}{0.66488546} \frac{-0.5 \times 3.14159}{180}\right) = 0.747859,$$

where $q_0 = 0$. From Eq. (7.31), we have

$$q_1 = (1 - 3a_1)q_0 + 2a_1f_0 \, \Delta\phi$$

$$= 0 + 2 \times 0.5 \left(\frac{-32.2014}{2.5} \frac{\sin 79°}{0.66488546} \frac{-0.5 \times 3.14159}{180}\right) = 0.165947,$$

$$\omega_2 = \omega_1 + a_2(f_1 \, \Delta\phi - q_1)$$

$$= 0.747859 + \left(1 - \frac{\sqrt{2}}{2}\right)$$

$$\times \left(\frac{-32.2014}{2.5} \frac{\sin 78.75°}{0.747859} \frac{-0.5 \times 3.14159}{180} - 0.165947\right) = 0.74243,$$

$$q_2 = \left(-2 + \frac{3}{\sqrt{2}}\right) z_0 + (2 - \sqrt{2})z_1$$

$$= \left(-2 + \frac{3}{\sqrt{2}}\right) \times 0.16594716 + (2 - \sqrt{2})$$

$$\times \left(\frac{-32.2014}{2.5} \frac{\sin 78.75°}{0.747859} \frac{-0.5 \times 3.14159}{180}\right) = 0.1065042,$$

$$\omega_3 = \omega_2 + a_3(f_2 \, \Delta\phi - q_2)$$

$$= 0.742431 + \left(1 + \frac{\sqrt{2}}{2}\right)$$

$$\times \left(\frac{-32.2014}{2.5} \frac{\sin 78.75°}{0.742431} \frac{-0.5 \times 3.14159}{180} - 0.1065042\right) = 0.814102,$$

$$q_3 = (1 - 3a_3)q_2 + 2a_3f_2 \, \Delta\phi$$

$$= \left[1 - 3\left(1 + \frac{\sqrt{2}}{2}\right)\right] \times 0.1065042 + 2\left(1 + \frac{\sqrt{2}}{2}\right)$$

$$\times \left(\frac{-32.2014}{2.5} \frac{\sin 78.75°}{0.742431} \frac{-0.5 \times 3.14159}{180}\right) = 0.0680443,$$

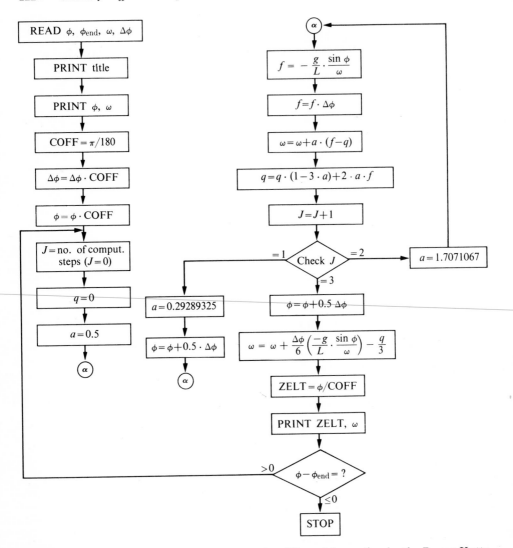

Fig. 7.7. Flow chart for solution of a first-order differential equation by the Runge-Kutta method using Gill's coefficients.

$$\omega_4 = \omega_3 + \tfrac{1}{6} f(\phi_n + \Delta\phi, \omega_3)\, \Delta\phi - \tfrac{1}{3} q_3$$

$$= 0.814102 + \frac{1}{6}\left(\frac{-32.2014}{2.5}\, \frac{\sin 78.5^{\circ}}{0.814102}\, \frac{-0.5 \times 3.14159}{180}\right) - \tfrac{1}{3}(0.0680443)$$

$$= 0.8139.$$

This is the value of ω at $\phi = 78.5°$. The process can be repeated for various ω-values. A flow chart and a FORTRAN program for this example are shown in Figs. 7.7 and 7.8, respectively. Table 7.3 lists the correct angular velocities.

TABLE 7.3. Angular Velocities by the Runge-Kutta-Gill Method

PHI	ANG. VELOCITY
79.0	.6648855
78.5	.8139816
78.0	.9395021
77.5	1.0499302
77.0	1.1496163
76.5	1.2411448
76.0	1.3261995
75.5	1.4059500
75.0	1.4812475
74.5	1.5527349
74.0	1.6209110
73.5	1.6861729
73.0	1.7488419
72.5	1.8091831
72.0	1.8674179
71.5	1.9237332
71.0	1.9782886
70.5	2.0312223
70.0	2.0826539
69.5	2.1326884
69.0	2.1814181
68.5	2.2289251
68.0	2.2752824
67.5	2.3205555
67.0	2.3648034
66.5	2.4080793
66.0	2.4504316
65.5	2.4919039
65.0	2.5325367
64.5	2.5723667
64.0	2.6114276

```
C    RUNGE-KUTTA-GILL METHOD TO SOLVE SIMPLE PENDULUM PROBLEM
C
C    PHI=INITIAL PHI    PHIN=PHI LAST    W=INITIAL OMEGA    DELTP=DELTA PHI
C
     READ 7,PHI,PHIN,W,DELTP
   7 FORMAT(F5.1,F5.1,F9.8,F3.1)
     PUNCH 500
 500 FORMAT(24X,3HPHI,5X,13HANG. VELOCITY//)
     PUNCH 5,PHI,W
   5 FORMAT(23X,F5.1,5X,F11.7)
     COFF=3.1415926/180.
     DELTP=DELTP*COFF
     PHI=PHI*COFF
   3 J=0
     Q=0.
     A=0.5
   6 F=-32.2014/2.*SINF(PHI)/W
     F=F*DELTP
     W=W+A*(F-Q)
     Q=Q*(1.-3.*A)+2.*A*F
     J=J+1
     GO TO(12,13,14),J
  12 A=0.29289325
     PHI=PHI+.5*DELTP
     GO TO 6
  13 A=1.7071067
     GO TO 6
  14 PHI=PHI+.5*DELTP
     W=W+(-32.2014/2.*SINF(PHI)/W*DELTP/6.)-(Q/3.)
     ZELT=PHI/COFF
     PUNCH5,ZELT,W
     IF(ZELT-PHIN)20,20,3
  20 STOP
     END
79.0 64.0.66488546-.5
```

Fig. 7.8.   FORTRAN program.

7.5   HIGHER-ORDER ORDINARY DIFFERENTIAL EQUATIONS; BOUNCING BALL PROBLEM

In the development of the previous sections in this chapter, computer solutions of differential equations *of first order* were discussed in considerable detail. In this and the next section, we shall examine how to apply these procedures to ordinary differential equations of higher orders.

The standard procedure for the computer solution of higher-order ordinary differential equations is to transform them to systems of simultaneous first-order equations. In this section, the first-order equations will be solved by an approximation similar to Euler's procedure. We shall consider a specific example of tracking a moving ball which has an initial horizontal velocity v_0 (Fig. 7.9).

The two governing differential equations are

$$\frac{dx}{dt} = v_0 \tag{7.33}$$

and

$$\frac{d^2y}{dt^2} = -g. \tag{7.34}$$

Equation (7.33) indicates that the horizontal velocity at any time is equal to a constant, v_0; Eq. (7.34) expresses the fact that the gravitational acceleration is equal to $g = 32.2$ ft/sec^2 throughout the motion.

If we let

$$v = \frac{dy}{dt},$$

then

$$\frac{dv}{dt} = \frac{d^2y}{dt^2},$$

and Eqs. (7.33) and (7.34) may be recast in the following system of three *first-order equations*:

$$\frac{dx}{dt} = v_0, \tag{7.35a}$$

$$\frac{dv}{dt} = -32.2, \tag{7.35b}$$

$$\frac{dy}{dt} = v. \tag{7.35c}$$

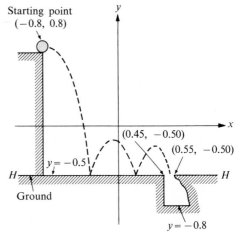

Fig. 7.9.   Bouncing ball problem: initial horizontal velocity $= v_0$, initial vertical velocity $= 0$.

In the following discussion we shall be concerned only with Eq. (7.35).

As the ball collides with the horizontal plane *HH*, it either bounces or falls through the hole. If it bounces, the horizontal velocity remains constant as v_0, and the vertical velocity v after one bounce is equal to the negative value of 85% of the vertical velocity before the bounce.

Our problem is to find the v_0 required to ensure that the ball falls into the hole. We first take $v_0 = 0.78$ ft/sec. If the ball misses the hole, we then try $v_0 = 0.775$ ft/sec, and so forth, decreasing v_0 by 0.005 ft/sec each time.

If the ball misses the hole, we continue the computation until $x = +0.58$. On the other hand, if the ball falls into the hole, the computation should go on until $y = -0.8$, and at this point this particular set of computation should be repeated. During this repeated computation, the step-by-step position of the ball, together with the corresponding time in seconds and the v_0-value, will be printed out. We shall use $\Delta t = 0.005$ sec.

Solution: For computer solutions, Eqs. (7.35) may be replaced by the following equations:

$$x_{j+1} = x_j + v_0(\Delta t), \quad \text{hori zontal position} \tag{7.36a}$$
$$v_{j+1} = v_j - 32.2(\Delta t), \quad \text{slope of curve.} \tag{7.36b}$$
$$y_{j+1} = y_j + \tfrac{1}{2}(v_j + v_{j+1})\,\Delta t. \quad \text{vertical position} \tag{7.36c}$$

Substituting the value of v_{j+1} in Eq. (7.36b) into Eq. (7.36c), one obtains

$$x_{j+1} = x_j + v_0(\Delta t),$$
$$v_{j+1} = v_j - 32.2(\Delta t),$$
$$y_{j+1} = y_j - [\tfrac{1}{2}g(\Delta t) - v_j]\,\Delta t. \tag{7.37}$$

The actual computational form may be arranged as follows:

$$v_x = 0.775$$

j	t	x	v_y	y
0	0	-0.8	0	0.8
1	0.005	-0.76125	-0.161	0.7987925
2	0.01	⋮	⋮	⋮

A sample flow chart and a FORTRAN program are shown in Figs. 7.11 and 7.12, respectively. This program is written to determine what initial velocity v_0 will cause the ball to drop into the hole. For this purpose, the following information is read in as data:

$$v_0 = 0.780, \qquad \Delta v = -0.005,$$
$$\Delta t = -0.005, \qquad e = 0.850.$$

So far as the problem is concerned, e means that the vertical velocity after the impact is 0.850 times as large as the vertical velocity before the impact (see Fig. 7.10).

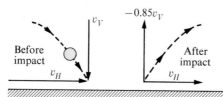

Figure 7.10

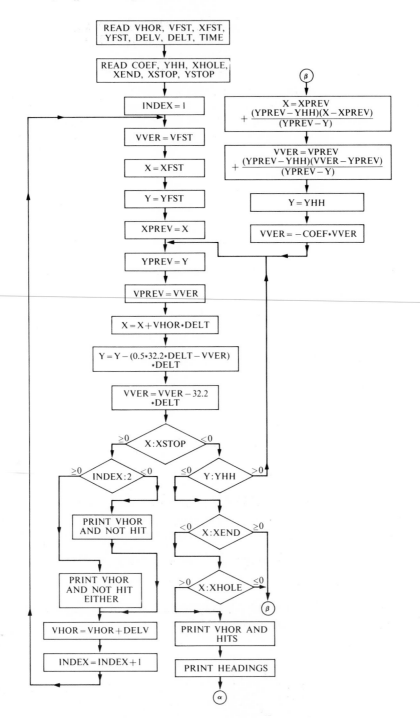

Fig. 7.11.   Flow chart for bouncing ball problem.

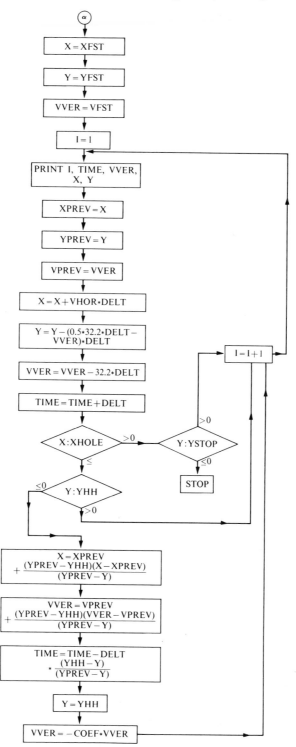

Fig. 7.11 (*cont.*)

```
C      BOUNCING BALL PROBLEM
C   VHOR=HORIZONTAL VELOCITY,  VFST=VERTICAL VELOCITY,
C   XFST=INITIAL X, YFST=INITIAL Y, DELV=DELTA V, DELT=DELTA T
C
       READ 1, VHOR, VFST, XFST, YFST, DELV, DELT, TIME
     1 FORMAT(F10.4,F10.4,F10.4,F10.4,F10.4,F10.4,F10.4)
C
C   COFF=COFF. OF RESTITUTION, YHH=Y FOR GROUND,XHOLE=LEFT SIDE OF HOLE,
C   XEND=RIGHT SIDE OF HOLE, XSTOP=MAXIMUM X IF BALL MISSES HOLE,
C   YSTOP=MAXIMUM Y IF BALL HITS HOLE
C
       READ 2, COEF,YHH, XHOLE, XEND, XSTOP, YSTOP
     2 FORMAT(F10.4,F10.4,F10.4,F10.4,F10.4,F10.4)
       INDEX=1
    10 VVER=VFST
       X=XFST
       Y=YFST
    12 XPREV=X
       YPREV=Y
       VPREV=VVER
       X=X+VHOR*DELT
       Y=Y-(0.5*32.2*DELT-VVER)*DELT
       VVER=VVER-32.2*DELT
       IF(X-XSTOP)16,14,14
    14 IF(INDEX-2)40,42,42
    40 PUNCH 3,INDEX,VHOR
     3 FORMAT(3X,3HRUN ,I3,7X,20HINITIAL VELOCITY IS ,F5.3)
       PUNCH 131                     MISTAKE
   131 FORMAT(44X,20HDID NOT HIT THE HOLE)
       GO TO 44
    42 PUNCH 3,INDEX,VHOR
       PUNCH 132
   132 FORMAT(44X,27HDID NOT HIT THE HOLE EITHER)
    44 VHOR=VHOR+DELV
       INDEX=INDEX+1
       GO TO 10
    16 IF(Y-YHH)20,20,12
    20 IF(X-XEND) 22,24,24
    22 IF(X-XHOLE)24,24,26
    24 X=XPREV+((YPREV-YHH)*(X-XPREV))/(YPREV-Y)
       VVER=VPREV+((VVER-VPREV)*(YPREV-YHH))/(YPREV-Y)
       Y=YHH
       VVER=-COEF*VVER
       GO TO 12
    26 PUNCH 3, INDEX, VHOR
       PUNCH 133
   133 FORMAT(44X,16HIT HITS THE HOLE/)
       PUNCH 6
     6 FORMAT(10X,45HTHE NEXT TRAJECTORY IS FOR THE SUCCESSFUL RUN///)
       PUNCH 7
     7 FORMAT(8X,1HJ,7X,4HTIME,5X,10HVERT. VEL.,9X,1HX,14X,1HY//)
       X=XFST
       Y=YFST
       VVER=VFST
       DO 34 I=1,1000
       PUNCH 8,I,TIME,VVER,X,Y
     8 FORMAT(6X,I4,F10.3,F15.6,F15.6,F15.6)
       XPREV=X
       YPREV=Y
       VPREV=VVER
```

Fig. 7.12.   FORTRAN program.

```
      X=X+VHOR*DELT
      Y=Y-(0.5*32.2*DELT-VVER)*DELT
      VVER=VVER-32.2*DELT
      TIME=TIME+DELT
      IF(X-XHOLE)30,30,28
   28 IF(Y-YSTOP)36,36,34
   30 IF(Y-YHH)32,32,34
   32 X=XPREV+((YPREV-YHH)*(X-XPREV))/(YPREV-Y)
      VVER=VPREV+((VVER-VPREV)*(YPREV-YHH))/(YPREV-Y)
      TIME=TIME-DELT*(YHH-Y)/(YPREV-Y)
      Y=YHH
      VVER=-COEF*VVER
   34 CONTINUE
   36 STOP
      END
```

+.7800	.0000	-.8000	+.8000	-.0050	+.0050	.0000
+.8500	-.5000	+.4500	+.5500	+.5800	-.8000	

Fig. 7.12 (*cont.*)

If the ball misses, the calculation is carried out to $x = 0.580$ ft. If it drops into the hole, the calculation is carried out until it strikes the bottom. To record the hits and misses, the following format is used (use a new sheet for these results):

RUN 1   INITIAL VELOCITY IS .780 DID NOT HIT THE HOLE

RUN 2   INITIAL VELOCITY IS .775 DID NOT HIT THE HOLE EITHER

RUN 3   INITIAL VELOCITY IS .770 DID NOT HIT THE HOLE EITHER

-----   ---------------------   ----------------------------

-----   ---------------------   ----------------------------

RUN X   -------------------------   IT HITS THE HOLE

After the correct v_0 for a hit is found, the next step is to print out the trajectory which the ball followed. Note that t is incremented by -0.005 sec, and that j is the number of iterations. (Use a new sheet for printing these results.)

J	T	X	VERT. VEL.	Y
1	0.000	-0.800	0.000	0.800
2	0.005	------	------	------
-	------	------	------	------
X	------	------	------	-0.800

TABLE 7.4.   Answers to Bouncing Ball Problem

```
RUN   1          INITIAL VELOCITY IS   .780
                                              DID NOT HIT THE HOLE
RUN   2          INITIAL VELOCITY IS   .775
                                              DID NOT HIT THE HOLE EITHER
RUN   3          INITIAL VELOCITY IS   .770
                                              DID NOT HIT THE HOLE EITHER
RUN   4          INITIAL VELOCITY IS   .765
                                              DID NOT HIT THE HOLE EITHER
RUN   5          INITIAL VELOCITY IS   .760
                                              DID NOT HIT THE HOLE EITHER
RUN   6          INITIAL VELOCITY IS   .755
                                              DID NOT HIT THE HOLE EITHER
RUN   7          INITIAL VELOCITY IS   .750
                                              DID NOT HIT THE HOLE EITHER
RUN   8          INITIAL VELOCITY IS   .745
                                              DID NOT HIT THE HOLE EITHER
RUN   9          INITIAL VELOCITY IS   .740
                                              DID NOT HIT THE HOLE EITHER
RUN  10          INITIAL VELOCITY IS   .735
                                              IT HITS THE HOLE


         THE NEXT TRAJECTORY IS FOR THE SUCCESSFUL RUN
```

J	TIME	VERT. VEL.	X	Y
1	.000	.00000000	-.80000000	.80000000
2	.005	-.16100000	-.79632500	.79959750
3	.010	-.32200000	-.79265000	.79839000
4	.015	-.48300000	-.78897500	.79637750
.....				
36	.175	-5.63500000	-.67137500	.30693750
.....				
57	.280	-9.01600000	-.59420000	-.46224000
58	.284	7.77721410	-.59114899	-.50000000
59	.289	7.61621410	-.58747399	-.46151643
.....				
79	.389	4.39621410	-.51397399	.13910497
.....				
105	.519	.21021410	-.41842399	.43852279
106	.524	.04921410	-.41474899	.43917136
107	.529	-.11178590	-.41107399	.43901494
.....				
144	.714	-6.06878590	-.27509899	-.13268785
.....				
154	.764	-7.67878590	-.23834899	-.47637715
155	.767	6.61029490	-.23611132	-.50000000
156	.772	6.44929490	-.23243632	-.46735103
.....				
176	.872	3.22929490	-.15893632	.01657840
.....				
196	.972	.00929490	-.08543632	.17850783
197	.977	-.15170510	-.08176132	.17815181
198	.982	-.31270510	-.07808632	.17699079
.....				

TABLE 7.4. (*cont.*)

219	1.087	-3.69370510	-.00091132	-.03334567
•••••				
237	1.177	-6.59170510	.06523868	-.49618906
238	1.177	5.61858210	.06565848	-.50000000
239	1.182	5.45758210	.06933348	-.47230959
•••••				
253	1.252	3.20358210	.12078348	-.16916885
•••••				
272	1.347	.14458210	.19060848	-.01013105
273	1.352	-.01641790	.19428348	-.00981064
274	1.357	-.17741790	.19795848	-.01029523
•••••				
289	1.432	-2.59241790	.25308348	-.11416407
•••••				
307	1.522	-5.49041790	.31923348	-.47789169
308	1.526	4.77547370	.32215034	-.50000000
309	1.531	4.61447370	.32582534	-.47652514
•••••				
326	1.616	1.87747370	.38830034	-.20061752
•••••				
337	1.671	.10647370	.42872534	-.14605906
338	1.676	-.05452630	.43240034	-.14592920
339	1.681	-.21552630	.43607534	-.14660433
•••••				
353	1.751	-2.46952630	.48752534	-.24058115
•••••				
370	1.836	-5.20652630	.55000034	-.56681336
•••••				
377	1.871	-6.33352630	.57572534	-.76876427

Linear interpolation is used to obtain the vertical velocity, x-distance, and time when the ball goes below the ground (*HH* in Fig. 7.9). The correct printout of these answers appears in Table 7.4.

7.6 HIGHER-ORDER EQUATIONS BY RUNGE-KUTTA METHOD

In the previous section, a higher-order equation was transformed into a system of first-order equations and then solved by an approximation similar to Euler's method. We shall now turn to the solution of higher-order equations using the Runge-Kutta method with Runge's coefficients. Regardless of what method we may choose, the first step is to transform the given higher-order equation to a system of first-order equations.

Consider the second-order differential equation,

$$\frac{d^2y}{dt^2} + c\,\frac{dy}{dt} + k^2y = 0, \tag{7.38}$$

where c and k are two given constants. To develop a procedure which can be easily used for a computer solution, we set

$$y_1 = y \quad \text{and} \quad y_2 = \frac{dy}{dt} = \frac{dy_1}{dt}.$$

We then let f_1 and f_2 stand for actual functions which are to be used to find the values of Δy_1 and Δy_2, respectively. We see that f_1 and f_2 can be easily obtained by transforming the original differential equation into two simultaneous first-order differential equations. If we set

$$f_1 = \frac{dy_1}{dt} = y_2, \tag{7.39}$$

we can easily solve (7.38) for f_2:

$$f_2 = \frac{dy_2}{dt} = -cy_2 - k^2 y_1. \tag{7.40}$$

To obtain a numerical solution for Eq. (7.38), we need a set of initial conditions. Here we take $y = 1$ and $dy/dt = 0$ at $t = 0$. Final values of t and Δt are also needed. These are taken as 3 and 0.2, respectively. The basic problem is, therefore, to determine the values of y_1 and y_2 as t increases by the increment Δt. We have already discussed one simple, but crude, method in Section 7.5. If we simply choose

$$\Delta y_1 = \Delta t f_1, \quad \text{at} \quad t = t_0 \quad \text{and} \quad \Delta y_2 = \Delta t f_2, \quad \text{at} \quad t = t_0,$$

then

$$y_1 \ (\text{at} \ t = t_0 + \Delta t) = y_1 \ (\text{at} \ t = t_0) \ + \Delta y_1,$$

$$y_2 \ (\text{at} \ t = t_0 + \Delta t) = y_2 \ (\text{at} \ t = t_0) \ + \Delta y_2. \tag{7.41}$$

This equation will directly give us approximations for y and $y'(y_1$ and $y_2)$ at $t + \Delta t$. These, in turn, will enable us to find new Δy_1 and Δy_2, which will give us y_1 and y_2 at $t = t_0 + 2 \Delta t$. The procedure can be carried on indefinitely.

Up to now, all that has been done toward developing the Runge-Kutta method is the transformation of Eq. (7.38) into two simultaneous first-order equations. We shall now

(1) further develop the notation,

(2) present the basic Runge-Kutta formula for solving simultaneous first-order equations,

(3) and, finally, use this for solving Eqs. (7.39) and (7.40).

Let us develop these steps.

(1) The notation used in Eq. (7.41) is awkward. We can simplify it by letting

$t_0 = $ initial value of t,

$t_n = n \Delta t + t_0$,

$y_n^{(2)} = y_2 \Big|_{t=t_n}$ (note that the superscript 2 is used to indicate the second ordinary differential equation of first order),

$m = $ the total number of first-order simultaneous equations that must be solved,

$y_n^{(i)} \ (i = 1, \ldots, m) = $ the value of any one of the dependent variables at $t = t_n$.

$$f^{(i)}(t_n, y_n^{(1)}, y_n^{(2)}, \ldots, y_n^{(m)}) = \frac{dy_n^{(i)}}{dt}.$$

(2) If the values of the dependent variables in the m first-order differential equations are given at $t = t_n$, we can use the following algorithm to find their numerical values at $t_{n+1} = t_n + \Delta t$:

$$y_{n+1}^{(i)} = y_n^{(i)} + \Delta y_n^{(i)}, \tag{7.42}$$

where

$$\Delta y_n^{(i)} = \frac{\Delta t}{6} (k_0^{(i)} + 2k_1^{(i)} + 2k_2^{(i)} + k_3^{(i)})$$

and

$$k_0^{(i)} = f^{(i)}(t_n, y_n^{(i)}),$$

$$k_1^{(i)} = f^{(i)} \left(t_n + \frac{\Delta t}{2}, y_n^{(i)} + \frac{k_0^{(i)}}{2} \Delta t \right),$$

$$k_2^{(i)} = f^{(i)} \left(t_n + \frac{\Delta t}{2}, y_n^{(i)} + \frac{k_1^{(i)}}{2} \Delta t \right),$$

$$k_3^{(i)} = f^{(i)}(t_n + \Delta t, y_n^{(i)} + k_2^{(i)} \Delta t),$$

and the superscript $i = 1, 2, 3, \ldots, m$ serves to indicate the m first-order differential equations.

If, for example, we have two simultaneous equations of first order, $m = 2$, then

$$\dot{y} = f(t, y, v), \qquad \dot{v} = g(t, y, v). \tag{7.43}$$

Equation (7.42) now takes the form

$$y_{n+1} = y_n + \tfrac{1}{6}(k_0 + 2k_1 + 2k_2 + k_3)\Delta t,$$

$$v_{n+1} = v_n + \tfrac{1}{6}(m_0 + 2m_1 + 2m_2 + m_3)\Delta t, \tag{7.44}$$

where

$$k_0 = f(t_n, y_n, v_n),$$
$$k_1 = f(t_n + \Delta t/2, y_n + k_0 \Delta t/2, v_n + m_0 \Delta t/2),$$
$$k_2 = f(t_n + \Delta t/2, y_n + k_1 \Delta t/2, v_n + m_1 \Delta t/2),$$
$$k_3 = f(t_n + \Delta t, y_n + k_2 \Delta t, v_n + m_2 \Delta t),$$
$$m_0 = g(t_n, y_n, v_n),$$
$$m_1 = g(t_n + \Delta t/2, y_n + k_0 \Delta t/2, v_n + m_0 \Delta t/2),$$
$$m_2 = g(t_n + \Delta t/2, y_n + k_1 \Delta t/2, v_n + m_1 \Delta t/2),$$
$$m_3 = g(t_n + \Delta t, y_n + k_2 \Delta t, v_n + m_2 \Delta t).$$

(3) We now turn to the evaluation of Eq. (7.42), the basic Runge-Kutta procedure. A subprogram RUNGE is provided for this purpose (see Fig. 7.13), in which the given initial conditions for the N dependent variables are used as solutions at $t = t_0$. RUNGE performs the computation necessary to find the solution for the new value of the independent variable T. The following symbols are used:

  T = independent variable,

DT = step size,

  N = number of dependent variables,

```
      SUBROUTINE RUNGE(T,DT,N,Y,DY,F,L,M,J)
      DIMENSION DY(2),Y(2),F(14)
      GO TO (100,110,300),L
100   GO TO (101,110) ,IG
101   J = 1
      L = 2
      DO 106 K = 1,N
      K1 = K+3*N
      K2 = K1+N
      K3 = N + K
      F(K1) = Y(K)
      F(K3) = F(K1)
106   F(K2) = DY(K)
      GO TO 406
110   DO 140 K=1,N
      K1 = K
      K2 = K+5*N
      K3 = K2+N
      K4 = K + N
      GO TO (111,112,113,114),J
111   F(K1) = DY(K)*DT
      Y(K) = F(K4)+.5*F(K1)
      GO TO 140
112   F(K2) = DY(K)*DT
      GO TO 124
113   F(K3) = DY(K)*DT
      GO TO 134
114   Y(K) = F(K4) +(F(K1)+2.*(F(K2)+F(K3))+DY(K)*DT)/6.
      GO TO 140
124   Y(K) = .5*F(K2)
      Y(K) = Y(K)+F(K4)
      GO TO 140
134   Y(K) = F(K4)+F(K3)
140   CONTINUE
      GO TO (170,180,170,180),J
170   T = T + .5*DT
180   J = J+1
      IF(J-4)404,404,299
299   M=1
      GO TO 406
300   IG=1
      GO TO 405
404   IG=2
405   L=1
406   RETURN
      END
```

Fig. 7.13. Subprogram RUNGE.

Y = first dependent variable followed by the remaining N − 1 dependent variables (must be dimensioned),

DY = derivative of first dependent variable followed by the remaining N − 1 derivatives in the same order as the corresponding dependent variables (must be dimensioned),

F = storages (must be dimensioned as 7N),

L = a fixed-point variable controlled by subroutine RUNGE to exit to the proper section of the program calling RUNGE,

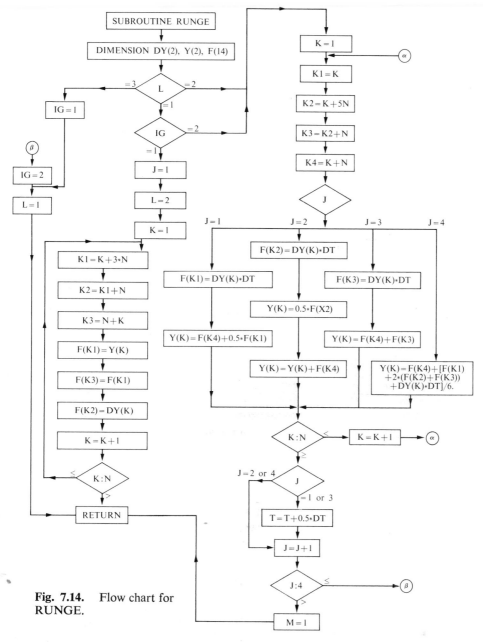

Fig. 7.14. Flow chart for RUNGE.

J = same as L,

M = a fixed-point variable used to return from subprogram RUNGE to the main program.

A flow chart for the subroutine RUNGE is shown in Fig. 7.14.

```
C       HIGHER ORDER EQUATIONS BY RUNGE-KUTTA METHOD
C       C = 0.1        K = 3.2      DT = 0.2
C       INITIAL CONDITIONS                  .00001
C               T = 0,           Y1 = 1.          Y2 = 0.
C       RANGE OF T                 0 TO 3  10
        DIMENSION DY(2),Y(2),F(14)
        N=2  v
        DT = 0.2
        T=0.
        Y(1)=1.  0.00001
        Y(2)=0.
 10  L=3
        M=0
 50  CALL RUNGE(T,DT,N,Y,DY,F,L,M,J)
        IF(M-1)75,10,75
 75  GO TO  (100,200,999),L
100  DY(1)=Y(2)
        DY(2) = -.1*Y(2)- 3.2*3.2*Y(1)
        GO TO 50
200  PUNCH 800,T,Y(1),Y(2)
250  IF(T-3.)260,999,999
260  GO TO 50
800  FORMAT(10X,3E15.8)
999  STOP
        END
```

Fig. 7.15. Main program.

Example

Write a main program, together with the required data cards, to numerically solve Eqs. (7.39) and (7.40), where

$$c = 0.1, \qquad k = 3.2, \qquad \Delta t = 0.2,$$

the initial conditions are $t = 0$, $y_1 = 1$, $y_2 = 0$, and the range of t is $0 \le t \le 3$.

This main program is used to (a) call the subroutine RUNGE; (b) read in Eqs. (7.39) and (7.40); (c) write out answers; and (d) terminate the calculations. Figures 7.15 and 7.16 show a possible main program and a flow chart, respectively. The calling sequence in the main program to call subroutine RUNGE consists of the three statements

```
       L = 3
S      CALL RUNGE (T, DT, N, Y, DY, L, M, J)
       GO TO (BOXA, BOXB, BOXC), L
```

where

S = a statement number,

BOXA = statement number for derivative computations,

BOXB = statement number for print routine and check
               for end of program,

BOXC = statement number for STOP.

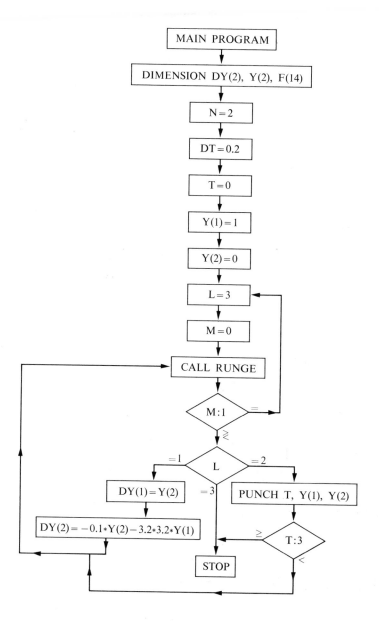

Fig. 7.16. Main program flow chart.

TABLE 7.5.   Computer Solutions

T	Y	DY/DT
.00000000E-99	.10000000E+01	.00000000E-99
.20000000E+00	.80354910E+00	-.18892436E+01
.40000000E+00	.29713235E+00	-.30013440E+01
.60000000E+00	-.31497695E+00	-.29177088E+01
.80000000E+00	-.79140636E+00	-.16956232E+01
.10000000E+01	-.94877030E+00	.16392680E+00
.12000000E+01	-.73213954E+00	.19211571E+01
.14000000E+01	-.23386334E+00	.28914892E+01
.16000000E+01	.34554886E+00	.27119313E+01
.18000000E+01	.77800717E+00	.14763096E+01
.20000000E+01	.89754080E+00	-.31079540E+00
.22000000E+01	.66387740E+00	-.19396786E+01
.24000000E+01	.17559422E+00	-.27770667E+01
.26000000E+01	-.37126041E+00	-.25120137E+01
.28000000E+01	-.76178357E+00	-.12707790E+01
.30000000E+01	-.84658468E+00	.44150700E+00

The statements related with BOXA, BOXB, and BOXC are:

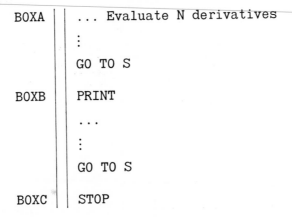

BOXA	... Evaluate N derivatives
	⋮
	GO TO S
BOXB	PRINT
	...
	⋮
	GO TO S
BOXC	STOP

The computer solutions are shown in Table 7.5.

BIBLIOGRAPHY

General

BENNETT, A. A., W. E. MILNE, and H. BATEMAN, *Numerical Integration of Differential Equations.* Dover, New York, 1956.

CLENSHAW, C. W., and F. W. J. OLIVER, "Solution of Differential Equations by Recurrence Relations," *Math. Tab., Wash.*, **5**, pp. 34–39 (1951).

COLLATZ, L., *The Numerical Treatment of Differential Equations*, 3rd edition (1st edition 1951), translated by P. G. WILLIAMS. Springer, Berlin, 1960.

Fox, L., "A Note on the Numerical Integration of First-order Differential Equations," *Quart. J. Mech.*, **7**, pp. 367–378 (1954).

Fox, L., *The Numerical Solution of Two-Point Boundary Problems in Ordinary Differential Equations*. Oxford University Press, London, 1957.

Gorn, S., and R. Moore, "Automatic Error Control, the Initial-Value Problem in Ordinary Differential Equations," *Ballistic Research Laboratory Report* 893 (1954).

Hull, T. E., and A. C. R. Newberry, "Integration Procedures Which Minimize Propagated Errors," *J. Soc. Ind. Appl. Math.*, **9**, pp. 31–47 (1961).

Levy, H., and E. A. Baggott, *Numerical Studies in Differential Equations*. Dover, New York, 1950.

Lindelof, E., "Remarques sur l'intégration numérique des équations différentielles ordinaires," *Acta Soc. Sci. Fennic. Nova Ser. A.*, **2**, pp. 1–21 (1938).

Milne, W. E., *Numerical Solution of Differential Equations*. John Wiley and Sons, New York, 1953.

National Physical Laboratory, *Modern Computing Methods, Notes on Applied Science*, No. 16, 2d ed. H. M. Stationery Office, London, 1961.

Ralston, A., "Numerical Integration Methods for the Solution of Ordinary Differential Equations," pp. 95–109, in *Mathematical Methods for Digital Computers*. A. Ralston and H. S. Wilf, Eds. John Wiley and Sons, New York, 1960.

Todd, J. "Notes on Modern Numerical Analysis, I, Solution of Differential Functions by Recurrence Relations," *Math. Tables Aids Comput.*, **4**, pp. 39–44 (1950).

von Mises, R., "Zur Numerischen Integration von Differentialgleichungen," *Z. Angew. Math. Mech.*, **10**, pp. 81–92 (1930).

Runge-Kutta Method

Conte, S. D., and R. F. Reeves, "A Kutta Third-Order Procedure for Solving Differential Equations Requiring Minimum Storage," *J. Assoc. Comput. Mach.*, **3**, pp. 22–25 (1956).

Gill, S., "A Process for the Step-by-Step Integration of Differential Equations in an Automatic Digital Computing Machine," *Proc. Cambridge Phil. Soc.*, **47**, pp. 96–108 (1951).

Heun, K., "Neue Methode zur Approximativen Integration der Differentialgleichungen einer Unabhängigen Variable," *Z. Math. Phys.*, **45**, pp. 23–38 (1900).

Kutta, W., "Beitrag zur Naherungsweisen Integration Totaler Differentialgleichungen," *Z. Math. Phys.*, **46**, pp. 435–453 (1901).

Martiń, D. W., "Runge-Kutta Methods for Integrating Differential Equations on High-Speed Digital Computers," *Comput. J.*, **1**, pp. 118–123 (1958).

Rice, J. R., "Split Runge-Kutta Method for Simultaneous Equations," *J. Res. Nat. Bur. Std.*, **64B**, pp. 151–170 (1960).

Romanelli, M. J., "Runge-Kutta Methods for the Solution of Ordinary Differential Equations," in *Mathematical Methods for Digital Computers*, A. Ralston and H. S. Wilf, Eds. John Wiley and Sons, New York, pp. 110–120, 1960.

Runge, C., "Über die Numerische Auflösung von Differentialgleichungen," *Math. Ann.*, **46**, pp. 167–178 (1895).

Runge, C., "Über die Numerische Auflösung Totaler Differentialgleichungen," *Nachr. K. Ges. Wiss. Göttingen*, pp. 252–257 (1905).

Adams' Method

ALONSO, R.,   A Starting Method for the Three-Point Adams Predictor-Corrector Method,"
J. Assoc. Comput. Mach., **7,** pp. 176–180 (1960).

Predictor-Corrector Procedures

FORRINGTON, C. V. D., "Extensions of the Predictor-Corrector Method for the Solution of
Systems of Ordinary Differential Equations," *Comput. J.*, **4,** pp. 80–84 (1961).

HAMMING, R. W., "Stable Predictor-Corrector Methods for Ordinary Differential Equations," *J. Assoc. Comput. Mach.*, **6,** pp. 37–47 (1959).

RALSTON, A., "Some Theoretical and Computational Matters Relating to Predictor-
Corrector Methods of Numerical Integration," *Comput. J.*, **4,** pp. 64–67 (1961).

SOUTHARD, T. H., and E. C. YOWELL, "An Alternative Predictor-Corrector Process," *Math.
Tables Aids Comput.*, **6,** pp. 253–254 (1952).

Miscellaneous Methods

BROCK, P., and F. J. MURRAY, "The Use of Exponential Sums in Step-by-Step Integration,"
Math. Tables Aids Comput., **6,** pp. 63–78 (1952).

CLENSHAW, C. W., "The Numerical Solution of Linear Differential Equations in Chebyshev
Series," *Proc. Cambridge Phil. Soc.*, **53,** pp. 134–149 (1957).

CURTISS, J. H., "Sampling Methods Applied to Differential and Integral Equations," in
Proceedings, Seminar on Scientific Computation. IBM Corporation, New York, 1949.

DENNIS, S. C., "The Numerical Integration of Ordinary Differential Equations Possessing
Exponential Type Solutions," *Proc. Cambridge Phil. Soc.*, **56,** pp. 240–246 (1960).

DE VOGELAERE, R., "A Method for the Numerical Integration of Differential Equations of
Second Order Without Explicit First Derivatives," *J. Res. Nat. Bur. Std.*, **54,** pp. 119–125
(1955).

FOX, L., "The Solution by Relaxation Methods of Ordinary Differential Equations," *Proc.
Cambridge Phil. Soc.*, **45,** pp. 50–68 (1949).

FOX, L., and E. T. GOODWIN, "Some New Methods for the Numerical Integration of Ordinary
Differential Equations," *Proc. Cambridge Phil. Soc.*, **45,** pp. 373–388 (1949).

HAMMER, P. C., and J. W. HOLLINGSWORTH, "Trapezoidal Methods of Approximating
Solutions of Differential Equations," *Math. Tables Aids Comput.*, **9,** pp. 92–96 (1955).

KEITEL, G. H., "An Extension of Milne's Three-Point Method," *J. Assoc. Comput. Mach.*,
3, pp. 212–222 (1956).

LOTKIN, M., "A New Integrating Procedure of High Accuracy," *J. Math. Phys.*, **31,** pp.
29–34 (1952).

SALZER, H. E., "Osculatory Extrapolation and a New Method for the Numerical Integration
of Differential Equations," *J. Franklin Inst.*, **262,** pp. 111–119 (1956).

STOLLER, L., and D. MORRISON, "A Method for the Numerical Integration of Ordinary
Differential Equations," *Math. Tables Aids Comput.*, **12,** pp. 269–272 (1958).

WILF, H. S., "An Open Formula for the Numerical Integration of First-Order Differential
Equations," *Math. Tables Aids Comput.*, **11,** pp. 201–203 (1957); **12,** pp. 55–58 (1958).

PROBLEMS

In the following problems compare the Runge-Kutta solution with the closed form solution; or compare the Runge-Kutta solution with the Euler's solution, when the analytic solution is not available. In many of these problems, the choice of increment size and interval length in the Runge-Kutta and Euler procedures has been left to the reader.

1. A hemispherical tank of radius R is initially filled with water. At the bottom of the tank there is a hole of radius r through which the water drains under the influence of gravity. The differential equation expressing the depth of water as function of time has been obtained as

$$\frac{dy}{dt} + \frac{r^2\sqrt{2g}}{2Ry^{1/2} - y^{3/2}} = 0,$$

where $g = 32.2 \text{ ft/sec}^2$, $R = 10 \text{ ft}$, $r = 1/12 \text{ ft}$. The initial condition is that at $t = 0$, $y = 0$.

Find the relation between y and t using Runge-Kutta and Euler procedures.

2. A cylindrical tank with a small hole at its bottom is full of water (Fig. 7.17). Water is flowing out through the hole due to gravity. The differential equation expressing the depth in time is

$$\frac{-dh}{dt} = \frac{d^2}{D^2}\sqrt{2gh}.$$

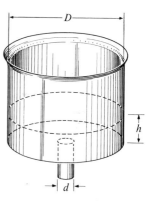

Find the h-t relation by Euler and Runge-Kutta procedures. Given: $D = 5 \text{ ft}$, $d = 2 \text{ in.}$, and $h_0 = 10 \text{ ft}$. Compare your results with the analytical solution

$$t = (2/c_1)(\sqrt{h_0} - \sqrt{h}),$$

where $h_0 = 10 \text{ ft}$, $c_1 = (d^2/D^2)\sqrt{2g}$.

Figure 7.17

3. Under the tank described in Problem 2, a second tank of diameter $D_b(D_b < D)$ is placed. At the bottom of the second tank, there is a hole of diameter d_b. Overflow is possible as the first tank empties the water into the bottom one. Given: $D_b = 4 \text{ ft}$, $d_b = 1.5 \text{ in.}$, $H_b = 10 \text{ ft}$.

Determine the height to which the top tank can be filled without causing the bottom one to overflow.

4. Let x be the temperature at time t of a body immersed in a medium of temperature described by the expression

$$G(t) = -100(t - 4).$$

The temperature satisfies the differential equation

$$dx/dt + kx = kG(t),$$

where k is a proportionality constant equal to 0.005.

and the initial condition is that at

$$t = 0, \quad x = 1000°F$$

Obtain the x-t relation by the Runge-Kutta procedure and compare the result with the analytical solution

$$x = 400 - \left(\frac{100}{k}\right)(kt - 1) + \left(600 - \frac{100}{k}\right)e^{-kt}.$$

5. Find the relation between velocity v and altitude r for a projectile that has been fired with initial velocity v_0 from the surface of the earth. The equation is

PLOT both forms.

$$v\frac{dv}{dr} = -g\frac{R^2}{r^2},$$

where $R = 20{,}908{,}800$ ft, $g = 32.2$ ft/sec^2, and the initial condition is $v_0 = 10{,}000$ ft/sec at $r = R$.

Use the Runge-Kutta procedure and compare your answers with the analytical solution

$$v = \sqrt{(2gR^2/r) + v_0^2 - 2gR}.$$

6. The current i in the driven RL circuit at any time t after a switch is thrown at $t = 0$ can be expressed by the equation

$$di/dt = (E\sin \omega t - Ri)/L,$$

where $E = 100$ volts, $L = 1$ henry, $\omega = 600$, $R = 100$ ohms and the initial condition is that at $t = 0$, $i = 0$.

Solve the differential equation numerically using the Runge-Kutta method and compare your answers with the analytical solution.

$$i = \frac{E}{Z^2}(R\sin \omega t - \omega L\cos \omega t + \omega Le^{-Rt/L}),$$

where

$$Z = \sqrt{R^2 + \omega^2 L^2}.$$

7. A quantity of 20 lb of sugar is dumped into a vessel containing 120 lb of water. The concentration of the solution, c, in percentage at any time t, is expressed as

$$(120 - 1.212c)\,dc/dt = (k/3)(200 - 14c)(100 - 4c),$$

where k, the mass transfer coefficient, is equal to 0.05889. The initial condition is that at $t = 0$, $c = 0$.

Find the c-t relation by the Runge-Kutta and Euler methods.

8. The oxygen sag curve represents the change in the amount of dissolved oxygen in a stream due to the introduction of a pollutional load. This change is brought about by two major effects, oxygen depletion due to the presence of organic wastes and oxygen replenishment by atmospheric reaeration. Therefore

$$\frac{dD}{dt} = K_1 L - K_2 D,$$

where D is the oxygen deficit in mg/liter, L is the amount of organic matter remaining in the stream measured in terms of the biological oxygen demand (BOD), and K_1 and K_2 are the rates of deoxygenation and reaeration, respectively. Furthermore,

$$\frac{-dL}{dt} = K_1 L.$$

The oxygen sag curve is primarily used to determine the maximum oxygen deficit in the stream and the time required to reach this deficit. The maximum deficit allowable is used as the basis for determining maximum pollutional loads which may be introduced into the stream.

Write a program so that the data fed to the computer are as follows:

DZERO = the initial oxygen deficit at time zero = 2.43,

ZK1 = K_1 = 0.2,

ZK2 = K_2 = 0.3,

DM = maximum allowable oxygen deficit in stream = 8.14.

The value of L is to be represented by ZL; ZL is given a very high value initially, say 24, and is gradually decreased by the computer until the maximum deficit corresponds to the value for DM. The values obtained for L and the time T to reach the maximum deficit are then printed.

9. The reaction of NO with H_2 is known as a third-order reaction, and its rate is given by

$$\frac{dx}{dt} = k(P_{NO} - 2x)^2 (P_{H_2} - x),$$

where x is the partial pressure of the product; k is the velocity constant; P_{NO} and P_{H_2} denote the partial pressures of NO and H_2, respectively, in the reaction mixture before the reaction takes place; $P_{NO} - 2x$ is the partial pressure of NO in the reactor; and $P_{H_2} - x$ is the partial pressure of H_2 in the reactor at any time after the reaction has been started. In this problem

$$P_{NO} = 359 \text{ mm Hg},$$
$$P_{H_2} = 400 \text{ mm Hg},$$
$$k = 1.12 \times 10^{-7} \text{ mm}^{-2}\text{sec}^{-1},$$

and the initial condition is that $x_0 = 0, 0 \leq t \leq 3$ min.

Find the x-t relation by the Runge-Kutta procedure and compare the result with the analytical solution.

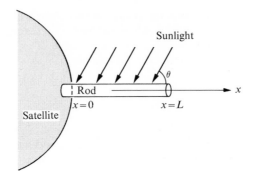

Figure 7.18

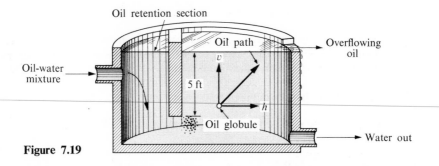

Figure 7.19

10. A rod protrudes from a satellite into a solar radiation field (see Fig. 7.18). The differential equation based on a one-dimensional heat-condition model is

$$\frac{dT}{dx} = \sqrt{\frac{2\sigma\epsilon CT^4}{5kA} - \frac{2S\alpha DT\sin\theta}{kA}} + K,$$

where

$\quad \alpha =$ absorptivity $= 0.4$,

$\quad \epsilon =$ emissivity $= 0.4$,

$\quad \sigma =$ Stefan-Boltzmann constant
$\quad\quad = 0.173 \times 10^{-8}$ Btu/hr $\cdot$ ft^2 °R^4,

$\quad A =$ cross-sectional area of the rod,

$\quad C =$ circumference of the rod,

$\quad D =$ diameter of the rod $= 1$ in.,

$\quad K =$ constant of integration,

$\quad L =$ length of rod $= 3.0$ ft,

$\quad S =$ solar radiation constant $= 425$ Btu/hr $\cdot$ ft^2,

$\quad T =$ temperature of the rod °R,

$\quad k =$ thermal conductivity of rod $= 100$ Btu/hr $\cdot$ ft $\cdot$ °R,

$\quad \theta = 30°$.

The initial condition is that at $x = 3.0$ ft, $T = 637.6285$ °R, and $dT/dx = 0$. Using the Runge-Kutta and Euler procedures, find the T-x relation.

11. A standard oil separator is used to separate an oil-water mixture. The overflow level of oil is 5 ft above the lower end of the retention wall (see Fig. 7.19). Obtain the v-t relation by using the equation

$$\frac{dv}{dt} = \left[\frac{(\rho_w - \rho_o)}{\rho_o}\right] g - \left[\frac{3 f\rho_w}{4\, D\rho_o}\right] v^2,$$

where

D = average diameter of oil globule = $\frac{1}{16}$ in.,

v = vertical velocity of oil globule,

ρ_o = density of oil = $0.6\rho_w$,

ρ_w = density of water,

g = acceleration due to gravity = 32.2 ft/sec^2,

f = coefficient of viscous friction = 0.06.

The initial condition is that at

$$t = 0, \qquad v = 0 \qquad (0 \le t \le 0.03 \text{ sec}).$$

Use Euler and Runge-Kutta procedures to solve numerically the following first order differential equations. Compare the results with the analytical solutions.

12. $dy/dx = x + \sin x + y$. Initial condition: $x = 0$, $y = 0.5$.
Analytical solution: $y = 2e^x - x - 1 - (\cos x + \sin x)/2$.

13. $dy/dx = yx/(y^2 + x^2)$. Initial condition: $x = 0.1223$, $y = 0.05$.
Analytical solution: $y = e^{x^2/2y^2}$.

14. $dy/dx = (x^2 \sin x)/y$. Initial condition: $x = 0$, $y = 1$.
Analytical solution: $y = \sqrt{\frac{2}{3}x^2 - 2\cos x + 3}$.

15. $dv/dx = (3x^2 + 2x)/8v$. Initial condition: $x = 3$, $v = 3$.
Analytical solution: $v = (x/2)\sqrt{x + 1}$.

16. The differential equation that describes a sphere in which heat is generated by a heat source at its center is expressed as

$$d^2T/dr^2 + (2/r)(dT/dr) + w/k = 0,$$

where T indicates the temperature inside the sphere and k is the thermal conductivity of the sphere in Btu/ft $\cdot$ °F $\cdot$ hr. The temperature of the heat source is kept at a constant temperature T_c, while the temperature gradient dT/dr is zero at the center. Let the diameter of the sphere equal 2 ft. Other values are

$$w = 100 \text{ Btu/hr} \cdot \text{ft}^3,$$
$$k = 212 \text{ Btu/ft} \cdot °F \cdot hr,$$
$$T_c = 900° \text{ F.}$$

What is the axial temperature distribution of the sphere? Use the Runge-Kutta procedure and $\Delta r = 0.1$ ft.

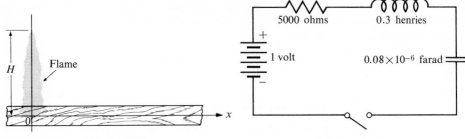

| Figure 7.20 | Figure 7.21 |

17. A long, horizontal strip of wood is burned at one end as shown in Fig. 7.20. The differential equation of temperature profile ahead of the flame front is

$$\frac{d^2T}{dx^2} + \frac{Vs\rho}{k} \cdot \frac{dT}{dx} - \frac{2U}{kL}(T - T_a) - \frac{2\sigma\epsilon}{kL}(T^4 - T_a^4)$$

$$+ \frac{1}{2}\frac{\sigma\epsilon_f}{kL}(T_f^4 - T_a^4)\left(1 - \frac{x}{\sqrt{x^2 + H^2}}\right) = 0,$$

where

V = velocity of the flame propagation along the x-axis = 11.010 ft/hr,

s = specific heat of wood = 0.55 Btu/°R · lb$_m$,

ρ = density of wood = 20.362 lb$_m$/ft^3,

k = thermal conductivity of wood = 0.2 Btu/ft · hr · °R,

U = mean heat transfer coefficient between the wood and air = 2.0 Btu/ft^2 · hr · °R,

L = thickness of the wooden strip = 0.00526 ft,

T_a = temperature of surrounding air = 530 °R,

T_f = temperature of the flame = 2160 °R,

σ = Stefan-Boltzmann constant = 0.173 × 10^{-8} Btu/°R^4 · hr · ft^2,

ϵ = radiant emissivity of wood = 0.9,

ϵ_f = radiant emissivity of flame = 0.85,

H = height of flame = 0.87 in. (0.0725 ft).

The experimental data show that

$$T = 1200 \text{ °R} \quad \text{at} \quad x = 0.5 \text{ in.}$$

and

$$dT/dx = -280761.72 \quad \text{at} \quad x = 0.5 \text{ in.}$$

Integrate the equation from $x = 0.5$ in. into $x = 1.0$ in. by use of the Runge-Kutta procedure.

18. Use the Runge-Kutta procedure to integrate the equation

$$0.3\frac{d^2Q}{dt^2} + 5000\frac{dQ}{dt} + \frac{Q}{0.08 \times 10^{-6}} = 1,$$

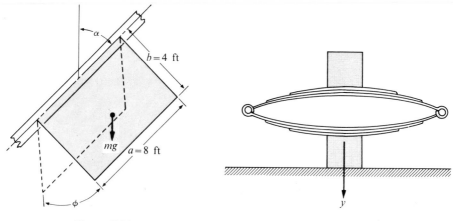

Figure 7.22   **Figure 7.23**

which describes the electric circuit shown in Fig. 7.21. The charge Q is initially zero ($t = 0$); that is, $Q_0 = 0$, $Q'_0 = 0$.

Obtain also the current $i = dQ/dt$ of the circuit at any time t ($0 \le t \le 1.5 \times 10^{-3}$ sec).

19. A gate is hung on a frictionless inclined support as shown in Fig. 7.22. The differential equation expressing the oscillation of the gate is

$$\frac{d^2\phi}{dt^2} + \frac{3g}{2b} \sin \alpha \sin \phi = 0,$$

where $g = 32.2$ ft/sec^2. Let the initial values be $\phi_0 = 90°$, $(d\phi/dt)_{t=0} = 4\pi$ rad/sec. Integrate the equation over the interval $0 \le t \le 3$ sec.

20. The differential equation of a simple pendulum is given by

$$\frac{d^2\theta}{dt^2} + \frac{g}{L} \sin \theta = 0,$$

Let the initial values be

$$L = 3.0 \text{ ft,}$$
$$g = 32.2 \text{ ft/sec}^2,$$
$$\theta_0 = 80°,$$
$$\dot{\theta}_0 = (d\theta/dt)_{t=0} = 2\pi \text{ rad/sec.}$$

Evaluate numerically the quantities θ and $\dot{\theta}$ ($0 \le t \le 3$ min).

21. The motion of a nonlinear spring (Fig. 7.23) is expressed by the equation

$$\frac{d^2y}{dt^2} = -\frac{a}{4k^2}[(1 - k^2)y + 2k^2y^3].$$

Solve the equation by taking $a = 4$, $k = 5$, $y'_0 = 0.04$, and $y_0 = 0$.

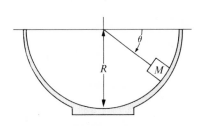

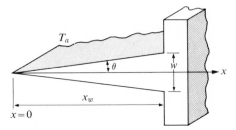

Figure 7.24   Figure 7.25

22. In a hemispherical bowl of radius R, a body with mass M starts from rest on its rim and slides down under the influence of gravity (see Fig. 7.24). The differential equation of the motion of the body is given by

$$\frac{d^2\theta}{dt^2} + \frac{g}{R}(f\sin\theta - \cos\theta) = 0,$$

where f is the coefficient of friction. Let $f = 0.006$, $R = 7$ in.; at $t = 0$, $d\theta/dt = 0$ and $\theta = 0$.

Integrate the equation by the Runge-Kutta procedure ($0 \le t \le 6$ sec).

23. The Bessel equation

$$x\frac{d^2y}{dx^2} + \frac{dy}{dx} - \left(2hx_w\frac{\sec\theta}{kw}\right)y = 0$$

expresses the temperature distribution of a triangular fin of an air heater (Fig. 7.25), where

$y = T - T_a = $ temperature distribution of fin temperature of air,

$h = $ heat transfer coefficient between the fin and air $= 2.5$ Btu/ft$^2 \cdot$ hr $\cdot$ °F,

$k = $ heat conductivity of the fin $= 212$ Btu/ft $\cdot$ hr $\cdot$ °F.

Initial conditions are that at $x = 1$ ft, $T = 170°$ and $dy/dx = 20$. Also, $\theta = 10°$.

Integrate the above equation by letting $x_w = 3$ ft and $T_a = 70$ °F. Use the Runge-Kutta procedure.

24. In the study of bubble motion, the second-order nonlinear differential equation

$$\frac{d^2y}{dt^2} = \frac{c_1y}{(1 + y^2)^3} - c_2\frac{dy}{dt}$$

is used. The initial conditions are that at $t = 0$, $dy/dt = 0$ and $y = 0.00001$.

Find the y-t and $(dy/dt) - t$ relations, using the Runge-Kutta procedure from $t = 0$ to $t = 10$ with $\Delta t = 0.2$. Assume that $c_1 = c_2 = 1$.

25. The following nonlinear differential equation is the well-known van der Pol equation

$$\ddot{x} - (1 - x^2)\dot{x} + x = 0.$$

Initial conditions are as follows: $t = 0$, $x = 0.5$, $t = 0$, $\dot{x} = 0$.

Write a FORTRAN main program to find the x vs. t, $\dot{x}$ vs. t, and $\ddot{x}$ vs. t relations from $t = 0$ to $t = 5$. The increment of t, Δt, equals 0.1. Use the Runge-Kutta method.

note if Runge-Kutta not available for simultaneous equations use Euler and do by hand.

26. Obtain the relation between radial velocity $\overline{V}$ of a particle and radial distance r from the center of a disk used in a spray drier. The differential equation is

$$\overline{V}(d\overline{V}/dr) + A\overline{V}^3 - Br = 0,$$

where $A = 1.66 \times 10^{-4}$, $B = 3.6 \times 10^7$, and $r = 0$ to 4 in.

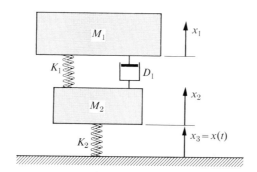

Figure 7.26

27. The differential equations of motion of a single wheel of an automobile suspension system (Fig. 7.26) are

$$\frac{d^2 x_1}{dt^2} = -\frac{D_1}{m_1}\frac{dx_1}{dt} - \frac{dx_2}{dt} - \frac{K_1}{m_1}(x_1 - x_2),$$

$$\frac{d^2 x_2}{dt^2} = -\frac{D_1}{m_2}\frac{dx_2}{dt} - \frac{dx_1}{dt} - \frac{K_1}{m_2}(x_2 - x_1) - \frac{K_2}{m_2}(x_2 - x_3),$$

where

m_1 = one-fourth the mass of the automobile = 25 slugs,
m_2 = mass of the wheel and axle = 2 slugs,
K_1 = spring constant of the main auto spring = 1000 lb/ft,
K_2 = spring constant of the tire (assumed linear) = 4500 lb/ft
D_1 = shock-absorber damping constant = 20 lb · sec/ft,
x_1 = displacement of the auto body,
x_2 = displacement of the wheel,
x_3 = roadway profile displacement.

The initial conditions and forcing functions are as follows:

$$x_1 = x_2 = \frac{dx_1}{dt} = \frac{dx_2}{dt} = 0 \quad \text{at} \quad t = 0;$$

$$x_3 = 1, \quad 0 \le t \le 35 \text{ msec};$$

$$= 0, \quad t > 35 \text{ msec}.$$

Obtain the x_1-t and x_2-t relations by the Runge-Kutta method. Use $\Delta t = 0.1$ sec and $0 \le t \le 4$ sec.

28. In the three-body system consisting of a projectile, the earth, and the moon, we can calculate the path of the projectile by using the following position, velocity, and acceleration relationships:

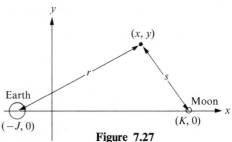

$$\frac{dx}{dt} = u + \omega y, \qquad \frac{dy}{dt} = v - \omega x,$$

$$\frac{du}{dt} = \omega v - \frac{m_1 G(x + J)}{r^3}$$

$$\qquad - \frac{m_2 G(x - K)}{s^3},$$

$$\frac{dv}{dt} = \omega u - \frac{m_1 Gy}{r^3} - \frac{m_2 Gy}{s^3}.$$

Figure 7.27

The coordinate system which defines the values of x and y has as its origin the centers of mass of the earth and moon, with the earth and moon along the x-axis at $-J$ and K, respectively (see Fig. 7.27). The constants ω, m_1, m_2, G, K, and J are defined as

$$m_1 = \text{mass of the earth} = 5.975 \times 10^{27} \text{ gm,}$$
$$m_2 = \text{mass of the moon} = 7.343 \times 10^{25} \text{ gm,}$$
$$G = \text{gravitational constant} = 6.67 \times 10^{-8} \text{ dyne-cm}^2/\text{gm}^2,$$
$$\omega = \text{angular velocity of rotation of the moon and earth}$$
$$\qquad \text{about each other} = 2.662 \times 10^{-6} \text{ rad/sec,}$$
$$K = 3.797 \times 10^{10} \text{ cm,}$$
$$J = 4.667 \times 10^{8} \text{ cm.}$$

The quantities r and s are determined by the formulas

$$r = \sqrt{(x + J)^2 + y^2}, \qquad s = \sqrt{(x - K)^2 + y^2}.$$

Indicate the projectile's distance from the earth and moon, respectively. Given that at $t = 0$, $x = -J$, $y = 0$, $u = 2.3 \times 10^5$ cm/sec and $v = 2.0 \times 10^5$ cm/sec, find the position and velocity of the projectile after 20 sec.

CHAPTER 8

MATRIX ALGEBRA AND
SIMULTANEOUS EQUATIONS

8.1 INTRODUCTION

In this chapter we discuss the solution of simultaneous linear equations and the related topics of matrices and determinants. Many physical problems are expressed in terms of simultaneous linear equations. Many other problems are expressed in the form of simultaneous linear differential equations which may be readily transformed into simultaneous algebraic equations. We shall limit our discussion to two widely used procedures, the Gauss-Jordan method and the Gauss-Seidel method. The elements of matrix algebra will also be introduced.

8.2 ELEMENTARY OPERATIONS OF MATRICES

As mentioned in Section 3.4 and illustrated in Fig. 3.8(b), a matrix is an array of numbers which may be either rectangular or square. A matrix is indicated by brackets and written in the following form:

$$[A] = \begin{bmatrix} a_{11} & a_{12} & a_{13} \\ a_{21} & a_{22} & a_{23} \\ a_{31} & a_{32} & a_{33} \end{bmatrix}. \tag{8.1}$$

The first subscript of the elements of the matrix corresponds to the row containing the element and the second subscript corresponds to the column. The rules for addition, subtraction, and multiplication of two matrices are stated below.

Consider matrix $[A]$ in Eq. (8.1) and matrix $[B]$,

$$[B] = \begin{bmatrix} b_{11} & b_{12} & b_{13} \\ b_{21} & b_{22} & b_{23} \\ b_{31} & b_{32} & b_{33} \end{bmatrix}. \tag{8.2}$$

If matrices $[A]$ and $[B]$ are added, a matrix $[C]$ is obtained in a 3×3 array of numbers:

$$[C] = \begin{bmatrix} c_{11} & c_{12} & c_{13} \\ c_{21} & c_{22} & c_{23} \\ c_{31} & c_{32} & c_{33} \end{bmatrix}. \tag{8.3}$$

Each element of $[C]$ is obtained by adding the corresponding elements of $[A]$ and $[B]$. Thus, the elements of $[C]$ are computed as follows:

$$
\begin{aligned}
c_{11} &= a_{11} + b_{11}, \\
c_{12} &= a_{12} + b_{12}, \\
&\;\;\vdots \\
c_{21} &= a_{21} + b_{21}, \\
&\;\;\vdots \\
c_{32} &= a_{32} + b_{32}, \\
c_{33} &= a_{33} + b_{33}.
\end{aligned}
\tag{8.4}
$$

Subtraction of matrices is done in the same manner.

The following numerical examples illustrate the processes of addition and subtraction. Given

$$[E] = \begin{bmatrix} 1 & 4 \\ 3 & 2 \end{bmatrix} \quad \text{and} \quad [F] = \begin{bmatrix} 2 & 1 \\ 3 & 6 \end{bmatrix},$$

then

$$[G] = [E] + [F] = \begin{bmatrix} 3 & 5 \\ 6 & 8 \end{bmatrix}, \quad = \begin{bmatrix} 1+2 & 4+1 \\ 3+3 & 2+6 \end{bmatrix}$$

and

$$[H] = [F] - [E] = \begin{bmatrix} 1 & -3 \\ 0 & 4 \end{bmatrix}. \quad = \begin{bmatrix} 2-1 & 1-4 \\ 3-3 & 6-2 \end{bmatrix}$$

If matrices $[A]$ and $[B]$ are multiplied, a matrix $[P]$ is obtained in a 3×3 array of numbers:

$$[A][B] = [P],$$

in which

$$[P] = \begin{bmatrix} p_{11} & p_{12} & p_{13} \\ p_{21} & p_{22} & p_{23} \\ p_{31} & p_{32} & p_{33} \end{bmatrix}. \tag{8.5}$$

The elements of $[P]$ are computed from the elements of $[A]$ and $[B]$ by the following definition:

$$
\begin{aligned}
p_{11} &= a_{11}b_{11} + a_{12}b_{21} + a_{13}b_{31}, \quad \text{Row x Column} \\
p_{12} &= a_{11}b_{12} + a_{12}b_{22} + a_{13}b_{32}, \\
p_{13} &= a_{11}b_{13} + a_{12}b_{23} + a_{13}b_{33}, \\
p_{21} &= a_{21}b_{11} + a_{22}b_{21} + a_{23}b_{31},
\end{aligned}
\tag{8.6}
$$

B is row

and in general,

$$p_{ij} = a_{i1}b_{1j} + a_{i2}b_{2j} + a_{i3}b_{3j}.$$

Each column of A to first row of B multiplied by first row of P

The following numerical examples illustrate the process of multiplication, where
[E] and [F] are as given above:

$$[E][F] = \begin{bmatrix} 1 & 4 \\ 3 & 2 \end{bmatrix}\begin{bmatrix} 2 & 1 \\ 3 & 6 \end{bmatrix} = \begin{bmatrix} 14 & 25 \\ 12 & 15 \end{bmatrix},$$

$$[F][E] = \begin{bmatrix} 2 & 1 \\ 3 & 6 \end{bmatrix}\begin{bmatrix} 1 & 4 \\ 3 & 2 \end{bmatrix} = \begin{bmatrix} 5 & 10 \\ 21 & 24 \end{bmatrix}.$$

These examples show the importance of the order of multiplication. The two examples below illustrate the process of multiplying rectangular matrices:

$$\begin{bmatrix} 1 & 4 & -1 \\ 3 & 2 & 2 \end{bmatrix}\begin{bmatrix} 2 & 1 \\ 3 & 6 \\ 4 & 5 \end{bmatrix} = \begin{bmatrix} 10 & 20 \\ 20 & 25 \end{bmatrix}$$

(handwritten notes in right margin):
$P_{11} = 1\times2 + 4\times3 + (-1)(+4) = 10$
$P_{12} = 3\times2 + 2\times3 + 2\times4 = 20$
$P_{21} = 1\times1 + 2\times4 + (-1)\times5 = 20$
$P_{22} = 1\times3 + 2\times6 + 2\times5 = 25$

$$\begin{bmatrix} 1 & 4 & -1 \\ 3 & 2 & 2 \end{bmatrix}\begin{bmatrix} 2 \\ 3 \\ 4 \end{bmatrix} = \begin{bmatrix} 10 \\ 20 \end{bmatrix}.$$

(handwritten notes in left margin): does not agree with statement — what is the significance of this?

It is important that the first matrix in a multiplication have the same number of
columns as there are rows in the second matrix. If this number is designated as m,
the multiplication of matrices can be defined as

$$[P] = [A][B], \tag{8.7}$$

where

$$p_{ij} = \sum_{k=1}^{k=m} a_{ik}b_{kj},$$

and the orders of the matrices [A], [B], and [P] are (n, m), (m, l), and (n, l), respectively.
The multiplication of two matrices may readily be carried out by the following
FORTRAN subprogram MATMPY:

```
SUBROUTINE MATMPY(A,N,M,B,L,C)
DIMENSION A(12,12),B(12,12),C(12,12)
  DO 5 I=1,N
  DO 5 J=1,L
  C(I,J)=0.
  DO 5 K=1,M
5 C(I,J)=C(I,J)+A(I,K)*B(K,J)
  RETURN
  END
```

In this subroutine, the three matrices are dimensioned as 12 × 12. These dimensions
may be changed but they must agree with the dimensions used in the main program.
If a matrix is to be multiplied by a constant (*scalar* multiplication), then each
element of the matrix must be multiplied by that constant. Thus

$$3\begin{bmatrix} 1 & 4 \\ 3 & 2 \end{bmatrix} = \begin{bmatrix} 3 & 12 \\ 9 & 6 \end{bmatrix}.$$

In the remainder of this section we shall introduce several definitions which are related to a square matrix.

(a) The *principal diagonal* of a square matrix $[A]$ of order n consists of the n elements $a_{11}, a_{22}, \ldots, a_{nn}$.

(b) The *transpose* of $[A]$ is obtained by interchanging the rows and columns of $[A]$ A transpose is indicated by a prime or a T. Thus,

$$[A] = \begin{bmatrix} 1 & 2 & 5 \\ 3 & 4 & 6 \\ 7 & 8 & 9 \end{bmatrix} \quad \text{and} \quad [A]^T = \begin{bmatrix} 1 & 3 & 7 \\ 2 & 4 & 8 \\ 5 & 6 & 9 \end{bmatrix}.$$

If $[B] = [A]^T$, then $b_{ij} = a_{ji}$. Note that the principal diagonal is not altered in the above example.

(c) A *symmetric matrix* is one in which the elements $a_{ij} = a_{ji}$, or $[A] = [A]^T$.

(d) A *diagonal matrix* is one in which all the elements other than those in the principal diagonal are zero; thus

$$[D] = \begin{bmatrix} 1 & 0 & 0 \\ 0 & 4 & 0 \\ 0 & 0 & 2 \end{bmatrix}.$$

(e) The *unit matrix*, or identity matrix $[I]$, is a matrix in which the elements of the principal diagonal are ones and the remaining elements are zeros; thus

$$[I] = \begin{bmatrix} 1 & 0 & 0 \\ 0 & 1 & 0 \\ 0 & 0 & 1 \end{bmatrix}.$$

8.3 GAUSS-JORDAN ELIMINATION METHOD—DIRECT METHOD

The usefulness of matrix algebra will be explained in the remainder of this chapter.† Consider the following system of three equations in three unknowns:

$$\begin{aligned} 3x_1 - 6x_2 + 7x_3 &= 3, \\ 9x_1 \qquad\quad - 5x_3 &= 3, \\ 5x_1 - 8x_2 + 6x_3 &= -4. \end{aligned} \tag{8.8}$$

The above equation can be expressed by using matrices in the following manner:

$$\begin{bmatrix} 3 & -6 & 7 \\ 9 & 0 & -5 \\ 5 & -8 & 6 \end{bmatrix} \begin{bmatrix} x_1 \\ x_2 \\ x_3 \end{bmatrix} = \begin{bmatrix} 3 \\ 3 \\ -4 \end{bmatrix}, \tag{8.9}$$

where the leftmost square matrix is commonly known as the *coefficient matrix*.

---

† Matrix algebra also plays an important part in eigenvalue problems (Chapter 9) and in linear programming (Chapter 15).

If the column matrix, representing the constant terms on the right-hand side, is combined with the coefficient matrix, then the resulting matrix is called the *augmented matrix*. Thus the augmented matrix in our example is

$$\begin{bmatrix} 3 & -6 & 7 & 3 \\ 9 & 0 & -5 & 3 \\ 5 & -8 & 6 & -4 \end{bmatrix}. \tag{8.10}$$

The Gauss-Jordan elimination method is used to reduce the augmented matrix to the form

$$\begin{bmatrix} a_{11} & 0 & 0 & c_1 \\ 0 & a_{22} & 0 & c_2 \\ 0 & 0 & a_{33} & c_3 \end{bmatrix}. \tag{8.11}$$

The solution is

$$x_1 = c_1/a_{11}, \qquad x_2 = c_2/a_{22}, \qquad x_3 = c_3/a_{33}.$$

The procedure involved is essentially a simple, direct process, one which is easily learned by a beginner and readily adapted to digital computers.

The reduction from Eq. (8.10) to Eq. (8.11) is based on three elementary operations which are well known for any system of linear equations:

(a) interchange any two equations;
(b) multiply any equation by a nonzero number;
(c) add to one equation *d* times a second equation, where *d* is any real number.

The new system of linear equations, resulting from any of these three operations, has exactly the same solution as the original system of linear equations. These two systems are known as *equivalent*.

We will now demonstrate the step-by-step operations as they are used to reduce Eq. (8.10) to Eq. (8.11). In this procedure, the given augmented matrix is first written

$$\begin{bmatrix} 3 & -6 & 7 & 3 \\ 9 & 0 & -5 & 3 \\ 5 & -8 & 6 & -4 \end{bmatrix}.$$

Next, we eliminate the *first* element in each row, except the *first* row. In other words, we wish to eliminate a_{21} and a_{31}. To reduce a_{21} from 9 to zero, we obtain a new second row by using the following expression:

The new second row = $a_{11} \cdot$ (the present second row) $- a_{21} \cdot$ (the first row).

Our matrix, after this first step, looks like this:

$$\begin{bmatrix} 3 & -6 & 7 & 3 \\ 0 & 54 & -78 & -18 \\ 5 & -8 & 6 & -4 \end{bmatrix}.$$

To reduce a_{31} to zero, a new third row is obtained by the following expression:

The new third row = $a_{11} \cdot$ (the present third row) $- a_{31} \cdot$ (the first row).

TABLE 8.1.   Gauss-Jordan Elimination Method

Given Matrix	$\begin{matrix} a_{11} & a_{12} & a_{13} & a_{14} \\ a_{21} & a_{22} & a_{23} & a_{24} \\ a_{31} & a_{32} & a_{33} & a_{34} \end{matrix}$	$\begin{matrix} 3 & -6 & 7 & 3 \\ 9 & 0 & -5 & 3 \\ 5 & -8 & 6 & -4 \end{matrix}$	

	PASS 1		
	$k = 1$, i.e., pivot row = row 1; pivot element = a_{11}		

	New row 2 = $a_{11} \times$ row 2 − $a_{21} \times$ row 1		
$i = 2$ $j = 1, 2, 3, 4$	$\begin{matrix} ⓐ_{11} & a_{12} & a_{13} & a_{14} \\ 0 & a'_{22} & a'_{23} & a'_{24} \\ a_{31} & a_{32} & a_{33} & a_{34} \end{matrix}$	$\begin{matrix} 3 & -6 & 7 & 3 \\ 0 & 54 & -78 & -18 \\ 5 & -8 & 6 & -4 \end{matrix}$	

	New row 3 = $a_{11} \times$ row 3 − $a_{31} \times$ row 1		
$i = 3$ $j = 1, 2, 3, 4$	$\begin{matrix} ⓐ_{11} & a_{12} & a_{13} & a_{14} \\ 0 & a'_{22} & a'_{23} & a'_{24} \\ 0 & a'_{32} & a'_{33} & a'_{34} \end{matrix}$	$\begin{matrix} 3 & -6 & 7 & 3 \\ 0 & 54 & -78 & -18 \\ 0 & 6 & -17 & -27 \end{matrix}$	

	PASS 2		
	$k = 2$, i.e., pivot row = row 2; pivot element = a'_{22}		

	New row 1 = $a'_{22} \times$ row 1 − $a_{12} \times$ row 2		
$i = 1$ $j = 1, 2, 3, 4$	$\begin{matrix} a'_{11} & 0 & a'_{13} & a'_{14} \\ 0 & ⓐ'_{22} & a'_{23} & a'_{24} \\ 0 & a'_{32} & a'_{33} & a'_{34} \end{matrix}$	$\begin{matrix} 162 & 0 & -90 & 54 \\ 0 & 54 & -78 & -18 \\ 0 & 6 & -17 & -27 \end{matrix}$	

	New row 3 = $a'_{22} \times$ row 3 − $a'_{32} \times$ row 2		
$i = 3$ $j = 1, 2, 3, 4$	$\begin{matrix} a'_{11} & 0 & a'_{13} & a'_{14} \\ 0 & ⓐ'_{22} & a'_{23} & a'_{24} \\ 0 & 0 & a''_{33} & a''_{34} \end{matrix}$	$\begin{matrix} 162 & 0 & -90 & 54 \\ 0 & 54 & -78 & -18 \\ 0 & 0 & -450 & -1350 \end{matrix}$	

	PASS 3		
	$k = 3$, i.e., pivot row = row 3; pivot element = a''_{33}		

	New row 1 = $a''_{33} \times$ row 1 − $a'_{13} \times$ row 3		
$i = 1$ $j = 1, 2, 3, 4$	$\begin{matrix} a''_{11} & 0 & 0 & a''_{14} \\ 0 & a'_{22} & a'_{23} & a'_{24} \\ 0 & 0 & ⓐ''_{33} & a''_{34} \end{matrix}$	$\begin{matrix} 72{,}900 & 0 & 0 & -1{,}458{,}000 \\ 0 & 54 & -78 & -18 \\ 0 & 0 & -450 & -1350 \end{matrix}$	

	New row 2 = $a''_{33} \times$ row 2 − $a'_{23} \times$ row 3		
$i = 2$ $j = 1, 2, 3, 4$	$\begin{matrix} a''_{11} & 0 & 0 & a''_{14} \\ 0 & a''_{22} & 0 & a''_{24} \\ 0 & 0 & ⓐ''_{33} & a''_{34} \end{matrix}$	$\begin{matrix} -72{,}900 & 0 & 0 & -1{,}458{,}000 \\ 0 & -24{,}300 & 0 & -97{,}200 \\ 0 & 0 & -450 & -1350 \end{matrix}$	

Solutions	$\begin{matrix} a''_{11}x_1 = a''_{14} \\ a''_{22}x_2 = a''_{24} \\ a''_{33}x_3 = a''_{34} \end{matrix}$	$\begin{matrix} x_1 = 2 \\ x_2 = 4 \\ x_3 = 3 \end{matrix}$	

This completes the second step and yields the matrix

$$\begin{bmatrix} 3 & -6 & 7 & 3 \\ 0 & 54 & -78 & -18 \\ 0 & 6 & -17 & -27 \end{bmatrix}.$$

For the sake of discussion, the above two steps of eliminating a_{21} and a_{31}, but not a_{11}, are referred to as the first pass. In this pass, the element a_{11} plays such a prominent role that we shall call it the pivot element for this pass. The first row is called the pivot row. It should be noted that the above matrix, representing a system of simultaneous linear equations, is completely equivalent to the given augmented matrix, as shown in Eq. (8.10).

Let us now return to our problem and initiate the second pass, consisting of two steps, whose purpose is to eliminate the *second* element in each row except the *second* row. This pass is shown in Table 8.1, where the pivot element is circled, and the row involved in the elimination is shaded. A third and final pass eliminates the *third* element in each row except the *third* row. This pass is also shown in Table 8.1. Our original system of equations, (8.8), is now seen to be equivalent to the following new set of equations:

$$-72{,}900x_1 = -1{,}458{,}000,$$
$$-24{,}300x_2 = -97{,}200,$$
$$-450x_3 = -1350.$$

The values of x_1, x_2, and x_3 can readily be obtained.

In recapitulation, the Gauss-Jordan elimination method as illustrated in this example has three passes. In each of the three passes, two elements are reduced to zero. Thus in pass one ($k = 1$), a_{21} and a_{31} are reduced to zero. In pass two ($k = 2$), the elements eliminated are a_{12} and a'_{32}, and in the final pass ($k = 3$), a'_{13} and a'_{23} are eliminated.

We note that in each pass ($k = 1, 2$, or 3) a pivot element a_{kk} is first selected. The kth row, or the pivot row, is then used to eliminate the coefficients in the kth column except the pivot element itself. In general, if we take a_{kk} as the pivot element, then the kth row, or the pivot row, is used to eliminate the elements a_{ij} where $i = 1, 2, 3, \ldots, n$ but $i \neq k$ ($j = 1, 2, 3, \ldots, n$). When the last pass has been completed, the values of the x's in the system of linear equations can be easily determined, as shown in the last step of Table 8.1.

8.4 NECESSITY OF NORMALIZATION

In the numerical example shown in the previous section (Table 8.1), the numbers increased greatly as we proceeded through each step. If the given system of simultaneous equations begins with large coefficients, overflow may occur. This difficulty can be solved if a slight modification is made on the Gauss-Jordan method by simply dividing the pivot row by the value of the pivot element prior to the elimination in each pass. Each pivot element is then equal to one. This process is commonly known as *normalization*. It should be noted that normalization does not alter the equivalence of the system, since an elementary operation, division, is used.

TABLE 8.2.   Elimination Method With Normalization

Given augmented matrix	a_{11} a_{12} a_{13} a_{14} a_{21} a_{22} a_{23} a_{24} a_{31} a_{32} a_{33} a_{34}	3 -6 7 3 9 0 -5 3 5 -8 6 -4

	PASS 1 $k = 1$, i.e., pivot row = row 1; pivot element $= a'_{11} = 1$	

$i = 1$
$j = 1, 2, 3, 4$
	New row 1 = row 1/a_{11}
	   1 a'_{12} a'_{13} a'_{14}
	   a_{21} a_{22} a_{23} a_{24}
	   a_{31} a_{32} a_{33} a_{34}
		1 -2 2.33 1
		9 0 -5 3
		5 -8 6 -4

$i = 2$
$j = 2, 3, 4$
	New row 2 = 1 $\times$ row 2 $- a_{21} \times$ row 1
	  ① a'_{12} a'_{13} a'_{14}
	  0 a'_{22} a'_{23} a'_{24}
	  a_{31} a_{32} a_{33} a_{34}
		1 -2 2.33 1
		0 18 -26 -6
		5 -8 6 -4

$i = 3$
$j = 2, 3, 4$
	New row 3 = 1 $\times$ row 3 $- a_{31} \times$ row 1
	  ① a'_{12} a'_{13} a'_{14}
	  0 a'_{22} a'_{23} a'_{24}
	  0 a'_{32} a'_{33} a'_{34}
		1 -2 2.33 1
		0 18 -26 -6
		0 2 -5.65 -9

	PASS 2 $k = 2$, i.e., pivot row = row 2; pivot element $= a''_{22} = 1$	

$i = 2$
$j = 2, 3, 4$
	New row 2 = row 2/a'_{22}
	  1 a'_{12} a'_{13} a'_{14}
	  0 1 a''_{23} a''_{24}
	  0 a'_{32} a'_{33} a'_{34}
		1 -2 2.33 1
		0 1 -1.44 -0.33
		0 2 -5.65 -9

$i = 1$
$j = 3, 4$
	New row 1 = 1 $\times$ row 1 $- a'_{12} \times$ row 2
	  1 0 a''_{13} a''_{14}
	  0 ① a''_{23} a''_{24}
	  0 a'_{32} a'_{33} a'_{34}
		1 0 -0.55 0.33
		0 1 -1.44 -0.33
		0 2 -5.65 -9

$i = 3$
$j = 3, 4$
	New row 3 = 1 $\times$ row 3 $- a'_{32} \times$ row 2
	  1 0 a''_{13} a''_{14}
	  0 ① a''_{23} a''_{24}
	  0 0 a''_{33} a''_{34}
		1 0 -0.55 0.33
		0 1 -1.44 -0.33
		0 0 -2.77 -8.33

TABLE 8.2. (*Cont.*)

	Pass 3 $k = 3$, i.e., pivot row = row 3; pivot element = $a_{33}''' = 1$		
$i = 3$ $j = 3, 4$	New row 3 = row 3/a_{33}'' $\begin{array}{cccc} 1 & 0 & a_{13}'' & a_{14}'' \\ 0 & 1 & a_{23}'' & a_{24}'' \\ 0 & 0 & 1 & a_{34}''' \end{array}$		$\begin{array}{cccc} 1 & 0 & -0.55 & 0.33 \\ 0 & 1 & -1.44 & -0.33 \\ 0 & 0 & 1 & 3.01 \end{array}$
$i = 1$ $j = 4$	New row 1 = 1 × row 1 − a_{13}'' × row 3 $\begin{array}{cccc} 1 & 0 & 0 & a_{14}''' \\ 0 & 1 & a_{23}'' & a_{24}'' \\ 0 & 0 & 1 & a_{34}''' \end{array}$		$\begin{array}{cccc} 1 & 0 & 0 & 1.99 \\ 0 & 1 & -1.44 & -0.33 \\ 0 & 0 & 1 & 3.01 \end{array}$
$i = 1$ $j = 4$	New row 2 = 1 × row 2 − a_{23}'' × row 3 $\begin{array}{cccc} 1 & 0 & 0 & a_{14}''' \\ 0 & 1 & 0 & a_{24}''' \\ 0 & 0 & 1 & a_{34}''' \end{array}$		$\begin{array}{cccc} 1 & 0 & 0 & 1.99 \\ 0 & 1 & 0 & 4.00 \\ 0 & 0 & 1 & 3.01 \end{array}$
Solutions	$\begin{array}{l} 1(x_1) = a_{14}''' \\ 1(x_2) = a_{24}''' \\ 1(x_3) = a_{34}''' \end{array}$		$\begin{array}{l} 1(x_1) = 1.99 \\ 1(x_2) = 4.00 \\ 1(x_3) = 3.01 \end{array}$

Table 8.2 shows a new tabulation for the Gauss-Jordan method with normalization. In each of the three passes ($k = 1, 2, 3$), there are now three operations. The first is a normalization step and the second and third operations are elimination steps.

When a pivot element is equal to zero, difficulty arises from normalization. This will be discussed in the next section.

8.5 ZERO DIAGONAL ELEMENT

Consider the following system of simultaneous equations:

$$- 6y + 9z = -3, \tag{8.12a}$$

$$7x \qquad\qquad - 5z = \quad 3, \tag{8.12b}$$

$$5x \quad - 8y + 6z = -4. \tag{8.12c}$$

If the Gauss-Jordan elimination method with normalization is to be used for Eqs. (8.12), the augmented matrix appears as

$$[A] = \begin{bmatrix} 0 & -6 & 9 & -3 \\ 7 & 0 & -5 & 3 \\ 5 & -8 & 6 & -4 \end{bmatrix}, \tag{8.13}$$

and we proceed to operate on it as discussed in Section 8.3. However, with zero as the first diagonal element, we would run into difficulty with the normalization process.

TABLE 8.3. Elimination Method With Interchange of Rows

Given augmented matrix	a_{11} a_{12} a_{13} a_{14} a_{21} a_{22} a_{23} a_{24} a_{31} a_{32} a_{33} a_{34}	0 -6 9 -3 7 0 -5 3 5 -8 6 -4
	PASS 1 Pivot row = row 3	
Interchange of rows	Find the element a_{ij} which has the largest absolute value $(i = 1, 2, 3; j = 1, 2, 3)$. Interchange rows i and j.	$i = 1,$ $j = 3$ Interchange rows 1 and 3
	a'_{11} a'_{12} a'_{13} a'_{14} a_{21} a_{22} a_{23} a_{24} a'_{31} a'_{32} a'_{33} a'_{34}	5 -8 6 -4 7 0 -5 3 0 -6 9 -3
$i = 3$ $j = 1, 2, 3, 4$	New row 3 = row $3/a'_{33}$ a'_{11} a'_{12} a'_{13} a'_{14} a_{21} a_{22} a_{23} a_{24} a''_{31} a''_{32} 1 a''_{34}	Normalize row j = row 3 5 -8 6 -4 7 0 -5 3 0 -0.66 1 -0.33
$i = 1$ $j = 1, 2, 4$	New row 1 = row 1 $- a'_{13}$ row 3 a''_{11} a''_{12} 0 a''_{14} a_{21} a_{22} a_{23} a_{24} a''_{31} a''_{32} 1 a''_{34}	Elimination 5 -4.04 0 -2.02 7 0 -5 3 0 -0.66 1 -0.33
$i = 2$ $j = 1, 2, 4$	New row 2 = row 2 $- a_{23}$ row 3 a''_{11} a''_{12} 0 a''_{14} a'_{21} a'_{22} 0 a'_{24} a''_{31} a''_{32} 1 a''_{34}	Elimination 5 -4.04 0 -2.02 7 -3.30 0 1.35 0 -0.66 1 -0.33
	PASS 2 Pivot row = row 1	
Interchange of rows	Find max $\|a_{ij}\|$ $i = 1, 2$ $j = 1, 2$ Interchange rows i and j a'''_{11} a'''_{12} 0 a'''_{14} a''_{21} a''_{22} 0 a''_{24} a''_{31} a''_{32} 1 a''_{34}	$i = 2$ $j = 1$ Interchange rows 1 and 2 7 -3.30 0 1.35 5 -4.04 0 -2.02 0 -0.66 1 -0.33
$i = 1$ $j = 1, 2, 4$	New row 1 = row $1/a'''_{11}$ 1 a^{iv}_{12} 0 a^{iv}_{14} a''_{21} a''_{22} 0 a''_{24} a''_{31} a''_{32} 1 a''_{34}	Normalize row j = row 1 1 -0.47 0 0.19 5 -4.04 0 -2.02 0 -0.66 1 -0.33

TABLE 8.3. (*Cont.*)

$i=2$ $j=2,4$	New row 2 = row 2 $-\ a''_{21}$ Row 1				Elimination			
	1	a^{iv}_{12}	0	a^{iv}_{14}	1	-0.47	0	0.19
	0	a'''_{22}	0	a'''_{24}	0	-1.69	0	-2.97
	a''_{31}	a''_{32}	1	a''_{34}	0	-0.66	1	-0.33
$i=3$ $j=2,4$	New row 3 = row 3 $-\ a''_{31}$ row 1				Elimination			
	1	a^{iv}_{12}	0	a^{iv}_{14}	1	-0.47	0	0.19
	0	a'''_{22}	0	a'''_{24}	0	-1.69	0	-2.97
	0	a''_{32}	1	a''_{34}	0	-0.66	1	-0.33

PASS 3
Pivot row = row 2

	Find max $\lvert a_{ij}\rvert$ $i=2,\ j=2$				No interchange needed			
$i=2$ $j=2,4$	New row 2 = row 2$/a''_{22}$				Normalization			
	1	a^{iv}_{12}	0	a^{iv}_{14}	1	-0.47	0	0.19
	0	1	0	a'''_{24}	0	1	0	1.76
	0	a''_{32}	1	a''_{34}	0	-0.66	1	-0.33
$i=1$ $j=4$	New row 1 = row 1 $-\ a'_{12}$ row 2				Elimination			
	1	0	0	a^{v}_{14}	1	0	0	1.03
	0	1	0	a^{iv}_{24}	0	1	0	1.76
	0	a''_{32}	1	a''_{34}	0	-0.66	1	-0.33
$i=3$ $j=4$	New row 3 = row 3 $-\ a''_{32}$ row 2				Elimination			
	1	0	0	a^{v}_{14}	1	0	0	1.03
	0	1	0	a^{iv}_{24}	0	1	0	1.76
	0	0	1	a'''_{34}	0	0	1	0.83
Solutions	$x_1 = a^{v}_{14}$ $x_2 = a^{iv}_{24}$ $x_3 = a'''_{34}$				$x_1 = 1.03$ $x_2 = 1.76$ $x_3 = 0.83$			

This situation can be remedied by the elementary operation of interchanging two equations, for example, Eq. (8.12a) with Eqs. (8.12b) or (8.12c).

A practical way to alleviate the difficulty arising from the presence of zero diagonal elements is to find the largest absolute number $\lvert a_{ij}\rvert$ in the given coefficient matrix. Since this is found to be the element a_{13}, or 9, row 3 and row 1 are interchanged. In general, we interchange rows i and j if the element a_{ij} has the largest absolute value. After the interchange of two rows, we normalize the original row i (or the new row j). When the two elements a_{ij} and a_{kl} are equal to each other and have the largest absolute value, we use a_{ij}, where $j \leq l$.

Table 8.3 shows in detail the interchange of rows before each of three regular passes. As mentioned in Table 8.2, each regular pass consists of one normalization and two elimination steps.

8.6 DETERMINANTS

We shall now discuss the evaluation of the value of a given determinant. It is known* that the value of a determinant is unchanged if each element of any row is added c times to the corresponding element of some other row, where c is a known constant. In other words, the following relation is valid:

$$\begin{vmatrix} a_1 & b_1 \\ a_2 & b_2 \end{vmatrix} = \begin{vmatrix} a_1 & b_1 \\ (a_2 + ca_1) & (b_2 + cb_1) \end{vmatrix}. \tag{8.14}$$

Using this relation, we will show that the value of the determinant of the coefficient matrix

$$\begin{bmatrix} 3 & -6 & 7 \\ 9 & 0 & -5 \\ 5 & -8 & 6 \end{bmatrix},$$

which has the same elements as those in the coefficient matrix (not the augmented matrix) in Table 8.2 or in Eq. (8.9), is simply equal to $(3)(18)(-2.77) = -149.58\dagger$.

In Table 8.2 each pass consists of two different operations, normalization and elimination. The combined effect of these is to reduce the coefficient matrix to a unit matrix.

We now wish to examine what effect each of the two operations has on the value of the determinant of the coefficient matrix. The elimination process does not alter the value of the determinant, as can be seen from Eq. (8.14). However, with each normalization process, the value of the given determinant is reduced by its normalization factor, for example, a_{11}, a'_{22}, or a''_{33} in Table 8.2. Hence the true value of the determinant is the product of the normalizing factors a_{11}, a'_{22}, and a''_{33}.

Before we begin the next section, it is important to note that the zero determinant, or a determinant having zero value, plays an important role in matrix inversion (see Section 8.7). For example, it is known that the following determinant‡ has zero value:

$$\begin{vmatrix} 1 & 4 & 13 & 16 \\ 15 & 14 & 3 & 2 \\ 12 & 9 & 8 & 5 \\ 6 & 7 & 10 & 11 \end{vmatrix}.$$

A square matrix $[A]$ having a zero determinant is called *singular*. If $|A| \neq 0$, then $[A]$ is called *nonsingular*.

When a determinant of order two is zero, we have one of the following two cases:

Case 1: There is no solution of the associated simultaneous equations if the equations are *incompatible* or *inconsistent*. For example, the following given linear

---

* For example, see Thomas, G. B., *Calculus and Analytic Geometry*, 3rd ed. Addison-Wesley, Reading, Mass., 1960, p. 422.
† The calculation of this determinant which would, in the usual way, yield -150.0 involves round-off errors. They will be discussed in Chapter 13.
‡ This is a 4×4 magic square.

equations are incompatible:

$$x_1 + 2x_2 = 6,$$
$$2x_1 + 4x_2 = 11.$$

Here, the lines are parallel, and no pair of numbers x_1 and x_2 can satisfy both equations.

Case 2: There are infinitely many solutions if the given linear equations coincide. For example, the following simultaneous equations represent only one straight line:

$$x_1 + 2x_2 = 6,$$
$$2x_1 + 4x_2 = 12.$$

Similarly, when a determinant of order three is zero, we have one of the following four cases:

(1) any two of the three planes are parallel,

(2) any two of the three planes coincide,

(3) the intersecting line of any two of the planes is parallel to the third plane, or

(4) the intersecting line lies in the third plane.

8.7   MATRIX INVERSION

As mentioned in Section 8.2, a unit matrix [*I*] is one in which the elements on the principal diagonal are ones and the remaining elements are zeros. We shall now define the inverse of a matrix [*A*]. The inverse of [*A*], or $[A]^{-1}$, is a matrix which has the property

$$[A][A]^{-1} = [A]^{-1}[A] = [I].$$

The basic problem in this section is to find $[A]^{-1}$ when [*A*] is given. The method we discuss below is essentially the Gauss-Jordan elimination method (Sections 8.3 through 8.5). When applied to a system of *n* simultaneous equations, the method consists of *n* passes, each having the following three steps:

(1) interchange of rows (discussed in Section 8.5),

(2) normalization (discussed mainly in Section 8.4), and

(3) elimination (discussed mainly in Section 8.3).

We shall now consider the inversion process using the Gauss-Jordan reduction. For the sake of clarity we shall temporarily ignore the interchange of rows.

If the matrix [*A*] is known and its inverse is to be found, we append a unit matrix of the same order, forming a double square matrix as follows:

$$\begin{bmatrix} a_{11} & a_{12} & a_{13} & 1 & 0 & 0 \\ a_{21} & a_{22} & a_{23} & 0 & 1 & 0 \\ a_{31} & a_{32} & a_{33} & 0 & 0 & 1 \end{bmatrix}. \tag{8.15}$$

TABLE 8.4.   Matrix Inversion

Given coefficient matrix and appended unit matrix	3	−6	7		1	0	0
	9	0	−5		0	1	0
	5	−8	6		0	0	1

Subtract using the pivot row

New rown = old n − pivot row

PASS 1
$k = 1$, pivot row = row 1

	New row 1 = (row 1)/3						
$i = 1$	1	−2	2.33		0.33	0	0
$j = 1, 2, 3, 4$	9	0	−5		0	1	0
	5	−8	6		0	0	1

	New row 2 = row 2 − 9 × row 1						
$i = 2$	1	−2	2.33		0.33	0	0
$j = 2, 3, 4$	0	18	−26		−3	1	0
	5	−8	6		0	0	1

	New row 3 = row 3 − 5 × row 1						
$i = 3$	1	−2	2.33		0.33	0	0
$j = 2, 3, 4$	0	18	−26		−3	1	0
	0	2	−5.65		−1.65	0	1

PASS 2
$K = 2$, pivot row = row 2

	New row 2 = (row 2)/18						
$i = 2$	1	−2	2.33		0.33	0	0
$j = 2, 3, 4$	0	1	−1.44		−0.17	0.06	0
	0	2	−5.65		−1.65	0	1

	New row 1 = row 1 − (−2) × row 2						
$i = 1$	1	0	−0.55		−0.01	0.12	0
$j = 3, 4$	0	1	−1.44		−0.17	0.06	0
	0	2	−5.65		−1.65	0	1

	New row 3 = row 3 − 2 × row 2						
$i = 3$	1	0	−0.55		−0.01	0.12	0
$j = 3, 4$	0	1	−1.44		−0.17	0.06	0
	0	0	−2.77		−1.31	−0.12	1

TABLE 8.4. (*Cont.*)

			Pass 3 $K = 3$, pivot row = row 3				
			New row 3 = (row 3)/−2.77				
$i = 3$ $j = 3, 4$		1	0	−0.55	−0.01	0.12	0
		0	1	−1.44	−0.17	0.06	0
		0	0	1	0.48	0.04	−0.36
			New row 2 = row 2 − (−1.44) × row 3				
$i = 2$ $j = 4$		1	0	−0.55	−0.01	0.12	0
		0	1	0	0.52	0.12	−0.52
		0	0	1	0.48	0.04	−0.36
			New row 1 = row 1 − (−0.55) × row 3				
$i = 1$ $j = 4$		1	0	0	0.26	0.14	−0.2
		0	1	0	0.52	0.12	−0.52
		0	0	1	0.48	0.04	−0.36

We proceed to normalize row 1 and eliminate a_{21} and a_{31} as shown in pass 1 of Table 8.2. The result of the first elimination is

$$\begin{bmatrix} 1 & a_{12}/a_{11} & a_{13}/a_{11} & 1/a_{11} & 0 & 0 \\ 0 & a_{22} - a_{21}(a_{12}/a_{11}) & a_{23} - a_{21}(a_{13}/a_{11}) & -a_{21}/a_{11} & 1 & 0 \\ 0 & a_{32} - a_{31}(a_{12}/a_{11}) & a_{33} - a_{31}(a_{13}/a_{11}) & -a_{31}/a_{11} & 0 & 1 \end{bmatrix}.$$

By continuing the process to eliminate the other variables, we obtain the following form:

$$\begin{bmatrix} 1 & 0 & 0 & b_{11} & b_{12} & b_{13} \\ 0 & 1 & 0 & b_{21} & b_{22} & b_{23} \\ 0 & 0 & 1 & b_{31} & b_{32} & b_{33} \end{bmatrix}.$$

In this resultant matrix, the matrix $[B]$ is the inverse of $[A]$. Table 8.4 shows a step-by-step numerical computation for obtaining the matrix $[A]^{-1}$, where

$$[A] = \begin{bmatrix} 3 & -6 & 7 \\ 9 & 0 & -5 \\ 5 & -8 & 6 \end{bmatrix}.$$

We note that the answer is

$$[A]^{-1} = \begin{bmatrix} 0.26 & 0.14 & -0.2 \\ 0.52 & 0.12 & -0.52 \\ 0.48 & 0.04 & -0.36 \end{bmatrix}.$$

Turning to the relation between the solution of simultaneous equations and matrix inversion, let us consider Eq. (8.9) which, in matrix form, becomes

$$[A][X] = [C]. \tag{8.16}$$

This equation is solved by multiplying through by $[A]^{-1}$. Thus

$$[A]^{-1}[A][X] = [A]^{-1}[C]$$

or

$$[X] = [A]^{-1}[C] \tag{8.17}$$

Equation (8.17) gives the values of all the unknown X's by a simple multiplication of matrices, provided that $[A]^{-1}$ is determined. In the example shown in Tables 8.1 and 8.2, Eq. (8.17) becomes

$$\begin{bmatrix} x_1 \\ x_2 \\ x_3 \end{bmatrix} = \begin{bmatrix} 0.26 & 0.14 & -0.2 \\ 0.52 & 0.12 & -0.52 \\ 0.48 & 0.04 & -0.36 \end{bmatrix} \begin{bmatrix} 3 \\ 3 \\ -4 \end{bmatrix} = \begin{bmatrix} 2 \\ 4 \\ 3 \end{bmatrix},$$

or

$$x_1 = 2, \qquad x_2 = 4, \qquad x_3 = 3,$$

which agree with the solutions obtained in Table 8.1.

It should be noted that $[A]^{-1}$ does not always exist. This is indeed the case if $[A]$ is singular, or $|A| = 0$. In addition, when the determinant $|A|$ has a very small value, the overflow problem usually occurs in computing $[A]^{-1}$. Suppose, for example, the absolute value of an element in floating point turns out to be larger than 10^{99} in FORTRAN II; we then have an overflow condition.

8.8 MATRIX INVERSION IN PLACE

In the last section we discussed matrix inversion through the use of an appended unit matrix. We shall now proceed to show how this powerful method can be modified to save a portion of computer storage. In this modified method each element of $[A]^{-1}$ is to be stored, as computed, in a location in $[A]$, and hence the appended matrix is not needed. To understand this procedure, it is necessary to inspect Table 8.4. We note that (1) at the end of each step, one of the elements in the left-hand column of the given matrix $[A]$ is made either zero or one, and (2) this element, once reduced to zero or one remains unaffected by later operations.

In pass 1, for example, the elements a_{11} in step 1, a_{12} in step 2, and a_{13} in step 3 are reduced to a value of one, zero, and zero, respectively, and these values are kept unchanged. At each step it is therefore possible to store the value of the corresponding element of the appended matrix in these locations. Thus the element b_{11} of the appended matrix, now having the value 0.33, can be stored in the location of the element a_{11} in place of the value of one. Similarly, the element b_{12}, now having the value -3.0, is stored in a_{12} in place of the value zero, etc.

Table 8.5 shows a step-by-step storage map of $[A]$ and compares this modified method with the method discussed in Table 8.4. In the left column of Table 8.5, matrix $[A]$ at each of the nine steps is reproduced from Table 8.4. These values may be compared with their counterparts, which are shown in the right column. We note that at each step, each of the nine elements of $[A]$ is replaced, one by one, by an

TABLE 8.5. Matrix Inversion in Place

Column 1 [A] reproduced from Table 8.4			Column 2 Inversion in place		
PASS 1, Step 1					
[1]	−2	2.33	[0.33]	−2	2.33
9	0	−5	9	0	−5
5	−8	6	5	−8	6
Step 2					
1	−2	2.33	0.33	−2	2.33
[0]	18	−26	[−3]	18	−26
5	−8	6	5	−8	6
Step 3					
1	−2	2.33	0.33	−2	2.33
0	18	−26	−3	18	−26
[0]	2	−5.65	[−1.65]	2	−5.65
PASS 2, Step 1					
1	−2	2.33	0.33	−2	2.33
0	[1]	−1.44	−0.17	[0.06]	−1.44
0	2	−5.65	−1.65	2	−5.65
Step 2					
1	[0]	−0.55	−0.01	[0.12]	−0.55
0	1	−1.44	−0.17	0.06	−1.44
0	2	−5.65	−1.65	2	−5.65
Step 3					
1	0	−0.55	−0.01	0.12	−0.55
0	1	−1.44	−0.17	0.06	−1.44
0	[0]	−2.77	−1.31	[−0.12]	−2.77
PASS 3, Step 1					
1	0	−0.55	−0.01	0.12	−0.55
0	1	−1.44	−0.17	0.06	−1.44
0	0	[1]	0.48	0.04	[−0.36]
Step 2					
1	0	−0.55	−0.01	0.12	−0.55
0	1	[0]	0.52	0.12	[−0.52]
0	0	1	0.48	0.04	−0.36
Step 3					
1	0	[0]	0.26	0.14	[−0.20]
0	1	0	0.52	0.12	−0.52
0	0	1	0.48	0.04	−0.36

element of the required $[A]^{-1}$-matrix. In other words, the inversion is done within $[A]$ itself, and no storages for the appended unit matrix are needed. This modified method is frequently referred to as matrix inversion in place.

Before we turn to the next section for a FORTRAN program, we shall define an orthogonal matrix. A square matrix $[T]$ is called *orthogonal* if $[T][T]' = [T]'[T] = [I]$. In other words, if $[T]' = [T]^{-1}$, then $[T]$ is said to be orthogonal. For example, the matrix

$$[T] = \begin{bmatrix} \cos \theta & \sin \theta \\ -\sin \theta & \cos \theta \end{bmatrix}$$

```
C     THIS SUBPROGRAM IS FOR MATRIX INVERSION AND SIMULT. LINEAR EQS.
      SUBROUTINE CHAP8 (A,N,B,M,DET)
      DIMENSION A(30,30),B(30,30),IPVOT(30),INDEX(30,2),PIVOT(30)
      COMMON IPVOT,INDEX,PIVOT
      EQUIVALENCE (IROW,JROW), (ICOL,JCOL)
C     FOLLOWING 3 STATEMENTS FOR INITIALIZATION
   57 DET=1.
      DO 17 J=1,N
   17 IPVOT(J)=0
      DO 135 I=1,N
C     FOLLOWING 12 STATEMENTS FOR SEARCH FOR PIVOT ELEMENT
      T=0.
      DO 9 J=1,N
      IF(IPVOT(J)-1) 13,9,13
   13 DO 23 K=1,N
      IF(IPVOT(K)-1) 43,23,81
   43 IF(ABSF(T)-ABSF(A(J,K))) 83,23,23
   83 IROW=J
      ICOL=K
      T=A(J,K)
   23 CONTINUE
    9 CONTINUE
      IPVOT(ICOL)=IPVOT(ICOL)+1
C  FOLLOWING 15 STATEMENTS TO PUT PIVOT ELEMENT ON DIAGONAL
      IF(IROW-ICOL) 73,109,73
   73 DET=-DET
      DO 12 L=1,N
      T=A(IROW,L)
      A(IROW,L)=A(ICOL,L)
   12 A(ICOL,L)=T
      IF(M) 109,109,33
   33 DO 2 L=1,M
      T=B(IROW,L)
      B(IROW,L)=B(ICOL,L)
    2 B(ICOL,L)=T
  109 INDEX(I,1)=IROW
      INDEX(I,2)=ICOL
      PIVOT(I)=A(ICOL,ICOL)
      DET=DET*PIVOT(I)
C     FOLLOWING 6 STATEMENTS TO DIVIDE PIVOT ROW BY PIVOT ELEMENT
      A(ICOL,ICOL)=1.
      DO 205 L=1,N
  205 A(ICOL,L)=A(ICOL,L)/PIVOT(I)
      IF(M) 347,347,66
   66 DO 52 L=1,M
   52 B(ICOL,L)=B(ICOL,L)/PIVOT(I)
```

Fig. 8.1. Subprogram CHAP8.

is an orthogonal matrix because it has the following property:

$$[T]' = [T]^{-1} = \begin{bmatrix} \cos\theta & -\sin\theta \\ \sin\theta & \cos\theta \end{bmatrix}.$$

$[T]' = [T]^T$

The orthogonal matrix plays an important role in Chapter 9. However, we impart a word of warning: the inverse of a nonsingular matrix is not always equal to the transpose of the given matrix.

8.9 FORTRAN PROGRAM FOR MATRIX INVERSION AND SIMULTANEOUS LINEAR EQUATIONS

A tested FORTRAN subprogram to carry out the matrix inversion with accompanying solution of simultaneous linear equations $[A][X] = [B]$ appears in Fig. 8.1. The procedure used is similar to the one discussed in Sections 8.5, 8.6, and 8.8. The arguments in the subprogram CHAP8 are as follows:

A = the given coefficient matrix A; A^{-1} will be stored in this matrix at return to the main program;

N = order of A; $N \geq 1$;

B = matrix of constant vector, used for solution of simultaneous equations only;

M = the number of column vectors in the matrix of constant vectors (M = 0 if inversion is the sole aim; M = 1, 2, ... for solution of simultaneous equations);

DET = value of the determinant $|A|$.

```
C       FOLLOWING 10 STATEMENTS TO REDUCE NON-PIVOT ROWS
    347 DO 135 LI=1,N
        IF(LI-ICOL) 21,135,21
     21 T=A(LI,ICOL)
        A(LI,ICOL)=0.
        DO 89 L=1,N
     89 A(LI,L)=A(LI,L)-A(ICOL,L)*T
        IF(M) 135,135,18
     18 DO 68 L=1,M
     68 B(LI,L)=B(LI,L)-B(ICOL,L)*T
    135 CONTINUE
C       FOLLOWING 11 STATEMENTS TO INTERCHANGE COLUMNS
    222 DO 3 I=1,N
        L=N-I+1
        IF (INDEX(L,1)-INDEX(L,2)) 19,3,19
     19 JROW=INDEX(L,1)
        JCOL=INDEX(L,2)
        DO 549 K=1,N
        T=A(K,JROW)
        A(K,JROW)=A(K,JCOL)
        A(K,JCOL)=T
    549 CONTINUE
      3 CONTINUE
     81 RETURN
        END
```

Fig. 8.1. *(cont.)*

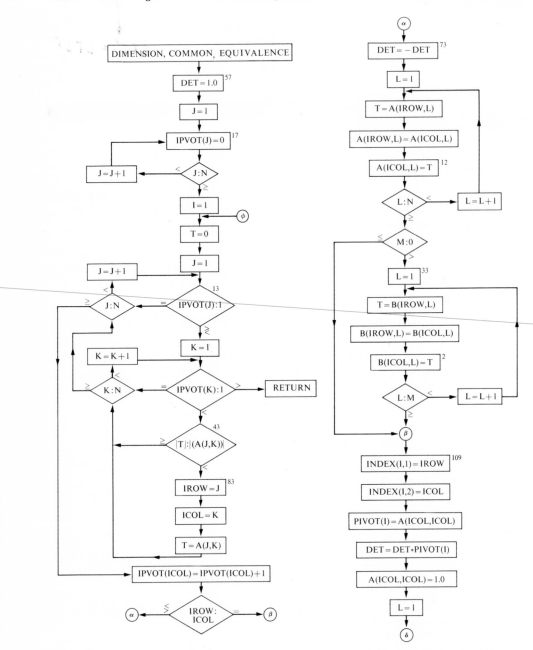

Fig. 8.2.   Flow chart for matrix inversion and solutions of simultaneous equations.

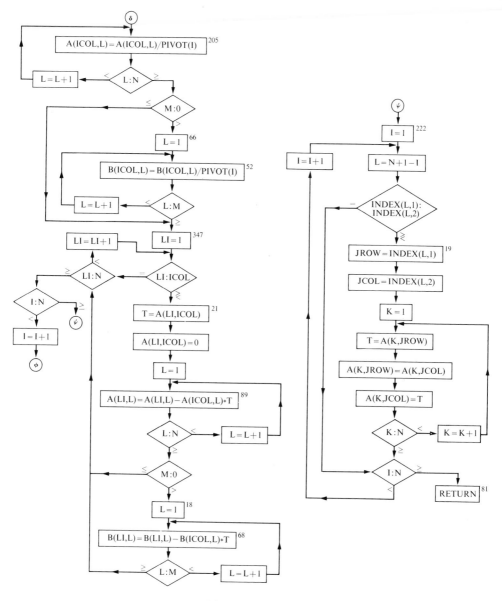

Fig. 8.2.   *(cont.)*

It should be noted that the column index for the argument INDEX is 2. IPVOT is an array used to prevent duplicate pivotings on any single row. Figure 8.2 shows the corresponding flow chart.

The EQUIVALENCE and COMMON statements used in this subprogram have not been discussed before and need some explanation.

```
C       MATRIX INVERSION.  MAIN PROGRAM   FOR EXAMPLE 8.1
        DIMENSION C(30,30), D(30,30)
        COMMON IPVOT,INDEX,PIVOT
        PUNCH 1
    1 FORMAT (10X, 16HGIVEN  MATRIX  C)
        READ5,N,M
    5 FORMAT(I2,I2)
        DO 10 I=1,N
   10 READ 15, (C(I,J), J=1,N)
   15 FORMAT (7F10.4)
        DO 20 I=1,N
   20 PUNCH 15,(C(I,J), J=1,N)
   30 CALL CHAP8 (C,N,D,M,DETERM)
        PUNCH 35
   35 FORMAT (10X, 22HINVERSE  OF  MATRIX  C)
        DO 40 I=1,N
   40 PUNCH 45, (C(I,J), J=1,N)
   45 FORMAT (7F10.4)
   50 STOP
   55 END
0300
0.0        -6.0        9.0
7.0         0.0       -5.0
5.0        -8.0        6.0
```

Fig. 8.3. Main program for matrix inversion.

The EQUIVALENCE statement conserves storage locations. This statement allows two or more variables which are never needed at the same time in the program to share the *same* storage location. For example, the statement

$$\text{EQUIVALENCE (IROW, JROW)}$$

means that the variables IROW and JROW are to share the same storage location. In general, the statement

$$\text{EQUIVALENCE } (a_1, a_2, \ldots, a_n), (b_1, b_2, \ldots, b_m)$$

will cause variables a_1 through a_n to share one location, and variables b_1 through b_m to share *another* storage location.

The COMMON statement is also used to conserve locations. As mentioned in Sections 5.7 and 5.8, if a variable V appears in both the main program and a subprogram, these two V's are not at all related. In fact, a separate storage area is set up for each one. It is clear that storage locations are wasted if these two V's are actually the same variable. To eliminate this waste, COMMON statements can be used in a FORTRAN II program. For example, in Figs. 8.2 and 8.3, the FORTRAN statement

$$\text{COMMON IPVOT, INDEX, PIVOT}$$

is put in both the subprogram CHAP8 and its main program. The variables are now the same for both programs and therefore storages are not wasted.

In this example, the three subscripted variables,

IPVOT, INDEX, and PIVOT,

are assigned to the same locations in a continuous special section of the storage which is set aside by the compiler. This is the special common area in the storage for the main program and its required subprograms. In this common area, the arrays IPVOT, INDEX, and PIVOT are assigned sequentially and by columns for each of the three arrays.

As shown in Fig. 8.2, the COMMON and EQUIVALENCE usually immediately follow the DIMENSION statement in the subroutine. They should precede all executable statements.

A COMMON statement also shows whether there is any correspondence between variables in the main program and the subprogram; it stores these variables in the same storage location even if they do not have the same name. For example, in the subroutine:

COMMON (A, B)

in the main program:

COMMON (D, E)

Then A and D, as well as B and E, have the same storage location.

Example 8.1

Write a main program, together with the necessary data cards, to compute $[C]^{-1}$, where $[C]$ is the coefficient matrix shown in Table 8.4. This main program will be used to call the subroutine CHAP8 shown in Fig. 8.1; it will also serve to read in $[C]$ and print out $[C]^{-1}$.

TABLE 8.6.   Answers for Example 8.1

```
              GIVEN   MATRIX   C
       0.0000      -6.0000      9.0000
       7.0000       0.0000     -5.0000
       5.0000      -8.0000      6.0000


              INVERSE   OF   MATRIX   C
        .3921        .3529      -.2941
        .6568        .4411      -.6176
        .5490        .2941      -.4117
```

Figure 8.3 illustrates a possible main program which calls for the subroutine CHAP8. After the first transfer (statement 30 in the main program) to the subprogram CHAP8, values in matrix C and matrix D will be substituted for the dummy variables A and B, respectively, 3 will be substituted for N, and 0 for M.

An echo print and the answers are shown in Table 8.6.

```
C        SOLUTION OF SIMULTANEOUS LINEAR EQUATIONS, MAIN PROGRAM
         DIMENSION C(30,30), D(30,30)
         COMMON IPVOT,INDEX,PIVOT
   71 READ 5,N,M
    5 FORMAT (I2,I2)
      IF(N) 77,60,77
   77 PUNCH 1
    1 FORMAT(10X, 16HGIVEN   MATRIX   C)
      DO 10 I=1,N
   10 READ 15, (C(I,J), J=1,N)
   15 FORMAT (7F10.4)
      DO 20 I=1,N
   20 PUNCH 15, (C(I,J), J=1,N)
      PUNCH 25
   25 FORMAT (10X, 16HGIVEN   MATRIX   D)
      DO 30 I=1,N
   30 READ 15, (D(I,J), J=1,M)
      DO 35 I=1,N
   35 PUNCH 15, (D(I,J), J=1,M)
      CALL CHAP8 (C,N,D,M,DET)
      PUNCH 40
   40 FORMAT (10X, 30HSOLUTION   OF   GIVEN   EQUATIONS)
      DO 45 I=1,N
   45 PUNCH 15, (D(I,J), J=1,M)
      PUNCH 50
   50 FORMAT (10X, 22HVALUE   OF   DETERMINANT)
      PUNCH 55, DET
   55 FORMAT (F10.4//)
      GO TO 71
   60 STOP
   65 END
0401
      .5000      .3300      .2500      .5000
      .5000      .2500      .2000     1.0000
     1.0000     1.0000     1.0000     1.0000
     2.0000     3.0000     1.0000     5.0000
    13.0000
    11.5000
    40.0000
    75.0000
0301
     2.0000     -7.0000      4.0000
     1.0000      9.0000     -6.0000
    -3.0000      8.0000      5.0000
     9.0000
     1.0000
     6.0000
0000
```

Fig. 8.4.   Main program for solutions of simultaneous equations.

Example 8.2

Write a FORTRAN main program to solve a set of simultaneous linear equations by calling on the subprogram CHAP8 shown in Fig. 8.1. The first input card after the heading print out should be N. If N is zero, terminate the computation; if it is not zero, read in the given matrices.

TABLE 8.7.   Answers for Example 8.2

```
        GIVEN  MATRIX   C
    •5000       •3300      •2500       •5000
    •5000       •2500      •2000      1•0000
   1•0000      1•0000     1•0000      1•0000
   2•0000      3•0000     1•0000      5•0000
        GIVEN  MATRIX   D
  13•0000
  11•5000
  40•0000
  75•0000
        SOLUTION   OF   GIVEN  EQUATIONS
   7•2290
  12•0654
  19•7954
    •9100
        VALUE   OF   DETERMINANT
  -•2445



        GIVEN  MATRIX   C
   2•0000    -7•0000     4•0000
   1•0000     9•0000    -6•0000
  -3•0000     8•0000     5•0000
        GIVEN  MATRIX   D
   9•0000
   1•0000
   6•0000
        SOLUTION   OF   GIVEN  EQUATIONS
   3•9999
    •9999
   1•9999
        VALUE   OF   DETERMINANT
 234•9999
```

The output should include:

(1) name and date (this is an echo print of an input card);
(2) an echo print of the given matrices;
(3) answers—a field of F7.3 will suffice;
(4) value of the determinants.

The following two sets of equations should be solved:

Set 1	Set 2
$x/2 + y/3 + z/4 + w/2 = 13.0,$	$2x - 7y + 4z = 9.0,$
$x/2 + y/4 + z/5 + w = 11.5,$	$x + 9y - 6z = 1.0,$
$x + y + z + w = 40.0,$	$-3x + 8y + 5z = 6.0.$
$2x + 3y + z + 5w = 75.0;$	

A possible main program is shown in Fig. 8.4, and the corresponding results
(FORTRAN II) are tabulated in Table 8.7.

```
C      MATRIX INVERSION ACCOMPANYING WITH DETERMINANT AND
C      SOLVING FOR SIMULTANEOUS EQUATIONS
C      FOR INVERSION ONLY  M=0,LDET=0,INV=0
C      FOR DETERMINANT ONLY  M=-1,LDET=0,INV=0
C      FOR SOLUTION ONLY   M=1 OR MORE,LDET=0,INV=1
C      FOR INVERSION AND DETERMINANT  M=0,LDET=1,INV=0
C      FOR SOLUTION AND DETERMINANT  M=1 OR MORE,LDET=0,INV=0
C      FOR INVERSION AND SOLUTION  M=1 OR MORE,LDET=0,INV=1
C      FOR ALL VALUE  M=1 OR MORE,LDET=1,INV=1
       DIMENSION A(20,20),B(20,20),IPVOT(20),INDEX(20,2),PIVOT(20)
       PUNCH 7
     7 FORMAT(10X,16HGIVEN  MATRIX  A//)
       READ 1, N, M, LDET, INV
     1 FORMAT(4I2)
       DO 14 I=1,N
       READ 5, (A(I,J),J=1,N)
       PUNCH 5, (A(I,J),J=1,N)
     5 FORMAT (7F10.4)
    14 CONTINUE
       IF(M) 57,57,10
    10 PUNCH 8
     8 FORMAT(10X, 35HGIVEN  MATRIX  OF  CONSTANT  VECTOR//)
       DO 4 I=1,N
       READ 5, (B(I,J),J=1,M)
       PUNCH 5, (B(I,J),J=1,M)
     4 CONTINUE
    57 DET=1.
       .................
       .................
       .................                SAME AS SHOWN IN FIG. 8.1.
       .................
       .................
     3 CONTINUE
       IF(M) 1003,1001,1004
  1001 PUNCH 1011
  1011 FORMAT(10X,22HINVERSE  OF  MATRIX  A//)
       DO 1002 I=1,N
       PUNCH 5, (A(I,J),J=1,N)
  1002 CONTINUE
       IF(LDET) 9009,9009,1003
  1003 PUNCH 1033
  1033 FORMAT(10X,22HVALUE  OF  DETERMINANT//)
       PUNCH 5, DET
       GO TO 9009
  1004 PUNCH 1044
  1044 FORMAT(10X,30HSOLUTION  OF  GIVEN  EQUATIONS//)
       DO 1005 I=1,N
       PUNCH 5, (B(I,J),J=1,M)
  1005 CONTINUE
       IF(INV) 9009,1003,1001
  9009 STOP
       END
```

Fig. 8.5. Main program for matrix inversion and linear equations.

TABLE 8.8.   Answers for Example 8.3

INPUT
```
03010101
      0.0000    -6.0000     9.0000
      7.0000     0.0000    -5.0000
      5.0000    -8.0000     6.0000
     -4.0000
      7.0000
      3.0000
```

OUTPUT
GIVEN   MATRIX   A
```
      0.0000    -6.0000     9.0000
      7.0000     0.0000    -5.0000
      5.0000    -8.0000     6.0000
```
GIVEN   MATRIX   OF   CONSTANT   VECTOR
```
     -4.0000
      7.0000
      3.0000
```
SOLUTION   OF   GIVEN   EQUATIONS
```
       .0196
     -1.3922
     -1.3725
```
INVERSE   OF   MATRIX   A
```
       .3922       .3529      -.2941
       .6569       .4412      -.6176
       .5490       .2941      -.4118
```
VALUE   OF   DETERMINANT
```
   -102.0000
```

INPUT
```
03000000
      2.0000     1.0000     1.0000
      1.0000     2.0000     3.0000
      3.0000     2.0000     1.0000
```

OUTPUT
GIVEN   MATRIX   A
```
      2.0000     1.0000     1.0000
      1.0000     2.0000     3.0000
      3.0000     2.0000     1.0000
```
INVERSE   OF   MATRIX   A
```
     -1.6000      .2000       .8000
       .6000     -.2000       .2000
      -.2000      .4000       .6000
```

Example 8.3

Modify the subroutine CHAP8 (see Fig. 8.1) to a *main* program and find the inverse of the matrix

$$A = \begin{bmatrix} 2 & 1 & 1 \\ 1 & 2 & 3 \\ 3 & 2 & 1 \end{bmatrix}.$$

We combine Figs. 8.1 and 8.3 to make a main program, shown in Fig. 8.5. Statements 57 through 3 inclusive are taken directly from subroutine CHAP8. The answers for $[A]^{-1}$ are shown in Table 8.8.

8.10   GAUSS-SEIDEL ITERATIVE METHOD

The elimination method discussed in Sections 8.3 through 8.5 is a direct method, not an iterative procedure. When the numerical values of diagonal elements in the given coefficient matrix are large compared with those of the remaining elements, an iterative procedure, the Gauss-Seidel method, is generally favored. This type of coefficient matrix arises frequently in numerical or partial differential equations of scientific and engineering problems. Let us consider the linear system

$$
\begin{aligned}
a_{11}x_1 + a_{12}x_2 + a_{13}x_3 + \cdots + a_{1n}x_n &= c_1, \\
a_{21}x_1 + a_{22}x_2 + a_{23}x_3 + \cdots + a_{2n}x_n &= c_2, \\
&\vdots \\
a_{n1}x_1 + a_{n2}x_2 + a_{n3}x_3 + \cdots + a_{nn}x_n &= c_n.
\end{aligned}
\tag{8.18}
$$

Equation (8.18) can be rewritten so that the ith equation is solved for x_i:

$$
x_1 = -\,\frac{a_{12}x_2 + a_{13}x_3 + \cdots + a_{1n}x_n - c_1}{a_{11}},
$$

$$
x_2 = -\,\frac{a_{21}x_1 + a_{23}x_3 + \cdots + a_{2n}x_n - c_2}{a_{22}},
$$

$$
x_3 = -\,\frac{a_{31}x_1 + a_{32}x_2 + \cdots + a_{3n}x_n - c_3}{a_{33}},
\tag{8.19}
$$

$$
\vdots
$$

$$
x_n = -\,\frac{a_{n1}x_1 + a_{n2}x_2 + \cdots + a_{nn}x_n - c_n}{a_{nn}}.
$$

The procedure is to assume a set of starting values for x_i ($i = 1, 2, \ldots, n$) and then to calculate new values by substitution into Eq. (8.19) for $i = 1, 2, \ldots, n$. These values are used as new estimates and iterations are continued until some criterion is met.

Consider the following numerical example of two simultaneous linear equations

$$
\begin{aligned}
3x_1 + x_2 &= 5, \\
x_1 + 2x_2 &= 5,
\end{aligned}
\tag{8.20}
$$

which may be rewritten as follows:

$$
x_1 = \frac{-x_2}{3} + \frac{5}{3},
$$

$$
x_2 = \frac{-x_1}{2} + \frac{5}{2}.
$$

Assuming as an initial approximation that

$$
x_1 = 0, \qquad x_2 = 0,
$$

we obtain the iterative solutions shown in the following table:

Step number	x_1	x_2
1	0	0
2	$\frac{5}{3}$	$\frac{5}{2}$
3	$\frac{5}{6}$	$\frac{5}{3}$
4	$\frac{10}{9}$	$\frac{25}{12}$
$\vdots$		
(True solution)	1	2

If the above iteration is modified so that the most recently computed values are used, then the iterative procedure will converge more rapidly, as can be seen:

Step number	x_1	x_2
1	0	0
2	$\frac{5}{3}$	$-(\frac{1}{2})(\frac{5}{3}) + \frac{5}{2} = \frac{5}{3}$
3	$-(\frac{1}{3})(\frac{5}{3}) + \frac{5}{3} = \frac{10}{9}$	$-(\frac{10}{9})(9) + \frac{5}{2} = \frac{35}{18}$

The Gauss-Seidel method suffers from its slow convergence for ill-conditioned systems. An ill-conditioned system is very sensitive to small variations in the values of the coefficients; such systems may be interpreted geometrically in terms of the two straight lines in the upper portion of Fig. 8.6. Here the intersecting angle is very acute, and the intersecting point P is not sharply defined.

To illustrate slow convergence, let us take the following singular system (the parallel lines shown in Fig. 8.6):

$$4x_1 + 3x_2 = 7,$$

$$8x_1 + 6x_2 = 14. \tag{8.21}$$

Using the Gauss-Seidel Method, we have at first

$$x_1 = \frac{7 - 3x_2}{4},$$

$$x_2 = \frac{14 - 8x_1}{6} \tag{8.22}$$

$$= \frac{7 - 4x_1}{3}.$$

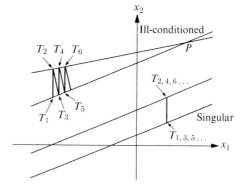

Fig. 8.6. Ill-conditioned system and singular system.

```
C       THE GAUSS-SEIDEL METHOD FOR SOLVING SIMULTANEOUS EQUATIONS
C       FOR USE OF FORTRAN II OR FORGO
C       THE EQUATIONS MUST BE PUT INTO THE FORM    A  X  X  =  B
C       READ IN N-THE NUMBER OF UNKNOWNS, ITRTE-THE MAXIMUM NUMBER OF
C       ITERATIONS, DELTA-THE TOLERANCE WITHIN WHICH THE RATIO OF TWO
C       SUCCESSIVE ITERATIONS MUST LIE (DELTA LESS THAN 1, USE .9 OR .99).
C       READ IN  A  MATRIX ROW BY ROW, SIX TO A CARD, F10.4 FORMAT.
C       READ IN  B  (COLUMN) MATRIX FROM THE TOP, SIX TO A CARD, F10.4.
        DIMENSION A(30,30), B(30), X(30), OLDX(30)
C       READ IN N, ITRTE, DELTA, A , B
        READ 5001, N, ITRTE, DELTA
 5001 FORMAT(I2,I3,F10.7)
        READ 5002, ((A(I,J), J=1,N), I=1,N)
 5002 FORMAT(6F10.4)
        READ 5002, (B(I), I=1,N)
C
C       BEGIN GAUSS-SEIDEL METHOD
C
C       INITIALIZATION
        KOUNT=0
        DO 5003 I=1,N
        OLDX(I)=0.0
 5003 X(I)=0.0
C
C       COMPUTE NEW VALUES FOR X(I)
C
 5011 DO 5004 I=1,N
        DIL=0.0
        DO 5006 J=1,N
        IF(I-J) 5005,5006,5005
 5005 DIL=DIL+A(I,J)*X(J)
 5006 CONTINUE
 5004 X(I)=(B(I)-DIL)/A(I,I)
        KOUNT=KOUNT+1
C
C       TEST TO SEE IF ITRTE HAS BEEN EXCEEDED
        IF(ITRTE-KOUNT) 5013, 5010, 5010
C       COMPARE EACH X TO ITS PREDECESSOR OLDX
 5010 DO 5007 I=1,N
        IF (ABSF(X(I))-ABSF(OLDX(I))) 5020, 5007, 5021
 5020 IF (DELTA-ABSF(X(I)/OLDX(I))) 5007, 5008, 5008
 5021 IF (DELTA-ABSF(OLDX(I)/X(I))) 5007, 5008, 5008
 5007 CONTINUE
        GO TO 5009
 5008 DO 5012 I=1,N
 5012 OLDX(I)=X(I)
        GO TO 5011
 5013 PUNCH 5014, ITRTE
 5014 FORMAT(15X,5HAFTER,I3,32H ITERATIONS THE VALUES OF X ARE )
 5009 DO 5015 I=1,N
        IF (I-10) 5016, 5019, 5019
 5019 PUNCH 5017, I, X(I)
 5017 FORMAT(25X,2HX(,I2,3H) =,E16.8)
        GO TO 5015
 5016 PUNCH 5018, I, X(I)
 5018 FORMAT(25X,2HX(,I1,3H) =,E16.8)
 5015 CONTINUE
        STOP
        END
```

Fig. 8.7. FORTRAN program for the Gauss-Seidel method.

The table below shows the iterative processes using the most recently computed values:

Step number	x_1	x_2
1	$\frac{7}{4}$	0
2	$\frac{7}{4}$	0
3	$\frac{7}{4}$	0
4	$\frac{7}{4}$	0

It is clear that no improvement is expected. Similarly for other ill-conditioned systems (see Fig. 8.6), the rate of convergence is very slow indeed.

In this connection, we might use the following convergence criterion:

$$\left| \frac{x_i^{(k+1)}}{x_i^{(k)}} \right| < \delta, \quad \text{if} \quad |x_i^{(k+1)}| < |x_i^{(k)}|,$$

where k = step number,

   i = number of variables ($i = 1, 2, \ldots, n$),

   δ = tolerance which is less than 1, say, between 0.9 and 0.999.

A FORTRAN program for the Gauss-Seidel method is shown in Fig. 8.7.

BIBLIOGRAPHY

Determinants and Matrices

AITKEN, A. C., *Determinants and Matrices*, 9th ed. (1st ed. 1939). Oliver and Boyd, Edinburgh; Interscience, New York, 1956.

BECKENBACH, E. F., Ed., *Modern Mathematics for the Engineer*. McGraw-Hill, New York, 1956.

BELLMAN, R., *Introduction to Matrix Algebra*. McGraw-Hill, New York, 1960.

BODEWIG, E., *Matrix Calculus*. North Holland, Amsterdam; Interscience, New York, 1956.

"Conference on Matrix Computations," *J. Assoc. Comput. Mach.*, **4**, pp. 100–115 (1958).

FRAZER, R. A., W. J. DUNCAN, and A. R. COLLAR, *Elementary Matrices*. Cambridge Univ. Press, London, 1947.

HOUSEHOLDER, A. S., "The Approximate Solution of Matrix Problems," *J. Assoc. Comp. Mach.*, **5**, pp. 205–243 (1958).

MARCUS, M., "Basic Theorems in Matrix Theory," *Nat. Bur. of Std. Appl. Math. Ser.*, **57** (1960).

OSBORNE, E. E., "On Acceleration and Matrix Deflation Processes Used with the Power Method," *J. Soc. Ind. Appl. Math.*, **6**, pp. 279–287 (1958).

Matrix Inversion

Fox, L., "Practical Solution of Linear Equations and Inversion of Matrices," *Appl. Math. Ser. U.S. Bur. Std.*, **39**, pp. 1–54 (1954).

Fox, L., and J. G. Hayes, "More Practical Methods for the Inversion of Matrices," *J. Roy. Stat. Soc. B*, **13**, pp. 83–91 (1951).

Goldstine, H. H., and J. von Neumann, "Numerical Inverting of Matrices of High Order." *Proc. Am. Math. Soc.*, **2**, pp. 188–202 (1951).

Householder, A. S., "A Survey of Some Closed Methods for Inverting Matrices," *J. Soc. Ind. Appl. Math.*, **5**, pp. 155–169 (1957).

Newman, M., and J. Todd, "The Evaluation of Matrix Inversion Programs," *J. Soc. Ind. Appl. Math.*, **6**, pp. 466–476 (1958).

von Neumann, J., and H. H. Goldstine, "Numerical Inverting of Matrices of High Order," *Bull. Am. Math. Soc.*, **53**, pp. 1021–1099 (1947), *Proc. Am. Math. Soc.*, **2**, pp. 188–202 (1951)

Linear Algebra and Simultaneous Equations

Dwyer, P. S., *Linear Computations.* John Wiley and Sons, New York, 1951.

Faddeeva, V. N., *Computational Methods in Linear Algebra*, translated by C. D. Benster. Dover, New York, 1959.

Forsythe, G. E., "Solving Linear Equations Can be Interesting," *Bull. Am. Math. Soc.*, **59**, pp. 299–329 (1953).

Forsythe, G. E., "Tentative Classification of Methods and Bibliography on Solving Systems of Linear Equations," *Inst. Numer. Anal. Rpt.* 52–7, Nat. Bur. Std., Los Angeles, Calif. (Multilith Typescript, 1951); *Appl. Math. Ser.*, **29**, Nat. Bur. Std., Washington, D. C., pp. 1–28 (1953).

Hestenes, M. R., and E. L. Stiefel, "Methods of Conjugate Gradients for Solving Linear Systems," *J. Res. Nat. Bur. Std.*, **49**, No. 6, pp. 409–436 (1952).

Paige, L. J., and O. Taussky, Eds., "Simultaneous Linear Equations and the Determination of Eigenvalues," *Nat. Bur. Std. Appl. Math. Ser.*, **29** (1953).

Stiefel, E. L., P. Henrici, and H. Rutishauser, "Further Contributions to the Solution of Simultaneous Linear Equations and the Determination of Eigenvalues," *Nat. Bur. Std. Appl. Math. Ser.*, **49** (1958).

Taussky, O., Ed., "Contributions to the Solution of Systems of Linear Equations and the Determination of Eigenvalues," *Nat. Bur. Std. Appl. Math. Ser.*, **39** (1954).

Other References

Crandall, S. H., *Engineering Analysis.* McGraw-Hill, New York, 1956.

Householder, A. S., *Principles of Numerical Analysis.* McGraw-Hill, New York, 1953.

Lanczos, C., *Applied Analysis.* Prentice-Hall, Englewood Cliffs, N. J., Chaps. II and III, 1956.

National Physical Laboratory, *Modern Computing Methods.* H. M. Stationery Office, London, 1961.

Ostrowski, A. M., "Über näherungsweise Auflösung von Systemen Homogener Linearer Gleichungen," *Z. Angew. Math. Phys.*, **8**, pp. 280–285 (1957).

Varga, R. S., *Iterative Numerical Analysis.* Prentice-Hall, Englewood Cliffs, N. J., 1962.

PROBLEMS

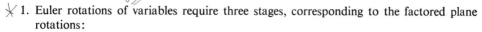

☆ 1. Euler rotations of variables require three stages, corresponding to the factored plane rotations:

$$
\begin{bmatrix} \bar{X} \\ \bar{Y} \\ \bar{Z} \end{bmatrix} = \begin{bmatrix} 1 & 0 & 0 \\ 0 & \cos\phi & \sin\phi \\ 0 & -\sin\phi & \cos\phi \end{bmatrix} \begin{bmatrix} \cos\theta & \sin\theta & 0 \\ -\sin\theta & \cos\theta & 0 \\ 0 & 0 & 1 \end{bmatrix} \begin{bmatrix} 1 & 0 & 0 \\ 0 & \cos\psi & \sin\psi \\ 0 & -\sin\psi & \cos\psi \end{bmatrix} \begin{bmatrix} X \\ Y \\ Z \end{bmatrix}
$$

Write a main program to call the subroutine MATMPY to find $\bar{X}$, $\bar{Y}$, $\bar{Z}$ if $\phi = 34°$, $\theta = 22.5°$, $\psi = 18°$, and $X = 1$, $Y = 2$, and $Z = 4$.

2. Solve the following simultaneous linear equations, using the Gauss-Jordan method:

$$ x_1 - x_2 + 2x_3 = 5, \qquad -2x_1 + 3x_2 + x_3 = 7, \qquad 3x_1 + 2x_2 + x_3 = 10. $$

3. Find $[A]^{-1}$ when

$$ [A] = \begin{bmatrix} 1 & 0 & 0 \\ 2 & -1 & 0 \\ 1 & 1 & -3 \end{bmatrix}. $$

4. In structural analysis, one may use the slope-deflection method to solve for moments in the various parts of a frame. In a typical skew frame problem one obtains

$$ \begin{bmatrix} 3 & 1 & 2.4 \\ 1 & 5 & 0.3 \\ -41 & 52 & -209.1 \end{bmatrix} \begin{bmatrix} \theta_b \\ \theta_c \\ \theta_a \end{bmatrix} = \begin{bmatrix} 0 \\ 0 \\ -500 \end{bmatrix}. $$

What is the value of θ_a?

☆ 5. Kirchhoff's law may be used to establish a set of linear equations for the circuit shown in Fig. 8.8. We have

$$ I_1 + I_2 + I_3 = A_1, $$
$$ I_8 + I_9 + I_{10} = A_2, $$
$$ -I_1 + I_4 - I_6 = 0, $$
$$ -I_3 + I_5 - I_9 = 0, $$
$$ I_6 + I_7 - I_{10} = 0, $$
$$ -R_7 I_7 + R_8 I_8 - R_{10} I_{10} = 0, $$
$$ -R_5 I_5 + R_8 I_8 - R_9 I_9 = 0, $$
$$ R_2 I_2 - R_3 I_3 - R_5 I_5 = 0, $$
$$ -R_1 I_1 + R_2 I_2 - R_4 I_4 = 0, $$
$$ -R_4 I_4 - R_6 I_6 + R_7 I_7 = 0, $$

where $R_1 = 1$, $R_2 = 10$, $R_3 = 35$, $R_4 = 23$, $R_5 = 100$, $R_6 = 25$, $R_7 = 50$, $R_8 = 75$, $R_9 = 5$, and $R_{10} = 50$ ohms. Solve for the current I_1 through I_{10}.

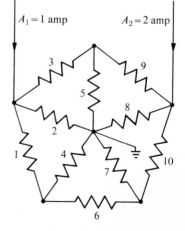

Figure 8.8

6. Two sets of equations are given as follows:

$$2x - 2y - 2z - 3w = 11.0, \qquad x/5 - y/2 - z/4 = 15.0,$$
$$x - y - z - 2w = 4.0, \qquad x - y - z = 57.0,$$
$$-x - y - 6w = -3.0, \qquad z/5 - x/2 - 3y = 2.5.$$
$$9x - 9y - 7z - 23w = 43.0,$$

Write a main program to solve the two given sets of equations by calling the subroutine CHAP8. Make the main program flexible enough to handle any number of sets of equations. The required format for ouput is:

1. Name, edition, date

2. Echo print of the first coefficient matrix:

$$
\begin{array}{ccccc}
2.00 & -2.00 & 2.00 & -3.00 & 11.00 \\
1.00 & \cdots & \cdots & \cdots & 4.00 \\
\vdots & & & & \vdots \\
9.00 & \cdots & \cdots & \cdots & 43.00
\end{array}
$$

Echo print of the second coefficient matrix:

$$
\begin{array}{cc}
0.20 & 0.50 \quad \cdots \\
\vdots
\end{array}
$$

3. Answers to the first set of equations:

$$x = \text{XXXX.XXX}, \quad y = \text{XXXX.XXX}, \quad z = \text{XXXX.XXX}, \quad w = \text{XXXX.XXX}.$$

Answers to the second set of equations: same.

7. Find the inverse and determinant of the following matrix (this is a 3 $\times$ 3 magic square):

$$
\begin{bmatrix}
2 & 7 & 6 \\
9 & 5 & 1 \\
4 & 3 & 8
\end{bmatrix}.
$$

8. Use the Gauss-Seidel method to solve

$$10x + 2y + 3z - w = 80,$$
$$x - 20y - z + 3w = 40,$$
$$x + y - 10z + 2w = 40,$$
$$2x - y - z + 30w = 120.$$

9. (a) Use the Gauss-Jordan procedure to find the inversion of the following matrix:

$$
\begin{bmatrix}
1 & 3 \\
4 & 2
\end{bmatrix}.
$$

Both normalization and possible zero element on diagonal should be considered.

(b) Do (a) by matrix inversion in place.

(c) Find the value of the related determinant by using the steps in (a).

CHAPTER 9

EIGENVALUES AND
EIGENVECTORS OF A
REAL SYMMETRIC MATRIX

9.1 INTRODUCTION

In many problems in applied mathematics it is necessary to solve linear equations having the form

$$\begin{bmatrix} a_{11} - \lambda & a_{12} & a_{13} \\ a_{21} & a_{22} - \lambda & a_{23} \\ a_{31} & a_{32} & a_{33} - \lambda \end{bmatrix} \begin{bmatrix} x_1 \\ x_2 \\ x_3 \end{bmatrix} = 0 \tag{9.1}$$

or the form

$$\begin{bmatrix} a_{11} & a_{12} & a_{13} \\ a_{21} & a_{22} & a_{23} \\ a_{31} & a_{32} & a_{33} \end{bmatrix} \begin{bmatrix} x_1 \\ x_2 \\ x_3 \end{bmatrix} = \begin{bmatrix} \lambda & 0 & 0 \\ 0 & \lambda & 0 \\ 0 & 0 & \lambda \end{bmatrix} \begin{bmatrix} x_1 \\ x_2 \\ x_3 \end{bmatrix}. \tag{9.2}$$

In general, Eq. (9.2) is expressed in the following matrix form,

$$[A][x] = \lambda[I][x], \tag{9.3}$$

where $[A]$ is a real symmetric matrix, $[x]$ is a column matrix of independent variables, and λ is a scalar parameter known as a *characteristic value* or *eigenvalue*.

Our problem is to find λ and its corresponding $[x]$, which is known as an *eigenvector*.

In this chapter only Jacobi's method will be discussed. The basic aim of the method is to transform Eqs. (9.2) or (9.3) into the following identity:

$$\begin{bmatrix} a'_{11} & 0 & 0 \\ 0 & a'_{22} & 0 \\ 0 & 0 & a'_{33} \end{bmatrix} \begin{bmatrix} \bar{x}_1 \\ \bar{x}_2 \\ \bar{x}_3 \end{bmatrix} \equiv \begin{bmatrix} \lambda_1 & 0 & 0 \\ 0 & \lambda_2 & 0 \\ 0 & 0 & \lambda_3 \end{bmatrix} \begin{bmatrix} \bar{x}_1 \\ \bar{x}_2 \\ \bar{x}_3 \end{bmatrix}, \tag{9.4}$$

where both $[a']$ and $[\lambda]$ are diagonal matrices. Once the transformation is completed, the eigenvalues and eigenvectors can readily be found. This will be discussed in the following three sections.

9.2 TRANSFORMATION OF COORDINATES

Before we discuss a step-by-step procedure of the Jacobi method, we will briefly review the basic concept of transformation of coordinates. For this purpose, we shall consider the column matrix $[x]$ in Eq. (9.3) as a column vector having two components x_1 and x_2, as shown in Fig. 9.1. If a new set of axes $\bar{x}_1$ and $\bar{x}_2$ with the same origin is introduced (Fig. 9.1), then the vector $\overline{OD}$ has two different components $\bar{x}_1$ and $\bar{x}_2$. By trigonometry, we have

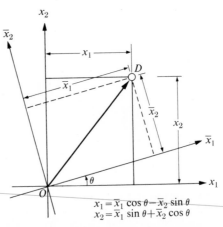

$$x_1 = \bar{x}_1 \cos \theta - \bar{x}_2 \sin \theta,$$
$$x_2 = \bar{x}_1 \sin \theta + \bar{x}_2 \cos \theta \qquad (9.5)$$

or, in matrix form,

$$\begin{bmatrix} x_1 \\ x_2 \end{bmatrix} = \begin{bmatrix} \cos \theta & -\sin \theta \\ \sin \theta & \cos \theta \end{bmatrix} \begin{bmatrix} \bar{x}_1 \\ \bar{x}_2 \end{bmatrix}. \qquad (9.6)$$

This is the transformation relation

$$[x] = [T][\bar{x}], \qquad (9.7)$$

Fig. 9.1. Transformation of coordinates.

which connects the two systems in x and $\bar{x}$.

The significance of matrix $[T]$ in Eq. (9.7) can be shown only after a general discussion on matrix operations in Eq. (9.3). Substituting Eq. (9.7) into Eq. (9.3), we have

$$[A][T][\bar{x}] = \lambda[T][\bar{x}], \qquad (9.8)$$

or

$$[T]'[A][T][\bar{x}] = \lambda[T]'[T][\bar{x}], \qquad (9.9)$$

where $[T]'$ is the transpose of $[T]$,

$$[T]'[A][T][\bar{x}] = \lambda[I][\bar{x}].$$
$$= [\lambda][\bar{x}] \qquad (9.10)$$

The relation $[T]'[T] = [I]$ can be verified by the following multiplication of the two matrices:

$$\begin{bmatrix} \cos \theta & \sin \theta \\ -\sin \theta & \cos \theta \end{bmatrix} \begin{bmatrix} \cos \theta & -\sin \theta \\ \sin \theta & \cos \theta \end{bmatrix} = \begin{bmatrix} 1 & 0 \\ 0 & 1 \end{bmatrix}.$$

We recall, from Section 9.1, that our basic aim is to alter the given $[A]$ so that all off-diagonal terms become zero. At this point, $[A]$ in Eq. (9.3) is already transformed to $[T]'[A][T]$, called $[B]$ for simplicity. We ask, Can this transformation possibly be used to eliminate one of the off-diagonal terms in $[A]$? The answer is affirmative provided that a proper angle of rotation θ is selected. To select θ properly, let us write out the matrix $[T]'[A][T]$, or $[B]$:

$$[B] = \begin{bmatrix} \cos\theta & \sin\theta \\ -\sin\theta & \cos\theta \end{bmatrix} \begin{bmatrix} a_{11} & a_{12} \\ a_{21} & a_{22} \end{bmatrix} \begin{bmatrix} \cos\theta & -\sin\theta \\ \sin\theta & \cos\theta \end{bmatrix}$$

$$= \begin{bmatrix} a_{11}\cos^2\theta + 2a_{12}\sin\theta\cos\theta + a_{22}\sin^2\theta \\ a_{12}(\cos^2\theta - \sin^2\theta) + \cos\theta\sin\theta(a_{22} - a_{11}) \end{bmatrix}$$

$$\begin{array}{r} a_{12}(\cos^2\theta - \sin^2\theta) + \sin\theta\cos\theta(a_{22} - a_{11}) \\ a_{11}\sin^2\theta - 2a_{12}\sin\theta\cos\theta + a_{22}\cos^2\theta \end{array} \Bigg].$$

$$(9.11)$$

We now wish to set the off-diagonal element b_{12} in Eq. (9.11) to zero. The necessary value is then found to be

$$a_{12}(\cos^2\theta - \sin^2\theta) + \cos\theta\sin\theta(a_{22} - a_{11}) = 0, \qquad (9.12)$$

or

$$\tan 2\theta = \frac{2a_{12}}{a_{11} - a_{22}}. \qquad (9.13)$$

For a symmetric $[A]$, both off-diagonal elements b_{12} and b_{21} in $[B]$ are reduced to zero by using the relation (9.13) and we find that

$$[B] = \begin{bmatrix} a_{11}\cos^2\theta + 2a_{12}\sin\theta\cos\theta + a_{22}\sin^2\theta & 0 \\ 0 & a_{11}\sin^2\theta - 2a_{12}\sin\theta\cos\theta + a_{22}\cos^2\theta \end{bmatrix}.$$

$$(9.14)$$

Hence the desired eigenvalues are the diagonal elements b_{11} and b_{22}, respectively.

Example 9.1

$$[A] = \begin{bmatrix} 4 & 1 \\ 1 & 2 \end{bmatrix}.$$

From Eq. (9.13) we have

$$\tan 2\theta = \frac{2(1)}{4 - 2} = 1, \qquad \theta = 22.5°$$

Since $[A]$ is symmetric, we can use Eq. (9.14), which establishes $[B]$ or $[T]'[A][T]$ as follows:

$$[B] = \begin{bmatrix} 4\cos^2\theta + 2\sin\theta\cos\theta + 2\sin^2\theta & 0 \\ 0 & 4\sin^2\theta - 2\sin\theta\cos\theta + 2\cos^2\theta \end{bmatrix}$$

$$= \begin{bmatrix} 4.414 & 0 \\ 0 & 1.5868 \end{bmatrix}.$$

From Eq. (9.10) we know that

$$[T]'[A][T] = [B] = [\lambda];$$

therefore, the eigenvalues are found to be

$$\lambda_1 = 4.414,$$
$$\lambda_2 = 1.586.$$

It is interesting to note that this example is closely related to the Mohr circle approach used in studying the strength of materials. Here, $\sigma_x = 4$, $\sigma_y = 2$, and $\tau_{xy} = \tau_{yx} = 1$ are the elements in $[A]$; the eigenvalues λ_1 and λ_2 are two principal stresses 4.414 and 1.586. The orientation of the principal axes is related to the eigenvectors to be considered in Section 9.4.

We shall now extend our discussion to the situation in which both $[A]$ and $[x]$ are of third order. Specifically, the column vector $[x]$ now has three components which are either x_1, x_2, and x_3 or $\bar{x}_1$, $\bar{x}_2$, and $\bar{x}_3$. As seen in Fig. 9.2, we have the following transformation relation for the three components in x and $\bar{x}$:

$$\begin{bmatrix} x_1 \\ x_2 \\ x_3 \end{bmatrix} = \begin{bmatrix} \cos\theta & -\sin\theta & 0 \\ \sin\theta & \cos\theta & 0 \\ 0 & 0 & 1 \end{bmatrix} \begin{bmatrix} \bar{x}_1 \\ \bar{x}_2 \\ \bar{x}_3 \end{bmatrix}, \quad (9.15)$$

or

$$[x] = [T][\bar{x}], \quad (9.7)$$

where $[T]$ is the transformation matrix, a square matrix.

Equation (9.10) can now be used to eliminate one of the off-diagonal elements. It should be emphasized that one such rotation is not sufficient to alter $[A]$ such that all off-diagonal terms become zero. In order to eliminate the remaining off-diagonal elements, a series of m plane rotations is necessary to transform $[A]$ successively to

$$[T_m]' \cdots [T_3]'[T_2]'[T_1]'[A][T_1][T_2][T_3] \cdots [T_m], \quad (9.16)$$

which converges to a diagonal matrix, the principal diagonal representing the eigenvalues λ. In other words, one off-diagonal element at a time is reduced to zero. The sole purpose for this reduction to zero and the many rotations of coordinates is to make *all* nondiagonal elements approach and eventually reach zero. The application of this concept will be discussed in the next section.

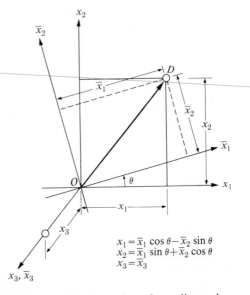

$$x_1 = \bar{x}_1 \cos\theta - \bar{x}_2 \sin\theta$$
$$x_2 = \bar{x}_1 \sin\theta + \bar{x}_2 \cos\theta$$
$$x_3 = \bar{x}_3$$

Fig. 9.2. Transformation of coordinates in a plane.

9.3 JACOBI'S METHOD FOR EIGENVALUES

We shall now consider the application of the concept of rotation of axes developed in Section 9.2. A practical procedure is to select the largest (in absolute value) off-diagonal element in [A]; the position of this element, which is to be eliminated, fixes the term $-\sin\theta$ in [T]. We develop [T] by placing the $(\sin\theta)$-term symmetrically opposite the term $-\sin\theta$, the $(\cos\theta)$-terms on the diagonal so as to form a square with the $(\sin\theta)$-terms, and finally by placing 1 on the remainder of the diagonal, and 0 elsewhere. For example, let us take

$$[A] = \begin{bmatrix} 2 & -1 & 0 \\ -1 & 2 & -1 \\ 0 & -1 & 2 \end{bmatrix}, \tag{9.17}$$

where a_{12} is selected as the largest off-diagonal element, since its absolute value is 1. We could have selected a_{23} as the largest off-diagonal element, since $|a_{23}| = |a_{12}|$; this would not affect the final answers. Following the above rule, $[T_1]$ will have the form

$$[T_1] = \begin{bmatrix} \cos\theta & -\sin\theta & 0 \\ \sin\theta & \cos\theta & 0 \\ 0 & 0 & 1 \end{bmatrix}. \tag{9.18}$$

Next we use Eq. (9.13) to determine θ and to evaluate the terms in Eq. (9.18). Thus

$$\tan 2\theta = \frac{-2}{2-2} = \frac{-2}{0}, \quad \text{or} \quad \theta = -45°;$$

and

$$[T_1] = \begin{bmatrix} \sqrt{2}/2 & \sqrt{2}/2 & 0 \\ -\sqrt{2}/2 & \sqrt{2}/2 & 0 \\ 0 & 0 & 1 \end{bmatrix}. \tag{9.19}$$

The matrix $[A_1] = [T_1]'[A][T_1]$ is thus determined. We repeat this procedure, assuming that $[A_1]$ is now the [A], and continue until a matrix $[A_m]$ is created such that all nondiagonal terms are zero. The diagonal terms of this $[A_m]$ will then be equal to the eigenvalues.

It can be seen from Table 9.1 that five successive rotations ($m = 5$) are performed. In each rotation first [A] is given and then the element to be eliminated from [A] is selected. Next, Eq. (9.13) is used to compute the angle of rotation θ, and [T] is written based on the rule mentioned above (see Eq. 9.19). A new [A] is then obtained from $[T]'[A][T]$.

The given [A] in Eq. (9.17) is symmetric and therefore only two off-diagonal elements need be eliminated. We note that $a_{13} = a_{31} = 0$, and hence no elimination is required. However, it takes five rotations, not two, to obtain the answers shown in Table 9.1, due to the fact that although any one rotation may set an off-diagonal element to zero, it does cause an element previously reduced to zero to attain a non-zero value. In other words, the number of rotations is by necessity greater than the number of off-diagonal nonzero terms. Fortunately, each rotation makes the

TABLE 9.1. Jacobi's Method for Eigenvalues

$[A_0]$ = given real symmetric matrix; $[A_m] = [T_m]'[A_{m-1}][T_m]$, $m = 1,2,3,4,5$

m	$[A_m]$			Element to be eliminated	$\tan 2\theta$	$\sin \theta$	$\cos \theta$	$[T_{m+1}]$		
0	2 −1 0	−1 2 −1	0 −1 2	(1,2)	−∞	−0.7071	0.7071	$\cos \theta$ $\sin \theta$ 0	$-\sin \theta$ $\cos \theta$ 0	0 0 1
1	3 0 0.7071	0 1 −0.7071	0.7071 −0.7071 2	(1,3)	1.4142	0.4597	0.8880	$\cos \theta$ 0 $\sin \theta$	0 1 0	$-\sin \theta$ 0 $\cos \theta$
2	3.3660 −0.3250 0	−0.3250 1 −0.6279	0 −0.6279 1.6339	(2,3)	1.9811	0.5241	0.8516	1 0 0	0 $\cos \theta$ $\sin \theta$	0 $-\sin \theta$ $\cos \theta$
3	3.3660 −0.1703 −0.2768	−0.1703 2.0204 0	−0.2768 0 0.6135	(1,3)	−0.2011	−0.0990	0.9950	$\cos \theta$ 0 $\sin \theta$	0 1 0	$-\sin \theta$ 0 $\cos \theta$
4	3.3935 −0.1695 0	−0.1695 2.0204 −0.0168	0 −0.0168 0.5859	(1,2)	−0.2469	−0.1207	0.9926	$\cos \theta$ $\sin \theta$ 0	$-\sin \theta$ $\cos \theta$ 0	0 0 1
5	3.4142 0 0.0020	0 1.9998 −0.0167	0.0020 −0.0167 0.5859							

maximum-valued off-diagonal element decrease in absolute value and $[A]$ generally converges to a diagonal matrix. Thus $[A]$ is diagonalized.

Before concluding this section, we shall examine Eq. (9.13), in which the angle of rotation θ is determined. If the components x_i and x_j are connected with $\bar{x}_i$ and $\bar{x}_j$, then Eq. (9.13) has the form

$$\tan 2\theta = \frac{2a_{ij}}{a_{ii} - a_{jj}}. \tag{9.20}$$

We recall from trigonometry that

$$\tan 2\theta = \frac{2 \tan \theta}{1 - \tan^2 \theta} = \frac{2a_{ij}}{a_{ii} - a_{jj}}$$

or

$$2a_{ij} \tan^2 \theta + 2(a_{ii} - a_{jj}) \tan \theta - 2a_{ij} = 0.$$

Solving, we have

$$\tan \theta = \frac{-(a_{ii} - a_{jj}) \pm \sqrt{(a_{ii} - a_{jj})^2 + 4a^2_{ij}}}{2a_{ij}}. \tag{9.21}$$

Multiplying both the denominator and the numerator of the right-hand side of Eq. (9.21) by

$$-(a_{ii} - a_{jj}) \mp \sqrt{(a_{ii} - a_{jj})^2 + 4a^2_{ij}},$$

we obtain

$$\tan \theta = \frac{2a_{ij}}{(a_{ii} - a_{jj}) \pm \sqrt{(a_{ii} - a_{jj})^2 + 4a_{ij}^2}}, \qquad (9.22)$$

or

$$\tan \theta = \frac{2a_{ij}}{|a_{ii} - a_{jj}| \pm \sqrt{(a_{ii} - a_{jj})^2 + 4a_{ij}^2}}, \qquad (9.23a)$$

if $a_{ii} \geq a_{jj}$; and

$$\tan \theta = \frac{-2a_{ij}}{|a_{ii} - a_{jj}| \pm \sqrt{(a_{ii} - a_{jj})^2 + 4a_{ij}^2}}, \qquad (9.23b)$$

if $a_{ii} < a_{jj}$. If we arbitrarily choose the plus sign in the denominators of both Eqs. (9.23a) and (9.23b), we have

$$\tan \theta = \frac{\pm 2a_{ij}}{|a_{ii} - a_{jj}| + \sqrt{(a_{ii} - a_{jj})^2 + 4a_{ij}^2}}, \qquad (9.24)$$

where the plus sign is used if $a_{ii} \geq a_{jj}$, the minus sign is used if $a_{ii} < a_{jj}$, and $\pi/2 \geq \theta \geq -\pi/2$. We also note that

$$\cos \theta = (1 + \tan^2 \theta)^{-1/2} \qquad (9.25)$$

and

$$\sin \theta = \cos \theta \tan \theta. \qquad (9.26)$$

Equations (9.24) through (9.26), rather than Eq. (9.13), will be used in discussing machine computation of the rotation of angles in Section 9.5.

9.4 EIGENVECTORS

Following our discussion on obtaining eigenvalues by Jacobi's method, we now turn to the numerical solution of eigenvectors. Eigenvectors are column matrices $[x]$ of the given matrix $[A]$, which are associated with the eigenvalue λ. Since there are n eigenvalues, $\lambda_1, \lambda_2, \ldots, \lambda_n$, the corresponding n column matrices for $[x]$ may be assembled together in a square matrix $[V]$. Let $[\lambda]$, a diagonal matrix, represent the known values of the eigenvalues. From Eq. (9.3), we have

$$[A][V] = [V][\lambda]. \qquad (9.27)$$

Premultiplying both sides by $[V]^{-1}$, the inverse of $[V]$, we obtain

$$[V]^{-1}[A][V] = [V]^{-1}[V][\lambda], \qquad (9.28)$$

and since $[V]^{-1}[V] = [I]$, the unit matrix, Eq. (9.28) becomes

$$[V]^{-1}[A][V] = [\lambda]. \qquad (9.29)$$

Comparing Eq. (9.29) with Eqs. (9.10) and (9.16), we see that $[V]$, a square matrix representing eigenvectors, is equal to the successive multiplication of the matrices $[T]$ used in obtaining the eigenvalues. Thus we have

$$[V] = [T_1][T_2] \cdots [T_m].$$

As a first example, let us consider the following symmetric matrix of second order from Example 9.1:

$$[A] = \begin{bmatrix} 4 & 1 \\ 1 & 2 \end{bmatrix}.$$

Since only one rotation is needed to diagonalize the matrix (see Example 9.1), $[V]$ is therefore equal to $[T]$, or

$$[V] = \begin{bmatrix} \cos\theta & -\sin\theta \\ \sin\theta & \cos\theta \end{bmatrix},$$

where $\theta = 22.5°$, as obtained in Example 9.1. Hence

$$[V] = \begin{bmatrix} 0.9238 & -0.3826 \\ 0.3826 & 0.9238 \end{bmatrix}.$$

As a second numerical example, the $[V]$ for the given $[A_0]$ in Table 9.1 is simply a succession of multiplications,

$$[V] = [T_1][T_2][T_3][T_4][T_5],$$

where $[T_1]$, $[T_2]$, ... are given in Table 9.1. Thus we have

$$[V] = \begin{bmatrix} 0.5 & 0.707 & 0.5 \\ -0.707 & 0 & 0.707 \\ 0.5 & -0.707 & 0.5 \end{bmatrix}.$$

We note that the first column, or the first *modal column*, corresponds to the first eigenvalue 3.4142. Similarly, the second and third modal columns correspond to the eigenvalues 1.9998 and 0.5859, respectively. These three eigenvalues are shown in Table 9.1 ($m = 5$).

9.5 MACHINE COMPUTATION

Following our discussion on Jacobi's method for obtaining eigenvalues and eigenvectors, we now examine the details for the development of a computer program. A subroutine JACOBI corresponding with the procedures described in the previous sections is written in FORTRAN II. In particular, Eqs. (9.24) through (9.26) are used to calculate the various trigonometric functions. The calculation stops when the following condition is met: the off-diagonal elements a_{ij} are smaller than a preassigned value $\epsilon = 10^{-8}$.

```
C       SUBPROGRAM FOR DIAGONALIZATION OF MATRIX Q BY SUCCESSIVE ROTATIONS
        SUBROUTINE JACOBI (N,Q,JVEC,M,V)
        DIMENSION Q(12,12), V(12,12), X(12), IH(12)
C
C       NEXT 8 STATEMENTS FOR SETTING INITIAL VALUES OF MATRIX V
C
        IF(JVEC) 10,15,10
    10  DO 14 I=1,N
        DO 14 J=1,N
        IF(I-J) 12,11,12
    11  V(I,J)=1.0
        GO TO 14
    12  V(I,J)=0.
    14  CONTINUE
C
    15  M=0
C
C       NEXT 8 STATEMENTS SCAN FOR LARGEST OFF DIAG. ELEM. IN EACH ROW
C       X(I) CONTAINS LARGEST ELEMENT IN ITH ROW
C       IH(I) HOLDS SECOND SUBSCRIPT DEFINING POSITION OF ELEMENT
C
    17  MI=N-1
        DO 30 I=1,MI
        X(I) = 0.
        MJ=I+1
        DO 30 J=MJ,N
        IF (X(I)-ABSF(Q(I,J))) 20,20,30
    20  X(I)=ABSF(Q(I,J))
        IH(I)=J
    30  CONTINUE
C
C       NEXT 7 STATEMENTS FIND FOR MAXIMUM OF X(I)S FOR PIVOT ELEMENT
C
    40  DO 70 I=1,MI
        IF (I-1) 60,60,45
    45  IF (XMAX-X(I)) 60,70,70
    60  XMAX=X(I)
        IP=I
        JP=IH(I)
    70  CONTINUE
C
C       NEXT TWO STATEMENTS TEST FOR XMAX. IF LESS THAN 10**-8,GO TO 1000
C
        EPSI=1.E-8
        IF (XMAX-EPSI) 1000,1000,148
C
   148  M=M+1
C
C       NEXT 11 STATEMENTS FOR COMPUTING TANG,SIN,COS,Q(I,I),Q(J,J)
C
        IF (Q(IP,IP)-Q(JP,JP)) 150,151,151
   150  TANG=-2.*Q(IP,JP)/(ABSF(Q(IP,IP)-Q(JP,JP))+SQRTF((Q(IP,IP)-Q(JP,JP
       1))**2+4.*Q(IP,JP)**2))
        GO TO 160
   151  TANG=+2.*Q(IP,JP)/(ABSF(Q(IP,IP)-Q(JP,JP))+SQRTF((Q(IP,IP)-Q(JP,JP
       1))**2+4.*Q(IP,JP)**2))
   160  COSN=1.0/SQRTF(1.0+TANG**2)
        SINE=TANG*COSN
        QII=Q(IP,IP)
        Q(IP,IP)=COSN**2*(QII+TANG*(2.*Q(IP,JP)+TANG*Q(JP,JP)))
```

Fig. 9.3. Subroutine JACOBI for diagonalization. (*Cont.*)

```
      Q(JP,JP)=COSN**2*(Q(JP,JP)-TANG*(2.*Q(IP,JP)-TANG*QII))
C
      Q(IP,JP)=0.
C
C     NEXT 4 STATEMENTS FOR PSEUDO RANK THE EIGENVALUES
C
      IF (Q(IP,IP)-Q(JP,JP)) 152,153,153
  152 TEMP=Q(IP,IP)
      Q(IP,IP)=Q(JP,JP)
      Q(JP,JP)=TEMP
C
C     NEXT 6 STATEMENTS ADJUST SIN,COS FOR COMPUTATION OF Q(I,K),V(I,K)
C
      IF (SINE) 154,155,155
  154 TEMP=+COSN
      GO TO 170
  155 TEMP=-COSN
  170 COSN=ABSF(SINE)
      SINE=TEMP
C
C     NEXT 10 STATEMENTS FOR INSPECTING T8E IHS BETWEEN I+1 AND N-1 TO
C     DETERMINE WHETHER A NEW MAXIMUM VALUE SHOULD BE COMPUTED SINCE
C     THE PRESENT MAXIMUM IS IN THE I OR J ROW
C
  153 DO 350 I=1,MI
      IF (I-IP) 210,350,200
  200 IF (I-JP) 210,350,210
  210 IF (IH(I)-IP) 230,240,230
  230 IF (IH(I)-JP) 350,240,350
  240 K=IH(I)
  250 TEMP=Q(I,K)
      Q(I,K)=0.
      MJ=I+1
      X(I)=0.
C
C     NEXT 5 STATEMENTS SEARCH IN DEPLETED ROW FOR NEW MAXIMUM
C
      DO 320 J=MJ,N
      IF (X(I)-ABSF(Q(I,J))) 300,300,320
  300 X(I)=ABSF(Q(I,J))
      IH(I)=J
  320 CONTINUE
      Q(I,K)=TEMP
  350 CONTINUE
C
      X(IP)=0.
      X(JP)=0.
C
C     NEXT 30 STATEMENTS FOR CHANGING THE OTHER ELEMENTS OF Q
C
      DO 530 I=1,N
C
      IF (I-IP) 370,530,420
  370 TEMP=Q(I,IP)
      Q(I,IP)=COSN*TEMP+SINE*Q(I,JP)
      IF (X(I)-ABSF(Q(I,IP))) 380,390,390
  380 X(I)=ABSF(Q(I,IP))
      IH(I)=IP
  390 Q(I,JP)=-SINE*TEMP+COSN*Q(I,JP)
      IF (X(I)-ABSF(Q(I,JP))) 400,530,530
```

Fig. 9.3 (*cont.*)

```
400 X(I)=ABSF(Q(I,JP))
    IH(I)=JP
    GO TO 530
C
420 IF (I-JP) 430,530,480
430 TEMP=Q(IP,I)
    Q(IP,I)=COSN*TEMP+SINE*Q(I,JP)
    IF (X(IP)-ABSF(Q(IP,I))) 440,450,450
440 X(IP)=ABSF(Q(IP,I))
    IH(IP)=I
450 Q(I,JP)=-SINE*TEMP+COSN*Q(I,JP)
    IF (X(I)-ABSF(Q(I,JP))) 400,530,530
C
480 TEMP=Q(IP,I)
    Q(IP,I)=COSN*TEMP+SINE*Q(JP,I)
    IF (X(IP)-ABSF(Q(IP,I))) 490,500,500
490 X(IP)=ABSF(Q(IP,I))
    IH(IP)=I
500 Q(JP,I)=-SINE*TEMP+COSN*Q(JP,I)
    IF (X(JP)-ABSF(Q(JP,I))) 510,530,530
510 X(JP)=ABSF(Q(JP,I))
    IH(JP)=I
530 CONTINUE
C
C    NEXT 6 STATEMENTS TEST FOR COMPUTATION OF EIGENVECTORS
C
    IF (JVEC) 540,40,540
540 DO 550 I=1,N
    TEMP=V(I,IP)
    V(I,IP)=COSN*TEMP+SINE*V(I,JP)
550 V(I,JP)=-SINE*TEMP+COSN*V(I,JP)
    GO TO 40
1000 RETURN
    END
```

Fig. 9.3 (*concl.*)

The arguments used in the subroutine JACOBI are defined as follows:

N = order of the given real symmetric matrix [Q], N $\geq$ 2,

Q = the matrix [Q] to be diagonalized (This input matrix is later destroyed),

JVEC = a fixed point index,

      JVEC = 0 when eigenvalues alone are to be found,

      JVEC = $\pm 1, \pm 2, \ldots$ and up when eigenvalues and eigenvectors are to be found,

M = the number of rotations performed,

V = storage for eigenvectors. This storage is required even for the case JVEC = 0.

A program and a flow chart for the subprogram JACOBI are shown in Figs. 9.3 and 9.4, respectively.

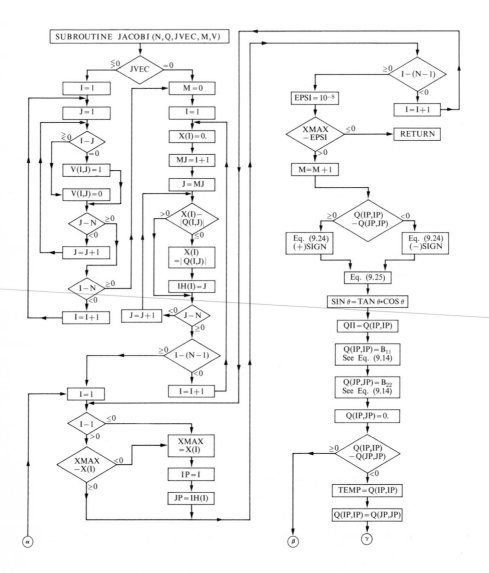

Fig. 9.4.   Flow chart of subroutine JACOBI.

Example 9.2

Write a main program to call the subroutine JACOBI and to satisfy the input and output requirements. The primary objective of this example is to find the eigenvalues and eigenvectors of the real symmetric matrix $[A]$ shown in Eq. (9.17). The first data card is for N, with format I2, where N is the order of the given $[A]$. Following the first data cards, there will be the data cards for the elements a_{ij}. They are punched row by row on cards for all elements in the upper triangular matrix.

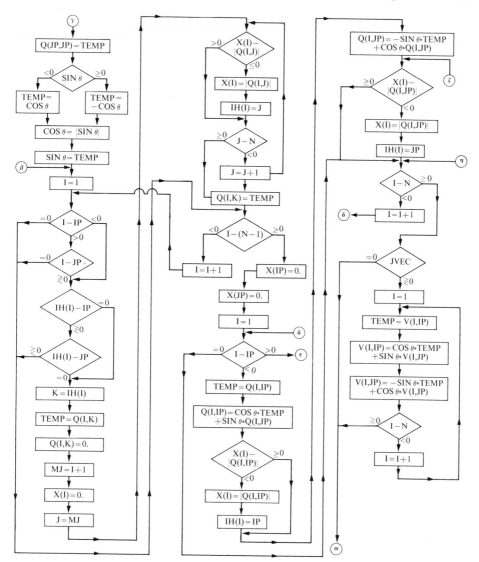

Fig. 9.4 *(cont.)*

An echo print of [A] is required before transferring the operation to the subroutine JACOBI. The required output is shown in Table 9.2, where the eigenvalue is printed first, followed by its associated eigenvectors. It is important that the size of each matrix in the main program agree with that in the subroutine. Figure 9.5 shows a possible main program. In the DIMENSION statement, both A and X are arbitrarily dimensioned as 12×12. Both the corresponding matrices Q and V in subroutine JACOBI must also be dimensioned as 12×12.

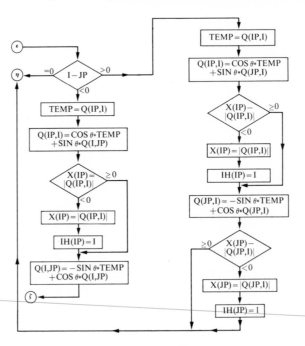

Fig. 9.4 (*concl.*)

TABLE 9.2.   Answers for Example 9.2

MATRIX A

2.00000	-1.00000	0.00000
-1.00000	2.00000	-1.00000
0.00000	-1.00000	2.00000

THE NUMBER OF ROTATION =   9

EIGENVALUE (1) =   3.41421

EIGENVECTORS
         .50000   -.70710   .50000

EIGENVALUE (2) =   2.00000

EIGENVECTORS
         .70710   0.00000   -.70710

EIGENVALUE (3) =   .58578

EIGENVECTORS
         .50000   .70710   .50000

```
C         THIS IS MAIN PROGRAM FOR EIGENVALUE PROBLEM IN THE FORM OF
C               AX = LX
C         A IS SYMMETRICAL MATRIX
C         L ARE EIGENVALUES, X ARE EIGENVECTORS
C
          DIMENSION A(12,12),X(12,12)
          READ 10,N
 10 FORMAT(I2)
          DO 11 I=1,N
 11 READ 20, (A(I,J),J=I,N)
 20 FORMAT(6F10.5)
          PUNCH 30
 30 FORMAT(9H MATRIX A/)
          DO 32 I=1,N
          DO 31 J=1,N
 31 A(J,I)=A(I,J)
 32 PUNCH 40, (A(I,J), J=1,N)
 40 FORMAT(5F15.5)
          CALL JACOBI(N,A,1,NR,X)
          PUNCH 80,NR
 80 FORMAT(//25H THE NUMBER OF ROTATION =,I3//)
          DO 46 J =1,N
 44 PUNCH 50, J,A(J,J)
 46 PUNCH 60, (X(I,J), I=1,N)
 50 FORMAT(/13H EIGENVALUE (,I2,4H ) =,F15.5)
 60 FORMAT(/13H EIGENVECTORS/5F15.5)
          STOP
          END
03
2.          -1.          0.
2.          -1.
2.
```

Fig. 9.5.   Main program $AX = LX$.

9.6   GENERAL EIGENVALUE PROBLEMS

In the previous sections we discussed the eigenvalue problem which can be expressed as

$$[A][x] = \lambda[B][x], \qquad (9.30)$$

where $[B]$ is a unit matrix. In this section we shall focus our attention on two cases: first, $[B]$ as a diagonal matrix and, second and this is the more general case, $[B]$ as a symmetric matrix.

Let us consider the case where $[B]$ is a diagonal matrix. We assume that

$$[B] = [G]'[G], \qquad (9.31)$$

where $[G]$ is also a diagonal matrix. We have

$$[B] = [G][G]; \qquad (9.32)$$

hence each element g_{ii} in $[G]$ is equal to the square root of the corresponding element b_{ii} in $[B]$, and this element is required to be positive:

$$g_{ii} = \sqrt{b_{ii}}.$$

Substituting Eq. (9.32) into

$$[A][x] = \lambda[B][x], \tag{9.33}$$

we obtain

$$[A][x] = \lambda[G][G][x]. \tag{9.34}$$

Premultiplying Eq. (9.34) by $[G]^{-1}$, we have

$$[G]^{-1}[A][x] = \lambda[G][x], \tag{9.35}$$

or

$$[G]^{-1}[A][G]^{-1}[G][x] = \lambda[G][x]. \tag{9.36}$$

If we define

$$[Y] = [G][x] \quad \text{and} \quad [Q] = [G]^{-1}[A][G]^{-1},$$

then Eq. (9.36) becomes

$$[Q][Y] = \lambda[Y]. \tag{9.37}$$

The above equation has precisely the same form as Eq. (9.3). Thus, the eigenvalues, obtained from diagonalization of $[Q]$, are the true eigenvalues. On the other hand, the true eigenvectors are obtained only after postmultiplying $[G]^{-1}$ by the resulting eigenvectors; that is,

$$[\text{true eigenvectors}] = [G]^{-1}[\text{resulting vectors}].$$

Each diagonal element in the diagonal matrix $[G]^{-1}$ is equal to the reciprocal of the square root of each diagonal element of $[G]$.

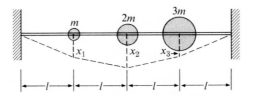

Fig. 9.6.   The three-mass system.

Example 9.3

We know from the study of the free vibrations of a system consisting of three masses (Fig. 9.6), that the equations of motion lead to the following eigenvalue formulation:

$$\begin{bmatrix} 2k - m\omega^2 & -k & 0 \\ -k & 2k - 2m\omega^2 & -k \\ 0 & -k & 2k - 3m\omega^2 \end{bmatrix} \begin{bmatrix} x_1 \\ x_2 \\ x_3 \end{bmatrix} = [0], \tag{9.38}$$

where

$$\omega = \text{frequency},$$
$$[x] = \text{displacement vector},$$
$$k = s/l,$$
$$s = \text{tension in string},$$
$$4l = \text{length of string}.$$

TABLE 9.3. Answers for Example 9.3

MATRIX A

2.00000	-1.00000	0.00000
-1.00000	2.00000	-1.00000
0.00000	-1.00000	2.00000

MATRIX B

1.00000	0.00000	0.00000
0.00000	2.00000	0.00000
0.00000	0.00000	3.00000

THE NUMBER OF ROTATION = 8

EIGENVALUE (1) =   2.38742

EIGENVECTORS
        .87134   -.33758   .06539

EIGENVALUE (2) =   1.00000

EIGENVECTORS
        .40824   .40824   -.40824

EIGENVALUE (3) =   .27924

EIGENVECTORS
        .27218   .46837   .40297

Letting $\lambda = mw^2/k$, we find that Eq. (9.38) becomes

$$\begin{bmatrix} 2 & -1 & 0 \\ -1 & 2 & -1 \\ 0 & -1 & 2 \end{bmatrix}\begin{bmatrix} x_1 \\ x_2 \\ x_3 \end{bmatrix} = \lambda \begin{bmatrix} 1 & 0 & 0 \\ 0 & 2 & 0 \\ 0 & 0 & 3 \end{bmatrix}\begin{bmatrix} x_1 \\ x_2 \\ x_3 \end{bmatrix},$$

or

$$[A][X] = \lambda[B][X], \tag{9.39}$$

which has precisely the same form as Eq. (9.33).

We wish to write a main program which will compute three λ's and associated model shapes (eigenvectors). The first data card is for N, the order of the given $[A]$. The data for elements A_{ij} are then read in row by row for all elements in the upper triangular matrix. Finally, the diagonal elements of $[B]$ are read in one per card.

An echo print of $[A]$ and $[B]$ is required. In the output, shown in Table 9.3, the rotation number is punched before each eigenvalue and its associated eigenvectors are punched. A possible main program is shown in Fig. 9.7. The program requires two subroutines: JACOBI and MATMPY. The subroutine MATMPY, which was discussed in Section 8.2, is used to multiply two given matrices.

```
C         THIS IS MAIN PROGRAM FOR EIGENVALUE PROBLEM IN THE FORM OF
C                   AX = LBX
C         A IS SYMMETRIC MATRIX
C         B IS DIAGONAL MATRIX
C         L ARE EIGENVALUES, X ARE EIGENVECTORS
C
          DIMENSION A(12,12), B(12,12),C(12,12),AA(12,12),X(12,12),XX(12,12)
          READ 10, N
   10 FORMAT(I2)
          DO 11 I=1,N
C         READ IN LOWER TRIANGULAR MATRIX
   11 READ 20, (A(I,J), J=I,N)
   20 FORMAT(7F10.5)
          DO 12 I = 1,N
          DO 12 J = 1,N
   12 B(I,J) = 0.
          DO 14 I=1,N
   14 READ 18, B(I,I)
   18 FORMAT(F10.5)
          PUNCH 30
   30 FORMAT(9H MATRIX A/)
          DO 32 I=1,N
          DO 32 J=1,N
          A(J,I)=A(I,J)
   32 PUNCH 40, (A(I,K), K=1,N)
   40 FORMAT(5F15.5)
          PUNCH 70
   70 FORMAT(//9H MATRIX B//)
          DO 75 I=1,N
   75 PUNCH 40, (B(I,J), J=1,N)
          DO 85 I=1,N
   85 B(I,I)=1./SQRTF(B(I,I))
          CALL MATMPY(B,N,N,A,N,C)
          CALL MATMPY(C,N,N,B,N,AA)
          CALL JACOBI(N,AA,1,NR,XX)
          CALL MATMPY(B,N,N,XX,N,X)
          PUNCH 80, NR
   80 FORMAT(//25H THE NUMBER OF ROTATION =,I3//)
          DO 46 J=1,N
   44 PUNCH 50, J,AA(J,J)
   46 PUNCH 60, (X(I,J), I=1,N)
   50 FORMAT(/13H EIGENVALUE (,I2,4H ) =,F15.5)
   60 FORMAT(/13H EIGENVECTORS/5F15.5)
          STOP
          END
03
2.        -1.        0.
2.        -1.
2.
1.
2.
3.
```

Fig. 9.7. Main program for Example 9.3.

We now turn to the general eigenvalue problem

$$[A][x] = \lambda[B][x], \tag{9.40}$$

where $[A]$ is real and symmetric, $[x]$ is a column matrix, λ is a scalar, and $[B]$ is real, symmetric, and positive definite.

At this point it is necessary to explain what is meant by *positive definite*. If we let $[B]$ be a real symmetric matrix, and $[x]$ be a real column matrix, then $[x]'[B][x]$ is a quadratic in n variables $x_1, x_2, \ldots, x_n$; that is,

$$\begin{aligned}
[x]'[B][x] = {}& b_{11}x_1^2 + 2b_{12}x_1x_2 + 2b_{13}x_1x_3 + \cdots + 2b_{1n}x_1x_n \\
&+ b_{22}x_2^2 + 2b_{23}x_2x_3 + \cdots + 2b_{2n}x_2x_n \\
&+ b_{33}x_3^2 + \cdots + 2b_{3n}x_3x_n + \cdots + b_{nn}x_n^2.
\end{aligned} \tag{9.41}$$

The quadratic form $[x]'[B][x]$ is called positive definite if its values are always positive for $x_i \neq 0$ ($i = 1, 2, \ldots, n$). Its value is zero for $x_i = 0$ ($i = 1, 2, \ldots, n$). Also, if $[x]'[B][x]$ is positive definite, then the real symmetric matrix $[B]$ is said to be *positive definite*.

To find the eigenvalues and eigenvectors in Eq. (9.40), we use a procedure similar to that described previously in this section, but with one difference: $[G]$ cannot be calculated directly from $[B]$. However, $[B]$ can be diagonalized beforehand so that

$$[B] = [V][D][V]', \qquad \text{\textit{Eigenvector}} \tag{9.42}$$

where $[D]$ is a diagonal matrix and $[V]$ is a square matrix representing the eigenvectors (see Eqs. 9.27 and 9.29). Substituting Eq. (9.42) into (9.40), we obtain

$$[A][x] = \lambda[V][D][V]'[x]. \tag{9.43}$$

Premultiplying both sides by $[V]'$, we get

$$[V]'[A][x] = \lambda[D][V]'[x], \tag{9.44}$$

or

$$[V]'[A][V][V]'[x] = \lambda[D][V]'[x]. \tag{9.45}$$

If we define $[H] = [V]'[A][V]$ and $[Y] = [V]'[x]$, then Eq. (9.45) takes the form

$$[H][Y] = \lambda[D][Y]. \tag{9.46}$$

So long as $[D]$ is positive definite, Eq. (9.46) can be solved readily by the method discussed in the first part of this section. In other words, we take

$$[D] = [G][G] \tag{9.47}$$

such that

$$[H][Y] = \lambda[G][G][Y] \tag{9.48}$$

or

$$[G]^{-1}[H][G]^{-1}[G][Y] = \lambda[G][Y]. \tag{9.49}$$

```
C    MAIN PROGRAM FOR GENERAL EIGENVALUE PROBLEM AX=LBX
C    A AND B ARE SYMMETRIC MATRICES. B + DEFINITE
C    L=EIGENVALUES    X=EIGENVEVTORS
     DIMENSION A(3,3),B(3,3),T(3,3),TP(3,3),S(3,3),X(3,3),BAB(3,3),
    1W(3,3),AA(3,3),AB(3,3),XX(3,3)
     READ 10, N
  10 FORMAT(I2)
     DO 11 I=1,N
  11 READ 20, (A(I,J), J=I,N)
  20 FORMAT(6F10.5)
     DO 12 I=1,N
  12 READ 20, (B(I,J), J=I,N)
     PUNCH 30
  30 FORMAT(9H MATRIX A/)
     DO 32 I=1,N
     DO 32 J=1,N
     A(J,I)=A(I,J)
  32 B(J,I)=B(I,J)
     DO 35 I=1,N
  35 PUNCH 20, (A(I,J), J=1,N)
     PUNCH 70
  70 FORMAT(//9H MATRIX B/)
     DO 75 I=1,N
  75 PUNCH 20, (B(I,J), J=1,N)
     CALL JACOBI(N,B,1,NR,T)
     PUNCH 25
  25 FORMAT(//22H DIAGONALIZED MATRIX B/)
     DO 24 I=1,N
     DO 24 J=1,N
  24 B(J,I)=B(I,J)
     DO 26 I=1,N
  26 PUNCH 20, (B(I,J), J=1,N)
     PUNCH 27
  27 FORMAT(//25H EIGENVECTORS OF MATRIX B/)
     DO 28 I=1,N
  28 PUNCH 20, (T(I,J), J=1,N)
     DO 76 I=1,N
     DO 76 J=1,N
  76 TP(I,J)=T(J,I)
     CALL MATMPY(TP,N,N,A,N,W)
     CALL MATMPY(W,N,N,T,N,AA)
     DO 85 I=1,N
     IF (B(I,I)) 84,85,85
  84 PUNCH 83
  83 FORMAT(//34H MATRIX B IS NOT POSITIVE DEFINITE)
     GO TO 100
  85 B(I,I)=1./SQRTF(B(I,I))
     CALL MATMPY(B,N,N,AA,N,AB)
     CALL MATMPY(AB,N,N,B,N,BAB)
     CALL JACOBI(N,BAB,1,NR,XX)
     CALL MATMPY(T,N,N,B,N,S)
     CALL MATMPY(S,N,N,XX,N,X)
     PUNCH 80, NR
  80 FORMAT(//25H THE NUMBER OF ROTATION =, I3//)
     DO 46 J=1,N
  44 PUNCH 50, J,BAB(J,J)
  46 PUNCH 60, (X(I,J), I=1,N)
  50 FORMAT(/13H EIGENVALUE (, I2, 4H ) =, F15.5)
  60 FORMAT(/13H EIGENVECTORS/5F15.5)
 100 STOP
     END
```

Fig. 9.8. Main program for $Ax = LBx$ when A and B are symmetric.

TABLE 9.4.   Output for $Ax = LBx$

MATRIX A

1.00000	1.00000	.50000
1.00000	1.00000	.25000
.50000	.25000	2.00000

MATRIX B

2.00000	2.00000	2.00000
2.00000	5.00000	5.00000
2.00000	5.00000	11.00000

DIAGONALIZED MATRIX B

14.43089	0.00000	0.00000
0.00000	2.61519	0.00000
0.00000	0.00000	.95390

EIGENVECTORS OF MATRIX B

.21493	-.50489	.83599
.49265	-.68305	-.53919
.84326	.52774	.10192

THE NUMBER OF ROTATION = 7

EIGENVALUE (1) =   .61064

EIGENVECTORS
  .52639   .28178   -.24794

EIGENVALUE (2) =   .31504

EIGENVECTORS
  .51459   -.40261   .31839

EIGENVALUE (3) =   -.00902

EIGENVECTORS
  .53984   -.50842   -.06174

We now let

$$[G]^{-1}[H][G]^{-1} = [Q] \tag{9.50}$$

and

$$[G][Y] = [Z], \tag{9.51}$$

and we have the final form

$$[Q][Z] = \lambda[Z], \tag{9.52}$$

which has the precise form of Eq. (9.3).

The eigenvalues obtained from the diagonalization of $[Q]$ are the true eigenvalues. The true eigenvectors can be obtained by using the relation

$$[x] = \cancel{[V][G][Z]}. \quad [V][G]^{-1}[Z] \tag{9.53}$$

Example 9.4

Write a main program to call the subroutines JACOBI (Fig. 9.2) and MATMPY (see Section 8.2) to compute the eigenvalues and eigenvectors in the equation

$$[A][x] = \lambda[B][x],$$

where

$$A = \begin{bmatrix} 1 & 1 & 0.5 \\ 0 & 1 & 0.25 \\ 0.5 & 0.25 & 2 \end{bmatrix} \quad \text{and} \quad B = \begin{bmatrix} 2 & 2 & 2 \\ 2 & 5 & 5 \\ 2 & 5 & 11 \end{bmatrix}.$$

A sample main program is shown in Fig. 9.8, where the first data card is for N, the order of both the given $[A]$ and $[B]$. Elements a_{ij} and b_{ij} are then punched row by row on input cards for all elements in the upper triangular positions. They are echo-printed as shown in Table 9.4.

BIBLIOGRAPHY

Eigenvalue Problems

GOLDSTINE, H. H., and L. P. HORWITZ, "A Procedure for the Diagonalization of Normal Matrices," *J. Assoc. Comput. Mach.*, **6**, pp. 176–195 (1959).

HOUSEHOLDER, A. S., and F. L. BAUER, "On Certain Methods for Expanding the Characteristic Polynomial," *Numer. Math.*, **1**, pp. 29–37 (1959).

OSTROWSKI, A. M., "On the Convergence of the Rayleigh Quotient Iteration for the Computation of the Characteristic Roots and Vectors," *I–VI, Arch. Rational Mech. Ann.*, **1**, pp. 233–241 (1958); **2**, pp. 423–428 (1959); **3**, pp. 325–340, 341–367, 472–481 (1959); **4**, pp. 153–165 (1960).

PARODI, M., *La localisation des valeurs caractéristiques des matrices et ses applications.* Gauthier-Villars, Paris, 1959.

RUTISHAUSER, H., "Solution of Eigenvalue Problems with the LR-Transformation," *Nat. Bur. Std. (U.S.), Appl. Math. Ser.*, **49**, pp. 47–81 (1958).

WHITE, P. A., "The Computation of Eigenvalues and Eigenvectors of a Matrix," *J. Soc. Ind. Appl. Math.*, **6**, pp. 393–437 (1958).

WILKINSON, J. H., "Householder's Method for the Solution of the Algebraic Eigenproblem," *Comput. J.*, **3**, pp. 23–27 (1960).

WILKINSON, J. H., "The Calculation of Eigenvectors by the Method of Lanczos," *Comput. J.*, **1**, pp. 148–152 (1958).

WILKINSON, J. H., "The Calculation of the Eigenvectors of Codiagonal Matrices," *Comput. J.*, **1**, pp. 90–96 (1958).

WILKINSON, J. H., "The Calculations of the Latent Roots and Vectors of Matrices on the Pilot Model of the A. C. E.," *Proc. Cambridge Phil. Soc.*, **50**, pp. 536–566 (1956).

WILKINSON, J. H., "The Use of Iterative Methods for Finding the Latent Roots and Vectors of Matrices," *Math. Tables Aids Comput.*, **9**, pp. 184–191 (1955).

The Symmetric Matrices

CAUSEY, R. L., and P. HENRICI, "Convergence of Approximate Eigenvectors in Jacobi Methods," *Numer. Math.*, **2**, pp. 67–78 (1960).

GREGORY, R. T., "Computing Eigenvalues and Eigenvectors of a Symmetric Matrix on the ILLIAC," *Math. Tables Aids Comput.*, **7**, pp. 215–220 (1953).

GIVENS, W., "A Method of Computing Eigenvalues and Eigenvectors Suggested by Classical Results on Symmetric Matrices," *Nat. Bur. Std. (U.S.), Appl. Math. Ser.*, **29**, pp. 117–122.

GIVENS, W., "Numerical Computation of the Characteristic Values of a Real Symmetric Matrix," *ORNL*-1574, Oak Ridge National Laboratory (1954).

GOLDSTINE, H. H., F. J. MURRAY, and J. VON NEUMANN, "The Jacobi Method for Real Symmetric Matrices," *J. Assoc. Comput. Mach.*, **6**, pp. 59–96 (1959).

HENRICI, P., "On the Speed of Convergence of Cyclic and Quasicyclic Jacobi Methods for Computing Eigenvalues of Hermitian Matrices," *J. Soc. Ind. Appl. Math.*, **6**, pp. 144–162 (1958).

KUO, S. S., "A Note on Jacobi's Method for Real Symmetric Matrices," *J. Aerospace Sci.*, **28**, No. 3 (1961).

POPE, D. A., and C. B. TOMPKINS, "Maximizing Functions of Rotations. Experiments Concerning the Speed of Diagonalization of Symmetric Matrices Using Jacobi's Method," *J. Assoc. Comput. Mach.*, **4**, pp. 459–466 (1957).

PROBLEMS

1. Find the eigenvalues and eigenvectors of the system

$$x_1 + x_2 + x_3 - \lambda x_1 = 0,$$
$$x_1 + 2x_2 + 2x_3 - \lambda x_2 = 0,$$
$$x_1 + 2x_2 + 3x_3 - \lambda x_3 = 0.$$

2. Find the principal moments of inertia and principal axes of rotation of a three-dimensional rigid body when the moment-of-inertia matrix is

$$I = mr^2 \begin{bmatrix} 10 & 0.134 & -0.866 \\ 0.134 & 6.5 & -1.0 \\ -0.866 & -1.0 & 7.5 \end{bmatrix}.$$

Note: The principal moments of inertia are the eigenvalues, the principal axes of rotation are the associated eigenvectors, and m and r are constants.

3. In a three-dimensional stress problem, we have the symmetric matrix

$$
\begin{bmatrix}
\sigma_x & \tau_{xy} & \tau_{zx} \\
\tau_{xy} & \sigma_y & \tau_{yz} \\
\tau_{zx} & \tau_{yz} & \sigma_z
\end{bmatrix}.
$$

Find the principal stresses (eigenvalues) and the associated direction cosines (eigenvectors). We are given that $\sigma_x = 120$, $\sigma_y = 200$, $\sigma_z = 150$, $\tau_{xy} = 65$, $\tau_{zx} = 180$, and $\tau_{yz} = 75$.

Figure 9.9

4. Using the finite-difference approach, we can treat the buckling of a column (Fig. 9.9) as an eigenvalue-eigenvector problem.

$$
\begin{bmatrix}
7 & -4 & 1 & 0 \\
-4 & 6 & -4 & 1 \\
1 & -4 & 5 & -2 \\
0 & 1 & -2 & 1
\end{bmatrix}
\begin{bmatrix}
w_b \\ w_c \\ w_d \\ w_e
\end{bmatrix}
=
\begin{bmatrix}
2k & -k & 0 & 0 \\
-k & 2k & -k & 0 \\
0 & -k & 2k & -k \\
0 & 0 & -k & k
\end{bmatrix}
\begin{bmatrix}
w_b \\ w_c \\ w_d \\ w_e
\end{bmatrix}.
$$

Find the buckling load $P = 16kEI/L^2$, where the k's are the eigenvalues, and relative values of w_b, w_c, w_d, and w_e are represented by the eigenvectors.

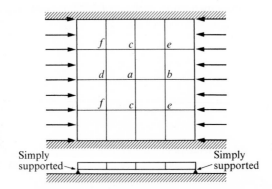

Simply supported   Simply supported

Figure 9.10

5. The buckling of a plate (see Fig. 9.10) can be treated as an eigenvalue problem:

$$
\begin{bmatrix}
20 & -8 & -16 & -8 & 4 & 4 \\
-8 & 19 & 4 & 1 & -16 & 0 \\
-16 & 4 & 44 & 4 & -16 & -16 \\
-8 & 1 & 4 & 19 & 0 & -16 \\
4 & -16 & -16 & 0 & 42 & 2 \\
4 & 0 & -16 & -16 & 2 & 42
\end{bmatrix}
\begin{bmatrix}
w_a \\ w_b \\ w_c \\ w_d \\ w_e \\ w_f
\end{bmatrix}
= k
\begin{bmatrix}
-2 & 1 & 0 & 1 & 0 & 0 \\
1 & -2 & 0 & 0 & 0 & 0 \\
0 & 0 & -4 & 0 & 2 & 2 \\
1 & 0 & 0 & -2 & 0 & 0 \\
0 & 0 & 2 & 0 & -2 & 0 \\
0 & 0 & 2 & 0 & 0 & -2
\end{bmatrix}
\begin{bmatrix}
w_a \\ w_b \\ w_c \\ w_d \\ w_e \\ w_f
\end{bmatrix}.
$$

Find the eigenvalues in terms of k and the eigenvectors.

6. Determine the frequency ω and the modes of the system shown in Fig. 9.11. The equation of motion is

$$\begin{bmatrix} y_1 \\ y_2 \\ y_3 \end{bmatrix} = \frac{\omega^2 \delta_{11}}{27} \begin{bmatrix} 27 & 14 & 4 \\ 14 & 8 & 2.5 \\ 4 & 2.5 & 1 \end{bmatrix}$$

$$\times \begin{bmatrix} M_1 & 0 & 0 \\ 0 & M_2 & 0 \\ 0 & 0 & M_3 \end{bmatrix} \begin{bmatrix} y_1 \\ y_2 \\ y_3 \end{bmatrix},$$

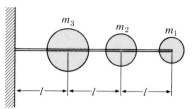

Figure 9.11

where $M_1 = M_2 = 2$, $M_3 = 3$ and δ_{11} is a constant.

CHAPTER 10

POLYNOMIAL INTERPOLATION

10.1 INTERPOLATION

Table 10.1 shows the values of a set of equally spaced data. It is sometimes necessary to determine the y-value at a given x between two known data points, for example, the y-value at $x = 6.3$. This type of problem is usually referred to as an *interpolation problem* for equally spaced data. As a *crude* estimate, it is possible to obtain the value y at $x = 6.3$ by linear interpolation.

TABLE 10.1. Given Data Points

k	0	1	2	3	4
x_k	0	2	4	6	8
y_k	−1	1	6	9	11

As shown in Fig. 10.1, we replace the true curve (which is actually unknown) between $x = 6$ and $x = 8$ by its chord, and then simply use $\overline{AB}$ as the required value:

$$\overline{AB} = y_{(\text{at } x=6)} + \tfrac{1}{2}(0.3)(y_{(\text{at } x=8)} - y_{(\text{at } x=6)}). \tag{10.1}$$

In general, $\overline{AB}$ represents the ordinate at

$$x = x_k + r\,\Delta x, \tag{10.2}$$

where Δx is the given interval, r represents the ratio $\overline{A'A}/\Delta x$, and k is the station number where point A' is located (see Fig. 10.1). We note that $0 \leq r \leq 1$. However, the true answer is $\overline{AC}$; and the difference $\overline{BC}$ between the two values $\overline{AB}$ and $\overline{AC}$ is the error produced by the linear interpolation.

As an improvement over the linear approximation, we now employ a second-order interpolation, as shown in Fig. 10.2. Here, three data points are given, namely,

210

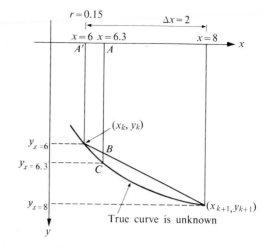

Fig. 10.1. Linear interpolation; BC is ignored.

(x_k, y_k), $(x_k + \Delta x, y_{k+1})$, and $(x_k + 2\,\Delta x, y_{k+2})$; and a parabola of the form

$$y = c_0 + c_1 x + c_2 x^2 \tag{10.3}$$

can be found to pass through the three given points.

To determine the coefficients c_0, c_1, and c_2, one substitutes the three given points into Eq. (10.3). The three resulting simultaneous equations yield the values

$$c_0 = \frac{y_{k+2}x_k}{2(\Delta x)^2}(x_k + \Delta x) - \frac{y_{k+1}x_k}{(\Delta x)^2}(x_k + 2\,\Delta x) + \frac{2y_k[x_k^2 + 2(\Delta x)x_k + 2(\Delta x)^2]}{2(\Delta x)^2},$$

$$c_1 = \frac{-y_{k+2}(2x_k + \Delta x) + 4y_{k+1}(x_k + \Delta x) - (2x_k + 3\,\Delta x)y_k}{2(\Delta x)^2}, \tag{10.4}$$

$$c_2 = \frac{y_{k+2} - 2y_{k+1} + y_k}{2(\Delta x)^2}.$$

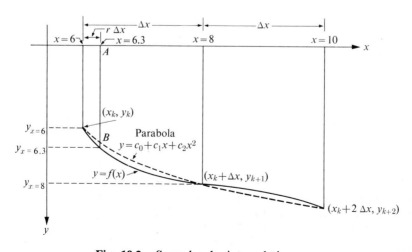

Fig. 10.2. Second-order interpolation.

Hence we can readily compute the interpolated value by substituting the appropriate x-value into Eq. (10.3).

It is not always necessary to use this cumbersome line of reasoning in order to obtain the coefficients for polynomials of higher order. One can arrive at these polynomials with the aid of the Lagrange polynomials. Before we present this procedure, which basically involves unequally spaced data, we will first introduce the Lagrange polynomials.

10.2   THE LAGRANGE POLYNOMIALS

Suppose that we are given $n + 1$ data points,

$$(x_0, y_0), \ (x_1, y_1), \ \ldots, \ (x_n, y_n),$$

and we wish to find the coefficient $c_0, c_1, \ldots, c_n$ of the polynomial

$$P_n(x) = c_0 + c_1 x + \cdots + c_n x^n, \tag{10.5}$$

such that the curve represented by Eq. (10.5) will pass through all $n + 1$ distinct points, that is,

$$P_n(x_k) = y_k \quad (k = 0, 1, \ldots, n). \tag{10.6}$$

We now define the Lagrange polynomial $L_k(x)$ of degree n as

$$L_k(x_i) = 0 \quad \text{if} \ \ i \neq k, \tag{10.7a}$$
$$= 1 \quad \text{if} \ \ i = k, \tag{10.7b}$$

where x_i $(i = 0, 1, \ldots, n)$ are the given $n + 1$ distinct arguments. We can now write $P_n(x)$ in the form

$$P_n(x) = L_0(x)y_0 + L_1(x)y_1 + \cdots + L_n(x)y_n$$
$$= \sum_{k=0}^{n} L_k(x)y_k, \tag{10.8}$$

as is readily seen since we can obtain Eq. (10.6) when each x_k-value $(k = 0, 1, \ldots, n)$ is substituted into Eq. (10.8) and when Eqs. (10.7) are taken into consideration. On the other hand, Eq. (10.7a) requires that each factor $x - x_i$, where $i \neq k$, must divide $L_k(x)$. We have

$$L_k(x) = \alpha(x - x_0)(x - x_1) \cdots (x - x_{k-1})(x - x_{k+1}) \cdots (x - x_n), \tag{10.9}$$

where the factor $(x - x_k)$ is *not* present on the right-hand side.

To determine α, we note that $L_k(x_k) = 1$, and so

$$\alpha = \frac{1}{(x_k - x_0)(x_k - x_1) \cdots (x_k - x_{k-1})(x_k - x_{k+1}) \cdots (x_k - x_n)}. \tag{10.10}$$

Substituting Eq. (10.10) into Eq. (10.9), we obtain

$$L_k(x) = \frac{(x - x_0)(x - x_1) \cdots (x - x_{k-1})(x - x_{k+1}) \cdots (x - x_n)}{(x_k - x_0)(x_k - x_1) \cdots (x_k - x_{k-1})(x_k - x_{k+1}) \cdots (x_k - x_n)}.$$

(10.11)

As a practical procedure, we note from Eq. (10.9) that

$$L_k(x) = \frac{\alpha(x - x_0)(x - x_1) \cdots (x - x_n)}{x - x_k},$$

(10.12)

and, using L'Hôpital's rule, we have

$$L_k(x_k) = \lim_{x \to x_k} \frac{(d/dx)[\alpha F_{n+1}(x)]}{(d/dx)(x - x_k)} = \frac{\alpha F'_{n+1}(x_k)}{1},$$

(10.13)

where

$$F_{n+1}(x) = (x - x_0)(x - x_1) \cdots (x - x_n).$$

(10.14)

Since $L_k(x_k) = 1$, we have

$$\alpha = 1/F'_{n+1}(x_k).$$

(10.15)

Substituting Eq. (10.15) into Eq. (10.12), we have

$$L_k(x) = \frac{1}{F'_{n+1}(x_k)} \frac{F_{n+1}(x)}{x - x_k} = \frac{G_k(x)}{F'_{n+1}(x_k)},$$

(10.16)

where

$$G_k(x) = \frac{F_{n+1}(x)}{x - x_k}.$$

(10.17)

Hence, a Lagrange polynomial of degree n can be constructed by the following steps:

(1) Set up $F_{n+1}(x) = (x - x_0)(x - x_1) \cdots (x - x_n)$.
(2) Find $F'_{n+1}(x)$ and then compute $F'_{n+1}(x_k)$; $k = 0, 1, \ldots, n$.
(3) Using Eq. (10.17), find $G_k(x)$ for $x = x_0, x_1, \ldots, x_n$.
(4) Finally, find $L_k(x)$ by use of Eq. (10.16).

Example 10.1

Find the Lagrange polynomials $L_0(x)$, $L_1(x)$, $L_2(x)$, and $L_3(x)$ from the unequally spaced data given below:

k	0	1	2	3
x_k	2	3	6	7

We have four data points; thus $n = 4 - 1 = 3$. We first set up $F_4(x)$ and $F'_4(x)$:

$$F_4(x) = (x - x_0)(x - x_1)(x - x_2)(x - x_3),$$

$$\begin{aligned} F'_4(x) = {} & (x - x_1)(x - x_2)(x - x_3) + (x - x_0)(x - x_2)(x - x_3) \\ & + (x - x_0)(x - x_1)(x - x_3) + (x - x_0)(x - x_1)(x - x_2). \end{aligned}$$

We then formulate $G_0(x)$ through $G_3(x)$:

$$G_0(x) = (x - x_1)(x - x_2)(x - x_3),$$
$$G_1(x) = (x - x_0)(x - x_2)(x - x_3),$$
$$G_2(x) = (x - x_0)(x - x_1)(x - x_3),$$
$$G_3(x) = (x - x_0)(x - x_1)(x - x_2).$$

It follows that

$$L_0(x) = \frac{(x - x_1)(x - x_2)(x - x_3)}{(x_0 - x_1)(x_0 - x_2)(x_0 - x_3)} = \frac{(x - 3)(x - 6)(x - 7)}{-20},$$

$$L_1(x) = \frac{(x - x_0)(x - x_2)(x - x_3)}{(x_1 - x_0)(x_1 - x_2)(x_1 - x_3)} = \frac{(x - 2)(x - 6)(x - 7)}{12},$$

$$L_2(x) = \frac{(x - x_0)(x - x_1)(x - x_3)}{(x_2 - x_0)(x_2 - x_1)(x_2 - x_3)} = \frac{(x - 2)(x - 3)(x - 7)}{-12},$$

$$L_3(x) = \frac{(x - x_0)(x - x_1)(x - x_2)}{(x_3 - x_0)(x_3 - x_1)(x_3 - x_2)} = \frac{(x - 2)(x - 3)(x - 6)}{20}.$$

10.3 LAGRANGE INTERPOLATION FORMULA FOR UNEQUALLY SPACED DATA

Let us examine Eq. (10.11) carefully:

$$L_k(x) = \frac{(x - x_0)(x - x_1) \cdots (x - x_{k-1})(x - x_{k+1}) \cdots (x - x_n)}{(x_k - x_0)(x_k - x_1) \cdots (x_k - x_{k-1})(x_k - x_{k+1}) \cdots (x_k - x_n)}. \tag{10.11}$$

At first glance, this expression appears to be very complicated. However, it is not difficult to see that Eq. (10.11) is equivalent to the following shorthand version:

$$L_k(x) = \prod_{\substack{i=0 \\ i \neq k}}^{n} \frac{x - x_i}{x_k - x_i}, \tag{10.18}$$

where the pi notation has the meaning

$$\prod_{k=1}^{n} x_k = x_1 \cdot x_2 \cdot x_3 \cdots x_n. \tag{10.19}$$

Substituting Eq. (10.18) into Eq. (10.8), we obtain

$$P_n(x) = \sum_{k=0}^{n} \left[\prod_{\substack{i=0 \\ i \neq k}}^{n} \left(\frac{x - x_i}{x_k - x_i} \right) \right] y_k. \tag{10.20}$$

This equation is known as the Lagrange interpolation formula for unequally spaced data.

Example 10.2

The following ten tabulated values are given:

x	y	x	y
0.1	0.9003	1.5	0.0158
0.3	0.7077	1.6	−0.0059
0.7	0.3798	1.8	−0.0376
1.0	0.1988	2.0	−0.0563
1.2	0.1091	2.4	−0.0669

```
C       EXAMPLE 10.2    LAGRANGIAN INTERPOLATION
C       L=NO. OF TABULATED POINTS CONSIDERED. LL=NO. OF GIVEN ARGUMENTS
C       X(K)=A GIVEN X ARGUMENT. ZX( )=A TABULATED VALUE OF X
C       Y( )=A TABULATED VALUE OF Y
C       E=DIFFERENCE BETWEEN EXACT VALUE AND LAGRANGIAN VALUE
        READ 4
4   FORMAT(7X,48H                                                 //)
        PUNCH 4
        PUNCH 8
8   FORMAT (8X,4H (1),14X,4H (2),15X,4H (3),14X,4H (4))
        PUNCH 10
10  FORMAT(7X,8HARGUMENT,9X,10HLAGRANGIAN,11X,5HEXACT,12X,7H(3)-(2)//)
        DIMENSION X(12), ZX(12), Y(12)
        READ 18, L,LL
18  FORMAT (I3,I3)
        DO 20 I=1,L
20  READ 22, ZX(I),Y(I)
22  FORMAT (F4.1,F8.4)
        DO 25 K=1,LL
25  READ 27, X(K)
27  FORMAT (F4.1)
        DO 62 K=1,LL
        XK=X(K)
        C=0.
        DO 52 I=1,L
        ZXI=ZX(I)
        P=1.
        DO 40 J=1,L
        IF (I-J) 35,40,35
35  ZXJ=ZX(J)
        A=(XK-ZXJ)/(ZXI-ZXJ)
        P=P*A
40  CONTINUE
        B=P*Y(I)
        C=C+B
52  CONTINUE
        YY=EXPF(-XK)*COSF(XK)
        E=YY-C
        PUNCH 60, XK, C, YY, E
60  FORMAT (7X,F4.1,12X,F9.5,10X,F9.5,9X,F9.5//)
62  CONTINUE
        PUNCH 65
65  FORMAT (23X,32H END OF LAGRANGIAN INTERPOLATION)
        STOP
        END
```

Fig. 10.3. FORTRAN program for Lagrangian interpolation. (*Cont.*)

```
                3RD EDITION IS PERFORMED ON 5/ 4/ 66

        10    6
        0.1    0.9003
        0.3    0.7077
        0.7    0.3798
        1.0    0.1988
        1.2    0.1091
        1.5    0.0158
        1.6   -0.0059
        1.8   -0.0376
        2.0   -0.0563
        2.4   -0.0669
        0.4
        0.6
        0.9
        1.4
        1.7
        1.9
```

Fig. 10.3 (*concl.*)

TABLE 10.2.   Output for Lagrangian Interpolation

```
        3RD EDITION IS PERFORMED ON 5/ 4/ 66
```

(1) ARGUMENT	(2) LAGRANGIAN	(3) EXACT	(4) (3)-(2)
.4	.61698	.61740	.00042
.6	.45273	.45295	.00022
.9	.25282	.25272	-.00009
1.4	.04192	.04191	0.00000
1.7	-.02357	-.02353	.00003
1.9	-.04836	-.04835	.00001

```
        END OF LAGRANGIAN INTERPOLATION
```

We are required (1) to compute the values of y corresponding to a given argument, and (2) to find the error resulting from the interpolation by subtracting the answer based on (1) from the answer using

$$y = e^{-x} \cos x.$$

The following six arguments are to be read in, one per data card.

$$0.4, \ 0.6, \ 0.9, \ 1.4, \ 1.7, \ 1.9.$$

Write a FORTRAN program to perform the Lagrangian interpolation. The program should be written in a flexible way so that a maximum of 12 given points can be considered. These points should also be read in via data cards. A possible FORTRAN program and the correct output are shown in Fig. 10.3 and Table 10.2, respectively.

BIBLIOGRAPHY

Interpolation

Interpolation and Allied Tables. H. M. Stationery Office, London, 1956.

KUNTZMANN, J., *Méthodes numériques, interpolation, dérivées.* Dunod, Paris, 1959.

LANCZOS, C., "Trigonometric Interpolation of Empirical and Analytic Functions," *J. Math. Phys.*, **17**, pp. 123–199 (1938).

SALZER, H. E., "A New Formula for Inverse Interpolation," *Bull. Amer. Math. Soc.*, **50**, pp. 513–516 (1946).

STEFFENSEN, J. F., *Interpolation.* Chelsea, New York, 1927.

SOUTHARD, T. H., "Everett's Formula for Bivariate Interpolation and Throw-Back of Fourth Differences," *Math. Tables Aids Comput.*, **10**, pp. 216–223 (1956).

THACHER, H. C., "Derivation of Interpolation Formulas in Several Independent Variables," *Ann. N. Y. Acad. Sci.*, **86**, pp. 758–775 (1960).

WALSH, J. L., *Interpolation and Approximation in the Complex Domain.* Am. Math. Soc., Providence, R. I., 1955.

Finite Differences

ABRAMOWITZ, M., "Note on Modified Second Differences for Use with Everett's Interpolation Formula," in *Tables of Bessel Functions of Fractional Order*, Nat. Bur. of Std. Columbia Univ. Press Ser., **10**, pp. XXXIII–XXXVI (1948).

BICKLEY, W. G., "Differences and Associated Operators, with Some Applications," *J. Math. Phys.*, **27**, pp. 182–192 (1948).

FREEMAN, H., *Finite Differences for Actuarial Students*, 2nd ed. (1st ed. published in 1939 as *Mathematics for Actuarial Students, Part II*), Cambridge University Press, London, 1960.

JORDAN, C., *Calculus of Finite Differences*, 2nd ed. (1st ed. 1939). Chelsea, New York, 1950.

MICHEL, J. G. L., "Central-Difference Formulae Obtained by Means of Operator Expansions," *J. Inst. Actu.*, **72**, pp. 470–480 (1946).

MILNE-THOMSON, L. M., *The Calculus of Finite Differences*, reprint (1st ed. 1933). Mac-Millan, London, 1951.

PROBLEMS

1. Find the Lagrange polynomials $L_0(x)$, $L_1(x)$, and $L_2(x)$ from the data given below:

i	0	1	2
x_i	2	4	6
y_i	3	4	5

Also find $P_2(x)$, using Eqs. (10.5) and (10.8) independently.

2. Ten tabulated values are given below:

x	y	x	y
0.1	0.9907	1.5	0.2384
0.3	0.9267	1.7	0.1576
0.7	0.6997	2.0	0.0667
0.9	0.5712	2.1	0.0439
1.2	0.3899	2.3	0.0080

Write a program in FORTRAN to compute the values of y at each of the eight x's, 0.2, 0.5, 0.6, 0.8, 1.0, 1.4, 1.8, 2.2. The values are to be computed by each of the following two methods: 1. Lagrangian interpolation. 2. Closed form solution: $y = e^{-x}(\cos x + \sin x)$. Compute the error resulting from the first method by comparing your results with those obtained by using the closed form.

Notes. (a) The ten tabulated values should be read in via data cards (one x and one y per card). (b) Each of the eight x's for which y must be computed should be read in via data cards (one x per card). (c) The program should be written to handle 12 given points.

3. If $v_t = (1/\sqrt{2\pi})\int_{-\infty}^{t} e^{-t^2/2} \, dt$, then we can construct the following table:

t	v_t	t	v_t
0	0.50000000	2.0	0.97724987
.5	0.69146246	2.5	0.99379033
1.0	0.84134475	3.0	0.99865010
1.5	0.93319280		

Find $v_{0.75}$, $v_{1.75}$, $v_{2.75}$, and $v_{3.75}$ using the Lagrangian interpolation equation.

4. Given the table below, find e^π.

x	e^x	x	e^x
3.10	22.197951	3.13	22.973980
3.11	22.421044	3.14	23.103867
3.12	22.646380	3.15	23.336065

CHAPTER 11

LEAST-SQUARES
CURVE FITTING

11.1 INTRODUCTION

In the previous chapter we demonstrated how to obtain the equation of a curve which passes exactly through all given points. This is accomplished by means of interpolation formulas, such as Eq. (10.20). We now ask for the equation of a smooth curve (Fig. 11.1) which does not pass through each of a number of given points, but which passes near each of them in a plane. The "nearness" is usually obtained by imposing the least-squares criterion, and the application of this criterion is the basis of the method of least squares, which we shall develop in Sections 11.2 and 11.3.

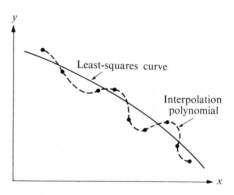

Fig. 11.1. Interpolation curve versus least-squares curve.

11.2 NORMAL EQUATIONS FOR CURVE FITTING

Let us begin by considering the problem of fitting a given number of function values (see Table 11.1) by a straight line in the form

$$Y = k_0 + k_1 x. \tag{11.1}$$

We first plot the values in Table 11.1 on a graph paper to see whether or not it is reasonable to approximate the given values by a straight line (Fig. 11.2). We next determine the coefficients k_0 and k_1 using the least-squares criterion which requires that $S = \sum (Y_i - y_i)^2$ be a minimum, where Y_i is evaluated from Eq. (11.1). The values $Y_i - y_i$ are called *residuals*.

TABLE 11.1. Seven function values ($n = 7$)

x	y	x	y
0	2	4	9
1	3	5	8
2	5	6	10
3	5		

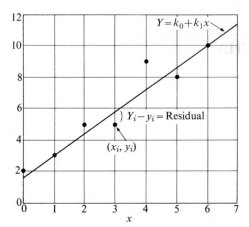

Fig. 11.2. Straight line representation for data in Table 11.1.

To obtain the minimum value for S, which is a function of two variables k_0 and k_1, we set the following two first partial derivatives to zero:

$$\frac{\partial S}{\partial k_0} = 0 \quad \text{and} \quad \frac{\partial S}{\partial k_1} = 0.$$

This yields the two simultaneous linear equations

$$\frac{\partial S}{\partial k_0} = \sum_{i=1}^{n} \frac{\partial}{\partial k_0} (k_0 + k_1 x_i - y_i)^2 = \sum_{i=1}^{n} 2(k_0 + k_1 x_i - y_i) = 0 \qquad (11.2a)$$

and

$$\frac{\partial S}{\partial k_1} = \sum_{i=1}^{n} \frac{\partial}{\partial k_1} (k_0 + k_1 x_i - y_i)^2 = \sum_{i=1}^{n} 2x_i(k_0 + k_1 x_i - y_i) = 0. \qquad (11.2b)$$

From Eqs. (11.2a) and (11.2b) one has

$$\sum_{i=1}^{n} y_i = nk_0 + k_1 \sum_{i=1}^{n} x_i \qquad (11.3a)$$

and

$$\sum_{i=1}^{n} x_i y_i = k_0 \sum_{i=1}^{n} x_i + k_1 \sum_{i=1}^{n} x_i^2. \qquad (11.3b)$$

Thus Eq. (11.3a) and (11.3b) represent two conditions which must be met in order to obtain the best fit of the straight line, based on the least-squares criterion.

Example 11.1

To illustrate the application of Eqs. (11.3a) and (11.3b), we shall now find k_0 and k_1, using the values in Table 11.1. We first compute $x_i y_i$, then x_i^2 for $i = 1, 2, \ldots, 7$, as shown in Table 11.2. Substituting the values of $\sum y_i, \sum x_i, \sum x_i y_i$, and $\sum x_i^2$ into Eqs. (11.3a) and (11.3b), we find that k_0 and k_1 satisfy the following two conditions, or *normal equations:*

$$42 = 7k_0 + 21k_1, \qquad 164 = 21k_0 + 91k_1.$$

TABLE 11.2. Computations for $\sum x_i y_i$ and $\sum x_i^2$

i	x_i	y_i	$x_i y_i$	$(x_i)^2$
1	0	2	0	0
2	1	3	3	1
3	2	5	10	4
4	3	5	15	9
5	4	9	36	16
6	5	8	40	25
7	6	10	60	36
Sum	21	42	164	91

TABLE 11.3. Residuals

(1)	(2)	(3)	(4)	(5)
x_i	y_i	Y_i	$Y_i - y_i$	$x_i \cdot$ (4)
0	2	1.929639	0.070361	0.000000
1	3	3.286426	-0.286426	-0.286426
2	5	4.643213	0.356787	0.713574
3	5	6.000000	-1.000000	-3.000000
4	9	7.356787	1.643213	6.572852
5	8	8.713574	-0.713574	-3.567870
6	10	10.070361	-0.070361	-0.422166
Sum			0.000000	0.009964

The solution of these equations yields

$$k_0 = 1.929639 \quad \text{and} \quad k_1 = 1.356787.$$

The equation for the required straight line is therefore

$$Y = 1.929639 + 1.356787x. \tag{11.4}$$

It is now possible to compute Y_i by means of Eq. (11.4). This is shown in column 3 of Table 11.3. Columns 4 and 5 are the values of $(Y_i - y_i)$ and $x_i(Y_i - y_i)$, respectively. As a check, note that the values of both $\sum(Y_i - y_i)$ and $\sum x_i(Y_i - y_i)$ should be equal to zero, as indicated in Eqs. (11.2a) and (11.2b).

After our discussion on fitting given data with a straight line, we turn now to fitting a set of data with a polynomial of mth degree. The procedure is quite similar to the straight-line case. Basically, we wish to find a minimum value of S, where

$$S = \sum_{i=1}^{n} (Y_i - y_i)^2 = \sum_{i=1}^{n} (k_0 + k_1 x_i + k_2 x_i^2 + \cdots + k_m x_i^m - y_i)^2.$$

To obtain the minimum value of S, which is now a function of $m + 1$ variables $k_0, k_1, \ldots, k_m$, we set the following $m + 1$ first partial derivatives to zero:

$$\frac{\partial S}{\partial k_0} = \sum_{i=1}^{n} 2(k_0 + k_1 x_i + k_2 x_i^2 + \cdots + k_m x_i^m - y_i) = 0,$$

$$\frac{\partial S}{\partial k_1} = \sum_{i=1}^{n} 2x_i(k_0 + k_1 x_i + k_2 x_i^2 + \cdots + k_m x_i^m - y_i) = 0, \tag{11.5}$$

$$\vdots$$

$$\frac{\partial S}{\partial k_m} = \sum_{i=1}^{n} 2x_i^m(k_0 + k_1 x_i + k_2 x_i^2 + \cdots + k_m x_i^m - y_i) = 0.$$

We then obtain the $m + 1$ simultaneous linear, or normal, equations

$$k_0 n + k_1 \sum x_i + k_2 \sum x_i^2 + \cdots + k_m \sum x_i^m - \sum y_i = 0,$$
$$k_0 \sum x_i + k_1 \sum x_i^2 + k_2 \sum x_i^3 + \cdots + k_m \sum x_i^{m+1} - \sum x_i y_i = 0,$$
$$k_0 \sum x_i^2 + k_1 \sum x_i^3 + k_2 \sum x_i^4 + \cdots + k_m \sum x_i^{m+2} - \sum x_i^2 y_i = 0, \quad (11.6)$$
$$\vdots$$
$$k_0 \sum x_i^m + k_1 \sum x_i^{m+1} + k_2 \sum x_i^{m+2} + \cdots + k_m \sum x_i^{m+m} - \sum x_i^m y_i = 0,$$

where the symbol $\sum$ implies summation for i from 1 to n.

It is convenient to express Eq. (11.6) in the following matrix notation,

$$[A][k] = [B], \quad (11.7)$$

where

$$[A] = \begin{bmatrix} n & \sum x_i & \sum x_i^2 & \cdots & \sum x_i^m \\ \sum x_i & \sum x_i^2 & \sum x_i^3 & \cdots & \sum x_i^{m+1} \\ \vdots & & & & \\ \sum x_i^m & \sum x_i^{m+1} & \sum x_i^{m+2} & \cdots & \sum x_i^{2m} \end{bmatrix},$$

is a symmetric matrix, and

$$[k] = \begin{bmatrix} k_0 \\ k_1 \\ \vdots \\ k_m \end{bmatrix}, \quad [B] = \begin{bmatrix} \sum y_i \\ \sum x_i y_i \\ \vdots \\ \sum x_i^m y_i \end{bmatrix}.$$

Example 11.2

We are to fit a parabola to a set of points (x_i, y_i) shown in columns 2 and 3 of Table 11.4. It should be noted that the given data are not equally spaced along the x-direction.

Normal equations can be obtained only after the values of the sum of the following expressions are known:

$$x_i, \; y_i, \; x_i y_i, \; x_i^2, \; x_i^3, \; x_i^4, \; \text{and} \; x_i^2 y_i.$$

These are tabulated in Table 11.4. From the table and Eq. (11.6), we see that three normal equations are

$$9k_0 + 53k_1 + 381k_2 = 76,$$
$$53k_0 + 381k_1 + 3017k_2 = 489,$$
$$381k_0 + 3017k_1 + 25317k_2 = 3547.$$

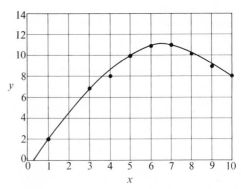

Fig. 11.3. Fitting a parabola to nine points.

TABLE 11.4.   Fitting a Parabola to a Set of Points

(1)	(2)	(3)	(4)	(5)	(6)	(7)	(8)
i	x_i	y_i	$x_i y_i$	x_i^2	$x_i^2 y_i$	x_i^3	x_i^4
1	1	2	2	1	2	1	1
2	3	7	21	9	63	27	81
3	4	8	32	16	128	64	256
4	5	10	50	25	250	125	625
5	6	11	66	36	396	216	1296
6	7	11	77	49	539	343	2401
7	8	10	80	64	640	512	4096
8	9	9	81	81	729	729	6561
9	10	8	80	100	800	1000	10000
Σ	53	76	489	381	3547	3017	25317

Solving the equations, we have

$$k_0 = -1.4597,$$

$$k_2 = -0.2676,$$

$$k_1 = 3.6053,$$

and the equation of the desired parabola is

$$y = -1.4597 + 3.6053x - 0.2676x^2.$$

The resulting parabola is plotted in Fig. 11.3.

So far in this section we have considered a given set of data points having equal importance. Very often, due to measuring instruments of differing precision, some of the y_i values are more accurate and are therefore considered more important than others and these points are necessarily assigned more "weight." In other words, we should assign a weight, or weighting coefficient w_i, to each point (x_i, y_i).

By means of the least-squares criterion discussed in Eq. (11.5), the expression

$$S = \sum_{i=0}^{n} w_i \left(y_i - \sum_{j=0}^{m} k_j x_i^j \right)^2$$

is minimized. The system of normal equations

$$\frac{\partial S}{\partial k_j} = 0 \qquad (j = 0, 1, \ldots, m)$$

is represented in matrix notation as

$$[A][k] = [B],\qquad\qquad (11.8)$$

where

$$[A] = \begin{bmatrix} \sum w_i & \sum w_i x_i & \sum w_i x_i^2 & \cdots & \sum w_i x_i^m \\ \sum w_i x_i & \sum w_i x_i^2 & \sum w_i x_i^3 & \cdots & \sum w_i x_i^{m+1} \\ \vdots & & & & \\ \sum w_i x_i^m & \sum w_i x_i^{m+1} & \sum w_i x_i^{m+2} & \cdots & \sum w_i x_i^{2m} \end{bmatrix},$$

$$[k] = \begin{bmatrix} k_0 \\ k_1 \\ \vdots \\ k_m \end{bmatrix}, \qquad [B] = \begin{bmatrix} \sum w_i y_i \\ \sum w_i x_i y_i \\ \vdots \\ \sum w_i x_i^m y_i \end{bmatrix}.$$

When $w_i = 1$ ($i = 1, \ldots, n$), Eq. (11.8) becomes identical to Eq. (11.7). It is noted that the column matrix $[k]$, also referred to as the regression coefficient vector, can be readily obtained by the Gauss-Jordan Method, as discussed in Chapter 8.

11.3   FORTRAN PROGRAM FOR LEAST-SQUARES POLYNOMIAL FIT

The main program shown in Fig. 11.4 may be used to fit polynomials of several different degrees to a given set of N data points (x_i, y_i). Each data point has a weighting coefficient w_i. This program may determine the coefficients of polynomials of degree $0, 1, 2, 3, \ldots, N - 1$. In other words, up to N different sets of polynomial coefficients can be found for the same set of data points. The variables used in this main program are:

N = the number of data points.

M = the degree of the polynomial to be fitted.

LL = the number of polynomials of different degrees which are to be fitted.

MM = an index to read data points for the first polynomial being fitted, to avoid rereading data points for the next polynomial, and to stop the program after fitting the last polynomial.

X(I) = the value of x at the ith data point.

W(I) = the weight of the ith data point. If all points are treated equally, W(I) = 1.

L = the number of y-values which correspond to each X(I) (in most cases, L = 1).

Y(I,J) = the jth value of y at the ith data point.

In Example 11.2, we were fitting a second-degree polynomial to nine points. If we wish to use this program to fit a fourth-degree polynomial to this set of points in the

```
C     MAIN PROGRAM FOR LEAST SQUARE POLYNOMIAL FIT     SECTION 11.3
      DIMENSION A(15,15),B(15,15),X(15),Y(15,4),W(15),C(15,15)
      MM = 0
      READ 100,LL
    5 IF(MM-LL) 10,1000,1000
   10 READ 200,N,M,L
      IF(MM) 25,15,25
   15 PUNCH 400
      DO 20 I=1,N
      READ 300,X(I),W(I),(Y(I,J),J=1,L)
      DO 20 J=1,L
   20 PUNCH 500,X(I),W(I),Y(I,J)
   25 DO 30 I = 1,N
   30 C(I,1) = 1.0
      MP1=M+1
      DO 35 J=2,MP1
      DO 35 I=1,N
   35 C(I,J) = C(I,J-1)*X(I)
      DO 40 I=1,MP1
      DO 40 J=1,MP1
      A(I,J) = 0.0
      DO 40 K=1,N
   40 A(I,J) = A(I,J) + C(K,I)*C(K,J)*W(K)
      DO 45 J =1,L
      DO 45 I=1,MP1
      B(I,J) = 0.0
      DO 45 K = 1,N
   45 B(I,J) = B(I,J) + C(K,I)*Y(K,J)*W(K)
      CALL CHAP8(A,MP1,B,L,DET)
      PUNCH 600,N
      PUNCH 700, M
      DO 50 J=1,L
      DO 50 I=1,MP1
      II = I-1
   50 PUNCH 800,II,B(I,J)
      PUNCH 900
      MM = MM+1
      GO TO 5
  100 FORMAT(I4)
  200 FORMAT(3I4)
  300 FORMAT(6F10.5)
  400 FORMAT(14X,1HX,20X,6HWEIGHT,22X,1HY,//)
  500 FORMAT(8X,E12.6,12X,E12.6,13X,E12.6/)
  600 FORMAT(///,30HNUMBER OF GIVEN DATA POINTS = ,I2)
  700 FORMAT(/7X,23HDEGREE OF POLYNOMIAL = ,I2,///)
  800 FORMAT(5X,I2,22H DEGREE COEFFICIENT = ,E14.8,/)
  900 FORMAT(/,49H - - - - -
 1000 STOP
      END
```

Fig. 11.4. Main program for the normal-equation method.

TABLE 11.5.   Normal-Equation Solutions

X	WEIGHT	Y
.100000E+01	.100000E+01	.200000E+01
.300000E+01	.100000E+01	.700000E+01
.400000E+01	.100000E+01	.800000E+01
.500000E+01	.100000E+01	.100000E+02
.600000E+01	.100000E+01	.110000E+02
.700000E+01	.100000E+01	.110000E+02
.800000E+01	.100000E+01	.100000E+02
.900000E+01	.100000E+01	.900000E+01
.100000E+02	.100000E+01	.800000E+01

```
NUMBER OF GIVEN DATA POINTS  =   9

    DEGREE OF POLYNOMIAL  =   2


        0 DEGREE COEFFICIENT  =  -.14596409E+01

        1 DEGREE COEFFICIENT  =   .36052985E+01

        2 DEGREE COEFFICIENT  =  -.26756969E+00


 -  -  -  -   -


NUMBER OF GIVEN DATA POINTS  =   9

    DEGREE OF POLYNOMIAL  =   4


        0 DEGREE COEFFICIENT  =   .44753310E+00

        1 DEGREE COEFFICIENT  =   .11041027E+01

        2 DEGREE COEFFICIENT  =   .61011515E+00

        3 DEGREE COEFFICIENT  =  -.11443138E+00

        4 DEGREE COEFFICIENT  =   .49863874E-02
```

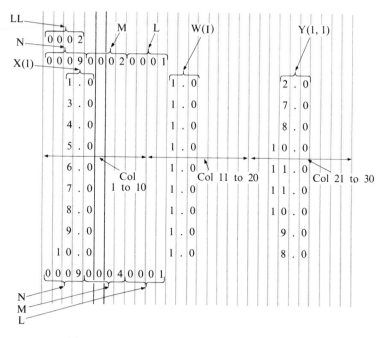

Fig. 11.5. Input format for the main program.

same run, the data would be read in the format shown in Fig. 11.5. This main program calls for the subprogram CHAP8, the subroutine for matrix inversion and simultaneous equations (see Section 8.9). The answers corresponding to the input (see Fig. 11.5) are listed in Table 11.5. We can see that the answers, obtained by machine computation for the polynomial of second degree, check closely with the known answers in Example 11.2.

11.4 ORTHOGONAL POLYNOMIALS

The normal-equation method discussed in the previous sections can be used to fit a number of function values by a polynomial in the form

$$Y = k_0 + k_1 x + k_2 x^2 + \cdots + k_m x^m.$$

To determine k_0 through k_m, we must solve a set of simultaneous linear equations. Unfortunately, this method fails when the resulting m normal equations are ill-conditioned, which is often the case when m becomes large. Another disadvantage of the normal-equation method lies in the fact that whenever the value of m is changed, a set of new values of k_0 through k_m must be computed, as can be seen in Examples 11.1 and 11.2.

In the remainder of this chapter, we shall discuss a method which makes it possible to overcome the two difficulties mentioned above. This technique is designed for digital computers using the Chebyshev polynomials $T_m(x)$ and fits the given data in the form

$$Y_m(x) = c_0 T_0(x) + c_1 T_1(x) + \cdots + c_m T_m(x). \tag{11.9}$$

Our immediate problem is to derive an expression for each of the coefficients c_j ($j = 0, 1, \ldots, m$). This derivation requires the knowledge of certain properties of orthogonal polynomials discussed below.

The following two sets of definite integrals are known as orthogonal conditions:

$$\int_0^\pi \sin mx \sin nx \, dx = 0, \qquad m \neq n,$$
$$= \pi/2, \qquad m = n; \tag{11.10}$$
$$\int_0^\pi \cos mx \cos nx \, dx = 0, \qquad m \neq n,$$
$$= \pi/2, \qquad m = n. \tag{11.11}$$

They are valid provided that m and n are nonnegative integers and are not both zero.

In general, a set of functions $\phi_0(x), \phi_1(x), \ldots, \phi_m(x)$ is known as orthogonal in an interval $a \leq x \leq b$ if

$$\int_a^b w(x)\phi_m(x)\phi_n(x) \, dx = 0, \qquad m \neq n, \tag{11.12}$$

where the weighting function $w(x)$ is nonnegative in the given interval (a,b). When all the *orthogonal* functions $\phi_m(x)$ are polynomials, they are known as *orthogonal polynomials*.

A particular example of such orthogonal polynomials is the set of Chebyshev polynomials.

11.5 CHEBYSHEV POLYNOMIALS

Chebyshev polynomials of degree r in x are defined by

$$T_r(x) = \cos (r \cos^{-1} x). \tag{11.13}$$

The first through sixth Chebyshev polynomials are

$$T_0(x) = 1,$$
$$T_1(x) = x,$$
$$T_2(x) = 2x^2 - 1,$$
$$T_3(x) = 4x^3 - 3x, \tag{11.14}$$
$$T_4(x) = 8x^4 - 8x^2 + 1,$$
$$T_5(x) = 16x^5 - 20x^3 + 5x,$$
$$T_6(x) = 32x^6 - 48x^4 + 18x^2 - 1.$$

Other Chebyshev polynomials can be readily obtained by using the recurrence relation

$$T_{r+1}(x) - 2xT_r(x) + T_{r-1}(x) = 0. \tag{11.15}$$

The set of Chebyshev polynomials, one of several classical orthogonal polynomials,† has the following important property:

$$\sum_{i=1}^{m+1} T_k(\bar{x}_i)T_l(\bar{x}_i) = \begin{cases} 0, & \text{for } k \neq l, \tag{11.16} \\ (m+1)/2, & \text{for } k = l \neq 0, \tag{11.17} \\ m+1, & \text{for } k = l = 0, \tag{11.18} \end{cases}$$

where

$$\bar{x}_i = \cos \frac{(2i-1)\pi}{2(m+1)}, \qquad i = 1, 2, \ldots, m+1. \tag{11.19}$$

For example, if $m = 3$, the values of $\bar{x}_i$, as determined by Eq. 11.19 and listed in Table 11.6, would satisfy Eqs. (11.16), (11.17), and (11.18).

TABLE 11.6.   Values of $\bar{x}_i$

i	1	2	3	4
$\bar{x}_i$	0.92388	0.38268	−0.38268	−0.92388

11.6   CHEBYSHEV POLYNOMIALS AND CURVE FITTING

We are now in a position to derive an expression for each of the coefficients c_j ($j = 0, 1, \ldots, m$) in the equation

$$Y_m(x) = c_0T_0(x) + c_1T_1(x) + \cdots + c_mT_m(x). \tag{11.20}$$

We shall assume that the given n data points $(x_1, y_1), (x_2, y_2), \ldots, (x_n, y_n)$ are *equally spaced*.

As with the normal-equation solution, we apply the least-squares criterion discussed in Eq. (11.5) to minimize the expression

$$S = \sum_{i=1}^{n} \left[y_i - \sum_{j=0}^{m} c_j T_j(x_i) \right]^2. \tag{11.21}$$

The system of simultaneous equations

$$\frac{\partial S}{\partial c_j} = 0, \qquad j = 0, 1, \ldots, m,$$

---

† Others are Laguerre, Legendre, Gegenbauer, Jacobi, Hermite, etc. The Legendre polynomials will be discussed in Section 12.2.

can then be written in the following matrix form:

$$
\begin{bmatrix}
\sum T_0^2(x_i) & \sum T_0(x_i)T_1(x_i) & \cdots & \sum T_0(x_i)T_m(x_i) \\
\sum T_1(x_i)T_0(x_i) & \sum T_1^2(x_i) & \cdots & \sum T_1(x_i)T_m(x_i) \\
\vdots & & & \vdots \\
\sum T_m(x_i)T_0(x_i) & \sum T_m(x_i)T_1(x_i) & \cdots & \sum T_m^2(x_i)
\end{bmatrix}
\begin{bmatrix}
c_0 \\ c_1 \\ \vdots \\ c_m
\end{bmatrix}
=
\begin{bmatrix}
\sum y_i T_0(x_i) \\ \sum y_i T_1(x_i) \\ \vdots \\ \sum y_i T_m(x_i)
\end{bmatrix},
$$

(11.22)

where $\sum$ implies $\sum_{i=1}^{n}$. This matrix equation can be expressed more simply as

$$[T][C] = [E]. \tag{11.23}$$

We would like to reduce $[T]$ to a diagonal matrix since there would then be no need to solve simultaneous equations, and the coefficients c_j could be obtained very easily. This reduction is indeed possible, and we shall now discuss the procedure used to perform it.

We observe that each off-diagonal element in $[T]$ is of the form

$$\sum_{i=1}^{n} T_k(x_i)T_l(x_i),$$

where $k \neq l$. We ask, Do the x_i's in each element meet the following two conditions, that is,

(1) do they lie in the interval $(-1, 1)$?
(2) do they satisfy Eq. (11.19)?

The answer is clearly negative. In order to meet these two conditions, the given data points $(x_1, y_1), (x_2, y_2), \ldots, (x_n, y_n)$ which lie in the interval (a, b) are first changed to a set of points $(x_1', y_1), (x_2', y_2), \ldots, (x_n', y_n)$, which lie in the interval $(-1, 1)$, by the following linear transformation:

$$x_i' = \frac{x_i - (b+a)/2}{(b-a)/2} = \frac{2x_i - (b+a)}{b-a}, \qquad i = 1, 2, \ldots, n. \tag{11.24}$$

We next employ Eq. (10.20), the Lagrange interpolation formula, to obtain $m + 1$ interpolated values for $\bar{y}_i$ which correspond to the values of $\bar{x}_i$ ($i = 1, \ldots, m + 1$) generated by Eq. (11.19).

For example, if we are to fit the equation ($m = 2$) $P_n(x) = \sum_{k=0}^{n} \prod_{\substack{i=0 \\ i \neq k}}^{n} \left(\frac{x - x_i}{x_k - x_i} \right) y_k$

$$Y_m(x) = c_0 T_0(x) + c_1 T_1(x) + c_2 T_2(x)$$

to a set of seven ($n = 7$) data points then the necessary transformation would be as indicated in Table 11.7.

Since the final set of modified $m + 1$ data points $(\bar{x}_1, \bar{y}_1), (\bar{x}_2, \bar{y}_2), \ldots, (\bar{x}_{m+1}, \bar{y}_{m+1})$ satisfies Eq. (11.16), the orthogonal relation of the Chebyshev polynomials,

TABLE 11.7. Relation Between x_i, x_i', $\bar{x}_i$, y_i, and $\bar{y}_i$

x_i	x_i'	$\bar{x}_i$	y_i	$\bar{y}_i$
Given	Using Eq. (11.24)	Using Eq. (11.19)	Given	Using Eq. (10.20)
1	-1		2	
		-0.866		3.1
2	-0.667		5	
3	-0.333		7	
4	0	0	8	8.0
5	$+0.333$		10	
6	$+0.667$		9	
		$+0.866$		7.7
7	$+1$		7	

then all off-diagonal elements of $[T]$ will be equal to zero. In other words,

$$
\begin{bmatrix}
\sum T_0^2(\bar{x}_i) & 0 & \cdots & 0 \\
0 & \sum T_1^2(\bar{x}_i) & \cdots & 0 \\
\vdots & & & \vdots \\
0 & 0 & & \sum T_m^2(\bar{x}_i)
\end{bmatrix}
\begin{bmatrix}
c_0 \\ c_1 \\ \vdots \\ c_m
\end{bmatrix}
=
\begin{bmatrix}
\sum \bar{y}_i T_0(\bar{x}_i) \\
\sum \bar{y}_i T_1(\bar{x}_i) \\
\vdots \\
\sum \bar{y}_i T_m(\bar{x}_i)
\end{bmatrix},
\qquad (11.25)
$$

where $\sum$ implies $\sum_{i=1}^{m+1}$. There is, consequently, no need to solve simultaneous equations, and we can compute by simple division a value for each coefficient c_j,

$$
c_j = \frac{\sum_{i=1}^{m+1} \bar{y}_i T_j(\bar{x}_i)}{\sum_{i=1}^{m+1} T_j^2(\bar{x}_i)}, \qquad j = 0, 1, \ldots, m. \qquad (11.26)
$$

Using the relation (11.17) and (11.18), we obtain

$$
c_j = \frac{2}{m+1} \sum_{i=1}^{m+1} \bar{y}_i T_j(\bar{x}_i), \qquad j \neq 0, \qquad (11.27)
$$

and

$$
c_j = \frac{1}{m+1} \sum_{i=1}^{m} \bar{y}_i T_j(\bar{x}_i), \qquad j = 0. \qquad (11.28)
$$

Once we know the coefficients c_j, the Chebyshev expansion of degree m for $Y_m(\bar{x})$ has been completely determined:

$$
Y_m(\bar{x}) = \sum_{j=0}^{m} c_j T_j(\bar{x}).
$$

The final answer may then be expressed as a Chebyshev series in the interval $(-1, 1)$ or, with the proper transformations, as a power series in the original interval (a, b).

For example, if $m = 2$, the Chebyshev series expansion for Y_m in the interval $(-1, 1)$ is

$$Y_2(\bar{x}) = c_0 T_0(\bar{x}) + c_1 T_1(\bar{x}) + c_2 T_2(\bar{x})$$
$$= (c_0 - c_2) + c_1 \bar{x} + 2c_2 \bar{x}^2.$$

In order to convert the Chebyshev series expansion for Y_2 in the interval $(-1, 1)$ to the interval (a, b), we use the transformation

$$x = \frac{(b - a)\bar{x}}{2} + \frac{(b + a)}{2} \tag{11.29}$$

and obtain $Y_2(x) = A_0 + A_1 x + A_2 x^2$, where

$$A_0 = c_0 - c_1 + c_1 \left(\frac{b + a}{b - a}\right) + 2c_2 \left(\frac{b + a}{b - a}\right)^2,$$

$$A_1 = \frac{2c_1}{b - a} - \frac{8(b + a)c_2}{(b - a)^2},$$

$$A_2 = \frac{8c_2}{(b - a)^2}.$$

At this point, $Y_2(x)$ has been expressed as a power series in the interval (a, b).

11.7   CHEBYSHEV-POLYNOMIAL CURVE FITTING WITH A COMPUTER

The procedure presented in the previous section is well suited to high-speed digital computation. The following seven steps are involved:

(1) Compute the $m + 1$ values of $\bar{x}_i$, where m is the degree of the polynomial Y_m.

(2) Normalize the initial values of x_i to the interval $(-1, 1)$.

(3) Perform the Lagrangian interpolation to obtain $m + 1$ values of $\bar{y}_i$ which correspond to the $m + 1$ values of $\bar{x}_i$.

(4) Compute the coefficients c_j.

(5) Convert the Chebyshev series for Y_m to its equivalent power series.

(6) Convert the power series from the interval $(-1, 1)$ to the interval (a, b).

(7) Punch the coefficients of the final series expansion.

A FORTRAN program written to carry out the above seven steps is shown in Fig. 11.7. The input variables for the FORTRAN program are defined as follows:

M = degree of the polynomial Y_m desired.

N = number of original data points.

XMIN = first value of x (smallest value of original x-coordinates).

DELTX = increment between values of x, that is, $(x_i - x_{i-1})$.

Y(J) = value of the original y corresponding to the jth value of x.

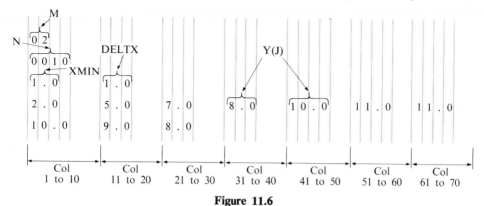

Figure 11.6

In the dimension statement we have

R(I) = the ith root, or $\bar{x}_i$.

V(I) = the ith value of x_i', or normalized x_i.

C(I) = the ith coefficient of the Chebyshev series in $(-1, 1)$.

F(I) = the intermediate storage used in computing interpolated $\bar{y}_i$, in computing C(I)'s, and in converting C(I)'s to final power-series coefficients in (a, b). The final coefficients are stored in Y(J).

Example 11.3

Using Chebyshev polynomials, we are to fit a parabola to the following ten data points:

x	y	x	y
1	2	6	11
2	5	7	11
3	7	8	10
4	8	9	9
5	10	10	8

This is the same set of data as that used in Example 11.2 and Table 11.4, except that a tenth point, (2, 5), has been added to make the x-coordinates equispaced. The results of this example may then be compared with those obtained by the normal-equation solution.

Applying the Chebyshev program to this example, the data would be read in the format shown in Fig. 11.6. A possible FORTRAN program for Chebyshev-polynomial curve fitting is shown in Fig. 11.7.

The output for the Chebyshev program gives the coefficients A_j for the polynomial Y_m in terms of the power series:

$$Y_m = \sum_{j=0}^{m} A_j x^j.$$

```
C        CHEBYSHEV POLYNOMIAL APPROXIMATION - EQUIDISTANT DATA
         DIMENSION R(25), V(500), Y(500), C(25), F(25)
         READ 5,M,N,XMIN,DELTX
       5 FORMAT(I2/I4/F10.5,F10.5)
         M = M + 1
C        COMPUTE ROOTS
         X2 = M
         DO 1000 I=1,M
         X1 = I
         ARG=1.5707963268*(2.0*X1-1.0)/X2
         MSUB = M+1-I
         R(MSUB) = COSF(ARG)
    1000 CONTINUE
C        NORMALIZE VECTORS
         X1=N-1
         DV=2.0/X1
         V(1)= -1.0
         L = N-1
         DO 1003 I=1,L
         V(I+1) =V(I)+DV
    1003 CONTINUE
         READ 10,(Y(J),J=1,N)
      10 FORMAT(7F10.5)
C        PERFORM LAGRANGIAN INTERPOLATION
         I=1
         DO 150 L=1,N
         IF(R(I)-V(L)) 151,151,150
     151 U=(R(I)-V(L-1))/(V(L)-V(L-1))
         IF(L-2)154,154,155
     154 F(I)=U*(Y(L)-Y(L-1)) + Y(L-1)
         GO TO 157
     155 IF(L-N)156,154,154
     156 ZIP = -U*(U-1.)*(U-2.)*Y(L-2)/6. + (U*U-1.)*(U-2.)*Y(L-1)/2.
         F(I) = ZIP - (U+1.)*(U-2.)*U*Y(L)/2. + U*(U*U-1.)*Y(L+1)/6.
     157 I=I+1
         IF(M+1-I)153,153,160
     160 IF(R(I)-V(L))151,151,150
     150 CONTINUE
C        COMPUTE COEFFICIENTS
     153 ZM = M
         DO 280 I=1,M
         SUM=0.0
         IF (I-2) 260, 265, 270
     260 DO 261 J=1,M
     261 SUM=SUM + F(J)
         GO TO 275
     265 DO 266 J=1,M
     266 SUM=SUM + R(J)*F(J)
         GO TO 275
     270 V(1)=1.0
         DO 272 J=1,M
         V(2)=R(J)
         DO 271 K=3,I
     271 V(K)=2.*R(J)*V(K-1) - V(K-2)
     272 SUM=SUM + F(J)*V(I)
     275 C(I) = 2.0*SUM/ZM
     280 CONTINUE
         C(1)=C(1)/2.0
```

Fig. 11.7. Chebyshev polynomial curve fitting.

```
         ZIP = XMIN
         NN = N-1
         DO 593 J=1,NN
C
   593 XMIN=XMIN + DELTX
         SUM1=(XMIN+ZIP)/2.
         SUM2=(XMIN-ZIP)/2.
         NN = M-1
         PUNCH 305, NN
   305 FORMAT(33HPOLYNOMIAL COEFFICIENTS - DEGREE ,I2,//)
C        CONVERT CHEBYSHEV SERIES TO IT'S EQUIVALENT POWER SERIES
         F(1)=C(1)
         F(2)=C(2)
         IF(M-2)597,597,596
   596 DO 598 K=1,M
         V(K)=0.0
         Y(K)=0.0
   598 F(K+2)=0.0
         V(2)=1.0
         DO 599 K=3,M
         ZIP=K-1
         Y(1)=COSF(3.14159265*ZIP/2.)
         DO 594 J=2,K
   594 Y(J)=2.*V(J-1) - Y(J)
         DO 595 J=1,K
         F(J) = F(J) + C(K)*Y(J)
         ZIP=V(J)
         V(J) = Y(J)
   595 Y(J) = ZIP
   599 CONTINUE
C        GO BACK TO ORIGINAL INTERVAL
   597 Y(1) = F(1)
         DO 580 K=2,M
   580 Y(K)=0.0
         DO 583 K=2,M
         L=K-1
         Y(K) = Y(K) + F(K)/SUM2**L
         SUM3=1.0
         ZIP=1.0
         X2=K
         DO 582 J=1,L
         X1=J
         SUM3=SUM3*X1
         DV=SUM3*SUM2**L
         ZIP=ZIP*(X2-X1)
   582 Y(K-J)=Y(K-J) + (ZIP*SUM1**J*(-1.)**J*F(K))/DV
   583 CONTINUE
C        COEFFICIENTS STORED IN Y(K)
         DO 584 K=1,M
         I=K-1
   584 PUNCH 585, I, Y(K)
   585 FORMAT(30X,2HA(,I2,3H) =,E16.8)
         STOP
         END
02
0010
1.0          1.0
2.0          5.0          7.0          8.0          10.0          11.0          11.0
10.0         9.0          8.0
```

Fig. 11.7 *(cont.)*

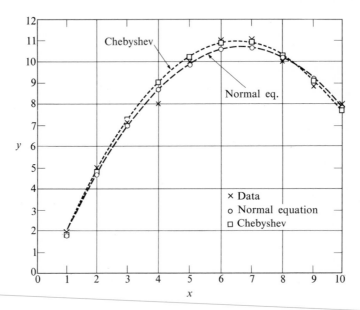

Fig. 11.8. Normal equation solution vs. Chebyshev polynomial solution.

For our specific example, the series is expressed in the interval (1, 10), and the resulting coefficients are

$$A(0) = -1.5601329, \quad A(1) = 3.8158582, \quad A(2) = -0.2909781.$$

Using the same set of data points with the normal-equation approach, we obtain the coefficients

$$A(0) = -1.2999683, \quad A(1) = 3.5651364, \quad A(2) = -0.2651502.$$

Although the two sets of coefficients appear to differ considerably, an evaluation of the polynomial Y_m at each of the x-coordinates with both sets of coefficients indicates that the curve fits are remarkably close. This similarity can be seen in Fig. 11.8.

BIBLIOGRAPHY

General References

ASCHER, M., and G. A. FORSYTHE, "SWAC Experiments on the Use of Orthogonal Polynomials for Data Fitting," *J. Assoc. Comput. Mach.*, 5 (1958).

BLUM, E. K., "Polynomial Approximation," *U. S. Naval Ordinance Laboratory Report 3740* (1956).

CLENSHAW, C. W., "Curve Fitting with a Digital Computer," in *Comput. J.*, **2**, pp. 170–173 (1960).

CLENSHAW, C. W., "Polynomial Approximations to Elementary Functions," *Math. Tables Aids Comput.*, **8**, pp. 143–147 (1954).

FORSYTHE, G. E., "Generation and Use of Orthogonal Polynomials for Data Fitting with a Digital Computer," *J. Soc. Ind. Appl. Math.*, **5**, pp. 74–88 (1957).

HAYES, J. G., and T. VICKERS, "The Fitting of Polynomials to Unequally Spaced Data," *Phil. Mag.*, **42**, pp. 1387–1400 (1951).

LANCZOS, C., *Approximations by Orthogonal Polynomials*. University of California, Los Angeles, 1952.

VON HOLDT, R. E., and R. J. BROUSSEAU, *Weighted Least-Squares Polynomial Approximation to a Continuous Function of a Single Value*. University of California Radiation Laboratory, Livermore, 1956.

Chebyshev Polynomials

CLENSHAW, C. W., "A Note on the Summation of Chebyshev Series," *Math. Tab., Wash.*, **9**, pp. 118–120 (1955).

LANCZOS, C., Introduction to "Tables of Chebyshev Polynomials," *Nat. Bur. Std. (U.S.) Appl. Math. Ser.*, **9** (1952); *Applied Analysis*, Prentice-Hall, Englewood Cliffs, N. J., 1956.

MURNAGHAN, F. D., and J. W. WRENCH, "The Determination of the Chebyshev Approximating Polynomial for a Differentiable Function," *Math. Tab., Wash.*, **13**, 185–193 (1959).

PROBLEMS

1. The number of graduate students enrolled in the College of Engineering of a major eastern university for a period of 11 years is tabulated below:

t	N	t	N
1952	920	1958	1260
1953	970	1959	1260
1954	940	1960	1325
1955	1000	1961	1350
1956	1100	1962	1360
1957	1180		

Fit these points to the polynomials

$$N = a_0 + a_1 t + a_2 t^2 + a_3 t^3,$$

by (a) normal equation method and (b) Chebyshev polynomials.

2. An oxyacetylene torch is used to cut a one-inch piece of metal of varying thickness. The following data are given.

Metal thickness, in. (t)	Time to cut 1 in., min (T)	Metal thickness, in. (t)	Time to cut 1 in., min (T)
$\frac{1}{4}$	0.036	$3\frac{1}{2}$	0.077
$\frac{3}{8}$	0.037	4	0.084
$\frac{1}{2}$	0.039	$4\frac{1}{2}$	0.091
$\frac{3}{4}$	0.042	5	0.100
1	0.046	$5\frac{1}{2}$	0.106
$1\frac{1}{4}$	0.050	6	0.111
$1\frac{1}{2}$	0.053	$6\frac{1}{2}$	0.118
2	0.059	7	0.125
$2\frac{1}{2}$	0.065	$7\frac{1}{2}$	0.134
3	0.072	8	0.143

Find coefficients for a least-squares curve of the form

(a) $T = c_0 + c_1 t$,

(b) $T = c_0 + c_1 t + c_2 t^2$,

(c) $T = c_0 + c_1 t + c_2 t^2 + c_3 t^3$.

3. A cooling fin is placed in an air stream and the center of the fin is heated by a heater to simulate an air-cooled engine cylinder. Twelve thermocouples are placed at equal distances radially on the fin for temperature measurements. During one test run, the following data were taken:

Radius, in. (R)	Temperature, °F (T)	Radius, in. (R)	Temperature, °F (T)
1	138.0	7	148.1
2	138.8	8	150.2
3	139.7	9	152.3
4	141.5	10	152.9
5	143.4	11	153.5
6	145.6	12	153.8

Fit the data into the following curve:

$$T = c_0 + c_1 R + c_2 R^2 + c_3 R^3.$$

Use normal equations and Chebyshev polynomials.

CHAPTER 12

NUMERICAL INTEGRATION

12.1 PRELIMINARY REMARKS

Two facts which relate to the evaluation of a definite integral are not commonly recognized:

(1) An integral does not always have its closed-form expression.

(2) Even when this closed-form expression is available, it is sometimes preferable to compute the integral by numerical methods.

For example, consider the integral

$$\int_0^x \sqrt{ax^2 + b}\, x^2\, dx = \frac{x}{4a} (ax^2 + b)^{3/2} - \frac{bx}{8a} \sqrt{ax^2 + b}$$

$$- \frac{b^2}{8a\sqrt{a}} \ln (x\sqrt{a} + \sqrt{ax^2 + b}), \qquad \text{when } a \geq 0;$$

$$= \frac{x}{4a} (ax^2 + b)^{3/2} - \frac{bx}{8a} \sqrt{ax^2 + b} \tag{12.1}$$

$$- \frac{b^2}{8a\sqrt{-a}} \sin^{-1} \left(x\sqrt{\frac{-a}{b}} \right), \qquad \text{when } a < 0.$$

When we are to compute the values corresponding to a large number of values of x, it is often advantageous to make a numerical evaluation of the integrals. Numerical integration is often known as *quadrature*.

The Gaussian quadrature procedure to evaluate a definite integral is in many ways better than other methods; it is accurate and requires fewer computational steps. However, a study of this procedure demands a complete understanding of the two types of special polynomials, namely, Lagrange polynomials and Legendre polynomials. The Lagrange polynomials and their associated interpolation formula were already discussed in Section 10.3, while a brief discussion was presented in Section 11.4 on general orthogonal polynomials, of which the Legendre polynomials are special cases.

To help build up background, we shall summarize the principal properties of the Legendre polynomials in the next section. Once they are fully understood, it is a relatively simple matter to study the Gaussian quadrature procedure.

12.2   LEGENDRE POLYNOMIALS

The first five orthogonal polynomials of Legendre are

$$
\begin{aligned}
P_0(x) &= 1, \\
P_1(x) &= x, \\
P_2(x) &= \tfrac{1}{2}(3x^2 - 1), \\
P_3(x) &= \tfrac{1}{2}(5x^3 - 3x), \\
P_4(x) &= \tfrac{1}{8}(35x^4 - 30x^2 + 3).
\end{aligned}
\tag{12.2}
$$

The Legendre polynomial of degree n can be† obtained from Rodrigues' formula

$$
P_n(x) = \frac{1}{2^n n!} \frac{d^n}{dx^n} (x^2 - 1)^n
\tag{12.3}
$$

or from the recurrence relation

$$
(n + 1)P_{n+1}(x) - (2n + 1)xP_n(x) + nP_{n-1}(x) = 0.
\tag{12.4}
$$

The orthogonality and normalization relations, with the weighting function equal to unity, are

$$
\int_{-1}^{1} P_n(x)P_m(x)\, dx =
\begin{cases}
0 & \text{if } n \neq m, & (12.5\text{a}) \\[2mm]
\dfrac{2}{2n + 1} & \text{if } n = m. & (12.5\text{b})
\end{cases}
$$

It is worth while to note that all the roots of each $P_n(x) = 0$ are real and distinct, and are between -1 and $+1$.

12.3   GAUSSIAN QUADRATURE

The purpose of this section is to discuss the Gaussian integration formula which approximates the definite integral

$$
\int_{-1}^{1} f(x)\, dx,
$$

and to show that by a simple change of variables, the procedure can be extended to limits of integration other than $(-1, 1)$.

---

† For example, see Hildebrand, F. B., *Advanced Calculus for Applications*. Prentice-Hall, Englewood Cliffs, N.J., p. 164, 1962.

This method serves to approximate the definite integral

$$\int_{-1}^{1} f(x)\, dx$$

by the expression

$$\int_{-1}^{1} f(x)\, dx = w_0 f(x_0) + w_1 f(x_1) + \cdots + w_n f(x_n) = \sum_{k=0}^{n} w_k f(x_k), \quad (12.6)$$

where $w_0, w_1, \ldots, w_n$ are the weighting coefficients and $x_0, x_1, \ldots, x_n$, are the associated points. The basic problem is to determine these $2n + 2$ constants and our basic assumption is that Eq. (12.6) should involve no approximations if the integrand $f(x)$ is a polynomial of degree $2n + 1$ or less.

We shall first show that the associated points x_k ($k = 0, 1, \ldots, n$) are equal to the values of the roots of a Legendre polynomial $P_{n+1}(x)$. These polynomials were discussed in Section 12.2.

Let us arbitrarily take a polynomial $g_n(x)$ of degree n. This polynomial can be written in terms of the Legendre polynomials as

$$g_n(x) = \beta_0 P_0(x) + \beta_1 P_1(x) + \cdots + \beta_n P_n(x). \quad (12.7)$$

As an illustration, let us suppose that

$$g_3(x) = 1 + 3x + 4x^2 - 7x^3. \quad (12.8)$$

From Eq. (12.7) we have

$$g_3(x) = \beta_0 + \beta_1 x + \frac{\beta_2}{2}(3x^2 - 1) + \frac{\beta_3}{2}(5x^3 - 3x). \quad (12.9)$$

Expanding the right-hand side of Eq. (12.9) and comparing the coefficients with Eq. (12.8), we find that

$$g_3(x) = \tfrac{7}{3}P_0(x) - \tfrac{6}{5}P_1(x) + \tfrac{8}{3}P_2(x) - \tfrac{14}{5}P_3(x).$$

This simple example serves to show that any polynomial $g_n(x)$ can be written in terms of the Legendre polynomials.

From Eq. (12.5a), the orthogonality relation, we have

$$\int_{-1}^{1} g_n(x)P_{n+1}(x)\, dx = \int_{-1}^{1} \beta_0 P_0(x)P_{n+1}(x)\, dx + \int_{-1}^{1} \beta_1 P_1(x)P_{n+1}(x)\, dx + \cdots$$

$$+ \int_{-1}^{1} \beta_n P_n(x)P_{n+1}(x)\, dx = 0. \quad (12.10)$$

It is worth while to note that $g_n(x)P_{n+1}(x)$ is a polynomial of degree $2n + 1$. Hence it satisfies the basic requirement in the selection of the weighting coefficients w_k and associated points x_k ($k = 0, 1, \ldots, n$). Comparing Eq. (12.10) with Eq. (12.6) and noting that $g_n(x)P_{n+1}(x)$ is the integrand, we have

$$w_0 g_n(x_0)P_{n+1}(x_0) + w_1 g_n(x_1)P_{n+1}(x_1) + \cdots + w_n g_n(x_n)P_{n+1}(x_n) = 0. \quad (12.11)$$

In the above equation, $g_n(x)$ is an *arbitrarily* chosen polynomial. For each value of x_k $(k = 0, 1, \ldots, n)$, we find that $g_n(x_k)$ has a corresponding value. Not all of these $n + 1$ corresponding values can be equal to zero, and not all of the $n + 1$ weighting coefficients w_k $(k = 0, 1, \ldots, n)$ can be equal to zero. Should this be so, then Eq. (12.6) would become identically zero, which is a trivial case. Therefore, the only condition which must be satisfied for Eq. (12.11) is that

$$P_{n+1}(x_0) = 0,$$
$$P_{n+1}(x_1) = 0,$$
$$\vdots$$
$$P_{n+1}(x_n) = 0.$$

In other words, the associated points $x_0, x_1, \ldots, x_n$ are the roots of the Legendre polynomial $P_{n+1}(x) = 0$. There are $n + 1$ distinct real roots in the interval $(-1, 1)$. For example, for $n = 2$, the roots of $P_3(x) = \frac{1}{2}(5x^3 - 3x) = 0$ are $-\sqrt{3/5}$, 0, and $\sqrt{3/5}$, respectively. In the remainder of this chapter we shall use the subscripted x, such as $x_0, x_1, \ldots, x_k, \ldots, x_n$ to indicate the roots of the Legendre polynomial $P_{n+1}(x)$.

Having selected the values of x_k, we now turn to the determination of the values of the weighting coefficients w_k $(k = 0, 1, \ldots, n)$. We recall that in accordance with our basic requirement, Eq. (12.6) must involve no approximation if the integrand $f(x)$ is a polynomial of degree $2n + 1$ or less. By the definition of the Lagrange polynomial, any polynomial $h_n(x)$ of degree n passing through x_k $(k = 0, 1, \ldots, n)$ points may be expressed in the form

$$h_n(x) = \sum_{k=0}^{n} h(x_k)L_k(x). \tag{12.12}$$

Hence

$$\int_{-1}^{1} h_n(x)\, dx = \int_{-1}^{1} \sum_{k=0}^{n} h(x_k)L_k(x), \tag{12.13}$$

and since $h(x_k)$ is a constant, we have

$$\int_{-1}^{1} h_n(x)\, dx = \sum_{k=0}^{n} h(x_k) \int_{-1}^{1} L_k(x)\, dx. \tag{12.14}$$

Comparing Eq. (12.6) with Eq. (12.14), we obtain

$$w_k = \int_{-1}^{1} L_k(x)\, dx, \qquad k = 0, 1, \ldots, n. \tag{12.15}$$

As a practical computational detail, one frequently calculates the weighting coefficients w_k in terms of the Legendre polynomials $P_n(x)$:

$$w_k = \frac{1}{P'_{n+1}(x_k)} \int_{-1}^{1} \frac{P_{n+1}(x)\, dx}{x - x_k}. \tag{12.16}$$

To see why Eq. (12.16) is valid, we first note that the polynomial

$$\frac{P_{n+1}(x)}{x - x_k}$$

has zero value for $x = x_j$ $(j \neq k, j = 0, 1, \ldots, n)$. Then, by L'Hôpital's rule, we have

$$\lim_{x \to x_k} \frac{P_{n+1}(x)}{x - x_k} = \left[\frac{dP_{n+1}(x)/dx}{d(x - x_k)/dx} \right]_{x=x_k} = P'_{n+1}(x_k), \qquad (12.17)$$

where the x_k is one of the $n + 1$ roots of the Legendre polynomial $P_{n+1}(x) = 0$. Hence the Lagrange polynomial can be written as

$$L_k(x) = \frac{1}{P'_{n+1}(x_k)} \frac{P_{n+1}(x)}{x - x_k}, \qquad (12.18)$$

since it assumes the value of 0 at $x = x_j$ $(j \neq k)$, and the value of 1 at $x = x_k$, where the derivative of $P_{n+1}(x_k)$ has been established in Eq. (12.17). Substituting Eq. (12.18) into Eq. (12.15), one readily obtains Eq. (12.16).

For purposes of illustration, we now use Eq. (12.16) to compute w_0, w_1, and w_2 $(n = 2)$. Since $n = 2$, we have

$$P_{n+1}(x) = P_3(x) = \tfrac{1}{2}(5x^3 - 3x),$$

whose roots are $x_0 = -\sqrt{\tfrac{3}{5}}$, $x_1 = 0$, $x_2 = \sqrt{\tfrac{3}{5}}$, and whose derivative is

$$P'_3(x) = \tfrac{3}{2}(5x^2 - 1).$$

Thus

$$w_0 = \frac{1}{\tfrac{3}{2}(5 \cdot \tfrac{3}{5} - 1)} \int_{-1}^{1} \frac{\tfrac{1}{2}(5x^3 - 3x)\,dx}{x + \sqrt{\tfrac{3}{5}}} = \frac{2}{3(3-1)} \int_{-1}^{1} \tfrac{1}{2}(x^2 - \sqrt{\tfrac{3}{5}}x) = \tfrac{5}{9},$$

$$w_1 = \frac{1}{\tfrac{3}{2}(5 \cdot 0 - 1)} \int_{-1}^{1} \frac{\tfrac{1}{2}(5x^3 - 3x)}{x - 0} = \tfrac{8}{9},$$

$$w_2 = \frac{1}{\tfrac{3}{2}(5 \cdot \tfrac{3}{5} - 1)} \int_{-1}^{1} \frac{\tfrac{1}{2}(5x^3 - 3x)}{x - \sqrt{\tfrac{3}{5}}} = \frac{2}{3(3-1)} \int_{-1}^{1} \tfrac{1}{2}(x^2 + \sqrt{\tfrac{3}{5}}x)\,dx = \tfrac{5}{9}.$$

Table 12.1 lists the w_k and x_k for a number of values of n (from $n = 2$ to $n = 5$).

Example 12.1

Approximate the following definite integral using Gaussian quadrature with $n = 2$:

$$I = \int_{-1}^{1} x^2 \cos x \, dx.$$

Solution: Let

$$f(x) = x^2 \cos x \quad \text{and} \quad I \doteq w_0 f(x_0) + w_1 f(x_1) + w_2 f(x_2).$$

TABLE 12.1. Weighting Coefficients w_k and Associated Points x_k for Gaussian Quadrature Formula

n	Weighting coefficients w_k	Associated points x_k
2	$\frac{8}{9}$	0
	$\frac{5}{9}$	$\pm 0.774\ 596\ 669$
3	0.652 145 154 9	$\pm 0.339\ 981\ 043\ 6$
	0.347 854 845 1	$\pm 0.861\ 136\ 311\ 6$
4	0.568 888 888 8	0
	0.478 628 670 5	$\pm 0.538\ 469\ 310\ 1$
	0.236 926 885 1	$\pm 0.906\ 179\ 845\ 9$
5	0.467 913 934 6	$\pm 0.238\ 619\ 186\ 1$
	0.360 761 573 0	$\pm 0.661\ 209\ 386\ 5$
	0.171 324 492 4	$\pm 0.932\ 469\ 514\ 2$

We then obtain the following:

Weighting coefficients	Associated points
$w_0 = \frac{5}{9}$	$x_0 = -\sqrt{\frac{3}{5}}$
$w_1 = \frac{8}{9}$	$x_1 = 0$
$w_2 = \frac{5}{9}$	$x_2 = \sqrt{\frac{3}{5}}$

Hence

$$I \doteqdot \tfrac{5}{9}(x_0^2 \cos x_0) + \tfrac{8}{9}(x_1^2 \cos x_1) + \tfrac{5}{9}(x_2^2 \cos x_2)$$
$$= 0.47650.$$

It may be noted that this integral has the following closed-form solution:

$$\int_{-1}^{1} x^2 \cos x \, dx = [2x \cos x + (x^2 - 2) \sin x]_{-1}^{1}$$
$$= 0.47830.$$

To extend our discussion to the case where the lower and upper limits of integration are a and b, respectively, we must first obtain a relation that holds for the limits of integration, -1 to 1. We do this by simply using

$$x = \frac{(b - a)t + (b + a)}{2}, \tag{12.19}$$

$$dx = \frac{b - a}{2} \, dt. \tag{12.20}$$

For example, suppose that we wish to approximate the following integral, using the three-point ($n = 2$) Gaussian quadrature:

$$I_1 = \int_0^3 x^2 \cos x \, dx.$$

We have $a = 0$ and $b = 3$; hence

$$x = 3(t + 1)/2, \quad \text{and} \quad dx = \tfrac{3}{2} \, dt.$$

Therefore

$$I_1 = \int_0^3 x^2 \cos x \, dx$$

$$= \frac{3}{2} \int_{-1}^1 \left[\frac{3(t + 1)}{2} \right]^2 \cos \left[\frac{3(t + 1)}{2} \right] dt.$$

Using the three-point Gaussian quadrature, we find that the associated points in terms of the new variable t are $t_0 = -\sqrt{\tfrac{3}{5}}, t_1 = 0$, and $t_2 = \sqrt{\tfrac{3}{5}}$. Therefore we have

$$I_1 = \frac{3}{2} \left(\frac{5}{9} \left\{ \left[\frac{3}{2} (t_0 + 1) \right]^2 \cos \frac{3(t_0 + 1)}{2} \right\} + \frac{8}{9} \left\{ \left[\frac{3}{2} (t_1 + 1) \right]^2 \cos \frac{3(t_1 + 1)}{2} \right\} \right.$$

$$\left. + \frac{5}{9} \left\{ \left[\frac{3}{2} (t_2 + 1) \right]^2 \cos \frac{3(t_2 + 1)}{2} \right\} \right) = -4.936.$$

For comparison, the closed-form solution is equal to

$$[2x \cos x + (x^2 - 2) \sin x]_0^3 = -4.952.$$

12.4   GAUSSIAN QUADRATURE IN FORTRAN LANGUAGE

We shall now develop a FORTRAN subprogram to evaluate the integration of $f(x) \, dx$ between the limits A and B by using Gaussian quadrature, which is expressed as

$$\int_A^B f(x) \, dx = \frac{B - A}{2} \sum_{i=1}^N w_i f \left(\frac{(B - A)t_i + (B + A)}{2} \right),$$

where $w_1, w_2, \ldots, w_N$ are weighting coefficients and $t_1, t_2, \ldots, t_N$ are the roots of the Legendre polynomial $P_N(t) = 0$. The value of N ranges from 3 to 6 in this program. The computation starts with $N = 3$. The program will first compare the result based on $N = 3$ with that based on $N = 4$. The results must satisfy the criterion

$$\epsilon \geq \frac{A_{n+1} - A_n}{A_n}, \tag{12.21}$$

where A_{n+1} is the answer based on $N + 1$ points, A_n is the answer based on N points, and ϵ is arbitrarily taken (in this program) to be 10^{-4}. If the result fails to pass the above test, the value of N will be increased by one. The maximum value of N is set to 6 in this program.

```
      SUBROUTINE GAUSS   (A, B, X, F, KOUNT)
C
C     INTEGRATION OF F(X).DX BY GAUSSIAN QUADRATUREBETWEEN THE
C     LIMITS A AND B.
C
C     NOMENCLATURE FOR THE ARGUMENTS
C          A = THE LOWER LIMIT OF INTEGRATION,
C          B = THE UPPER LIMIT OF INTEGRATION,
C          X = INDEPENDENT VARIABLE OF FUNCTION F(X),
C          F = F(X) UNDER INTEGRAL SIGN,
C          KOUNT = AN INTEGER USED TO CONTROL THE WAY OF EXECUTION,
C          ANS = ANSWER OF THE INTEGRATION.
C
      DIMENSION W(4,6), T(4,6)
      IF (KOUNT) 8, 10, 8
    8 GO TO 30
   10 ANS = 1.0
      IPOINT = 2
C
C     EPSILON FOR CONVERGENCE
C
      EPS = 10.E-05
C
C     STORE WEIGHTING COEFFICIENTS AND LEGENDRE ROOTS.
C
      DO 2 I=1, 4
      IP2 = I + 2
    2 READ 1, (W(I,K), K=1, IP2), (T(I,K), K=1, IP2)
    1 FORMAT (5F15.10)
C
C     CHANGE INTEGRATION LIMITS TO (-1 TO +1).
C
C     THE NEXT STATEMENT IS TO EVALUATE THE COEFFICIENT OF THE
C     NEW FUNCTION.
C
      C = (B - A)/2.
   18 IPOINT = IPOINT + 1
      TEMP = ANS
      ANS = 0.
      IPM2 = IPOINT - 2
      KOUNT = 1
C
C     EVALUATE NEW VARIABLES WHICH ARE EXPRESSED IN TERM OF
C     THE LEGENDRE ROOT.
C
   20 X =   C*T(IPM2,KOUNT) + (B + A)/2.
      RETURN
C
C     CARRY OUT INTEGRATION BY CALCULATING
C          ANS = C*(W1*F(X1) + W2*F(X2) + - - -).
C
   30 ANS = ANS + C*W(IPM2,KOUNT)*F
      KOUNT = KOUNT + 1
      IF (KOUNT - IPOINT) 20, 20, 40
   40 IF (IPOINT - 3) 18, 18, 50
C
```

Fig. 12.1. SUBROUTINE GAUSS. The 11 data cards must be used during the computing stage, but not during the compiling stage.

```
C       NEXT THREE STATEMENTS FOR DETERMINING WHETHER THE DEVIATION
C       OF ANSWER IS WITHIN THE LIMIT.
C       IF IT IS NOT, TAKE ONE MORE POINT GAUSSIAN INTEGRATION.
C
   50 DELT = ABSF(ANS - TEMP)
      RATIO = DELT/ABSF(TEMP)
    7 IF (RATIO - EPS) 70, 70, 80
C
C       PUNCH OUT THE ANSWER IF THE DEVIATION COMES WITHIN THE LIMIT.
C
   70 PUNCH 72, IPOINT, ANS
   72 FORMAT (///5X,16HBY CONVERGENCE, , I2,24H POINT GAUSS. QUADRARURE,
    1 15H GIVES ANSWER =,E14.8//)
      KOUNT = 7
      RETURN
   80 IF (IPOINT - 6) 18, 100, 100
  100 PUNCH 102, IPOINT, ANS
C
C       THE ANSWER IS PUNCHED OUT AFTER SIX POINT GAUSSIAN INTEGRATION
C       HAS BEEN EXECUTED AND THE DEVIATION IS STILL NOT WITHIN THE LIMIT.
C
  102 FORMAT (///5X,22HBY LIMITS OF PROGRAM, ,I2,14H POINT GAUSS. ,
    123HQUADRATURE GIVES ANS. =,E14.8//)
      KOUNT = 7
      RETURN
C
C       DATA FOR WEIGHTING COEFFICIENTS AND LEGENDRE ROOTS
C
      END
```

.5555555556	.8888888889	.5555555556	.7745966692	.0
-.7745966692				
.3478548451	.6521451549	.6521451549	.3478548451	.8611363116
.3399810436	-.3399810436	-.8611363116		
.2369268851	.4786286705	.5688888889	.4782686705	.2369268851
.9061798459	.5384693101	.0	-.5384693101	-.9061798459
.1713244924	.3607615730	.4679139346	.4679139346	.3607615730
.1713244924	.9324695142	.6612093865	.2386191861	-.2386191861
-.6612093865	-.9324695142			

Fig. 12.1   (*cont.*)

Nine data cards are provided here to be read in as the weighting coefficients and the roots of Legendre polynomials. They should not be used during the compilation stage, but only during execution. The subroutine GAUSS and its flow chart are shown in Figs. 12.1 and 12.2, respectively.

The output from this subroutine is in one of two forms:

(1) If the result passes the test shown in Eq. (12.21), an answer having the following format will be punched out:

```
BY CONVERGENCE, 5 POINT GAUSS. QUADRATURE GIVES ANSWER=-.49523118E+01
```

(2) If it does not pass the test when $N = 6$, the following answer will be punched out:

```
BY LIMITS OF PROGRAM, 6 POINT GAUSS. QUADRATURE GIVES ANS.=-.49521140E+01
```

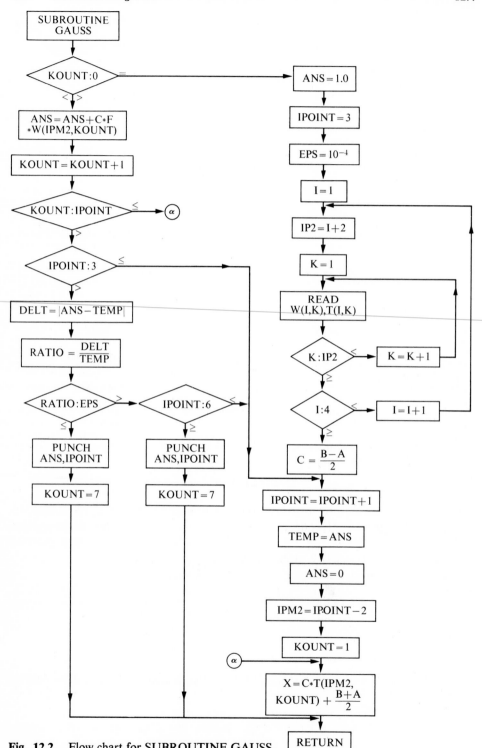

Fig. 12.2. Flow chart for **SUBROUTINE GAUSS.**

```
C        MAIN PROGRAM FOR GAUSSIAN INTEGRATION OF Z(X).DX BETWEEN THE
C        LIMITS A AND B.
C        YOU MUST CHANGE THE STATEMENTS 1,2 AND 5.
C        STATEMENT 1 IS FOR THE LOWER LIMIT OF INTEGRATION.
C        STATEMENT 2 IS FOR THE UPPER LIMIT OF INTEGRATION.
C        STATEMENT 5 IS FOR THE FUNCTION  UNDER THE INTEGRAL SIGN.
C        NEXT TWO STATEMENTS FOR LOWER AND UPPER LIMITS.
C        YOU CHANGE THE RIGHT HAND SIDE.
C
    1 A = 0.
    2 B = 3.
C
C        NEXT STATEMENT FOR INITIALIZATION
C
      KOUNT = 0
      X = 9.999
C
C        NEXT STATEMENT IS THE FUNCTION UNDER INTEGRAL SIGN.
C
    5 F = X*X*COSF(X)
    6 CALL GAUSS (A, B, X, F, KOUNT)
   14 GO TO (5, 5, 5, 5, 5, 5, 17), KOUNT
   17 STOP
      END
```

Fig. 12.3. Main program to call SUBROUTINE GAUSS.

Example 12.2

Using Gaussian quadrature, write a main program to approximate the integral

$$\int_0^3 x^2 \cos x \, dx.$$

This main program will be used to call the subroutine GAUSS, shown in Fig. 12.2; it will also serve to express the upper and lower limits and the integrand $f(x) = x^2 \cos x$.

Figure 12.3 illustrates a sample main program. Statements 1 and 2 serve to indicate the lower and upper limits of integration, respectively. Statement 5 is used to express the integrand $f(x)$. Statement 14 provides an easy method of taking care of multiple exits by using a computed GO TO statement. This statement,

GO TO (5,5,5,5,5,5;17),KOUNT

will transfer operations to statement 5 if KOUNT = 1, to statement 5 if KOUNT = 2,..., to statement 17 if KOUNT = 7. The output is

```
BY CONVERGENCE, 5 POINT GAUSS. QUADRATURE GIVES ANSWER=-.49523118E+01
```

It should be noted that this main program can be used for any integrand and for any given limits with only a slight modification. A change of only three statements is involved, namely, statements 1, 2, and 5. If, for example, we wish to approximate the integral

$$\int_{0.1}^{10} (x/\sqrt{1 + x}) \, dx,$$

then these three statements become

```
  C     . . .

  C     . . .

      1  A = 0.1
      2  B = 10.

         . . .

         . . .

      5  F = X/SQRTF(1.+X)

         . . .

         . . .

         . . .

        END
```

BIBLIOGRAPHY

General References

ABRAMOWITZ, M., "On the Practical Evaluation of Integrals," *J. Soc. Ind. Appl. Math.*, **2**, pp. 20–35 (1954).

BYRD, P. F., and M. D. FRIEDMAN, *Handbook of Elliptic Integrals for Engineers and Physicists.* Springer-Verlag, Berlin, 1954.

CLENSHAW, C. W., and A. R. CURTIS, "A Method for Numerical Integration on an Automatic Computer," *Numer. Math.*, **2**, pp. 197–205 (1960).

EBERLEIN, W. F., "Theory of Numerical Integration, I, Preliminary Report," *Bull. Am. Math. Soc.*, **60**, pp. 366–367 (1954).

FETTIS, H. E., "Numerical Calculation of Certain Definite Integrals by Poisson's Summation Formula," *Math. Tab. Wash.*, **9**, pp. 85–92 (1955).

GAUTSCHI, W., "Recursive Computation of Certain Integrals," *J. Assoc. Comput. Mach.*, **8**, pp. 21–40 (1961).

HAMMERLIN, G., "Zur Numerischen Integration Periodischer Funktionen," *Z. Angew. Math. Mech.*, **39**, pp. 80–82 (1959).

HARTREE, D. R., "The Evaluation of a Diffraction Integral," *Proc. Cambridge Phil. Soc.*, **50**, pp. 567–576 (1954).

LUKE, Y. L., "Evaluation of an Integral Arising in Numerical Integration Near a Logarithmic Singularity," *Math. Tab., Wash.*, **10**, pp. 14–21 (1956).

STROUD, A. H., "A Bibliography on Approximate Integration," *Math. Comp.*, **15**, pp. 52–80 (1961).

TODD, J., "Evaluation of the Exponential Integral for Large Complex Arguments," *J. Res. Nat. Bur. Std.*, **52**, pp. 313–317 (1956).

Gaussian Quadrature

DAVIS, P., and P. RABINOWITZ, "Abscissas and Weights for Gaussian Quadratures of High Order," *J. Res. Nat. Bur. Std.*, **56**, pp. 35–37 (1956).

DAVIS, P., and P. RABINOWITZ, "Additional Abscissas and Weights for Gaussian Quadratures of High Order . . . Values for *N*-64, 80, and 96," *J. Res. Nat. Bur. Std.*, **60**, pp. 613–614 (1958).

PROBLEMS

Write a complete FORTRAN program to evaluate the following integrals by using the Gaussian quadrature formula for three points:

1. $\int_0^3 x^2 \sin x^2 \, dx.$

2. $\int_0^2 \dfrac{t \sin t \, dt}{27 + t^3}.$

3. $\int_0^4 \dfrac{e^{-x^2/2}}{\sqrt{2\pi}}.$

4. $\int_0^1 \dfrac{dx}{1 + x^2}.$

5. $\int_0^\pi \dfrac{\sin x}{x} \, dx.$

6. It is desired to generate a certain waveform in an electric circuit. The waveform $f(t)$ is defined by

$$f(t) = 50 \cos (2\pi/200)t, \quad -50 \le t \le 50;$$
$$f(t) = 0, \quad -100 \le t \le -50, \quad 50 \le t \le 100.$$

Thus the period T is seen to be 200. The waveform will be represented by the first 10 terms in the Fourier series expansion of f(t). We seek

$$f(t) = A_0 + \sum_{n=1}^{9} [2A_n \cos (n\omega t)],$$

where $\omega = 2\pi/T$. Given that

$$A_n = (2/T) \int_0^{T/2} f(t) \cos (n\omega t) \, dt; \quad n = 0, 1, 2, \dots,$$

find $A_0, A_1, A_2, \dots, A_9$.

7. Given the integral $\int_0^3 3x^2 \sin x \, dx$, and the closed solution

$$\int 3x^2 \sin x \, dx = 3[2x \sin x - (x^2 - 2) \cos x],$$

write a program in FORTRAN to evaluate the given integral by using the Gaussian quadrature formula both for four points and for five points. The output should be in the following form:

```
    NAME                  DATE                 EDITION 3
 4-POINT GAUSSIAN QUADRATURE
             T(0) = X.XXXXXXXX     W(0) = X.XXXXXXXX
             T(1) = X.XXXXXXXX     W(1) = X.XXXXXXXX
               ⋮                     ⋮
             T(3) = X.XXXXXXXX     W(3) = X.XXXXXXXX
 5-POINT GAUSSIAN QUADRATURE
             T(0) = X.XXXXXXXX     W(0) = X.XXXXXXXX
               ⋮                     ⋮
             T(4) = X.XXXXXXXX     W(4) = X.XXXXXXXX
 ANSWER FROM CLOSED-FORM EXPRESSION = X.XXXXX
 ANSWER FROM 4-POINT GAUSSIAN QUADRATURE = X.XXXXX
 ANSWER FROM 5-POINT GAUSSIAN QUADRATURE = X.XXXXX
```

8. Evaluate the integral

$$\int_0^2 \frac{x}{27 + x^3}\, dx$$

by (a) using the closed-form solution; (b) using the Gaussian quadrature formula for three points, and (c) using the Gaussian quadrature formula for four points. It is known that the following closed-form expression exists:

$$\int_0^x \frac{t}{a^3 + t^3}\, dt = \frac{1}{\sqrt{3}\, a} \tan^{-1} \frac{\sqrt{3}\, x}{2a - x} + \frac{1}{6a} \log_e \frac{a^2 - ax + x^2}{(a + x)^2}, \quad -a < x < 2a.$$

The output should be in the following form:

```
 YOUR NAME       ED. 3.       4/25/66
 Answer from closed-form expression = XXX.XXXXXX
 Answer from three-point Gaussian quad. Eq. = XXX.XXXXXX
 Answer from four-point Gaussian quad. Eq. = XXX.XXXXXX
```

CHAPTER 13

ERRORS

13.1 PRELIMINARY REMARKS

Aside from possible mistakes in the initial data, there may also be round-off and truncation errors in machine computations. Round-off errors stem from a finite number of digits in a computer word, while truncation errors are due mainly to finite approximations of limiting processes.

This chapter summarizes the elements of these two types of errors. Error analysis for complicated computations is subject to continuing research. The interested reader is referred to the bibliography at the end of this chapter for further information.

13.2 ROUND-OFF ERRORS

If we are given a decimal number which contains a fractional part and we attempt to convert it to its binary equivalent, a conversion error due to the finite word length of the computer may be introduced, particularly if there is no *exact* binary equivalent.

For example, the decimal number 0.625 can be represented as a binary number without conversion error since it has an exact binary equivalent:†

$$0.625 = \tfrac{5}{8} = (\tfrac{1}{2})^1 + (\tfrac{1}{2})^3$$

$$= \boxed{.\,|\,1\,|\,0\,|\,1\,}$$

However, if we attempt to convert the decimal number 0.626 to its binary equivalent, we find that an infinite series is needed:

$$0.626 = (\tfrac{1}{2})^1 + (\tfrac{1}{2})^3 + (\tfrac{1}{2})^{10} + (\tfrac{1}{2})^{16} + (\tfrac{1}{2})^{17} + (\tfrac{1}{2})^{21} + \cdots$$

$$= \boxed{.\,|\,1\,|\,0\,|\,1\,|\,0\,|\,0\,|\,0\,|\,0\,|\,0\,|\,0\,|\,1\,|\,0\,|\,0\,|\,0\,|\,0\,|\,0\,|\,1\,|\,1\,|\,0\,|\,0\,|\,0\,|\,1\,|\,.\,|\,.\,|\,.\,}$$

---

† See Appendix B for a discussion of decimal-binary conversion.

Assuming that the binary machine has twenty bits available for representing the binary mantissa, we can read 0.626 as either

| . | 1 | 0 | 1 | 0 | 0 | 0 | 0 | 0 | 0 | 1 | 0 | 0 | 0 | 0 | 0 | 1 | 1 | 0 | 0 | 0 | (without rounding),

or

| . | 1 | 0 | 1 | 0 | 0 | 0 | 0 | 0 | 0 | 1 | 0 | 0 | 0 | 0 | 0 | 1 | 1 | 0 | 0 | 1 | (with rounding).

When either of these values is reconverted to an exact decimal equivalent with eight-digit accuracy, the error introduced by the initial decimal-binary conversion is clearly shown:

| . | 1 | 0 | 1 | 0 | 0 | 0 | 0 | 0 | 0 | 1 | 0 | 0 | 0 | 0 | 0 | 1 | 1 | 0 | 0 | 0 | = 0.62599945,

| . | 1 | 0 | 1 | 0 | 0 | 0 | 0 | 0 | 0 | 1 | 0 | 0 | 0 | 0 | 0 | 1 | 1 | 0 | 0 | 1 | = 0.62600040.

Even though no decimal-binary conversion may be necessary, another source of round-off error may be introduced if the calculation requires more digits than available through a machine or compiler. For example, if a decimal computer has a capacity of eight significant digits and we attempt to add the number 0.33333333 to itself four times, we find that the last significant digit will be truncated:

$$
\begin{array}{r}
0.33333333 \\
+0.33333333 \\
\hline
0.66666666 \\
+0.33333333 \\
\hline
0.99999999 \\
+0.33333333 \\
\hline
\end{array}
$$

Truncated to

True value $\longrightarrow$ 1.33333332 $\longrightarrow$ 1.3333333

Error = 0.00000002

After 3000 such additions, the error becomes 0.00908:

Expected value: 999.99999
Rounded-off value: 999.99091
Error: 0.00908

The study of round-off errors is important in high-speed digital computations and may be needed to:

(1) Estimate the final round-off error made in solving a given problem by a specific numerical method.

(2) Compare the round-off errors made in solving a given problem by different numerical methods.

(3) Examine the effect which the round-off errors of a particular numerical method may have upon the given problem in order to determine whether or not computation by that numerical method is worth while.

13.3 TRUNCATION ERRORS

Round-off errors were discussed in the previous section. We now consider the second type of errors—truncation errors—which stem from finite approximations of limiting processes. We will also discuss propagation of errors.

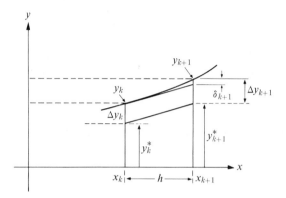

Fig. 13.1. Truncation errors.

The truncation error and its propagation will be treated by means of an initial-value problem (see Chapter 7). In this type of problem it may be given that at $x = x_0$, $y = y_0$; and knowing that $dy/dx = f(y, x)$, we may be asked to find the value of y corresponding to $x = x_m$. We might attempt to solve this problem by using a finite-difference approach in which a succession of ordinates $(y_1^*, y_2^*, \ldots, y_k^*, y_{k+1}^*, \ldots, y_m^*)$ corresponding to a set of abscissas $(x_1, x_2, \ldots, x_k, x_{k+1}, \ldots, x_m)$, spaced at equal intervals of length h, are approximated according to the relation

$$y_{k+1}^* - y_k^* = h \cdot f(y_k^*, x_k). \tag{13.1}$$

Corresponding to each approximated ordinate y_k^*, there is a true value y_k on the given curve, as shown in Fig. 13.1. The difference of the values can be expressed by

$$\Delta y_k = y_k - y_k^*. \tag{13.2}$$

If we attempt to apply Eq. (13.1) to the true ordinates y_k and y_{k+1}, we find that an additional error, which may be called δ_{k+1}, is introduced because we are approximating the slope of the given curve by a straight line:

$$y_{k+1} - y_k = h \cdot f(y_k, x_k) + \delta_{k+1}. \tag{13.3}$$

To determine the total error Δy_{k+1} at step $k + 1$, we can subtract Eq. (13.1) from

Eq. (13.3) and obtain:

$$(y_{k+1} - y_k) - (y_{k+1}^* - y_k^*) = h \cdot f(y_k, x_k) + \delta_{k+1} - h \cdot f(y_k^*, x_k).$$

After rearranging terms, we obtain

$$(y_{k+1} - y_{k+1}^*) - (y_k - y_k^*) = h[f(y_k, x_k) - f(y_k^*, x_k)] + \delta_{k+1};$$

and applying Eq. (13.2), we get

$$\Delta y_{k+1} - \Delta y_k = h[f(y_k^* + \Delta y_k, x_k) - f(y_k^*, x_k)] + \delta_{k+1}$$

or

$$\Delta y_{k+1} = \Delta y_k + h[f(y_k^* + \Delta y_k, x_k) - f(y_k^*, x_k)] + \delta_{k+1}. \tag{13.4}$$

We have thus obtained an expression for Δy_{k+1}, the total error accumulated after $k + 1$ steps, in terms of the total error Δy_k, after k steps, the error caused by Δy_k in making the $(k + 1)$-step (the second term on the right-hand side), and the error introduced strictly because of the truncation in the finite series approximation at step $k + 1$, or δ_{k+1}.

We recall that the Taylor series expansion can be written

$$f(y + k, x + h) = \sum_{n=0}^{N-1} \frac{1}{n!} \left(k \frac{\partial}{\partial y} + h \frac{\partial}{\partial x} \right)^n f(y, x) + R_N,$$

where the remainder after N terms is

$$R_N = \frac{1}{N!} \left(k \frac{\partial}{\partial y} + h \frac{\partial}{\partial x} \right)^N f(y + \theta k, x + \theta h), \qquad 0 \le \theta \le 1.$$

In applying this expansion we may rewrite the following function as two terms and a remainder:

$$f(y_k^* + \Delta y_k, x_k) = f(y_k^*, x_k) + f_y(y_k^*, x_k)(\Delta y_k) + f_{yy}(y_k^* + \theta \Delta y_k, x_k)(\Delta y_k)^2/2,$$

$$0 \le \theta \le 1.$$

Substituting this expansion into Eq. (13.4), we obtain

$$\Delta y_{k+1} = \Delta y_k + h[f(y_k^*, x_k) + f_y(y_k^*, x_k)(\Delta y_k)$$
$$+ f_{yy}(y_k^* + \theta \Delta y_k, x_k)(\Delta y_k)^2/2 - f(y_k^*, x_k)] + \delta_{k+1}$$
$$= \Delta y_k + h \Delta y_k [f_y(y_k^*, x_k)] + h(\Delta y_k)^2 f_{yy}(y_k^* + \theta \Delta y, x_k)/2 + \delta_{k+1}.$$

Since the second derivative term involves the small value $(\Delta y)^2$, it can often be ignored; thus the total error at the $(k + 1)$-step is expressed as

$$\Delta y_{k+1} = \Delta y_k + h \Delta y_k f_y(y_k^*, x_k) + \delta_{k+1}. \tag{13.5}$$

It should be noted that in our discussion we have considered the error introduced by, and solely due to, the $(k + 1)$-step as simply the truncation error δ_{k+1}. At each step, however, there are other errors introduced; e.g., round-off errors. Although we have ignored these other factors in our calculations, the total error introduced by the $(k + 1)$-step is actually different from δ_{k+1}.

In calculating the value of Δy_m in terms of the errors $\delta_1, \delta_2, \ldots, \delta_i, \ldots, \delta_m$, we begin at the given initial point and use Eq. (13.5) with $k = 0$ to evaluate successively:

$$\Delta y_0 = 0, \quad \text{at initial point } y = y_0 = y_0^*,$$

$$\Delta y_1 = \delta_1,$$

$$\begin{aligned}\Delta y_2 &= \Delta y_1[1 + hf_y(y_1^*, x_1)] + \delta_2 \\ &= \delta_1[1 + hf_y(y_1^*, x_1)] + \delta_2,\end{aligned}$$

$$\begin{aligned}\Delta y_3 &= \Delta y_2[1 + hf_y(y_2^*, x_2)] + \delta_3 \\ &= \delta_1[1 + hf_y(y_1^*, x_1)][1 + hf_y(y_2^*, x_2)] + \delta_2[1 + hf_y(y_2^*, x_2)] + \delta_3,\end{aligned}$$

$$\vdots$$

$$\begin{aligned}\Delta y_m &= \delta_1[1 + hf_y(y_1^*, x_1)][1 + hf_y(y_2^*, x_2)] \cdots [1 + hf_y(y_{m-1}^*, x_{m-1})] \\ &\quad + \delta_2[1 + hf_y(y_2^*, x_2)] \cdots [1 + hf_y(y_{m-1}^*, x_{m-1})] + \cdots \\ &\quad + \delta_i[1 + hf_y(y_i^*, x_i)] \cdots [1 + hf_y(y_{m-1}^*, x_{m-1})] + \cdots + \delta_m.\end{aligned}$$

$$(13.6)$$

We can see that the error contributed by δ_i to Δy_m can be expressed as

$$\delta_{im} = \delta_i \prod_{n=i}^{m-1} [1 + hf_y(y_n^*, x_n)], \quad i = 1, \ldots, m - 1. \quad (13.7)$$

Thus Eq. (13.6) may be rewritten as

$$\Delta y_m = \sum_{i=1}^{m-1} \delta_{im} + \delta_m. \quad (13.8)$$

Example 13.1

We wish to find the value of y at $x = 1$ for the initial-value problem where

$$dy/dx = f(y, x) = -y \quad (13.9)$$

and $y_0 = 1$ at $x_0 = 0$. Euler's method will be used to reach an approximate answer with $h = 0.001$. We can compare this answer with the analytic solution and obtain the *actual error*, which in turn can then be contrasted to the error Δy_m as derived above.

We approximate δ_i by the following term in the Taylor series expansion:

$$\delta_i = \frac{h^2}{2}\left(\frac{d^2 y}{dx^2}\right)_{x=x_{i-1}}$$

Using the given condition in Eq. (13.9), we have

$$\delta_i = \frac{h^2}{2}\left[\frac{d}{dx}\left(\frac{dy}{dx}\right)\right]_{x=x_{i-1}} = \frac{h^2}{2}\left[\frac{d}{dx}(-y)\right]_{x=x_{i-1}}$$

$$= h^2\,\frac{y_{i-1}^*}{2}. \quad (13.10)$$

In order to obtain an expression for y_{i-1}^* in terms of the given initial conditions, we can apply the finite-difference formula, Eq. (13.1):

$$
\begin{aligned}
y_1^* &= y_0 + hf(y_0, x_0) = y_0 + h(-y_0) = y_0(1 - h), \\
y_2^* &= y_1^* + hf(y_1^*, x_1) = y_1^* + h(-y_1^*) \\
&= y_1^*(1 - h) = y_0(1 - h)^2, \\
y_3^* &= y_0(1 - h)^3, \\
&\vdots \\
y_{i-1}^* &= y_0(1 - h)^{i-1}.
\end{aligned}
$$

Substituting this expression into Eq. (13.10) we obtain

$$
\delta_i = y_0(1 - h)^{i-1}(h^2/2). \tag{13.11}
$$

Equation (13.6) now becomes

$$
\delta_{im} = y_0(1 - h)^{i-1}(h^2/2) \prod_{n=i}^{m-1} [1 + hf_y(y_n^*, x_n)]. \tag{13.12}
$$

From Eq. (13.9) we have

$$
f_y(y_n^*, x_n') = (d/dy)[f(y, x)]_{x=x_n} = (d/dy)(-y)_{x=x_n} = -1,
$$

and so Eq. (13.12) can be further reduced to

$$
\begin{aligned}
\delta_{im} &= y_0(1 - h)^{i-1}(h^2/2) \prod_{n=i}^{m-1} (1 - h,) \qquad i = 1, \ldots, m - 1, \\
&= y_0(1 - h)^{i-1}(h^2/2)(1 - h)^{m-i} \\
&= y_0(h^2/2)(1 - h)^{m-1}. \tag{13.13}
\end{aligned}
$$

Substituting Eq. (13.11) with $i = m$ and Eq. (13.13) in Eq. (13.8), we have

$$
\begin{aligned}
\Delta y_m &= \sum_{i=1}^{m-1} y_0 \left(\frac{h^2}{2}\right)(1 - h)^{m-1} + y_0\left(\frac{h^2}{2}\right)(1 - h)^{m-1} \\
&= \frac{my_0(h^2/2)(1 - h)^m}{1 - h}. \tag{13.14}
\end{aligned}
$$

If we define the interval length A as

$$
A = mh = x_m - x_0 = 1 - 0 = 1,
$$

then Eq. (13.14) becomes

$$
\Delta y_m = \frac{y_0(h/2)(1 - h)^{1/h}}{1 - h}. \tag{13.15}
$$

Since

$$
\lim_{h \to 0} \frac{1}{1 - h} = 1 \qquad \text{and} \qquad (1 - h)^{1/h} = e^{-1},
$$

TABLE 13.1. Truncation Errors

Row	Item Interval	$h = 0.001$	$h = 0.0001$
1	e^{-1}	0.36787946	0.36787946
2	Eulerian approximation on IBM 1620	0.36769549	0.36786087
3	Actual error, row 1 − row 2	0.00018397	0.00001859
4	Theoretical error Δy_m	0.00018394	0.00001839
5	Difference between rows 3 and 4	0.00000003	0.00000020

Eq. (13.15) becomes

$$\Delta y_m = \frac{y_0 h e^{-1}}{2}.$$

Since we chose $h = 0.001$ and were given that $y_0 = 1$, we have

$$\Delta y_m = \frac{1 \times 0.001 e^{-1}}{2} = 0.00018394.$$

The actual error as determined by subtracting the Euler approximation from the analytic solution e^{-1} was found to be

$$0.36787946 - 0.36769549 = 0.00018397,$$

which compares remarkably well with the theoretical error, Δy_m. The results for this example and the same example with $h = 0.0001$ are summarized in Table 13.1. We would expect that with a smaller increment ($h = 0.0001$) the round-off errors would increase. As seen in the last column of Table 13.1, this expectation is confirmed by the slight increase in the difference between the actual error (truncation, round-off, and other errors) and the theoretical error (truncation only) discussed in this section.

BIBLIOGRAPHY

Error in Interpolation

OSTROWSKI, A. M., "On the Rounding-off of Difference Tables for Linear Interpolation," *Math. Tables Aids Comput.*, **6**, pp. 212–214 (1952).

Error in Numerical Integration

HULL, T. E., and A. C. R. NEWBERRY, "Error Bounds for a Family of Three-Point Integration Procedures," *J. Soc. Ind. Appl. Math.*, **7**, pp. 402–412 (1959).

HUSKEY, H. D., "On the Precision of a Certain Process of Numerical Integration" (with an appendix by D. R. Hartree), *J. Res. Nat. Bur. Std.*, **42**, pp. 57–62 (1949).

LOTKIN, M., "The Propagation of Error in Numerical Integration," *Proc. Am. Math. Soc.*, **5**, pp. 869–887 (1954).

RADEMACHER, H., "On the Accumulation of Errors in Processes of Integration on High-Speed Calculating Machines," *Ann. Comput. Lab. Harvard Univ.*, **16**, pp. 176–187 (1948).

Error in the Approximation of Analytical Functions

DAVIS, P., "Errors of Numerical Approximation for Analytic Functions," *J. Rational Mech. Anal.*, **2**, pp. 303–313 (1953).

DAVIS, P., and P. RABINOWITZ, "On The Estimation of Quadrature Errors for Analytic Functions," *Math. Tables Aids Comput.*, **8**, pp. 193–202 (1954).

Error in Matrix Calculation

TURING, A. M., "Rounding-off Errors in Matrix Processes," *Quart. J. Mech. Appl. Math.*, **1**, pp. 287–308 (1948).

WILKINSON, J. H., "Error Analysis of Direct Methods of Matrix Inversion," *J. Assoc. Comput. Mach.*, **8**, pp. 281–330 (1961).

Error in the Numerical Integration of Differential Equations

CARR, J. W., III, "Error Bounds for the Runge-Kutta Single-Step Integration Process," *J. Assoc. Comput. Mach.*, **5**, pp. 39–44 (1958).

HENRICI, P., "Theoretical and Experimental Studies on the Accumulation of Error in the Numerical Solution of Initial-Value Problems for Systems of Ordinary Differential Equations," in *Proc. Intern. Conf. on Information Processing*, Paris (1959), UNESCO, Paris, pp. 36–44 (1960).

LOTKIN, M., "On the Accuracy of Runge-Kutta's Method," *Math. Tables Aids Comput.*, **5**, pp. 128–133 (1951).

MURRAY, F. J., "Planning and Error Consideration for the Numerical Solution of a System of Differential Equations on a Sequenced Calculator," *Math. Tables Aids Comput.*, **4**, pp. 133–144 (1950).

STERNE, T. E., "The Accuracy of Numerical Solutions of Ordinary Differential Equations," *Math. Tab., Wash.*, **7**, pp. 159–164 (1953).

WASOW, W., "On the Truncation Error in the Solution of Laplace's Equation by Finite Differences," *J. Res. Nat. Bur. Std.*, **48**, pp. 345–348 (1952).

Other References on Errors

DAVIS, P. J., and P. RABINOWITZ, "On the Estimation of Quadrature Errors for Analytic Functions," *Math. Tables Aids Comput.*, **8**, pp. 193–203 (1954).

MACON, N., and M. BASKERVILLE, "On the Generation of Errors in Digital Evaluation of Continued Fractions," *J. Assoc. Comp. Mach.*, **3**, pp. 199–202 (1956).

WASOW, W., "The Accuracy of Difference Approximations to Plane Dirichlet Problems with Piecewise Analytic Boundary Values," *Quart. Appl. Math.*, **15**, pp. 53–63 (1957).

WEEG, G. P., "Truncation Error in the Graeffe Root Squaring Method," *J. Assoc. Comp. Mach.*, **7**, pp. 69–71 (1960).

WILKINSON, J. H., "Error Analysis of Floating-Point Computation," *Numer. Math.*, **2**, pp. 319–340 (1960).

WILKINSON, J. H., *Rounding Errors in Algebraic Processes, Information Processing*. UNESCO, Paris; Oldenbourg, Munich; Butterworths, London; pp. 44–53, 1960.

ZONDEK, B., and J. W. SHELDON, "On the Error Propagation in Adams' Extrapolation Method," *Math. Tables Aids Comput.*, **13**, pp. 52–55 (1959).

MODERN METHODS

Many numerical methods devised before the advent of high-speed computers and merely adapted for computer usage were discussed in Part II. However, application of some new methods has grown so extensively in recent years that an understanding of the underlying principles of the techniques is indispensable in handling certain scientific and engineering problems. Two of these methods, the Monte-Carlo method and linear programming, have been selected for discussion in PART III.

CHAPTER 14

MONTE CARLO METHOD AND RANDOM NUMBERS

14.1 MONTE CARLO METHOD

One of the most powerful features of the digital computer is its high speed, which makes possible the performance of many repeated arithmetic operations within a short period of time. The Monte Carlo method is a new procedure which takes advantage of this speed in solving complex problems in science and engineering where analytical formulation is not available and experimental procedure is not possible. The Monte Carlo method is mainly used to predict the final consequence of a series of occurrences, each having its own probability. We shall illustrate this procedure by considering the simple example of obtaining the shaded area under the curve $f(x) = L \sin x$, where $L = 0.876$ (see Fig. 14.1).

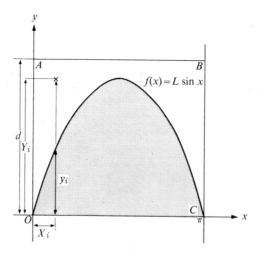

Fig. 14.1. Area under a given curve.

265

To "solve" this problem by the Monte Carlo method, we begin by asking, If a series of darts are thrown at random onto a rectangular board having dimensions $d \times \pi$, what is the probability P_a that the darts will hit the shaded area?

$$P_a = \frac{\text{Number of darts hitting the shaded area}}{\text{Total number of darts thrown}} . \tag{14.1}$$

This probability is clearly related to the shaded area itself. For example, a low probability of hitting the shaded area implies that this area is relatively small:

$$\text{The shaded area} = P_a \cdot (\text{total area OABC}). \tag{14.2}$$

A hit or a miss can readily be expressed by the following expressions: if

$$Y_i > y_i, \quad \text{it is a miss,} \tag{14.3}$$

and if

$$Y_i \leq y_i, \quad \text{it is a hit,} \tag{14.4}$$

where

$\quad y_i = \text{ordinate of the curve at a given } X_i,$

$\quad Y_i = \text{ordinate of the point of impact (see Fig. 14.1),} \quad 0 \leq Y_i \leq d.$

In order to calculate the shaded area by the Monte Carlo method, we follow these steps:

(1) We adopt two random input values for X_i and Y_i representing the abscissa and ordinate, respectively, for an impact point ($0 \leq X_i \leq \pi$ and $0 \leq Y_i \leq d$).

(2) We compare Y_i with the value of y_i corresponding to X_i. If Eq. (14.4) is satisfied, we register a hit.

(3) We calculate P_a, using Eq. (14.1).

(4) We repeat steps 1, 2, and 3 N times, where N is some large integer.

It should be mentioned that in order to repeat step 1 many times, we must be able to generate a large supply of random numbers, and since this in itself is a rather involved process, we will defer its discussion to the next section. We may state here, however, that many subprograms have been written to generate floating-point random numbers between 0 and 1, and that by a simple transformation these subprograms can be made to generate numbers randomly in some other interval, such as $(0, \pi)$ or $(0, d)$. For example, if we wanted to generate numbers randomly between 0 and π and if a subprogram called RANUM(A) had already been written to generate random numbers between 0 and 1,

$$Z = \text{RANUM(A)}, \quad 0 \leq Z \leq 1,$$

then we could simply multiply by the factor π to obtain

$$X = \text{RANUM(A)} * \pi, \quad 0 \leq X \leq \pi.$$

```
*1010
C        PROGRAM TO FIND AREA UNDER SINE CURVE
C        WITH RANUM(IU,IN) SUB-PROGRAM
C
         IN = 1
         READ 2,IU,HIT,XL,D,N
         PUNCH 20
         PUNCH 30
         PI = 3.14159265
         TA=PI*D
         DO 18 K=1,50
         DO 15 I=1,100
         U = RANUM(IU,IN)
         Y = U*D
         U = RANUM(IU,IN)
         Z = XL*SINF(U*PI)
         IF(Y-Z) 10,15,15
      10 HIT = HIT + 1.
      15 CONTINUE
         N = N + 100
         ZN = N
         P = HIT/ZN
         SA = TA*P
         PUNCH 120,N,P,SA
      18 CONTINUE
       2 FORMAT(I10,5X,F15.3,5X,F10.5,5X,F10.5,5X,I5)
      20 FORMAT(12X,43HAREA UNDER SINE CURVE BY MONTE CARLO METHOD)
      30 FORMAT(/,6X,1HN,22X,11HPROBABILITY,22X,4HAREA,/)
     120 FORMAT(3X,I5,21X,F8.6,21X,F9.6)
      90 STOP
         END
9876543219          0.                       .876              1.123
```

Fig. 14.2. Area under a sine curve.

An actual run on a digital computer has been made to compute the shaded area of Fig. 14.1. The associated FORTRAN program for the Monte Carlo method is listed in Fig. 14.2. The first line of the program, *1010, needs some explanation. This type of parameter card, always denoted by an asterisk in its first column, is used to add flexibility to the IBM 1620 FORTRAN II system. By simply placing a parameter card as the first card in the source program, one can increase the floating-point precision to as many as 28 (as against 8 places in normal cases) and the fixed-point precision to 10 places (as compared with 5 places in normal cases). In Fig. 14.2, the second and third columns of the first line indicate that the floating-point precision will be 10 digits throughout the program, while the fourth and fifth columns indicate that each fixed-point computation is also carried out to 10-digit accuracy.

The results, as shown in Table 14.1, were obtained by following the four steps mentioned previously. We begin by enclosing the sine curve in a rectangle of length π and of arbitrarily chosen height $d = 1.123$. After every 100 darts thrown, the results for the probability P_a and the computed area are printed out. Thus, after the first 100 throws there are 53 hits; $P_a = 53/100 = 0.53$, and the first estimate for the shaded area is $1.123 \times 0.53 = 1.8698$. This value for the area is far from the true area 1.752; however, from Table 14.1, we note that the results may fluctuate in the beginning but tend to converge to 1.752 as N gets large. This fluctuation can be observed in Fig. 14.3.

TABLE 14.1.   Area Under Sine Curve by Monte Carlo Method

N	PROBABILITY	AREA
100	.530000	1.869844
200	.490000	1.728724
300	.493333	1.740484
400	.500000	1.764004
500	.506000	1.785172
600	.501666	1.769884
700	.502857	1.774084
800	.502500	1.772824
900	.504444	1.779684
1000	.502000	1.771060
1100	.496363	1.751175
1200	.495000	1.746364
1300	.496923	1.753148
1400	.495000	1.746364
1500	.498000	1.756948
1600	.496250	1.750774
1700	.497647	1.755703
1800	.497222	1.754204
1900	.497368	1.754720
2000	.499500	1.762240
2100	.498571	1.758964
2200	.494545	1.744760
2300	.489565	1.727190
2400	.492500	1.737544
2500	.492000	1.735780
2600	.495000	1.746364
2700	.496296	1.750937
2800	.495000	1.746364
2900	.493448	1.740889
3000	.494000	1.742836
3100	.492580	1.737828
3200	.494062	1.743056
3300	.493333	1.740484
3400	.496470	1.751552
3500	.498000	1.756948
3600	.496111	1.750284
3700	.496756	1.752562
3800	.496052	1.750077
3900	.496410	1.751339
4000	.498500	1.758712
4100	.498292	1.757980
4200	.497142	1.753924
4300	.497674	1.755799
4400	.496590	1.751976
4500	.495777	1.749108
4600	.496086	1.750199
4700	.496808	1.752744
4800	.494791	1.745629
4900	.496122	1.750324
5000	.497800	1.756242

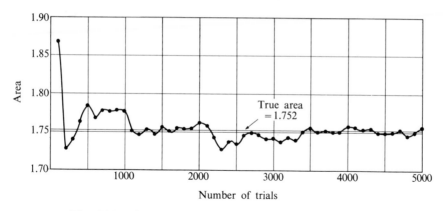

Fig. 14.3.   Area under a sine curve by Monte Carlo procedure.

14.2   BUFFON NEEDLE PROBLEM

As a second illustration of the Monte Carlo method, let us consider the classic *buffon needle* problem. The physical situation is quite simple. We are given a level plane surface with many parallel lines drawn a distance x_l apart and a thin needle of length x_N. The question is, If we drop the needle on the plane at random a great many times (Fig. 14.4), what is the ratio of the number of times it hits one of the lines to the number of times it is dropped? According to statistical theory† the answer is known as $2x_N/\pi x_l$; we would like to check this result by the Monte Carlo procedure.

From Fig. 14.4 it is obvious that if

$$x \le \frac{x_N}{2} \sin \theta,$$

then the needle is touching the line; and if $x > (x_N/2) \sin \theta$, it is not touching. We know that if the needle were actually dropped on the plane, then the values of x would occur at random. This act of dropping the needle may be simulated by picking random input values for θ and x. Clearly, in this case θ would lie between 0 and π, while x would lie between 0 and $x_l/2$. After dropping the needle many times we are able to calculate the following ratio,

$$\frac{\text{Number of hits}}{\text{Number of times dropped}},$$

which should be approximately equal to $2x_N/\pi x_l$.

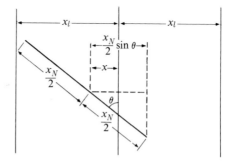

Fig. 14.4.   Buffon needle problem.

---

† For example, see Gredenko, B. V., *The Theory of Probability*. Chelsea, New York, pp. 41–43, 1962.

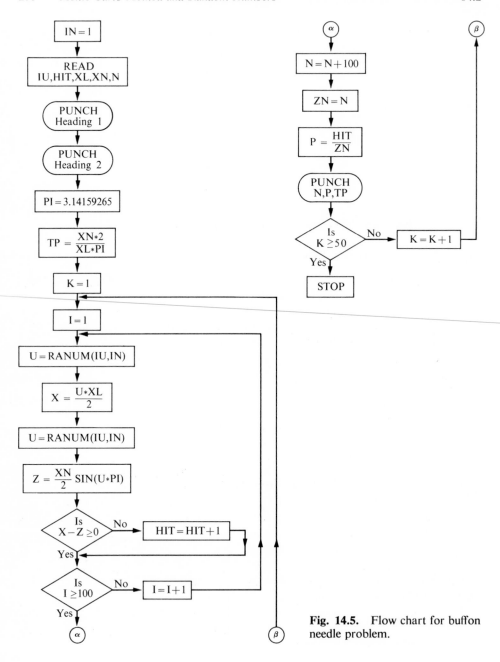

Fig. 14.5. Flow chart for buffon needle problem.

```
*1010
C       PROGRAM TO SOLVE BUFFON  NEEDLE PROBLEM
C       USING RANUM(IU,IN) SUB-PROGRAM
C
C       XL = DISTANCE BETWEEN PARALLEL LINES OF THE GRID
C       XN = LENGTH OF THE NEEDLE
        IN = 1
        READ 2, IU, HIT, XL, XN, N
        PUNCH 20
        PUNCH 30
        PI = 3.14159265
        TP = XN*2./(XL*PI)
        DO 18 K=1,50
        DO 15 I=1,100
        U = RANUM(IU,IN)
        X = U*XL/2.
        U = RANUM(IU,IN)
        Z = (XN/2.)*SINF(U*PI)
        IF(X-Z) 10,15,15
     10 HIT = HIT + 1.
     15 CONTINUE
        N = N + 100
        ZN = N
        P = HIT/ZN
        PUNCH 50,N,P,TP
     18 CONTINUE
      2 FORMAT(I10,5X,F15.3,5X,F10.5,5X,F10.5,5X,I5)
     20 FORMAT(30X,21HBUFFON NEEDLE PROBLEM)
     30 FORMAT(/,6X,1HN,22X,11HPROBABILITY,19X,10HTRUE PROB.,/)
     50 FORMAT(3X,I5,21X,F8.6,21X,F8.6)
     90 STOP
        END
9876543219    0.              2.5           1.48              0
```

Fig. 14.6. FORTRAN program for buffon needle problem.

Figures 14.5 and 14.6 are, respectively, a flow chart and a **FORTRAN** program for solving the buffon needle problem, i.e., determining the ratio of the number of trials to hits. We take

$$x_l = 2.5 \quad \text{and} \quad x_N = 1.48.$$

A recommended output format is shown below where N is the number of random sets tested.

BUFFON NEEDLE PROBLEM

(Skip 1 line)

N	PROBABILITY	TRUE PROB.
(Skip 1 line)		
100	X.XXXXXX	X.XXXXXX
⋮		
5000	X.XXXXXX	X.XXXXXX

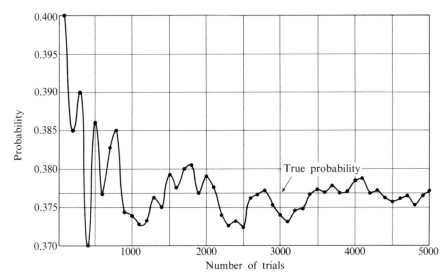

Fig. 14.7. Buffon needle problem.

The relation of the number of throws to the corresponding probability of hitting a line based on the computer output is depicted in Fig. 14.7. It is seen that the computer answers converge well to the true answer, which is known to be $2x_N/\pi x_l = 0.376878$. The time for computing 5000 throws on an IBM 1620 is about one hour.

We have illustrated how the Monte Carlo method is used to evaluate *approximately* a definite integral and to solve the buffon needle problem. The method can be used to find approximate answers for problems in such simulation studies as a job shop or automobile traffic flow, and for problems in nuclear physics (see references listed at the end of this chapter). It cannot be overemphasized that answers obtained by the Monte Carlo method are not very accurate when the sample size is small; increased accuracy may come only with a large number of trials.

A need for random numbers is evidenced by the two examples in the preceding sections. We shall proceed to discuss the available methods for generation of such random numbers, present a FORTRAN program for implementing it, and touch briefly on other possible procedures for generation of random numbers.

14.3   GENERATION OF RANDOM NUMBERS—POWER RESIDUE METHOD

Of the many methods attempted in the past for generating random numbers with the aid of computers, the most widely used one is believed to be the power-residue method. Before this method is presented, a brief introduction to some notations and concepts in number theory is necessary.

When the difference of two numbers s and t is *evenly* divisible by an integer M, then s is said to be "congruent to t modulo M," or

$$s = t \bmod M. \tag{14.5}$$

For example, in the expression

$$19 = 9 \bmod 5,$$

$s = 19$, $t = 9$, and their difference, 10, is evenly divisible by 5. In other words, the quotient $(s - t)/M$ is an integer:

$$(19 - 9)/5 = 2.$$

If s, t and M satisfy Eq. (14.5), then the following two relations exist:

(a) s and t must have the same remainder after division by M. For example,

$$19 = 9 \bmod 5,$$
$$\tfrac{19}{5} = 3\tfrac{4}{5} \quad \text{and} \quad \tfrac{9}{5} = 1\tfrac{4}{5}.$$

(b) $s - t = i \cdot M$, where i = integer. For example,

$$19 = 9 \bmod 5, \quad 19 - 9 = 2 \cdot 5.$$

In relation (b) it is seen that given t and M, s may have many possible solutions which are known as a *collection* (see Table 14.2).

TABLE 14.2.　A Collection of s for the Relation $s = 26$ Mod 6

i	1	0	−1	−2	−3	−4	−5
s	32	26	20	14	8	2	−4

In the following, we choose s to be the smallest positive number in the collection, known as the *least positive residue*. Thus in Table 14.2, the least positive residue is equal to 2.

If the value of t and M are given, then the least positive residue s can readily be evaluated by the relation

$$s = t - (t/M)M, \tag{14.6}$$

where (t/M) is a truncated-integer division; that is, any fractional part of the quotient (t/M) is ignored, *leaving only the integral part*.

Suppose, for example, that we wish to evaluate the value of s when $t = 10$ and $M = 4$. Then

$$s = 10 \bmod 4,$$

or

$$s = 10 - (\tfrac{10}{4})4 = 10 - (2)4 = 10 - 8 = 2.$$

Note that only the integral part, that is, 2, of the quotient 2.5 is used; the decimal part (.5) of the quotient is discarded.

We also define the set of power residues s_n as

$$s_n = t^n \pmod{M} \quad \text{for} \quad n = 1, 2, 3, \ldots$$

For example, if $t = 5$ and $M = 31$, then

$$s_1 = 5^1 \,(\text{mod } 31) = 5 - (\tfrac{5}{31})31 = 5 - 0 = 5,$$
$$s_2 = 5^2 \,(\text{mod } 31) = 25 - (\tfrac{25}{31})31 = 25 - 0 = 25,$$
$$s_3 = 5^3 \,(\text{mod } 31) = 125 - (\tfrac{125}{31})31 = 125 - 124 = 1,$$
$$s_4 = 5^4 \,(\text{mod } 31) = 625 - (\tfrac{625}{31})31 = 625 - 620 = 5,$$
$$\vdots \qquad\qquad\qquad\qquad\qquad\qquad\qquad \vdots$$

(this sequence repeats)

Here we see that 5, 25, and 1 are the power residues.

In using the power-residue concept to obtain random numbers with a decimal computer, we frequently generate the random number u_{n+1} by the relation

$$u_{n+1} = xu_n \,(\text{mod } 10^d),$$

where u_n is the previous random number, d represents the number of significant digits in a computer word, and x is a constant multiplier chosen so as to obtain the longest possible sequence of random numbers without repetition. This choice of x is determined by a more involved power-residue theory than presented above. It will suffice to state here, however, that the proper choice of x will produce a nonrepeating sequence, or period, of 0.5 billion numbers (for $d = 10$).

```
*1010
          FUNCTION RANUM(IU,IN)
  C       RANDOM NUMBER GENERATOR
  C
          IF(IN) 30,40,30
       30 IN=0
          IX = 100003
          SHIFT = 10.**(-10.)
       40 IU=IX*IU
          RU = IU
          RANUM = RU*SHIFT
          RETURN
          END
```

Fig. 14.8.   FUNCTION RANUM.

A subprogram called FUNCTION RANUM, shown in Fig. 14.8, is designed to generate random numbers according to the power-residue method with $d = 10$ and $x = 100003$. The calculations for each random number are made in fixed-point arithmetic, the 10 rightmost digits are retained after each operation, and the answer is converted to a 10-digit floating-point number between 0 and 1. We note that the first card of the program is a parameter card, as discussed in the previous section, and that the variable IN, which must be initially defined in the main program as any integer other than zero, is used to avoid redefining variables in the subprogram after the first number has been generated.

For the binary computer, the following generation formula is found to be statistically sound and to have a long period:

$$u_n = u_{n-1}(2^{18} + 3)(\mod 2^{35}),$$

where u_0 is any odd number (for example, 1). The number generated, u_n, is then converted to a number between 0 and 1.0.

BIBLIOGRAPHY

Random Numbers

ARTHUR, A. O., "Random Digit Generation," *Computing News* (Sept. 1956).

BOX, G. P., and M. E. MULLER, "A Note on the Generation of Random Number Deviates," *Ann. Math. Stat.*, **29**, pp. 610–611 (1958).

HORTON, H. BURKE, "A Method for Obtaining Random Numbers," *Annals of Mathematical Statistics*, **XIX,** No. 1, p. 81 (1948).

JUCOSA, M. L., "Random Number Generation on the BRL High-Speed Computing Machines," *BRL Report No. 855* (1953).

KAHN, H., "Random Sampling (Monte Carlo) Techniques in Neutron Attenuation Problems," *Nucleonics*, **6,** No. 5, pp. 27–33, 37 (May 1950); **6,** No. 6, pp. 60–65 (June 1950).

ROTENBERG, A., "A New Pseudo-Random Number Generator," *J. Assoc. Comput. Mach.*, **7,** No. 1, pp. 75–77 (1960).

SCHEID, F., "Radial Distribution of the Center of Gravity of Random Points on a Unit Circle," *J. Res. Nat. Bur. Std*, **60,** pp. 307–308 (1958).

PEARSON, E. S., and H. O. HARTLEY, *Biometrika Tables for Statistician I*. University Press, Cambridge, 1954.

PECK, L. G., "On Uniform Distribution of Algebraic Numbers," *Proc. Amer. Math. Soc.*, **4,** pp. 440–443 (1953).

Monte Carlo Method

BAUER, W. F., "The Monte Carlo Method," *J. Soc. Ind. Appl. Math.*, **6,** pp. 438–451 (1958).

BECKENBACK, E. F., Ed., *Modern Mathematics for the Engineer*. University of California, Engineering Extension Series. McGraw-Hill, Chapter 12 (1956).

HAMMERSLEY, J. M., and K. W. MORTON, "Poor Man's Monte Carlo," *J. Roy. Statist. Soc.*, Ser. B., **16,** pp. 23–38 (1954).

HOUSEHOLDER, A. S., G. E. FORSYTHE, and H. H. GERMOND, Eds., "Monte Carlo Method," *Nat. Bur. Std. Appl. Math. Ser.*, **12** (1951).

McCRACKEN, D. D., "The Monte Carlo Method," *Sci. Am.*, **192,** p. 90 (May 1955).

MEYER, H. A., Ed., *Symposium on Monte Carlo Methods*. John Wiley and Sons, New York, 1956.

Application of Monte Carlo Method

Davis, P. J., and P. Rabinowitz, "Some Monte Carlo Experiments in Computing Multiple Integrals," *Math. Tables Aids Comput.*, **10**, pp. 1–7 (1956).

Hammersley, J. M., "Monte Carlo Methods for Solving Multivariable Problems," *Ann. N. Y. Acad. Sci.*, **86**, pp. 844–874 (1960).

King, G. T., "Monte Carlo Method for Solving Diffusion Problems," *Industrial and Engineering Chemistry*, **43**, No. 11, pp. 2475–2478 (Nov. 1951).

Richtmyer, R. D., "The Evaluation of Definite Integrals and a Quasi-Monte Carlo Method Based on the Properties of Algebraic Numbers," *Los Alamos Scientific Laboratory Report* LA1342 (1951–1952).

Todd, J., "Experiments in the Solution of Differential Equations by Monte Carlo Methods," *J. Wash. Acad. Sci.*, **44**, pp. 377–381 (1954).

Other References

Dixon, W. J., and F. J. Massey, Jr., *Introduction to Statistical Analysis.* McGraw-Hill, New York, 2nd ed., 1957.

Hoel, P. G., *Introduction to Mathematical Statistics.* John Wiley and Sons, New York, 1956.

Lehmer, D. H., "Mathematical Methods in Large-Scale Computing Units," *Proceedings of a Second Symposium* (1949) *on Large-Scale Digital Calculating Machinery.* Harvard University Press, Cambridge, Mass. (1951).

Nagell, Trygve, *Introduction to Number Theory.* John Wiley and Sons, New York, 1951.

"Proceedings of a Second Symposium on Large Scale Digital Calculating Machinery," *Ann. Comput. Lab. Harvard Univ.*, **XXVI** (1951).

PROBLEMS

1. Using FUNCTION RANUM, generate 5000 numbers between 0 and 1, calculate their mean, and compare the calculated mean with the expected mean (0.5) as a test of randomness.

2. Calculate the distribution in intervals of (0.1) for 5000 numbers generated by FUNCTION RANUM, i.e., find the percentage of numbers between 0 and 0.1, between 0.1 and 0.2, etc. Compare these results with the expected distribution of 10% in each interval.

3. Use the Monte Carlo method to calculate the volume of the sphere

$$x^2 + y^2 + z^2 = 1.$$

4. Find the area under the bell-shaped curve $y = e^{-x^2/2}/\sqrt{2\pi}$ by using the Monte Carlo method with $0 \le x \le 4$.

5. In each play of a particular game, a pair of dice are thrown and the sum of the spots on the upper sides of the dice are counted. Using random numbers, find the probability that each of the different possible sums will occur.

6. A drunk starts off at a lamppost and takes 16 steps, each of length 2 and each in a random direction θ, where $0° \le \theta \le 360°$. Use the Monte Carlo method to find his most probable distance from the lamppost after the 16 steps and compare your results with the correct answer, $2\sqrt{16} = 8$. What is the distance after 200 steps?

7. On an American roulette wheel there are 38 slots, 36 for the digits 1 to 36, one for 0, and one for 00. The slots corresponding to the odd numbers in the ranges 1 through 10 and 19 through 28 and to the even numbers in the ranges 11 through 18 and 29 through 36 are colored red. The 0 and 00 slots are colored green and the rest are black. Using random numbers, write a FORTRAN program to simulate the operation of the roulette wheel and to print out the number and color for a succession of spins.

8. Bernoulli's lemniscate is described by the equation $\rho^2 = a^2 \cos 2\theta$, where ρ and θ are polar coordinates, and the constant a denotes the size of the lemniscate (see Fig. 14.9). Use the Monte Carlo method to find the area under one loop of this curve and compare your result with the analytical solution.

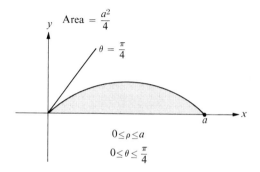

Figure 14.9

9. By playing a simple card game, it is possible to use random numbers and multiply two proper functions n_1/d_1 and n_2/d_2. In two decks each containing d cards, n of them are marked. Each deck is then shuffled separately and one card from each is chosen at random. If both of the cards chosen are marked, a win is recorded; if not, a loss. The cards are then replaced, the decks reshuffled, and after the procedure has been repeated many times the number of wins would approximate the product

$$\frac{n_1}{d_1} \cdot \frac{n_2}{d_2}.$$

Approximate the product $\frac{2}{3} \times \frac{5}{9}$ by adapting this game to the Monte Carlo procedure.

CHAPTER 15

LINEAR PROGRAMMING

15.1 CONSTRAINT, NONNEGATIVE CONDITION, AND OBJECTIVE FUNCTION

In Chapter 8 we introduced the Gauss-Jordan method for solving a system of simultaneous equations:

$$a_{11}x_1 + a_{12}x_2 + a_{13}x_3 = c_1,$$
$$a_{21}x_2 + a_{22}x_2 + a_{23}x_3 = c_2, \qquad (15.1)$$
$$a_{31}x_3 + a_{32}x_2 + a_{33}x_3 = c_3,$$

or

$$[A][x] = [C], \qquad (15.2)$$

and we observed that in each instance $[A]$ was a nonsingular square matrix. In other words, the number of unknowns was the same as the number of independent linear equations. In this chapter we shall extend our discussion to an important class of linear inequalities:

$$a_{11}x_1 + a_{12}x_2 + \cdots + a_{1n}x_n \geq c_1 \qquad (\text{or } \leq c_1),$$
$$a_{21}x_1 + a_{22}x_2 + \cdots + a_{2n}x_n \geq c_2 \qquad (\text{or } \leq c_2),$$
$$\vdots \qquad\qquad\qquad (15.3)$$
$$a_{m1}x_1 + a_{m2}x_2 + \cdots + a_{mn}x_n \geq c_m \qquad (\text{or } \leq c_m),$$

where we have $n \geq m$ or $n \leq m$, and an infinite number of solutions. In order to choose an optimal solution from all the possible solutions, we must introduce two additional conditions:

$$x_i \geq 0, \qquad i = 1, 2, \ldots, n \qquad (15.4)$$

and

$$z = b_1x_1 + b_2x_2 + \cdots + b_nx_n, \qquad (15.5)$$

where all the coefficients, a, b, and c, are known. We also wish to minimize z in Eq. (15.5).

For the sake of discussion, we shall refer to Eq. (15.3) as the constraints of the system, Eq. (15.4) as the nonnegative condition, and Eq. (15.5) as the objective function. We note that Eqs. (15.3) and (15.5) are assumed to be linear. This fact should not be overlooked since the linear programming method is used to optimize a linear function, such as Eq. (15.5), is subject to a set of linear constraints, such as given in Eq. (15.3), and is restricted by a set of nonnegative conditions, as expressed in Eq. (15.4).

15.2 CONVERSION TO THE STANDARD MINIMIZATION FORM

We noted that constraints (15.3) are a set of linear equations involving inequalities. Each inequality sign can be eliminated simply by adding or subtracting a new variable which must be nonnegative. To illustrate this point, let us consider the two constraints

$$x_1 + 2x_2 \le 3, \tag{15.6}$$

$$2x_1 + x_2 \ge 4. \tag{15.7}$$

If we add a nonnegative variable x_3 to the left-hand side of the constraint (15.6), we have

$$x_1 + 2x_2 + x_3 = 3. \tag{15.6a}$$

Similarly, if the term x_4 is subtracted from the left-hand side of the constraint (15.7), we obtain

$$2x_1 + x_2 - x_4 = 4, \tag{15.7a}$$

where x_4 is a nonnegative variable. In the above example, we have introduced two new variables x_3 and x_4 which have to be determined. They are called *slack* variables. Thus the constraint (15.3) can be rewritten as

$$
\begin{aligned}
a_{11}x_1 + a_{12}x_2 + \cdots + a_{1n}x_n + x_{n+1} &= c_1, \\
a_{21}x_1 + a_{22}x_2 + \cdots + a_{2n}x_n + \quad x_{n+2} &= c_2, \\
\vdots \qquad\qquad\qquad\qquad & \\
a_{m1}x_1 + a_{m2}x_2 + \cdots + a_{mn}x_n + \qquad\quad x_{n+m} &= c_m.
\end{aligned}
\tag{15.8}
$$

Our problem of linear programming set forth in the previous section may now be stated in the following standard minimization form. Determine

$$x_i \ge 0, \qquad i = 1, 2, \ldots, n + m, \tag{15.9}$$

so that

$$z = [B] \cdot [x] \tag{15.10}$$

is a minimum and

$$[A][x] = [C], \tag{15.11}$$

where $[A]$ is a matrix of m rows and $n + m$ columns; $[x]$ and $[C]$ are column matrices of degree $n + m$ and m, respectively; and $[B]$ is a row matrix of degree $n + m$.

We now proceed to examine the cases in which the objective function is to be maximized, rather than minimized. In order to transform the given objective function to the standard minimization form, we can multiply it by -1; the resulting equation will have the precise form of Eq. (15.10). For example, consider the objective function z,

$$z = 3x_1 - 6x_2, \tag{15.12}$$

which is to be maximized. By changing the sign of each term, we can reduce this to the following equation, where we wish to determine x_1 and x_2 such that

$$-z = -3x_1 + 6x_2 \quad \text{is a minimum.}$$

15.3 TWO-VARIABLE PROBLEM—GRAPHICAL SOLUTION

Let us examine a specific problem using the graphical method. We note that there are two variables and three constraints. Determine

$$x_1 \geq 0, \qquad x_2 \geq 0, \tag{15.13}$$

such that

$$z = 10x_1 + 11x_2 \tag{15.14}$$

is a maximum, and such that the two variables will satisfy the following three constraints:

$$3x_1 + 4x_2 \leq 9, \tag{15.15a}$$

$$5x_1 + 2x_2 \leq 8, \tag{15.15b}$$

$$x_1 - 2x_2 \leq 1. \tag{15.15c}$$

We shall now draw a graph representing the two nonnegative conditions and the three constraints. From Eq. (15.13) it is clear that any possible point representing solutions for x_1 and x_2 must be confined to the first quadrant (Fig. 15.1), including the points on both the x_1- and x_2-axes. Next we consider the three constraints (15.15). It is evident that the set of points satisfying Eq. (15.15a) must be below the line

$$3x_1 + 4x_2 = 9,$$

as shown in Fig. 15.2, where no solution is possible in the shaded portion. The other two constraints are readily plotted in the same way. An area bounded by the lines

$$x_1 = 0, \qquad x_2 = 0,$$
$$3x_1 + 4x_2 = 9, \qquad 5x_1 + 2x_2 = 8, \qquad x_1 - 2x_2 = 1$$

is thus formed, as shown in Fig. 15.3.

Our problem now is to select, from all points in the unshaded area (Fig. 15.3), one corresponding to the maximum z in Eq. (15.14). This task can be readily accomplished by plotting a family of straight lines representing

$$10x_1 + 11x_2 = \text{constant},$$

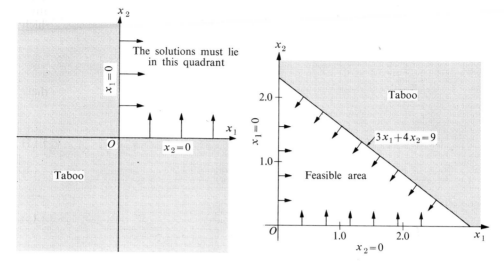

Fig. 15.1. Feasible solutions for $x_1 \geq 0$, $x_2 \geq 0$.

Fig. 15.2. Feasible solutions for $3x + 4x \leq 9$.

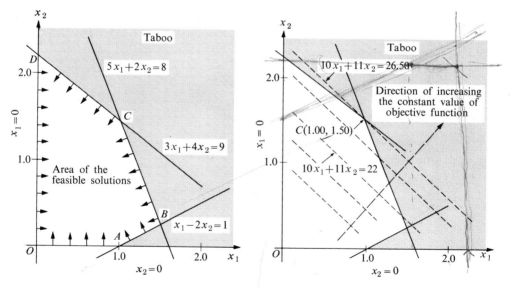

Fig. 15.3. Graph for three constraints.

Fig. 15.4. The optimal solution.

as shown in Fig. 15.4. The solution of this example clearly occurs at point C, where

$$x_1 = 1.0, \qquad x_2 = 1.5.$$

Hence $z = 10x_1 + 11x_2 = 26.5$.

Before proceeding to the next section, it would be useful to introduce, with the aid of Fig. 15.3, the concepts of *feasible* and *optimum* solutions.

Feasible solutions are represented by all points confined inside the polygon $OABCD$ (including the points on the five sides). In other words, a feasible solution is one in which all variables satisfy the three constraints, Eqs. (15.15), and the nonnegative condition, Eq. (15.13). The optimum solution is one of the feasible solutions which maximizes the objective function, Eq. (15.14).

15.4 BASIC FEASIBLE SOLUTIONS AND VERTICES

In this section, we introduce the concept of *basic feasible solutions* and discuss their relation with the vertices of a polygon (Fig. 15.3) in a two-variable case.

Let us reexamine the example discussed in the previous section. Determine

$$x_1 \geq 0, \qquad x_2 \geq 0, \tag{15.13}$$

so that

$$z = 10x_1 + 11x_2 \tag{15.14}$$

is a maximum, and so that

$$3x_1 + 4x_2 \leq 9,$$
$$5x_1 + 2x_2 \leq 8, \tag{15.15}$$
$$x_1 - 2x_2 \leq 1.$$

By introducing additional slack variables x_3, x_4, and x_5, we can convert the problem into the following standard form. Determine

$$x_i \geq 0, \qquad i = 1, 2, \ldots, 5, \tag{15.16}$$

so that the variables will maximize the objective function

$$z = 10x_1 + 11x_2, \tag{15.17}$$

and will satisfy the linear equations

$$
\begin{aligned}
3x_1 + 4x_2 + x_3 \qquad\quad &= 9, \\
5x_1 + 2x_2 + \quad + x_4 \quad &= 8, \\
x_1 - 2x_2 \qquad + x_5 &= 1.
\end{aligned}
\tag{15.18}
$$

Equations (15.18) involve five unknowns and, therefore, have an infinite number of solutions. However, if we arbitrarily assign the value zero to two of the five variables and solve for the other three, then there are ten possible solutions. These ten solutions, known as *basic solutions*, are calculated and tabulated in Table 15.1, which will be found helpful in our discussion. An inspection of the table will indicate that the solutions numbered 3, 4, 5, 6, and 9 contain negative values of the variables and are therefore not feasible, because they do not satisfy the nonnegative requirement in Eq. (15.16).

The remaining five solutions are called *basic feasible solutions*, since they satisfy two conditions: the condition of nonnegativity, as expressed in Eq. (15.16), and the constraints, Eqs. (15.18). It is important to note that these five basic feasible solutions have a one-to-one correspondence to the five vertices shown in Fig. 15.3. This correspondence is properly marked in the last column of Table 15.1.

TABLE 15.1. Ten Possible Solutions for Assigning Two Variables to be Zero and Solving for the Other Three

Number of possible solutions	Five variables					Vertex in Fig. 15.3
	x_1	x_2	x_3	x_4	x_5	
1	0	0	9.00	8.00	1.00	O
2	0	2.25	0	3.50	5.50	D
3	0	4.00	-7.00	0	9.00	—
4	0	-0.50	11.00	9.00	0	—
5	3.00	0	0	-7.00	-2.00	—
6	1.60	0	4.20	0	-0.60	—
7	1.00	0	6.00	3.00	0	A
8	1.00	1.50	0	0	3.00	C
9	2.20	0.60	0	-4.20	0	—
10	1.50	0.25	3.50	0	0	B

TABLE 15.2. Five Basic Feasible Solutions

Vertex	x_1	x_2	x_3	x_4	x_5
O	0	0	9.00	8.00	1.00
A	1.00	0	6.00	3.00	0
B	1.50	0.25	3.50	0	0
C	1.00	1.50	0	0	3.00
D	0	2.25	0	3.50	5.50

In retrospect, we have ten basic solutions. They are obtained by arbitrarily assigning the value zero to two variables and then solving for the other three. Out of these ten basic solutions, there exist only five basic feasible solutions which meet the non-negativity requirement. Finally, these five basic feasible solutions correspond to the five vertices of the polygon $OABCD$ of Fig. 15.3; they are arranged in Table 15.2.

15.5 SIMPLEX METHOD FOR AN OPTIMUM SOLUTION

One of the special features of all linear programming problems is the discrepancy between the number of constraints and the number of variables. Frequently, the number of variables is several times the number of constraints. When both m and n are large, the graphical method presented in Section 15.3 becomes useless and other methods must be used. Of the several computational methods available, Dantzig's Simplex method is probably the most widely used. We shall now introduce this method by means of the previous example, which involves two variables and three constraints; see Eqs. (15.16) through (15.18).

The first step of the Simplex method is to get rid of the inequality signs. As mentioned before, this can be accomplished readily by adding the so-called nonnegative slack variables x_3, x_4, and x_5. The problem is then converted to the following form. Determine

$$x_i \geq 0, \quad i = 1, 2, 3, 4, 5, \tag{15.19}$$

so that

$$-z = -10x_1 - 11x_2 + 0x_3 + 0x_4 + 0x_5 \tag{15.20}$$

is as small as possible and

$$3x_1 + 4x_2 + x_3 \qquad\qquad = 9, \tag{15.21a}$$
$$5x_1 + 2x_2 \qquad + x_4 \qquad = 8, \tag{15.21b}$$
$$x_1 - 2x_2 \qquad\qquad + x_5 = 1. \tag{15.21c}$$

The second step is to set x_1 and x_2 equal to zero and solve for the other three variables, x_3, x_4, and x_5. At this moment, x_1 and x_2 are called *nonbasic variables*; x_3, x_4, and x_5 are called *basic variables*. We know from Solution 1 of Table 15.1 that

$$x_3 = 9, \qquad x_4 = 8, \qquad x_5 = 1.$$

It should be noted that the value of $-z$ based on this basic feasible solution just computed is equal to zero. Clearly, it is not the best solution. We attempt to improve this situation in the third step described below. From Eq. (15.20), it is evident that the value of $-z$ can be decreased by increasing either x_1 or x_2. We then ask, Which one should be chosen? Since x_2 in Eq. (15.20) has a smaller (more negative) coefficient (that is, -11), it should be allowed to increase; x_1 should be kept at zero. Now that x_2 is no longer zero, we can replace it by x_3, x_4, or x_5. In other words, knowing that $x_1 = 0$ and $x_2 \neq 0$, we select x_3, x_4, or x_5 and set the chosen variable equal to zero in order to obtain a second set of basic feasible solutions.

We next select one of the three variables and set it equal to zero. We observe that this increase in the value of x_2 will have the following effects:

(1) It will increase the value of z; that is, decrease the value of $-z$ (see Eq. 15.20).
(2) It will decrease the values of x_3, x_4, and x_5.

The second effect can be seen from Eqs. (15.21) which can now be written as

$$4x_2 + x_3 \qquad\qquad = 9, \tag{15.22a}$$
$$2x_2 \qquad + x_4 \qquad = 8, \tag{15.22b}$$
$$-2x_2 \qquad\qquad + x_5 = 1, \tag{15.22c}$$

where all the variables are nonnegative. In particular, x_3 in Eq. (15.22a) cannot be negative. This condition forces us to increase the value of x_2 by no more than $\frac{9}{4}$ or

$$x_2 \leq 2.25. \tag{15.23}$$

Similarly, from Eq. (15.22b) we have

$$x_2 \leq 4.00. \tag{15.24}$$

Since x_2 has a negative coefficient in Eq. (15.22c), x_5 will always be positive and no restriction is needed for x_2 in Eq. (15.22c).

Comparing Eq. (15.23) with Eq. (15.24), we find that the smaller value of x_2 is 2.25, and since this comes from Eq. (15.23), we now set $x_3 = 0$ (as the new nonbasic variable) in place of x_2. In other words, our new basic feasible solution is

$$x_1 = 0, \qquad x_2 = 2.25, \qquad x_3 = 0, \qquad x_4 = 3.50, \qquad x_5 = 5.50.$$

Substituting this solution into Eq. (15.20), we obtain

$$-z = -24.75.$$

We note that the value of $-z$ in this solution, is smaller than zero, which is a substantial improvement over the previous solution.

The remainder of this step is to eliminate x_2 from Eq. (15.21b) and (15.21c). This task is readily accomplished by first converting Eq. (15.21a) to the form

$$\tfrac{3}{4}x_1 + x_2 + \tfrac{1}{4}x_3 = \tfrac{9}{4}, \tag{15.25a}$$

and then using it to eliminate x_2 from the other two equations. At the end of this step, we have

$$\tfrac{3}{4}x_1 + x_2 + \tfrac{1}{4}x_3 \qquad\qquad = \tfrac{9}{4}, \tag{15.25a}$$
$$\tfrac{7}{2}x_1 \qquad - \tfrac{1}{2}x_3 + x_4 \qquad = \tfrac{7}{2}, \tag{15.25b}$$
$$\tfrac{5}{2}x_1 \qquad + \tfrac{1}{2}x_3 \qquad + x_5 = \tfrac{11}{2}. \tag{15.25c}$$

The fourth step in the Simplex method serves to further improve the z-value. We now try to increase the value of x_1 which can be easily accomplished by setting

$$x_3 = 0,$$
$$x_4 = 0,$$

since $x_1 \leq 1$ from Eq. (15.25b), and solving for the other three variables. This step results in

$$x_1 = 1.00, \qquad x_2 = 1.50, \qquad x_3 = 0, \qquad x_4 = 0, \qquad x_5 = 3.00.$$

Substituting the above into Eq. (15.20), we have $-z = -26.50$. In Fig. 15.4, we can see clearly that at vertex C the objective function is maximized, and that no further improvement is possible for the value of $-z$. Thus our answers are

$$x_1 = 1.0, \qquad x_2 = 1.5, \qquad \max z = 26.5.$$

In order to simplify the discussion in the previous sections, we chose a well-behaved problem to illustrate the Simplex method. There are, however, some problems which introduce further complications in the method. Among these exceptional cases is *degeneracy*, in which one or more of the basic variables become zero at the same time that the objective function is zero.

In addition to the problem of degeneracy, other complications may arise, such as (1) no obvious feasible solution or contradictory constraint equations, or (2) multiple solutions or an infinite number of solutions. For a more detailed explanation of these exceptional cases, we refer the interested reader to the references listed at the end of this chapter.

15.6 GAUSS-JORDAN PROCEDURE AND SIMPLEX TABLEAU

In Chapter 8, we introduced the Gauss-Jordan elimination method to solve a set of simultaneous equations. We shall now extend this method to the solution of a set of linear algebraic equations where the number of unknowns is not equal to the number of the equations; this extension is important to the computer solution of linear programming problems.

To illustrate this extension, let us consider the following three equations in five unknowns:

$$3x_1 + 4x_2 + x_3 + x_4 + x_5 = 9,$$
$$5x_1 + 2x_2 + x_3 + x_4 + x_5 = 8, \tag{15.26}$$
$$x_1 - 2x_2 + x_3 + x_4 + x_5 = 1.$$

It should be noted that this set of equations has no relation whatsoever with Eqs. (15.18) or Eqs. (15.21). We wish to solve for x_1, x_2, and x_3 in terms of x_4 and x_5. In other words, we wish to transform Eqs. (15.26) into the form

$$x_1 \qquad + a'_{14}x_4 + a'_{15}x_5 = c'_1,$$
$$x_2 \quad + a'_{24}x_4 + a'_{25}x_5 = c'_2, \tag{15.27}$$
$$x_3 + a'_{34}x_4 + a'_{35}x_5 = c'_3,$$

and to determine the nine coefficients (a's and c's) in Eqs. (15.27). This transformation can be readily accomplished by the procedures discussed in Chapter 8:

(1) interchange of rows if the coefficient of a pivot element is zero,

(2) normalization (see Section 8.4),

(3) elimination (see Section 8.3).

And Eqs. (15.26) are then transformed into the following form:

$$x_1 \qquad + 0x_4 + 0x_5 = \tfrac{5}{8},$$
$$x_2 \quad + 0x_4 + 0x_5 = \tfrac{9}{8}, \tag{15.28}$$
$$x_3 + x_4 + x_5 = \tfrac{21}{8}.$$

Hence, the solutions for x_1, x_2, and x_3 in terms of x_4 and x_5 are

$$x_1 = \tfrac{5}{8}, \qquad x_2 = \tfrac{9}{8}, \qquad x_3 = \tfrac{21}{8} - x_4 - x_5.$$

We are now in a position to apply the Simplex method using the above extension of the Gauss-Jordan elimination procedure. Special attention will be paid to the selection of a pivotal element. We consider once more the sample problem from the previous sections in which we attempted to determine

$$x_i \geq 0, \qquad i = 1, 2, 3, 4, 5, \tag{15.16}$$

so that

$$-10x_1 - 11x_2 + 0x_3 + 0x_4 + 0x_5 + z = 0, \tag{15.17}$$

where z is the value to be maximized, and

$$3x_1 + 4x_2 + x_3 \qquad\qquad = 9, \tag{15.18a}$$
$$5x_1 + 2x_2 \qquad + x_4 \qquad = 8, \tag{15.18b}$$
$$x_1 - 2x_2 \qquad\qquad + x_5 = 1. \tag{15.18c}$$

The above four equations can be written in the following matrix form, known as a *Simplex tableau*:

$$A = \begin{bmatrix} -10 & -11 & 0 & 0 & 0 & 1 & 0 \\ 3 & 4 & 1 & 0 & 0 & 0 & 9 \\ 5 & 2 & 0 & 1 & 0 & 0 & 8 \\ 1 & -2 & 0 & 0 & 1 & 0 & 1 \end{bmatrix}. \tag{15.29}$$

To initiate the computation, we set x_1 and x_2 equal to zero (nonbasic variables). Then, by inspecting the tableau, we arrive at the first basic feasible solution:

$$x_1 = 0, \qquad x_2 = 0, \qquad x_3 = 9 - 3x_1 - 4x_2 = 9,$$
$$x_4 = 8 - 5x_1 - 2x_2 = 8, \qquad x_5 = 1 - x_1 + 2x_2 = 1,$$
$$z = 0 + 10x_1 + 11x_2 = 0.$$

Since z is equal to zero, this is clearly not the optimal solution.

As discussed in the second step of the Simplex method (Section 15.5), the value of x_2 is the first to be increased since it is the nonbasic variable with the most negative coefficient in Eq. (15.17) and therefore has the most pronounced effect in the maximization of z. At this point the Gauss-Jordan elimination procedure can be used advantageously to obtain a set of basic feasible solutions. Each basic feasible solution is obtained by arbitrarily setting two variables equal to zero and solving for the other three. Since we chose x_2 as the variable to be increased, we must determine the pivot element from column 2 of the Simplex tableau (Eq. 15.29). This pivot element can be found by (1) dividing each positive element in column 2 into the rightmost element of the row in which it appears and (2) selecting as the pivot element the one which after division yields the smallest quotient (excluding row 1).

In our example we note that only the second and third elements in this column are positive. We therefore compute only the two quotients

$$c_2/a_{22} = \tfrac{9}{4} = 2.25, \qquad c_3/a_{32} = \tfrac{8}{2} = 4,$$

and observe that the smaller quotient, that is, 2.25, is associated with the element a_{22}. Here the coefficients, a's and c's, are defined in Eq. (15.8).

TABLE 15.3. Simplex Tableau

Pass	Selection of the pivot element	Matrix						
		x_1	x_2	x_3	x_4	x_5	z	
Given augmented matrix	$\dfrac{9}{4} = 2.25$ $\dfrac{8}{2} = 4.00$	$\rightarrow$ $\begin{pmatrix} -10 \\ 3 \\ 5 \\ 1 \end{pmatrix}$	$\begin{matrix} -11 \\ ④ \\ 2 \\ -2 \\ \uparrow \end{matrix}$	$\begin{matrix} 0 \\ 1 \\ 0 \\ 0 \end{matrix}$	$\begin{matrix} 0 \\ 0 \\ 1 \\ 0 \end{matrix}$	$\begin{matrix} 0 \\ 0 \\ 0 \\ 1 \end{matrix}$	$\begin{matrix} 1 \\ 0 \\ 0 \\ 0 \end{matrix}$	$\begin{pmatrix} 0 \\ 9 \\ 8 \\ 1 \end{pmatrix}$
First pass		New row 2 = row 2/4						
		$\rightarrow$ $\begin{pmatrix} -10 \\ 0.75 \\ 5 \\ 1 \end{pmatrix}$	$\begin{matrix} -11 \\ ① \\ 2 \\ -2 \\ \uparrow \end{matrix}$	$\begin{matrix} 0 \\ 0.25 \\ 0 \\ 0 \end{matrix}$	$\begin{matrix} 0 \\ 0 \\ 1 \\ 0 \end{matrix}$	$\begin{matrix} 0 \\ 0 \\ 0 \\ 1 \end{matrix}$	$\begin{matrix} 1 \\ 0 \\ 0 \\ 0 \end{matrix}$	$\begin{pmatrix} 0 \\ 2.25 \\ 8 \\ 1 \end{pmatrix}$
		New row 1 = row 1 − row 2 × (−11)						
		$\rightarrow$ $\begin{pmatrix} -1.75 \\ 0.75 \\ 5 \\ 1 \end{pmatrix}$	$\begin{matrix} 0 \\ ① \\ 2 \\ -2 \\ \uparrow \end{matrix}$	$\begin{matrix} 2.75 \\ 0.25 \\ 0 \\ 0 \end{matrix}$	$\begin{matrix} 0 \\ 0 \\ 1 \\ 0 \end{matrix}$	$\begin{matrix} 0 \\ 0 \\ 0 \\ 1 \end{matrix}$	$\begin{matrix} 1 \\ 0 \\ 0 \\ 0 \end{matrix}$	$\begin{pmatrix} 24.75 \\ 2.25 \\ 8 \\ 1 \end{pmatrix}$
		New row 3 = row 3 − row 2 × 2						
		$\rightarrow$ $\begin{pmatrix} -1.75 \\ 0.75 \\ 3.50 \\ 1 \end{pmatrix}$	$\begin{matrix} 0 \\ ① \\ 0 \\ -2 \\ \uparrow \end{matrix}$	$\begin{matrix} 2.75 \\ 0.25 \\ -0.50 \\ 0 \end{matrix}$	$\begin{matrix} 0 \\ 0 \\ 1 \\ 0 \end{matrix}$	$\begin{matrix} 0 \\ 0 \\ 0 \\ 1 \end{matrix}$	$\begin{matrix} 1 \\ 0 \\ 0 \\ 0 \end{matrix}$	$\begin{pmatrix} 24.75 \\ 2.25 \\ 3.50 \\ 1 \end{pmatrix}$
	$\dfrac{2.25}{0.75} = 3.00$ $\dfrac{3.50}{3.50} = 1.00$ $\dfrac{5.50}{2.50} = 2.20$	New row 4 = row 4 − row 2 × (−2)						
		$\rightarrow$ $\begin{pmatrix} -1.75 \\ 0.75 \\ ⟨3.50⟩ \\ 2.50 \\ \uparrow \end{pmatrix}$	$\begin{matrix} 0 \\ 1 \\ 0 \\ 0 \end{matrix}$	$\begin{matrix} 2.75 \\ 0.25 \\ -0.50 \\ 0.50 \end{matrix}$	$\begin{matrix} 0 \\ 0 \\ 1 \\ 0 \end{matrix}$	$\begin{matrix} 0 \\ 0 \\ 0 \\ 1 \end{matrix}$	$\begin{matrix} 1 \\ 0 \\ 0 \\ 0 \end{matrix}$	$\begin{pmatrix} 24.75 \\ 2.25 \\ 3.50 \\ 5.50 \end{pmatrix}$

TABLE 15.3 (*cont.*)

	New row 3 = row 3/3.50
	$\begin{pmatrix} -1.75 & 0 & 2.75 & 0 & 0 & 1 & 24.75 \\ 0.75 & 1 & 0.25 & 0 & 0 & 0 & 2.25 \\ \rightarrow \quad ① & 0 & -0.143 & 0.286 & 0 & 0 & 1.00 \\ 2.50 & 0 & 0.50 & 0 & 1 & 0 & 5.50 \end{pmatrix}$
	New row 1 = row 1 − row 3 × (−1.75)
	$\begin{pmatrix} 0 & 0 & 2.50 & 0.50 & 0 & 1 & 26.50 \\ 0.75 & 1 & 0.25 & 0 & 0 & 0 & 2.25 \\ \rightarrow \quad ① & 0 & -0.143 & 0.286 & 0 & 0 & 1.00 \\ 2.50 & 0 & 0.50 & 0 & 1 & 0 & 5.50 \end{pmatrix}$
Second pass	New row 2 = row 2 − row 3 × 0.75
	$\begin{pmatrix} 0 & 0 & 2.50 & 0.50 & 0 & 1 & 26.50 \\ 0 & 1 & 0.357 & -0.214 & 0 & 0 & 1.50 \\ \rightarrow \quad ① & 0 & -0.143 & 0.286 & 0 & 0 & 1.00 \\ 2.50 & 0 & 0.50 & 0 & 1 & 0 & 5.50 \end{pmatrix}$
	New row 4 = row 4 − row 3 × 2.50
	$\begin{pmatrix} 0 & 0 & 2.50 & 0.50 & 0 & 1 & 26.50 \\ 0 & 1 & 0.357 & -0.214 & 0 & 0 & 1.50 \\ \rightarrow \quad ① & 0 & -0.143 & 0.286 & 0 & 0 & 1.00 \\ 0 & 0 & 0.857 & -0.714 & 1 & 0 & 3.00 \end{pmatrix}$

We thus choose the element a_{22}, whose value is 4, as the pivot element in the next step of the procedure, normalization. Dividing each element in the second row by the value of the pivot element, we find that Eq. (15.29) becomes

$$A = \begin{bmatrix} -10 & -11 & 0 & 0 & 0 & 1 & 0 \\ 0.75 & ① & 0.25 & 0 & 0 & 0 & 2.25 \\ 5 & 2 & 0 & 1 & 0 & 0 & 8 \\ 1 & -2 & 0 & 0 & 1 & 0 & 1 \end{bmatrix}. \qquad (15.30)$$

The pivot element is indicated above by a circle and is used to eliminate the other elements in column 2. At the end of this first elimination step the tableau becomes

$$A = \begin{bmatrix} -1.75 & 0 & 2.75 & 0 & 0 & 1 & 24.75 \\ 0.75 & 1 & 0.25 & 0 & 0 & 0 & 2.25 \\ 3.50 & 0 & -0.50 & 1 & 0 & 0 & 3.50 \\ 2.50 & 0 & 0.50 & 0 & 1 & 0 & 5.50 \end{bmatrix}. \qquad (15.31)$$

The new basic feasible solution obtained from the above matrix is

$$x_1 = 0, \qquad x_3 = 0,$$
$$x_2 = \quad 2.25 - 0.75x_1 - 0.25x_3 = \quad 2.25,$$
$$x_4 = \quad 3.50 - 3.50x_1 + 0.50x_3 = \quad 3.50,$$
$$x_5 = \quad 5.50 - 2.50x_1 - 0.50x_3 = \quad 5.50,$$
$$z = 24.75 + 1.75x_1 - 2.75x_3 = 24.75.$$

Although the value of z has been increased from 0 to 24.75, it can be made still greater by increasing the value of x_1, since the coefficient of x_1 is positive, while at the same time x_3 is kept equal to zero. To perform this operation, we simply select the appropriate pivot element from column 1 and repeat the normalization and elimination procedures as before to obtain

$$A = \begin{bmatrix} 0 & 0 & 2.50 & 0.50 & 0 & 1 & 26.5 \\ 0 & 1 & 0.35 & -0.21 & 0 & 0 & 1.5 \\ \textcircled{1} & 0 & -0.14 & 0.28 & 0 & 0 & 1.0 \\ 0 & 0 & 0.85 & -0.71 & 1 & 0 & 3.0 \end{bmatrix}. \tag{15.32}$$

We have now arrived at the optimal solution:

$$x_3 = 0, \qquad x_4 = 0,$$
$$x_2 = \quad 1.50 - 0.35x_3 + 0.21x_4 = \quad 1.50,$$
$$x_1 = \quad 1.00 + 0.14x_3 - 0.28x_4 = \quad 1.00,$$
$$x_5 = \quad 3.00 - 0.85x_3 + 0.71x_4 = \quad 3.00,$$
$$z = 26.50 - 2.50x_3 - 0.50x_4 = 26.50.$$

We can see that we have reached the maximum value for z, since the coefficients of both x_3 and x_4 are negative and an increase in either variable would only decrease z. On the other hand, if we decreased x_3 or x_4, then they would be less than zero—in violation of the nonnegative requirement. Table 15.3 summarizes the two steps in the elimination procedure. The computations made to select the two pivot elements are listed, and the pivot elements at each step of the procedure are circled. In addition, the pivotal rows and columns at each step are indicated by arrows.

15.7   COMPUTER APPLICATION IN LINEAR PROGRAMMING

In recent years, the use of linear programming methods has grown rather extensively. One of the key factors contributing to this remarkable development has been the availability of computers and computer programs. Many case studies of practical applications of linear programming are listed in the references at the end of this chapter. The main purpose of this section is to introduce to the reader one of the possible FORTRAN programs for the Simplex method.

The FORTRAN program shown in Fig. 15.5 can be used to solve a linear programming problem containing up to 34 constraints and 85 variables.

```
C       SIMPLEX METHOD FOR SOLVING LINEAR PROGRAMMING PROBLEMS
C       FORTRAN II MUST BE USED
C
C       THE LIMIT OF THE PROGRAM IS AS FOLLOWS
C             MAX. NUMBER OF VARIABLES INCLUDING SLACK VARIABLES = 85 50
C             MAX. NUMBER OF EQUATIONS INCLUDING THE OBJECTIVE FUNCTION = 35
C       THE INITIAL SIMPLEX TABLEAU CORRESPONDING TO THE GIVEN EQUATIONS
C       MUST BE PUT INTO THE FORM
C
C             I--                                              I
C             I  A(1,1)    A(1,2)  . . . . . .  A(1,JJ)   I
C             I                                              I
C             I  A(2,1)    A(2,2)  . . . . . .  A(2,JJ)   I
C             I      .        .                    .      I
C             I      .        .                    .      I
C             I      .        .                    .      I
C             I A(II,1)  A(II,2)  . . . . . . A(II,JJ)  I
C             I                                              I
C             I A(III,1) A(III,2) . . . . . . A(III,JJ) I
C             I--                                              I
C
C       WHERE THE ELEMENTS WERE DEFINED IN EQ.(15.33).
C
        DIMENSION A(36,86), W(36), L(36)
C
C   -   READ IN
C             II = TOTAL NUMBER OF THE GIVEN EQUATION INCLUDING THE
C                  OBJECTIVE FUNCTION,
C                = TOTAL NUMBER OF ROWS OF THE ABOVE SIMPLEX TABLEAU - 1 ,
C             JJ = TOTAL NUMBER OF COLUMNS OF THE GIVEN ARGUMENTED TABLEAU.
C
  108 READ 1, II, JJ
    1 FORMAT (18I4)
      III = II + 1
      DO 10 I=1, III
      W(I) = 0.
   10 L(I) = 0
C
C       READ IN THE ELEMENTS OF THE MATRIX ROW BY ROW.
C
      DO 9 I=1, III
    9 READ 4, (A(I,J), J=1, JJ)
    4 FORMAT (7F10.4)
C
C       READ IN THE SUBSCRIPT FOR THE SLACK VARIABLE ON ROW(I) WHERE
C       I IS NOT EQUAL TO 1 AND III.
C
      READ 1, (L(I), I=2, II)
C
C       NEXT STATEMENT FOR INITIALIZATION
C
      KKK = 0
C
C       THE NEXT STATEMENTS ARE TO LOOK FOR THE ROW AT WHICH THERE IS
C       NO SLACK VARIABLE(NOT INCLUDING THE FIRST ROW).
C
   22 I = 1
   23 I = I + 1
```

Fig. 15.5. FORTRAN program for linear programming problems. (*Cont.*)

```
      IF (I - III) 24, 40, 40
   24 IF (L(I)) 23, 25, 23
C
C     CALCULATE
C          NEW LAST ROW = LAST ROW - THE ROW WITHOUT SLACK VARIABLE
C
   25 DO 27 J=1, JJ
      IF (A(I,J)) 26, 27, 26
   26 A(III, J) = A(III,J) - A(I,J)
   27 CONTINUE
      GO TO 23
C
C     NEXT STATEMENTS FOR SEARCHING FOR THE COLUMN AT WHICH THE MOST
C     NEGATIVE ENTRY APPEARS EITHER IN THE FORST(OBJECTIVE FUNCTION)
C     OR LAST(FORM P) ROW.
C
   40 K = III
   44 J = 0
      W(K) = 0.
      L(K) = 0
   42 J = J + 1
      IF (J - JJ) 41, 45, 45
   41 IF (A(K,J)) 43, 42, 42
   43 IF (W(K) - A(K,J)) 42, 42, 47
   47 W(K) = A(K,J)
      L(K) = J
      GO TO 42
C
C     TEST FOR L(K).  IF L(K) IS EQUAL TO ZERO, THAT IS, ALL THE THE
C     ENTRIES EXCEPT THE EXTREME RIGHT ONE EITHER IN THE FIRST OR LAST
C     ROW ARE POSITIVE. GO TO ST. 62 FOR FURTHER EXAMINATION.
C
   45 IF (L(K)) 46, 62, 46
C
C     FIND OUT THE PIVOT COLUMN
C
   46 KJ = L(K)
C
C     TEST EVERY ENTRY IN THE PIVOT COLUMN TO SEE IF IT IS POSITIVE
C     OR NOT. IF IT IS, GO TO ST. 121 TO COMPUTE THE RATIO DEFINED IN
C     THE LAST SECTION.
C
      DO 120 I=2, II
      IF (A(I,KJ)) 120, 120, 121
  120 CONTINUE
C
C     IF ALL THE ENTRIES IN THE PIVOT COLUMN ARE ZERO OR NEGATIVE
C     NUMBERS, 'UNBOUNDED' IS GOING TO BE TYPED.
C
      PUNCH 130
  103 FORMAT (8HFEASIBLE)
      GO TO 70
C
C     THE FOLLOWING STATEMENTS ARE FOR COMPUTING THE RATIO DEFINDED
C     IN SECTION 15.4, AND FOR DETERMINING THE LOCATION OF THE PIVOT.
C
  121 I = 1
      JK = 0
   50 I = I + 1
```

Fig. 15.5 (*cont.*)

```
      IF (I - II) 52, 52, 56
  52 IF (A(I,KJ)) 50, 50, 51

  51 X = A(I,JJ)/A(I,KJ)
      IF (JK) 55, 53, 55
  55 IF (X - XMIN) 53, 50, 50
  53 XMIN = X
      JK = I
      GO TO 50
C
C     THE NEXT STATEMENT INDICATES THE PIVOT ELEMENT BEFORE NORMALIZATION.
C
  56 X = A(JK, KJ)
      L(JK) = KJ
C
C     NEXT STATEMENTS FOR CALCULATING THE NEW ROWS ABOVE THE PIVOT ROW
C
      DO 57 I=1, III
  57 W(I) = A(I,KJ)
      IJ = JK - 1
      DO 59 I=1, IJ
      DO 59 J=1, JJ
      IF (A(JK,J)) 58, 59, 58
  58 IF (W(I)) 580, 59, 580
 580 A(I,J) = A(I,J) - W(I)*(A(JK,J)/X)
  59 CONTINUE
C
C     NEXT STATEMENTS FOR CALCULATING THE NEW ROWS BELOW THE PIVOT ROW
C
      IJ = JK + 1
      DO 61 I=IJ, III
      DO 61 J=1, JJ
      IF (A(JK,J)) 60, 61, 60
  60 IF (W(I)) 600, 61, 600
 600 A(I,J) = A(I,J) - W(I)*(A(JK,J)/X)
  61 CONTINUE
C
C     NEXT STATEMENTS FOR NORMALIZATION
C
      DO 205 J=1, JJ
 205 A(JK,J) = A(JK,J)/X
      KKK = KKK + 1
      PUNCH 105, KKK, A(K,JJ), L(JK)
 105 FORMAT (1X, I4, 6X, F15.2, 10X, I4)
      GO TO 44
C
C     NEXT STATEMENT FOR TESTING TO SEE IF IT IS THE FIRST ROW ON
C     WHICH ALL THE ENTRIES ARE POSITIVE EXCEPT THE EXTREME RIGHT ONE.
C     IF IT IS, THAT MEANS, NO FURTHER IMPROVEMENT ON THE SOLUTION
C     CAN BE MADE, GO TO ST. 70 AND THE ANSWER WILL BE TYPED OUT.
C
  62 IF (K - 1) 70, 70, 63
  63 IJ = JJ - 1
C
C     TEST TO SEE WHETHER ALL THE ELEMENTS ON THE LAST ROW(NOT
C     INCLUDING THE EXTREME RIGHT ONE) ARE CLOSE TO ZERO.
C     IT IS DEFINED IN THE NEXT STATEMENTS THAT THE PROBLEM IS
C     INFEASIBLE IF ONE(OR MORE) OF THEM IS LARGER THAN 0.0001.
C
      DO 65 J=1, IJ
```

Fig. 15.5 (*cont.*)

```
      IF (A(K,J) - .0001) 65, 65, 66
   65 CONTINUE
      PUNCH 103
  130 FORMAT (9HUNBOUNDED)
      PUNCH 101
  101 FORMAT (46HITERATION      OBJ. FUNCTION      NEW BASIC VAR.)
C
C     IF, AFTER ITERATIONS, ALL THE ELEMENTS IN THE LAST ROW HAVE
C     BECOME POSITIVE BUT NEAR ZERO, DEFINE ALL OF THEM TO BE ZERO.
C
      DO 140 J=1, JJ
  140 A(III,J) = 0.
C
C     IN CASE OF NONARTIFICAL PROBLEMS, DEFINE K=1, AND GO TO ST. 44
C     FOR SEARCHING FOR THE PIVOT COLUMN.
C
      K = 1
      KKK = 0
      GO TO 44
C
C     TYPE OUT THE SOLUTION
C
   66 PUNCH 6
    6 FORMAT (10HINFEASIBLE)
   70 PUNCH 8, A(1,JJ)
    8 FORMAT (///13HOBJ. FUNCTION, F20.8/)
      PUNCH 7
    7 FORMAT (23HVARIABLE          VALUE)
      DO 71 I=2, II
   71 PUNCH 5, L(I), A(I,JJ)
    5 FORMAT (I4, F20.8)
C
C     NEXT STATEMENTS FOR PRINTING THE FINAL MATRIX
C
      PUNCH 100
  100 FORMAT (/////16HTHE FINAL MATRIX)
      DO 78 I=1, III
      PUNCH 150, I
  150 FORMAT (//35X, 4HROW , I2/)
   78 PUNCH 4, (A(I,J), J=1, JJ)
      STOP
      END
```

Fig. 15.5 (*concl.*)

The Simplex tableau mentioned in the previous section is followed very closely in this program. A detailed flow chart is shown in Fig. 15.6.

The first step is to form the following matrix:

$$[\alpha] = \begin{bmatrix} a_{11} & a_{12} & \cdots & a_{1,n+1} \\ a_{21} & a_{22} & \cdots & a_{2,n+1} \\ \vdots & & & \\ a_{m+1,1} & a_{m+1,2} & \cdots & a_{m+1,n+1} \\ 0 & 0 & \cdots & 0 \end{bmatrix}. \tag{15.33}$$

The matrix $[\alpha]$ can be obtained from $[A]$ by simply deleting the column for z in Eq. (15.29). The column for z is the second column from the right. We can make the following observations.

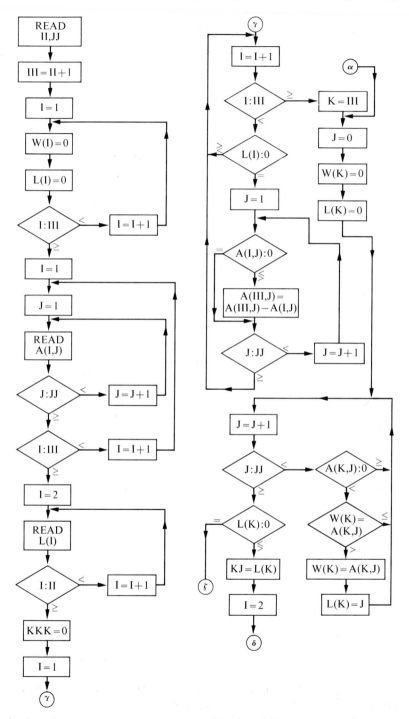

Fig. 15.6.   Flow chart for simplex method.   (*Cont.*)

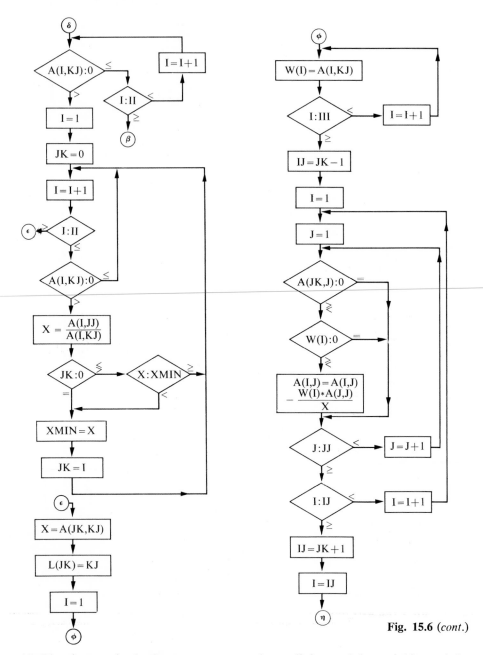

Fig. 15.6 (*cont.*)

(1) The elements in the first row represent the coefficients of the variables and the constant in the objective function.

(2) The elements in the second row through the $m + 1$ row represent the coefficients of the variables and the constant in the constraints.

(3) The elements in the last row (all zeros) are for artificial variable problems which will be discussed in the next section.

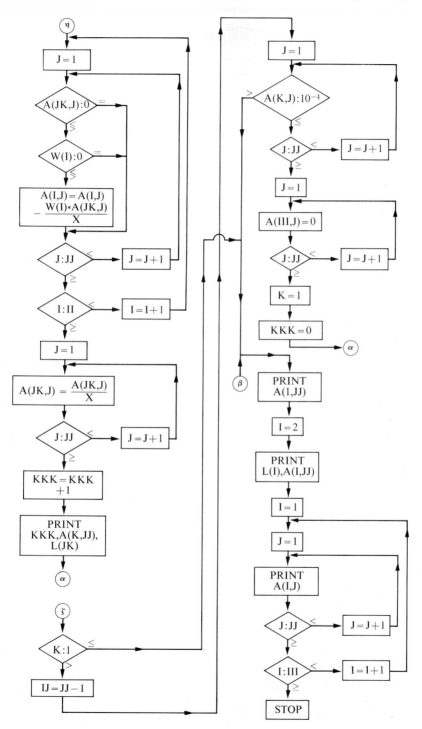

Fig. 15.6 (*concl.*)

TABLE 15.4. Output for Example 15.1

FEASIBLE

ITERATION	OBJ. FUNCTION	NEW BASIC VAR.
1	24.75	2
2	26.50	1

OBJ. FUNCTION   26.50000000

VARIABLE	VALUE
2	1.50000000
1	1.00000000
5	3.00000000

THE FINAL MATRIX

                                                ROW   1

| 0.0000 | 0.0000 | 2.5000 | .4999 | 0.0000 | 26.5000 |

                                                ROW   2

| 0.0000 | 1.0000 | .3571 | -.2142 | 0.0000 | 1.5000 |

                                                ROW   3

| 1.0000 | 0.0000 | -.1428 | .2857 | 0.0000 | 1.0000 |

                                                ROW   4

| 0.0000 | 0.0000 | .8571 | -.7142 | 1.0000 | 3.0000 |

                                                ROW   5

| 0.0000 | 0.0000 | 0.0000 | 0.0000 | 0.0000 | 0.0000 |

Example 15.1

As a sample problem we may apply this program to the example developed in Section 15.6. We would thus read in the data in the form shown in Fig. 15.7.

The required input are as follows.

Card 1

Columns 1 to 4 inclusive: Number of the constraints $+$ 1 (FORMAT I4).
Columns 5 to 8 inclusive: Number of columns in Eq. (15.33) (FORMAT I4).

Starting with Card 2

Matrix [@] as shown in Eq. (15.33), row by row in FORMAT(7F10.4).

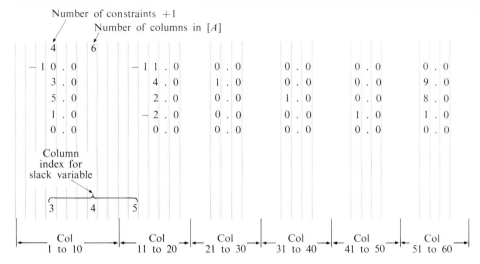

Figure 15.7

Last Card

Column index for the slack variable in each row (ignore the first and last rows) in FORMAT(18I4). We assume here that there are less than 18 slack variables.

Here the number of columns in $[\alpha]$ is 6, not 7, because the elements in the z-column, such as shown in Table 15.3, are not included in $[\alpha]$. Depending on the problem, one of the following three messages will be punched out as output for the program:

FEASIBLE,   INFEASIBLE,   or   UNBOUNDED.

In our particular example, the solution is feasible and the FEASIBLE message is punched out. Table 15.4 lists the complete output for Example 15.1.

15.8 ARTIFICIAL VARIABLES

In the previous section we used the Simplex procedure to solve a maximization problem involving constraints containing only inequalities of the "less than or equal to" type. The initial basic feasible solution that started off the iterations could be easily found by assigning x_1 and x_2 as nonbasic variables, and then setting them equal to zero. In general, however, not all linear programming problems are quite so simple. We shall now consider a more difficult example in which the objective function is subject to a set of constraints containing $\geq$-inequalities. This type of problem is known as the *artificial-variable* problem. In order to explain the artificial-variable technique, let us begin by stating the following example, which is actually the same as the sample problem in Section (15.7) except that the inequality sign in the second constraint has been reversed.

Determine

$$x_1 \geq 0, \qquad x_2 \geq 0, \tag{15.34}$$

so that

$$z = 10x_1 + 11x_2 \tag{15.35}$$

is a maximum and

$$3x_1 + 4x_2 \leq 9, \tag{15.36}$$

$$5x_1 + 2x_2 \geq 8, \tag{15.37}$$

$$x_1 - 2x_2 \leq 1. \tag{15.38}$$

By introducing the slack variables x_3, x_4, and x_5 as before, the problem is reformulated as follows. Determine

$$x_i \geq 0, \qquad i = 1, 2, 3, 4, 5, \tag{15.39}$$

so that

$$-z = -10x_1 - 11x_2 \tag{15.40}$$

is a minimum and

$$3x_1 + 4x_2 + x_3 \qquad\qquad = 9, \tag{15.41}$$

$$5x_1 + 2x_2 \qquad - x_4 \qquad = 8, \tag{15.42}$$

$$x_1 - 2x_2 \qquad\qquad + x_5 = 1. \tag{15.43}$$

The problem now is to evaluate the initial basic feasible solution. It is obvious that the origin, $x_1 = 0$, $x_2 = 0$, is not one of the basic feasible solutions to the above constraints, for it makes x_4 equal to -8, and this clearly violates the nonnegativity condition of Eq. (15.39). These equations must therefore be rearranged so that we can easily find a first feasible solution and the iterations will finally lead to an optimal solution satisfying the original as well as the rearranged set of equations. For this purpose, we introduce in Eq. (15.42) a new variable, x_6, which is called an *artificial variable*, since it has no direct connection with the original constraints. Having made this addition, we see that the constraints become

$$x_i \geq 0, \qquad i = 1, 2, 3, 4, 5, 6, \tag{15.44}$$

$$3x_1 + 4x_2 + x_3 \qquad\qquad\qquad = 9, \tag{15.45}$$

$$5x_1 + 2x_2 \qquad - x_4 \qquad + x_6 = 8, \tag{15.46}$$

$$x_1 - 2x_2 \qquad\qquad + x_5 \qquad = 1. \tag{15.47}$$

We immediately have a basic feasible solution by setting x_1, x_2, and x_4 equal zero:

$$x_1 = 0, \qquad x_2 = 0, \qquad x_4 = 0, \qquad x_3 = 9, \qquad x_5 = 1, \qquad x_6 = 8. \tag{15.48}$$

It should be mentioned, however, that the first basic feasible solution of Eqs. (15.45) through (15.47) is not necessarily a basic feasible solution to the original set of constraints, Eqs. (15.39) through (15.43). Any basic feasible solution of the constraints, Eqs. (15.44) through (15.47), which is also a basic feasible solution to the constraints,

Eqs. (15.39) through (15.43), must have $x_6 = 0$. In other words, the artificial variable must be assigned as a nonbasic variable.

Our next step is to use the Simplex method to search for a basic feasible solution common to both sets of constraints. However, in searching for a basic feasible solution for which $x_6 = 0$, we may ask, Can we improve the value of the objective function while the search is being made? The answer to this question is yes; we can by introducing in the objective function a quantity px_6, where p is chosen as an unspecified, yet extremely large, positive number. Let us define

$$-z' = -z + px_6 \tag{15.49a}$$
$$= -10x_1 - 11x_2 + 0x_3 + 0x_4 + 0x_5 + px_6, \tag{15.49b}$$

and then proceed to seek a minimum value for $-z'$ instead of $-z$. We now have the following problem. Determine

$$x_i \geq 0, \qquad i = 1, 2, 3, 4, 5, 6, \tag{15.44}$$

so that

$$-z' = -10x_1 - 11x_2 + 0x_3 + 0x_4 + 0x_5 + px_6 \tag{15.49b}$$

is a minimum and

$$3x_1 + 4x_2 + x_3 \qquad\qquad\qquad = 9, \tag{15.45}$$
$$5x_1 + 2x_2 \qquad - x_4 \qquad + x_6 = 8, \tag{15.46}$$
$$x_1 - 2x_2 \qquad\qquad + x_5 \qquad = 1. \tag{15.47}$$

If there is a solution at all to the original constraints, Eqs. (15.39) through (15.43), we shall eventually arrive at such a basic feasible solution with $x_6 = 0$, by applying the Simplex procedure to the above modified system. The large coefficient p will prevent the appearance of the artificial variable x_6 in the optimal solution to Eqs. (15.44) through (15.47) and (15.49b); and the value of $-z'$ will not reach its minimum while the search is being made for a basic feasible solution with $x_6 = 0$. It should be noted here that any optimal solution with $x_6 = 0$ for Eqs. (15.44) through (15.47) and (15.49b) is not necessarily the optimal solution to the original set of constraints, Eqs. (15.39) through (15.43); it is just one of the basic feasible solutions of the original constraints subject to the objective function $-z$. Having attained a basic feasible solution with $x_6 = 0$, we can therefore drop the artificial variable x_6 from the objective function and continue with the original variables, applying the Simplex procedure until either the minimum value of $-z'$ is found or $-z'$ is determined to have an infinite minimum.

The first Simplex tableau (see Section 15.6) can be written as

$$
A = \begin{array}{c} \begin{array}{ccccccc} x_1 & x_2 & x_3 & x_4 & x_5 & x_6 & z' \end{array} \\ \left(\begin{array}{ccccccc} -10 & -11 & 0 & 0 & 0 & p & 1 & 0 \\ 3 & 4 & 1 & 0 & 0 & 0 & 0 & 9 \\ 5 & 2 & 0 & -1 & 0 & 1 & 0 & 8 \\ 1 & -2 & 0 & 0 & 1 & 0 & 0 & 1 \end{array} \right). \end{array} \tag{15.50}
$$

It is convenient to separate the first row into two parts. The element p is transferred to a new row (the last one) in the following matrix:

$$
\begin{pmatrix}
x_1 & x_2 & x_3 & x_4 & x_5 & x_6 & z' & \\
-10 & -11 & 0 & 0 & 0 & 0 & 1 & 0 \\
3 & 4 & 1 & 0 & 0 & 0 & 0 & 9 \\
5 & 2 & 0 & -1 & 0 & 1 & 0 & 8 \\
1 & -2 & 0 & 0 & 1 & 0 & 0 & 1 \\
0 & 0 & 0 & 0 & 0 & p & 0 & 0
\end{pmatrix}.
\tag{15.51}
$$

Note that the first and last rows in the above tableau still represent a single objective function, Eq. (15.49b). We know that in this problem there are only three variables which can be taken as the nonbasic variables. Equation (15.51) does not yield a basic feasible solution because it contains four nonbasic variables, that is, x_1, x_2, x_4, and x_6. This difficulty can be easily solved by multiplying each entry of the third row in Eq. (15.51) by $-p$, and then adding the results to the fifth row in order to make x_6 a basic variable. The resulting matrix is

$$
\begin{array}{ll}
 & \begin{array}{ccccccc} x_1 & x_2 & x_3 & x_4 & x_5 & x_6 & z' \end{array} \\
\begin{array}{l} \\ \frac{9}{3} = 3 \\ \frac{8}{5} = 1.6 \\ \frac{1}{1} = 1 \\ \\ \end{array} &
\begin{pmatrix}
-10 & -11 & 0 & 0 & 0 & 0 & 1 & 0 \\
3 & 4 & 1 & 0 & 0 & 0 & 0 & 9 \\
5 & 2 & 0 & -1 & 0 & 1 & 0 & 8 \\
\rightarrow \textcircled{1} & -2 & 0 & 0 & 1 & 0 & 0 & 1 \\
-5p & -2p & 0 & p & 0 & 0 & 0 & -8p
\end{pmatrix}.
\end{array}
\tag{15.52}
$$

We have now reached the first basic feasible solution for Eqs. (15.45) to (15.47) and (15.49b), which can be taken from Eq. (15.52) as

$$
\begin{aligned}
&x_1 = 0, \quad x_2 = 0, \quad x_4 = 0, \\
&x_3 = 0, \quad x_5 = 1, \quad x_6 = 8, \quad z' = -8p.
\end{aligned}
\tag{15.53}
$$

Since the first and last row of the artificial tableau denote a single objective function, we have from Eq. (15.52),

$$
-z' = 8p - (10 + 5p)x_1 - (11 + 2p)x_2 + px_4.
\tag{15.54}
$$

This equation suggests that an increase in either x_1 or x_2 will decrease the value of $-z'$. From Section (15.5) it is known that the variable which has the smaller (more negative) coefficient should be increased first. Therefore, it is necessary to determine which variable has the smaller coefficient. Since the coefficient p is defined as an extremely large number, the coefficients -10 and -11 become negligible in comparison with $-5p$ and $-2p$, respectively. This leads us to the conclusion that the coefficient of x_1 is more negative than that of x_2, and that we should search in column 1 to locate the pivot element. By comparing the ratios of the rightmost elements to their corresponding entries in the pivot column, we choose element 1, encircled in

Eq. (15.52), as the pivot element. Once this choice has been made, we use the Gauss-Jordan elimination method to perform the first iteration, the results of which are indicated in the following matrix:

$$
\begin{array}{c}
\\
\tfrac{6}{10} = 0.6 \\
\tfrac{3}{12} = 0.25 \\
\\
\\
\\
\end{array}
\begin{array}{cccccccc}
x_1 & x_2 & x_3 & x_4 & x_5 & x_6 & z' & \\
0 & -31 & 0 & 0 & 10 & 0 & 1 & 10 \\
0 & 10 & 1 & 0 & -3 & 0 & 0 & 6 \\
0 & \boxed{12} & 0 & -1 & -5 & 1 & 0 & 3 \\
1 & -2 & 0 & 0 & 1 & 0 & 0 & 1 \\
0 & -12p & 0 & p & 5p & 0 & 0 & -3p \\
\end{array}
\qquad (15.55)
$$

with a basic feasible solution

$$
\begin{aligned}
x_2 &= 0, & x_4 &= 0, & x_5 &= 0, \\
x_1 &= 1, & x_3 &= 6, & x_6 &= 3, & z' &= 10 - 3p.
\end{aligned}
\qquad (15.56)
$$

The large negative entry, $-12p$, in the last row of Eq. (15.55) implies that $-z'$ may be further improved. The second iteration is therefore performed by using the element 12 as a pivot, which is marked by a circle in Eq. (15.55). The result is

$$
\begin{array}{ccccccc}
x_1 & x_2 & x_3 & x_4 & x_5 & x_6 & z' \\
0 & 0 & 0 & -\tfrac{31}{12} & -\tfrac{35}{12} & \tfrac{31}{12} & 1 & \tfrac{71}{4} \\
0 & 0 & 1 & \tfrac{5}{6} & \tfrac{7}{6} & -\tfrac{7}{6} & 0 & \tfrac{7}{2} \\
0 & 1 & 0 & -\tfrac{1}{12} & -\tfrac{5}{12} & \tfrac{1}{12} & 0 & \tfrac{1}{4} \\
1 & 0 & 0 & -\tfrac{1}{6} & \tfrac{1}{6} & \tfrac{1}{6} & 0 & \tfrac{3}{2} \\
0 & 0 & 0 & 0 & 0 & p & 0 & 0 \\
\end{array}
\qquad (15.57)
$$

with a basic feasible solution

$$
\begin{aligned}
x_4 &= 0, & x_5 &= 0, & x_6 &= 0, & x_1 &= \tfrac{3}{2} = 1.50, \\
x_2 &= \tfrac{1}{4} = 0.25, & x_3 &= \tfrac{7}{2} = 3.50 & & & z' &= \tfrac{71}{4} = 17.75.
\end{aligned}
\qquad (15.58)
$$

The artificial variable x_6 has now become nonbasic, namely, it is zero, and from Eq. (15.49b) it follows that z' becomes equal to z. The objective function may be now written as

$$
-z = -\tfrac{71}{4} - \tfrac{31}{12}x_4 - \tfrac{35}{12}x_5 + \tfrac{31}{12}x_6,
\qquad (15.59)
$$

which signifies that $-z$ can be improved further by increasing the value of x_5.

We have now come to the final phase of this problem in which we attempt to find the optimal solution for the original constraint. The last row in Eq. (15.57) may be ignored in this phase, because the large number p no longer influences the value of z.

By omitting the last row from Eq. (15.57), we have

$$\begin{array}{c} \frac{7}{2}=3.0 \\[4pt] \frac{7}{6} \\[2pt] \frac{3}{2}=9.0 \\[2pt] \frac{1}{6} \\[2pt] {} \\[2pt] {} \end{array} \begin{array}{cccccccc} x_1 & x_2 & x_3 & x_4 & x_5 & x_6 & z' & \\ \left(\begin{array}{ccccccc} 0 & 0 & 0 & -\frac{31}{12} & -\frac{35}{12} & \frac{31}{12} & 1 & \frac{71}{4} \\[4pt] 0 & 0 & 1 & \frac{5}{6} & \boxed{\frac{7}{6}} & -\frac{7}{6} & 0 & \frac{7}{2} \\[4pt] 0 & 1 & 0 & -\frac{1}{12} & -\frac{5}{12} & \frac{1}{12} & 0 & \frac{1}{4} \\[4pt] 1 & 0 & 0 & -\frac{1}{6} & \frac{1}{6} & \frac{1}{6} & 0 & \frac{3}{2} \\ & & & & \uparrow & & & \end{array} \right). \end{array}$$

(15.57a)

The next two iterations are

$$\begin{array}{c} \frac{3}{\frac{5}{7}}=4.2 \\[6pt] \frac{\frac{2}{3}}{\frac{3}{14}}=7.0 \\[6pt] {} \\[4pt] {} \end{array} \begin{array}{cccccccc} x_1 & x_2 & x_3 & x_4 & x_5 & x_6 & z' & \\ \left(\begin{array}{ccccccc} 0 & 0 & \frac{5}{2} & -\frac{1}{2} & 0 & \frac{1}{2} & 1 & \frac{53}{2} \\[4pt] 0 & 0 & \frac{6}{7} & \boxed{\frac{5}{7}} & 1 & -\frac{7}{5} & 0 & 3 \\[4pt] 0 & 1 & \frac{5}{14} & \frac{3}{14} & 0 & -\frac{3}{14} & 0 & \frac{3}{2} \\[4pt] 1 & 0 & -\frac{1}{7} & -\frac{2}{7} & 0 & -\frac{2}{7} & 0 & 1.0 \\ & & & \uparrow & & & & \end{array} \right), \end{array}$$

(15.60)

$$\left(\begin{array}{ccccccc} 0 & 0 & \frac{31}{10} & 0 & \frac{7}{10} & 0 & 1 & \frac{143}{5} \\[4pt] 0 & 0 & \frac{6}{5} & 1 & \frac{7}{5} & -1 & 0 & \frac{21}{5} \\[4pt] 0 & 1 & \frac{1}{10} & 1 & -\frac{3}{10} & 0 & 0 & \frac{3}{5} \\[4pt] 1 & 0 & \frac{1}{5} & 0 & \frac{2}{5} & 0 & 0 & \frac{11}{5} \end{array} \right),$$

(15.61)

from which the final solution to this artificial-variable problem is found to be

$$x_3 = 0, \qquad x_5 = 0,$$
$$x_6 = 0, \qquad x_1 = 2.2,$$
$$x_2 = 0.6, \qquad x_4 = 4.2,$$

(15.62)

$$\max z = 28.6.$$

Figure 15.8 indicates the graphical solution to the same problem.

Example 15.2

If we were to apply the FORTRAN program listed in Fig. 15.5 to the example discussed above, the input would be read in as shown in Fig. 15.9. The output for this example is listed in Fig. 15.10.

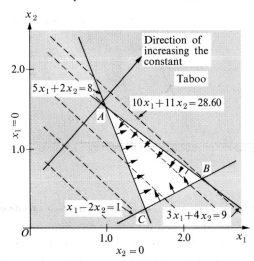

Fig. 15.8. Artificial variable problem.

Col 1 to 10	Col 10 to 20	Col 20 to 30	Col 30 to 40	Col 40 to 50	Col 50 to 60	Col 60 to 70
4 7						
−1 0.0	−1 1.0	0.0	0.0	0.0	0.0	0.0
3.0	4.0	1.0	0.0	0.0	0.0	9.0
5.0	2.0	0.0	−1.0	0.0	1.0	8.0
1.0	−2 2.0	0.0	0.0	1.0	0.0	1.0
0.0	0.0	0.0	0.0	0.0	0.0	0.0
3	6 5					

Figure 15.9

```
FEASIBLE
ITERATION        OBJ. FUNCTION      NEW BASIC VAR.
     1               24.75                2
     2               26.50                1
     3               28.59                4


OBJ. FUNCTION              28.59999900

VARIABLE              VALUE
    2                .60000010
    1              2.19999990
    4              4.20000000



THE FINAL MATRIX


                                    ROW   1

 0.0000      0.0000      3.1000      0.0000      .6999      0.0000     28.5999


                                    ROW   2

 0.0000      1.0000       .1000      0.0000     -.2999      0.0000       .6000


                                    ROW   3

 1.0000      0.0000       .1999      0.0000      .3999      0.0000      2.1999


                                    ROW   4

 0.0000      0.0000      1.2000      1.0000     1.4000     -1.0000      4.2000


                                    ROW   5

 0.0000      0.0000      0.0000      0.0000      0.0000      0.0000      0.0000
```

Fig. 15.10. Output for Example 15.2.

BIBLIOGRAPHY

Application of Linear Programming

BELLMAN, R., "The Theory of Dynamic Programming," Chap. 11 in *Modern Mathematics for the Engineer*, E. F. BECKENBACH, Ed. McGraw-Hill, New York, 1956.

BOWMAN, E. H., "Production Scheduling by the Transportation Method of Linear Programming," *Operations Res.*, **4**, (1956).

CHARNES, A., and W. W. COOPER, *Management Models and Industrial Application of Linear Programming*, **I** and **II**. John Wiley and Sons, New York, 1960.

CHARNES, A., W. W. COOPER, and D. FARR, "Linear Programming and Profit Preference Scheduling for a Manufacturing Firm," *Journal of the Operations Research Society of America* (now titled *Operations Res.*), **1** (1953).

CHARNES, A., W. W. COOPER, and B. MELLON, "Blending Aviation Gasolines—A Study in Programming Interdependent Activities in an Integrated Oil Company," *Econometrica*, **20** (1952).

DANTZIG, G. B., R. FULKERSON, and S. JOHNSON, "Solution of a Large Scale Traveling Salesman Problem," *Operations Res.*, **2**, pp. 293–404 (1954).

EISEMANN, K., "The Trim Problem," *Management Science*, **3**, No. 3 (1957).

EISEMANN, K., and J. R. LOURIE, *The Machine Loading Problem*. IBM Applications Library, New York, 1959.

HARRISON, J. O., Jr., "Linear Programming and Operations Research" in *Operations Research for Management*, J. F. MCCLOSKEY and F. N. TREFETHEN, Eds., **1**, pp. 217–237. Johns Hopkins Press, Baltimore, 1954.

JOSEPH, J. A., "The Application of Linear Programming to Weapon Selection and Target Analysis," *Technical Memorandum 42*, Operations Analysis Division, Headquarters, U. S. Air Force, Washington, D. C. (1954).

KATZMAN, IRWIN, "Solving Feed Problems through Linear Programming," *J. Farm Economics*, **38** (1956).

KOOPMANS, T. C., Ed., *Activity Analysis of Production and Allocation*, Cowles Commission Monograph 13. John Wiley and Sons, New York, 1951.

MUNKRES, J., "Algorithms for the Assignment and Transportation Problems," *J. Soc. Ind. Appl. Math.*, **5**, No. 1 (1957).

NEUMANN, J. VON, "A Numerical Method to Determine Optimum Strategy," *Naval Research Logistics Quarterly*, **1** (1954).

STANLEY, E. D., D. HONIG, and L. GAINEN, "Linear Programming in Bid Evaluation," *Naval Research Logistics Quarterly*, **1** (1954).

SUZUKI, G., "A Transportation Simplex Algorithm for Machine Computation Based on the Generalized Simplex Method," *Report 959*, The David W. Taylor Model Basin, Washington, D. C. (1955).

WAUGH, F. V., "The Minimum-Cost Dairy Feed," *J. Farm Economics* (Aug. 1951).

WOLFE, P., *A Technique for Resolving Degeneracy in Linear Programming*, Rand Report *RM-2995-PR*. The Rand Corporation, Santa Monica, Calif. (May 1962).

PROBLEMS

1. (a) Use the graphical method to find

$$x_1 \geq 0, \qquad x_2 \geq 0,$$

so that $P = 6x_1 + 9x_2$ is a maximum and

$$2x_1 + 3x_2 \leq 12,$$
$$4x_1 + x_2 \leq 8.$$

(b) Tabulate all basic solutions. (c) How many feasible basic solutions are there?

2. Due to a mistake in planning, a manufacturing firm finds that it has 120 hr of skilled labor and 140 hr of machine time available next week. Product A requires 5 hr of machine time and 2 hr of skilled labor per unit. Product B requires 3 hr of machine time and 3 hr of skilled labor per unit. Product A will give the company a profit of $5 per unit and product B yields a profit of $4 per unit. Use the Simplex method to find the amounts of A and B which should be produced for maximum profits.

3. The weekly production schedule for three plants of an automobile manufacturer must be prepared. Plant A has a maximum total weekly output of 9800 units of all models, plant B a capacity for all models of 9419 units, and plant C a total maximum plant capacity of 9996 units. A breakdown of plant capacity by model type is shown in Table 15.5. The associated manufacturing costs by model type for each plant are shown in Table 15.6. Assign assembly quotas by model type to each plant based on the demand outlined in Table 15.7, in such a fashion that (a) the demand by model type is satisfied;

TABLE 15.5. Maximum Plant Capacity by Model Type

Plant	Custom	J300	Wildcat	Special	Riviera	Total
A	7154	None	1568	None	1078	9800
B	3014	2543	1036	1884	0942	9419
C	3899	2099	1499	2499	None	9996
Total	14067	4642	4103	4383	2020	

TABLE 15.6. Unit Cost by Model

Plant	Custom	J300	Wildcat	Special	Riviera
A	$2281	None	$3220	None	$3367
B	2404	$3478	3421	$1954	3501
C	2197	3495	3217	1917	None

TABLE 15.7 Sales Orders for the Week of November 4th, 1964

Model type	Custom	Jumbo 300	Wildcat	Special	Riviera
Quantity	8990	3101	2421	3785	0980

(b) the plant capacity by model type is not exceeded; (c) the total manufacturing costs of all plants is a minimum, based on the cost data outlined in Table 15.6.

4. Two types of cakes may be made in a factory. The first item (cake *A*) requires 2 hr of furnace baking and 3 hr of finishing. The second item (cake *B*) needs 2 hr of baking and 4 hr of finishing. The profit for each cake *A* is $1 and that for each cake *B* is $3. The owner may put as many as 10 workers on the finishing job to work a regular eight-hour shift. He has one furnace which, to operate economically, should work 24 hr a day and which bakes one cake at a time. How many cakes *A* and how many cakes *B* should be made *per day* to produce a maximum profit? Use the Simplex method.

APPENDIXES

OPERATING INSTRUCTIONS
FOR IBM 1620 AND 1622

A.1 FOR FORTRAN PROGRAMS

Prerequisite

1. A thoroughly checked FORTRAN source program deck.
2. POWER READY light is ON on the 1620.†
3. Reserved machine time.

Three Stages

1. Precompiling phase. Debug your FORTRAN program automatically by the 1620 and 1622. Remember that the computer does not point out logical errors.
2. Compiling phase. The computer will translate the FORTRAN language into the machine language, and an OBJECT program deck is punched by the 1622 for you.
3. Computing phase. The OBJECT program is used to produce answers.

Precompiling Phase (debugging)

1. The 1620 *Console Switch Settings* (on the left side of the 1620):

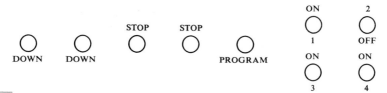

---

† To start the IBM 1620 system: (a) Set POWER SWITCH to OFF (1620). (b) Set switch on the wall box to ON. (c) THERMAL light (1620) will show. Depress RESET (1620) to turn off THERMAL light. (d) set POWER SWITCH (1620) to ON. POWER ON and MANUAL lights will go on. (e) Wait until POWER READY light shows (about five minutes). The 1620 system is ready for use.

2. Ready read hopper of the 1622 with (in sequence): (a) Precompiler (available at the Computer Center), (b) your FORTRAN deck.
3. Depress the 1620 RESET key.
4. Depress the 1620 INSERT key.
5. Type in 310000300002.
6. Depress RELEASE key (1620).
7. Depress START key (1620).
8. After 10 seconds, depress INSTANT STOP SCE key (1620).
9. Depress the 1620 RESET key.
10. Depress the 1622 LOAD key to read the precompiler.
11. The typewriter will type

ENTER SOURCE PROGRAM THEN PUSH START

   Push START key (1620).
12. Your FORTRAN program and errors will be listed on the typewriter.
13. The 1620 and 1622 will stop before the completion of precompiling. Depress the 1622 READER START key. This will process the last two cards of your FORTRAN program.
14. The typewriter will type

PROCESSING COMPLETE

15. Any error in your FORTRAN program has been typed in code *before* each related statement. Consult the list of error codes and correct your FORTRAN statements.
16. Put PRECOMPILER back in the proper place.

Compiling Phase (translation)

1. The 1620 *Console Switch Settings* (on the left side of the 1620):

2. Put about a three-inch stack of cards in the punch hopper of the 1622.
3. Ready read hopper of the 1622 with (in sequence): (a) FORTRAN Processor (available at the Computation Center), (b) your FORTRAN statements.
4. On the 1620:
   (a) RESET.
   (b) INSERT.
   (c) Type 310000300002.
   (d) RELEASE.
   (e) START.
   (f) After 10 seconds, depress the INSTANT STOP SCE key.

   }Zeroing the cores

5. RESET (1620).
6. Depress LOAD key (1622); it causes the 1622 to read FORTRAN processor.
7. After the typewriter types

ENTER SOURCE PROGRAM PUSH START

depress the START key (1620) and PUNCH START key (1622).
8. Machine will stop when the last card appears in the reader hopper. Depress the 1622 READER START key.
9. After the typewriter types

PROG SW 1 ON FOR SYMBOL TABLE PUSH START

push START key (1620).
10. After the typewriter types

SW 1 OFF TO IGNORE SUBROUTINES, PUSH START

push START key (1620).
11. After the typewriter types

PROCESSING COMPLETE

take the blank cards out of the punch hopper and depress downward the white NON PROC RUN OUT key on the punch side of the 1622 for several seconds. This will cause three more cards to drop to the punched card stacker (the left-most stacker). Discard the last two cards which are blank. The punched deck is the object program deck. Mark the deck (your name, object program, and date).
12. Put FORTRAN Processor back in its proper place.

Computing Phase

1. The 1620 *Console Switch Settings*:

					O OFF	O OFF
		STOP	STOP			
O DOWN	O DOWN	O	O	O PROGRAM	O OFF	O OFF

2. Ready read hopper of the 1622 with (in sequence): (a) LOADER 54 (available at the Computer Center), (b) Your object program. (c) Subroutine deck (available at the Computer Center). No data cards.
3. RESET (1620).
4. LOAD (1622).
5. After the typewriter types

ENTER SUBROUTINES, PUSH START

push START (1620).

6. After the typewriter types

1620 FORTRAN . . .

the reader will automatically read in the subroutine deck. When the 1622 stops reading, push READER START (1622).

7. The typewriter now will type

LOAD DATA

>   Case A—*No data cards needed for your program:*
>   Push START (1620).

>   Case B—*Data cards needed for your program:*
>   (a) Place them in the read hopper of the 1622.
>   (b) Push START (1620) and READER START (1622).
>   (c) Watch READER NO FEED light on the 1620. Whenever it is on, push READER START (1622).

8. Answers should appear either in typewritten or punched-card form according to your FORTRAN output statement.

9. Put back the LOADER 54 and the subroutine deck, and *clean up.*

A.2 FOR SYMBOLIC PROGRAMMING SYSTEM LANGUAGE (SPS)

Prerequisite

1. Checked SPS deck.
2. POWER READY light is ON (1620).†
3. Reserved machine time.

Two steps:

1. (a) Process—first pass; (b) second pass.
2. Run.

STEP 1(a)—FIRST PASS

1. Set switches as shown above (1620).
2. Press RESET key.‡

---

† To start the IBM 1620 system, see footnote on p. 311.
‡ All keys are on the 1620 console unless stated otherwise.

3. Press INSERT key.
4. Type 310000300002.
5. Press RELEASE key.
6. Press START key.
7. Wait five seconds and press INSTANT STOP key.
8. Press RESET key
9. Place SPS processor deck in the 1622 read hopper.
10. Place SPS source deck in the 1622 read hopper on top of SPS processor deck (no data cards).
11. Press LOAD key on the 1622.
12. When MANUAL light on the 1620 comes on, press START key.
13. When READER READY light on the 1622 goes out, press READER START key for last card to be read.
14. Typewriter should now print

END PASS 1

15. If any errors were found by the computer during pass 1, an error message will be printed out. This code may be translated from pp. 89 and 90 of IBM *SPS Reference Manual* which should be available in Computer Center (see also Froese, C., *Introduction to Programming the IBM 1620*. Addison-Wesley, Reading, Mass., 1964). Correct your errors and repeat step 1(a).
16. Replace SPS processor deck.
17. You must now proceed to step 1(b). (The information in the machine at this point is needed for step 1(b).)

STEP 1(b)—SECOND PASS

1. Set switches for desired results:

   (a) Punched object deck and listing of source program and assembled object program:

		STOP	STOP		ON	
					ON (ON)	OFF (OFF)
○ DOWN	○ DOWN	○ STOP	○ STOP	○ PROGRAM	○ ON	○ OFF

   (b) Listing of source program and assembled object program only:

		STOP	STOP		ON	
○ DOWN	○ DOWN	○ STOP	○ STOP	○ PROGRAM	○ ON	○ OFF (OFF)
					○ ON	○ ON

   (c) Punched object deck only:

		STOP	STOP		ON OFF	OFF
○ DOWN	○ DOWN	○ STOP	○ STOP	○ PROGRAM	○ ON	○ OFF

2. Place five inches of blank cards in the 1622 punch hopper.
3. Place SPS source deck in the 1622 hopper. No data cards.
4. Press READER START on the 1622.
5. Press PUNCH START on the 1622.
6. Press START key on the 1620. The object program will be punched and/or a listing will be typed, depending on the switch settings.
7. When the READER READY light goes out, press READER START (1622).
8. If subroutines are called for in the source program, the typewriter will print LOAD SUBROUTINES. Then:

    (a) Place SPS subroutine deck 1 into the 1622 read hopper.
    (b) Place SPS subroutine deck 2 on top of deck 1 in the 1622 read hopper.
    (c) Press READER START key on the 1622.
    (d) Press START key on the 1620.
    (e) When the next to the last card has been read, press READER START to read last card.
    (f) Typewriter will now print END PASS 2 and the symbol table.

9. Lift up the blank cards that are still in the 1622 punch hopper and then press NON PROCESS RUN OUT (on the left-hand side).
10. Remove the two blank cards from the back of the deck that was punched (object deck).
11. Remove source program from the 1622 and place subroutines, if used, in the storage rack.

STEP 2—RUN

1. Switch settings:

2. Set switches as shown above.†
3. Press RESET key.
4. Press INSERT key.
5. Type 310000300002.
6. Press RELEASE key.
7. Press START key.
8. Wait five seconds and press INSTANT STOP key.
9. Press RESET key.
10. Place object deck in the 1622 read hopper.
11. Place data cards (if any) on top of object deck in the 1622 read hopper.
12. Press LOAD key (1622).
13. When object deck has been fed in, MANUAL light will appear on the 1620. If there are no data cards, press READER START on the 1622 to feed in last object deck card.

---

† Unless program calls for sense switch operation.

14. Press START key.
15. Press READER START key if there are any data cards.
16. Computer will now execute program.
17. Clean up.

A.3 FOR REGULAR FORTRAN II COMPILATION

PASS I

1. Clear Memory:

    (a) Press RESET (1620).
    (b) Press INSERT (1620).
    (c) Type 310000300002.
    (d) Press RELEASE and START (1620).
    (e) After 5 seconds, press INSTANT STOP SCE (1620).

2. Set console switches (1620):

3. Check card level in punch hopper (1622).
4. Press RESET (1620).
5. Load FORTRAN II deck 1, or pass I deck, followed by your source program, into read hopper (1622).
6. Press LOAD (1622).
7. When

    ENTER SOURCE PROGRAM, PRESS START

    is typed, press START (1620).
8. When PUNCH NO FEED is lit on the 1620, press PUNCH START (1622).
9. When READER NO FEED is lit on the 1620, press READER START (1622).
10. When

    TURN SW 1 ON . . .

    is typed, press START (1620).
11. When

    END OF PASS 1

    is typed, lift blank cards in punch hopper (1622) and press NON PROC RUN OUT (1622). This will run out the last card of the intermediate output deck and the two blank cards. Remove the two blank cards.

12. If there are no errors in your source program, proceed immediately to Pass II, after replacing deck 1 in file because information sorted in the computer on pass I is required for pass II. Therefore they must be run together without clearing cores.

PASS II

1. Set console switches (1620):

		STOP	STOP	STOP	OFF	OFF
DOWN	DOWN				OFF	OFF

2. Press RESET (1620).
3. Check Punch Hopper for blank card supply.
4. Load pass II deck, or deck 2, into hopper (1622), followed by:
5. Intermediate output deck from pass I.
5. Press LOAD (1622).
6. When deck 2 has been read in and MANUAL (1620) is lit, press START (1620) and PUNCH START (1622).
7. Press READER START to read last card.
8. When

SW 1 ON . . .

is typed, press START (1620).
9. When

END OF PASS II

is typed, lift out blank cards in punch hopper and press NON PROC RUN OUT (1622). This will process the last subroutine card and the two blank cards. Remove the blank cards, return processing decks, and go on to pass III.

PASS III

1. Set switches (1620):

		STOP	STOP		OFF	OFF
DOWN	DOWN			PROGRAM	OFF	OFF

2. Load main line program deck from pass II into read hopper (1622).
3. Press RESET (1620) and LOAD (1622).
4. Press READER START (1622) to read last cards. If

LOAD SUBROUTINES

is typed, put deck III in read hopper and press START (1620), and READER START (1622).

5. When LOAD DATA is typed, place data cards in read hopper and press START (1620) and READER START (1622).

6. Press READER START (1622) to read last data card. Your solution will be processed.

A.4   FORGO OPERATING INSTRUCTIONS

		STOP	STOP		1 ○ OFF	2 ○ OFF
○ DOWN	○ DOWN	○	○	○ PROGRAM	ON ○ 3	4 ○ OFF

1. Set switches as shown above.

2. Check to see that the control card (C in columns 1 and 4) is the first card in your source deck and ready the read hopper (1622) with your source deck and your data cards.

3. Place a three-inch stack of cards in the punch hopper (1622).

4. Press RESET,
5. Press INSERT, } on the 1620.
6. Press RELEASE,
7. Press START,

8. Press READER START and PUNCH START (1622).

9. Your source statements will be read and compiled. For each statement in error, two cards will be punched. The first will have the appropriate error code and the second will be a copy of the statement in error.

10. The 1620 will not automatically read the last two cards in the source deck. The computer will stop with the last card in the read hopper. To read these last cards, depress READER START (1622).

11. If your program has compiled correctly, the typewriter will type

```
PROGRAM ACCEPTED
```

and the computer will automatically start executing your program.

12. If there were any errors during compilation, the typewriter will type PROGRAM NOT ACCEPTED. Remove the cards from the punch stack (1622). Do *NOT* press the NON-PROCESS RUNOUT key on the punch hopper; it is not necessary. All the required cards are in the stack. Place these cards in the 407 to obtain a listing; then correct your statements in error.

NUMBER SYSTEMS

B.1 INTRODUCTION

The most commonly used number system is the decimal system based on powers of ten. This system requires ten symbols:

$$0, 1, 2, 3, 4, 5, 6, 7, 8, 9.$$

The symbols 0 to 9 can be used to represent more than ten numbers by writing them in a particular order. To obtain the representation of a written integer such as 353, the digit farthest to the right is multiplied by $(10)^0$ or 1, and the succeeding digits to the left are multiplied by successively increased powers of 10. The products are then summed to give the integer 353. When numbers involve a decimal point, digits to the right are multiplied by successively increasing negative powers of 10, beginning with -1 at the digit adjacent to the decimal point. Digits to the left of the decimal point are multiplied by positive powers of 10, beginning with zero. As in the case of integers, the sum of these products is a representation of the value of the set of digits in this particular order.

Number systems involving bases other than 10 are also used. For instance, the binary system uses base 2, the octal system, base 8. Since the binary system has base 2, only two symbols are used, namely 1 and 0. Binary numbers can be represented in a manner similar to that applying to the number system based on 10. In binary, the symbols are multiplied by correct powers of 2 instead of 10, depending on their location with respect to the decimal point. The products are then added to obtain the decimal representation in the base-10 system. This concept will be further discussed in Section B.2.

In the octal system, eight symbols, 0 to 7, are used, and systems of numbers may be represented in the familiar base 10 system by summing the products of the digits and appropriate powers of 8 as governed by the digit's location with respect to the decimal. We shall discuss these two systems in some detail in the following two sections.

B.2 BINARY SYSTEM

The relation between the binary and decimal systems (base-10 system) can be best explained by Fig. B.1. The four dials imprinted with the binary symbols 0 and 1 represent the four digit locations to the left of the decimal point in a binary number. Each dial can rotate only half a revolution clockwise at one time. Thus the symbols can either occupy the positions shown or they can appear in the opposite position. Each time a dial moves through one complete revolution, the dial on its left rotates through half a revolution.

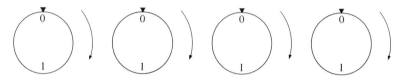

Fig. B.1. Binary number system.

If we begin with all dials set at 0, which is equivalent to 0 in the decimal system, a comparison of the binary and decimal system can easily be made by following the rule stated above. This has been done below.

Decimal system	Binary system	Decimal system	Binary system
0	000	7	111
1	001	8	1000
2	010	9	1001
3	011	10	1010
4	100	11	1011
5	101	12	1100
6	110		

Thus it can be seen that the decimal system of numbers can be represented by certain logical arrangements of only two symbols. As the decimal numbers become larger, the corresponding binary numbers become extremely long and cumbersome.

Binary numbers can be converted into decimal form by following the rules set forth in Section B.1. For instance, to represent the binary number 11011 in decimal form, the steps indicated by the example below must be carried out.

$$(11011)_2 = 1 \times 2^4 + 1 \times 2^3 + 0 \times 2^2 + 1 \times 2^1 + 1 \times 2^0$$

$$= 16 + 8 + 0 + 2 + 1 = (27)_{10}$$

Mathematical calculations in the binary system have their own rules corresponding to the familiar "carry" and "borrow" associated with the decimal system. These rules, along with simple examples, are given below. The decimal equivalents accompanying each example can be obtained by following the conversion process illustrated previously.

Rules for binary calculation

Addition

1. $(0)_2 + (0)_2 = (0)_2$,
2. $(0)_2 + (1)_2 = (1)_2$,
3. $(1)_2 + (1)_2 = (0)_2$ carry $(1)_2$ to the left.

Example

01011	Decimal system equivalent 11
+ 01110	+ 14
$(11001)_2$	25

Subtraction

1. $(0)_2 - (0)_2 = (0)_2$,
2. $(1)_2 - (1)_2 = (0)_2$,
3. $(1)_2 - (0)_2 = (1)_2$,
4. $(0)_2 - (1)_2 = (1)_2$,   with $(1)_2$ borrowed from the left.

Example

10101	Decimal system equivalent 21
− 01100	− 12
01001	9

Multiplication

1. $(0)_2 \times (0)_2 = (0)_2$,
2. $(0)_2 \times (1)_2 = (0)_2$,
3. $(1)_2 \times (1)_2 = (1)_2$.

Example

11101	Decimal system equivalent 29
× 1101	× 13
11101	377
00000	
11101	
11101	
101111001	

B.3 OCTAL SYSTEM

As mentioned previously, the octal system uses eight symbols. Groups of numbers may be represented by the sum of the products of the digits and the appropriate powers of 8. A comparison of the decimal, binary, and octal number systems is shown below.

Decimal system	Octal system	Binary system
0	0	000
1	1	001
2	2	010
3	3	011
4	4	100
5	5	101
6	6	110
7	7	111
8	10	1000
9	11	1001
10	12	1010
11	13	1011
12	14	1100

The value of the octal system is especially apparent in its relation with the binary system. Conversion of the large and cumbersome numbers of the binary system to the octal system is made simply by dividing the binary number into groups of three, beginning at the decimal point, as shown in the example below. These groups are then individually converted into octal numbers. If a decimal equivalent is required, the octal number can then be quite easily converted by multiplying each digit by the correct power of 8 and summing.

Example

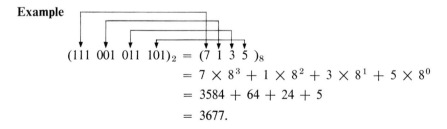

$$(111 \ 001 \ 011 \ 101)_2 = (7 \ 1 \ 3 \ 5 \ )_8$$
$$= 7 \times 8^3 + 1 \times 8^2 + 3 \times 8^1 + 5 \times 8^0$$
$$= 3584 + 64 + 24 + 5$$
$$= 3677.$$

B.4 NUMBER CONVERSIONS

The conversion of integers and fractions from one system to either of the others may best be explained by a set of examples. Table B.1 will illustrate these conversions between decimal, octal, and binary number systems.

TABLE B.1.

OPERATION: Decimal to octal		OPERATION: Octal to decimal	
INTEGERS	**FRACTIONS**	**INTEGERS**	**FRACTIONS**
Rule: Divide the decimal number by 8 and develop the octal number, as shown below.	Rule: Multiply the decimal number by 8 and develop the octal number as shown.	Rule: Multiply the octal number by 8 and add as shown below.	Rule: Express the octal number as powers of 8, add, and divide as shown.

INTEGERS (Decimal to octal)

$$(362)_{10} = (?)_8$$

$$
\begin{array}{l}
8\,\underline{|362} \quad \text{Remainder} \; 2 \\
\;\;8\,\underline{|45} \qquad\qquad\;\; ,, \quad 5 \\
\;\;\;\;8\,\underline{|5} \qquad\qquad\;\; ,, \quad 5 \\
\;\;\;\;\;\;\;0
\end{array}
$$

The octal number is read as directed by the arrow. Thus

$$(362)_{10} = (552)_8$$

FRACTIONS (Decimal to octal)

$$(0.362)_{10} = (?)_8$$

$$
\begin{array}{r}
0.362 \\
\times 8 \\
\hline
2.896 \\
\times 8 \\
\hline
7.168 \\
\times 8 \\
\hline
1.344 \\
\times 8 \\
\hline
2.752
\end{array}
$$

Only the portion of the number to the right of the decimal is multiplied by 8. The answer in octal is made up of the single digits to the left of the decimal point, as directed by the arrow. Thus

$$(0.362)_{10} = (0.2712)_8$$

INTEGERS (Octal to decimal)

$$(422)_8 = (?)_{10}$$

$$
\begin{array}{r}
422 \\
\times 8 \\
\hline
32 \\
+\;2 \\
\hline
34 \\
\times 8 \\
\hline
272 \\
+\;2 \\
\hline
274
\end{array}
$$

$$(422)_8 = (274)_{10}$$

FRACTIONS (Octal to decimal)

$$(0.1322)_8 = (?)_{10}$$

$$
\begin{aligned}
&= 1 \times 8^{-1} + 3 \times 8^{-2} \\
&\quad + 2 \times 8^{-3} + 2 \times 8^{-4} \\
&= \tfrac{1}{8} + \tfrac{3}{64} + \tfrac{2}{512} + \tfrac{2}{4096} \\
&= 0.17619
\end{aligned}
$$

$$(0.1322)_8 = (0.17619)_{10}$$

OPERATION: Decimal to binary		OPERATION: Binary to decimal	
INTEGERS	**FRACTIONS**	**INTEGERS**	**FRACTIONS**

OPERATION: Decimal to binary

INTEGERS

Rule: Divide the decimal number by 2 and proceed as shown.

$$(421)_{10} = (?)_2$$

```
2|421  remainder 1
2|210    "      0
2|105    "      1
2|52     "      0
2|26     "      0
2|13     "      1
2|6      "      0
2|3      "      1
2|1      "      1
  0
```

$$(421)_{10} = (110100101)_2$$

FRACTIONS

Rule: Multiply the decimal number by 2 and develop, as shown below.

$$(0.321)_{10} = (?)_2$$

```
      0.321
    ×     2
      0.642
    ×     2
      1.284
    ×     2
      0.568
    ×     2
      1.136
```

Only the portion of the number to the right of the decimal is multiplied by 2. The binary answer is made up of the single digits to the left of the decimal as directed by the arrow. Thus

$$(0.321)_{10} = (0.0101)_2$$

OPERATION: Binary to decimal

INTEGERS

Rule: Multiply the binary number by 2 and add as shown below.

$$(010111)_2 = (?)_{10}$$

```
0 1 0 1 1 1
      0
 ×2
 +1
  1
 ×2
  2
 +0
  2
 ×2
  4
 +1
  5
 ×2
 10
 +1
 11
 ×2
 22
 +1
 23
```

$$(010111)_2 = (23)_{10}$$

FRACTIONS

Rule: Express the binary number as powers of 2, then add and divide as shown.

$$(0.11011)_2 = (?)_{10}$$

$$= 1 \times 2^{-1} + 1 \times 2^{-2}$$
$$+ 0 \times 2^{-3} + 1 \times 2^{-4}$$
$$+ 1 \times 2^{-5}$$
$$= \frac{1}{2} + \frac{1}{4} + 0 + \frac{1}{16} + \frac{1}{32}$$
$$= 0.8437$$

$$(0.11011)_2 = (.8437)_{10}$$

(cont.)

TABLE B.1. (*concl.*)

OPERATION: Octal to binary		OPERATION: Binary to octal	
INTEGERS	**FRACTIONS**	**INTEGERS**	**FRACTIONS**
Rule: Represent each symbol in the octal number by an equivalent three-digit symbol in the binary system as follows:	Rule: Represent each symbol in the octal number by an equivalent three-digit symbol in the binary system, beginning at the decimal as shown.	Rule: Break up the binary number into groups of three, beginning at the right and convert each group to its equivalent octal form.	Rule: Break up the binary number into groups of three, beginning at the decimal point and convert each group into its equivalent octal form.
$(4602)_8$ $= (100\ 110\ 000\ 010)_2$	$(.2136)_8$ $= (.010\ 001\ 011\ 110)_2$	$(110\ 101\ 111\ 011)_2$ $= (6\ 5\ 7\ 3)_8$	$(.101\ 111\ 011\ 010)_2$ $= (.5\ 7\ 3\ 2)_8$

DERIVATION OF BAIRSTOW'S ITERATIVE EQUATIONS

Consider a nonlinear algebraic (polynomial) equation of the symbolic form

$$y^n + A_1 y^{n-1} + A_2 y^{n-2} + \cdots + A_{n-1} y + A_n = 0, \tag{C1}$$

where $A_1, \ldots, A_n$ are real. As was mentioned in Section 6.5, the problem is to find p and q in a quadratic factor of the form $(y^2 + py + q)$, by an iterative technique. If a polynomial of the form of Eq. (C1) is divided by the quadratic factor $(y^2 + py + q)$, it yields a polynomial of the form $y^{n-2} + B_1 y^{n-3} + B_2 y^{n-4} + \cdots + B_{n-3} y + B_{n-2}$ and a remainder of the form $Ry + S$.

Our objective is to reduce the remainders to zero, that is, $R = S = 0$. To do this we first establish the relationships between p, q, R, S, the A's, and the B's. This is a simple matter of rewriting Eq. (C1) in the factored form, expanding, and then equating coefficients of like powers.

If we let k denote the general term and n denote the last term, we have

$$
\begin{aligned}
y^n + A_1 y^{n-1} &+ \cdots + A_k y^{n-k} + \cdots + A_{n-1} y + A_n \\
&= (y^2 + py + q)(y^{n-2} + B_1 y^{n-3} + B_2 y^{n-4} + \cdots + B_{k-2} y^{n-(k)} \\
&\quad + B_{k-1} y^{n-(k+1)} + B_k y^{n-(k+2)} + \cdots + B_{n-3} y + B_{n-2}) \\
&\quad + Ry + S \tag{C2}
\end{aligned}
$$

$$
\begin{aligned}
&= y^n + (B_1 + p) y^{n-1} + (B_2 + B_1 p + q) y^{n-2} + \cdots \\
&\quad + (B_k + pB_{k-1} + qB_{k-2}) y^{n-(k)} + \cdots \\
&\quad + (pB_{n-2} + qB_{n-3} + R) y + (qB_{n-2} + S). \tag{C3}
\end{aligned}
$$

Equating coefficients of like powers, we obtain

$$A_k = B_k + pB_{k-1} + qB_{k-2}, \qquad k = 1, 2, \ldots, n - 2; \tag{C4}$$

$$A_{n-1} = R + pB_{n-2} + qB_{n-3}, \qquad k = n - 1; \tag{C5}$$

$$A_n = S + qB_{n-2}, \qquad k = n. \tag{C6}$$

There is no y^{n-1}-term on the right-hand side of Eq. (C2) since this would lead to a y^{n+1}-term when expanded, and hence $B_{-1} = 0$ and $B_0 = 1$. All other B's, however, vary with p and q. Therefore, B_{n-1} and B_n, although they do not exist in Eq. (C2), can be evaluated and are used to express R and S as functions of p, q, and the B's. Extending Eq. (C4) for $k = n - 1$, we have

$$A_{n-1} = B_{n-1} + pB_{n-2} + qB_{n-3},$$

and for $k = n$ we have

$$A_n = B_n + pB_{n-1} + qB_{n-2}.$$

From Eqs. (C5) and (C6) we now have

$$R = A_{n-1} - pB_{n-2} - qB_{n-3} = B_{n-1}, \tag{C7}$$

$$S = A_n - qB_{n-2} = B_n + pB_{n-1}. \tag{C8}$$

Thus our requirement becomes $R = f_1(p, q) = 0$ and $S = f_2(p, q) = 0$, where f_1 and f_2 are B_{n-1} and $B_n + pB_{n-1}$, respectively.

Now that we have R and S as functions of p and q, we need only find the particular values of p and q which make $R = S = 0$. This is done by expressing the functions of R and S in terms of their Taylor series, setting the Taylor series equal to zero, and then finding the particular values of p and q that satisfy this equality.

We shall next discuss the general form of the Newton-Raphson iteration for a function of two variables. Taylor's theorem for a function with one variable can be written compactly as†

$$f(p) = \sum_{k=0}^{\infty} \frac{f^{(k)}(p_0)(p - p_0)^k}{k!}, \tag{C9}$$

where $f^{(k)}(p_0)$ denotes the kth derivative of $f(p)$ evaluated at p_0, the point about which the expansion takes place. This theorem may be extended, and for a function with two variables we have‡

$$f(p, q) = f(p_0, q_0) + [(p - p_0)f_p(p_0, q_0) + (q - q_0)f_q(p_0, q_0)]$$
$$+ \frac{1}{2!} [(p - p_0)^2 f_{pp}(p_0, q_0) + 2(p - p_0)(q - q_0)f_{pq}(p_0, q_0)$$
$$+ (q - q_0)^2 f_{qq}(p_0, q_0)] + \cdots, \tag{C10}$$

where $f_p \equiv \partial f / \partial p$, $f_{pp} \equiv \partial^2 f / \partial p^2$ and $f_{pq} \equiv \partial^2 f / \partial p\, \partial q$, and all are evaluated at the point (p_0, q_0).§

---

† For example, see Thomas, G. B., *Calculus and Analytic Geometry*, 3rd ed. Addison-Wesley, Reading, Mass., p. 787, 1960.

‡ For example, see Hildebrand, F. B., *Advanced Calculus for Applications*. Prentice-Hall, Englewood Cliffs, N.J., p. 350, 1962.

§ In the case of one variable, p_0 is the p-coordinate of the point $(p_0, f(p_0))$ about which the expansion takes place, and we say, "the function is expanded about the point p_0." Similarly, for two variables we are expanding about $(p_0, q_0, f(p_0, q_0))$ we say, "the function is expanded about the point (p_0, q_0)."

We consider the Taylor series expansion about a point (p_k, q_k). If P and Q are the exact values of p and q for which $f(P, Q) = 0$, we have

$$f(P, Q) = 0 = f(p_k, q_k) + (P - p_k)f_p(p_k, q_k) + (Q - q_k)f_q(p_k, q_k) + \cdots .$$

$$(C11)$$

We see that $P = p_k$ and $Q = q_k$ would satisfy Eq. (C11) nicely, but since we have no idea of the values of P and Q, we have no idea of the location of (p_k, q_k) about which we should expand the series. Letting $\Delta p = P - p_k$ and $\Delta q = Q - q_k$, we see that if Δp and Δq are made small, then nonlinear terms may be dropped because the series rapidly converges. We may, therefore, get an approximation by dropping nonlinear terms as follows:

$$f(P, Q) = 0 \cong f(p_k, q_k) + (P - p_k)f_p(p_k, q_k) + (Q - q_k)f_q(p_k, q_k). \qquad (C12)$$

Letting p_k, q_k be initial "guesses" or estimates of the expansion point coordinates, we have for some other point (p_{k+1}, q_{k+1}),

$$f_1(P, Q) = 0 \approx f_1(p_k, q_k) + \Delta p f_{1p}(p_k, q_k) + \Delta q f_{1q}(p_k, q_k), \qquad (C13)$$

$$f_2(P, Q) = 0 \approx f_2(p_k, q_k) + \Delta p f_{2p}(p_k, q_k) + \Delta q f_{2q}(p_k, q_k), \qquad (C14)$$

where $\Delta p = p_{k+1} - p_k$ and $\Delta q = q_{k+1} - q_k$. Hence Δp and Δq may be found by simultaneous solution of Eqs. (C13) and (C14).

If p_k and q_k were good estimates, $f_1(p_k, q_k)$ would be almost equal to $f_1(P, Q)$, and Δp and Δq would be small. If the estimates were not good, then large values of Δp and Δq would imply that (p_{k+1}, q_{k+1}) is closer to the actual expansion point. Hence we next try

$$p_{k+1} = p_k + (p_{k+1} - p_k) = p_k + \Delta p$$

and

$$q_{k+1} = q_k + (q_{k+1} - q_k) = q_k + \Delta q.$$

We continue in this fashion until Δp and Δq are within preassigned limits.

Although Eqs. (C13) and (C14) are explicitly stated, we have as yet no means of calculating the following partial derivatives:

$$\frac{\partial f_1}{\partial p} = \frac{\partial B_{n-1}}{\partial p},$$

$$\frac{\partial f_1}{\partial q} = \frac{\partial B_{n-1}}{\partial q},$$

$$\frac{\partial f_2}{\partial p} = \frac{\partial B_n}{\partial p} + p\frac{\partial B_{n-1}}{\partial p} + B_{n-1},$$

$$\frac{\partial f_2}{\partial q} = \frac{\partial B_n}{\partial q} + p\frac{\partial B_{n-1}}{\partial q}.$$

$$(C15)$$

Equations (C13) and (14) may be simplified in the following manner.

(1) Substituting f_1, f_2, and the derivatives of Eqs. (C15) to give

$$B_{n-1} + \frac{\partial B_{n-1}}{\partial p} \Delta p + \frac{\partial B_{n-1}}{\partial q} \Delta q = 0, \tag{C16}$$

$$B_n + p_k B_{n-1} + \left(\frac{\partial B_n}{\partial p} + p_k \frac{\partial B_{n-1}}{\partial p} + B_{n-1}\right)\Delta p + \left(\frac{\partial B_n}{\partial q} + p_k \frac{\partial B_{n-1}}{\partial q}\right)\Delta q = 0; \tag{C17}$$

(2) subtracting p_k times Eq. (C16) from Eq. (C17) to give

$$B_{n-1} + \frac{\partial B_{n-1}}{\partial p} \Delta p + \frac{\partial B_{n-1}}{\partial q} \Delta q = 0, \tag{C18}$$

$$B_n + \left(\frac{\partial B_n}{\partial p} + B_{n-1}\right)\Delta p + \frac{\partial B_n}{\partial q} \Delta q = 0. \tag{C19}$$

Since we need the derivative of B at n and at $n - 1$, and since n may be any positive integer, it is clear that a recursion relationship for $\partial B_k/\partial p$ and $\partial B_k/\partial q$ must be obtained. The general term was given by Eq. (C4) and differentiating it, we have

$$\frac{\partial B_k}{\partial p} = -B_{k-1} - p \frac{\partial B_{k-1}}{\partial p} - q \frac{\partial B_{k-2}}{\partial p}, \tag{C20}$$

$$\frac{\partial B_k}{\partial q} = -B_{k-2} - p \frac{\partial B_{k-1}}{\partial q} - q \frac{\partial B_{k-2}}{\partial q}. \tag{C21}$$

Since both B_{-1} and B_0 are constant, we have

$$\frac{\partial B_{-1}}{\partial p} = \frac{\partial B_{-1}}{\partial q} = \frac{\partial B_0}{\partial p} = \frac{\partial B_0}{\partial q} = 0. \tag{C22}$$

Although the partial derivatives of Eqs. (C18) and (C19) could be calculated directly from the recursion relationship of Eqs. (C20) and (C21), we choose the following procedure which avoids the awkward notation.

Just as we factored Eq. (C1) to get Eq. (C2), so we may factor $(y^2 + py + q)$ from Eq. (C2) [Note: R and S are zero in the final form of (C2)] to get

$$(y^2 + py + q)(y^{n-4} + C_1 y^{n-5} + \cdots + C_{n-5}y + C_{n-4}) + R^*y + S^*,$$

where $R^*y + S^*$ is the linear remainder analogous to R and S in Eq. (C2). Expanding and equating coefficients of like powers as we did in Eq. (C2), we have for the general recursion relationship,

$$C_k = B_k - pC_{k-1} - qC_{k-2} \quad \text{with} \quad C_{-1} = 0 \quad \text{and} \quad C_0 = 1, \tag{C23}$$

which may be extended for $k = 1, \ldots, n$. Equation (C23) may be altered to give $-C_{k-1} = -B_{k-1} + pC_{k-2} + qC_{k-3}$. When this is compared with Eq. (C20), it is implied that

$$\partial B_k/\partial p = -C_{k-1}. \tag{C24}$$

Altering Eq. (C23) results in $-C_{k-2} = -B_{k-2} + pC_{k-3} + qC_{k-4}$, which may be compared with Eq. (C21) to yield

$$\partial B_k / \partial q = -C_{k-2}. \tag{C25}$$

Substituting Eqs. (C24) and (C25) into Eqs. (C18) and (C19), we have

$$C_{n-2}\,\Delta p + C_{n-3}\,\Delta q = B_{n-1}, \tag{C26}$$

$$-(\partial B_n / \partial p + B_{n-1})\,\Delta p + C_{n-2}\,\Delta q = B_n. \tag{C27}$$

Letting $-(\partial B_n / \partial p + B_{n-1}) = \overline{C}_{n-1}$, we have

$$\overline{C}_{n-1} = C_{n-1} - B_{n-1} = -pC_{n-2} - qC_{n-3},$$

from which we obtain the final forms of Bairstow's equations:

$$C_{n-2}\,\Delta p + C_{n-3}\,\Delta q = B_{n-1} \tag{C28}$$

and

$$\overline{C}_{n-1}\,\Delta p + C_{n-2}\,\Delta q = B_n. \tag{C29}$$

Equations (6.17) and (6.18) in Chapter 6 are obtained by solving Eqs. (C28) and (C29) simultaneously.

To recapitulate the computational procedure, we start with an initial assumption for p and q; then we calculate the B-terms from the A-terms using Eq. (C4) expanded for $k = 1, \ldots, n$; next we compute the C-terms from Eq. (C23), which need be extended only for $k = 1, \ldots, (n-1)$; and finally we calculate $\overline{C}_{n-1} = C_{n-1} - B_{n-1}$. The coefficients C_{n-2}, C_{n-3}, and C_{n-1}, are then substituted along with B_{n-1} and B_n into the two Bairstow equations, (C28) and (C29). These equations can be solved simultaneously for Δp and Δq. If Δp and Δq are smaller in magnitude than some preassigned positive number, say, $|\Delta p| + |\Delta q| < \epsilon$, where ϵ is usually between 0 and 1, then the solution has converged to a p and a q, which yield the desired quadratic factor $(y^2 + py + q)$; if the convergence test is not passed, p and q are modified by the amounts Δp and Δq, and the whole iterative process is repeated.

To compute the two roots associated with the factor $(y^2 + py + q)$ is an easy matter. If we let the two roots be of the form $(D + Ej)$ and $(D - Ej)$, then the quadratic factor would be $[y - (D + Ej)][y - (D - Ej)] = y^2 - 2\,Dy + (D^2 + E^2)$. Equating coefficients of like powers of y from the quadratic factor $y^2 + py + q$ yields

$$p = -2D, \quad q = (D^2 + E^2) \quad \text{or} \quad D = -p/2, \quad E = \sqrt{q - p^2/4}.$$

If the initial values of p and q are sufficiently close to the true values, then the method will always converge. Since this is Newton's process, convergence, once established, is quite rapid. In cases where the initial values of p and q are merely random guesses, the method may not converge. To protect against this possibility, an upper limit should be placed on the number of iterations.

ANSWERS TO SELECTED PROBLEMS

CHAPTER 6

1. 1.391 radians
2. (a) 0.14393, 4.4934, 7.7253, etc.   (b) 0.30677, 4.4939, 7.7254, etc.
3. *Case* 1: $t = 2.364$; *Case* 2: $t = 17.48$ 4. 2.3650   5. 4.4934   6. 2.2185
9. For $c = 0.8$, $t = -0.42548$; for $c = 0.9$, $t = -0.45851$
11. 0.4725   12. 0.00874   13. 0.8354   14. 0, ± 1, ± 2 15. $1 \pm j$, $2 \pm 3j$

CHAPTER 7

1. The closed-form solution is

$$t = \frac{\frac{4}{3}Ry^{3/2} - \frac{2}{5}y^{5/2}}{r^2\sqrt{2g}}.$$

   If $y = 0.1$, then $t = 0.1258$.
2. $t = 10$, $h = 9.7199$ for the closed-form solution.
3. *Hint.* The differential equation is

$$\frac{dH}{dt} = c_2 - c_3t - c_4\sqrt{H},$$

   and we wish to determine t for $H = 10$ ft.
4. $t = 2.5$, $x = 990.992$ from the closed-form solution.
7. $t = 5$ hours, $c = 1.4484$ for the closed-form solution.
8. $t = 3.6$ days, $L = 11.7$.
9. For $\Delta t = 0.125$: $t = 0.125$, $x = 0.718199$ (Runge-Kutta).
11. $t = 0.001$, $v = 0.021445$ from the closed-form solution.

12. $x = 0.2$, $y = 0.6534$ from the closed-form solution.

15. $x = 3.01$, $v = 3.01376$ for the closed-form solution.

16. For $\Delta r = 0.1$: at $r = 1$, $T = 899.212$, $dT/dr = -1.57$.

17. For $\Delta x = 0.05$ in.: at $x = 0.6$ in., $T = 1014.82$, $dT/dR = -18077.8$.

21. For $t = 0.1$: at $t = 3$, $y = 0.346$, $dy/dt = 0.306$.

22. For $t = 0.1$: at $t = 1$, $d\theta/dt = 1.484$.

23. For $x = 0.1$: at $x = 3$ ft, $y = 124.29$, $dy/dx = 8.456$.

24. For $\Delta t = 0.2$: at $t = 1.2$, $y = 0.0000156$, $y' = 0.00000874$.

25. At $t = 2$, $x = -0.8607$, $dx/dt = -1.2285$.

CHAPTER 8

2. $x_1 = 1$, $x_2 = 2$, $x_3 = 3$

3. $\begin{bmatrix} 1 & 0 & 0 \\ 2 & -1 & 0 \\ 1 & -\frac{1}{3} & -\frac{1}{3} \end{bmatrix}$

4. $\theta_a = 2.954$

5. $I_1 = 0.377$, $I_2 = 1.262$, $I_3 = -0.639$, $I_4 = 0.532$, $I_5 = 0.35$,
   $I_6 = 0.154$, $I_7 = 0.322$, $I_8 = 0.532$, $I_9 = 0.99$, $I_{10} = 0.477$

7. DET $= -360$, Inverse $= \begin{bmatrix} -0.1027 & 0.1055 & 0.0638 \\ 0.1888 & 0.0222 & -0.1444 \\ -0.0194 & -0.0611 & -0.1472 \end{bmatrix}$

8. $x = 9.26$, $y = -0.92$, $z = -2.51$, $w = 3.27$

CHAPTER 9

1. $\lambda_1 = 5.05$

2. Eigenvectors:

$$\begin{matrix} -0.080 & 0.339 & -0.937 \\ -0.831 & -0.544 & -0.119 \\ -0.555 & 0.767 & 0.330 \end{matrix}$$

CHAPTER 11

1. $Y = 948.184 - 40.18x + 19.3069x^2 - 1.1208x^3$ (based on $x = 1, 2, \ldots, 11$)

2. (a) $T = 0.0321 + 0.01346t$
   (b) $T = 0.0332 + 0.01237t + 0.000142t^2$
   (c) $T = 0.03192 + 0.01457t - 0.000586t^2 + 0.0000612t^3$

3. From normal equations:

$$T = 138.4505 - 0.8437R + 0.5120R^2 - 0.028R^3$$

From Chebyshev polynomials:

$$T = 139.0476 - 1.2933R + 0.6045R^2 - 0.033R^3$$

CHAPTER 12

3. 0.499968   4. 0.7854   5. 1.8518

6. $A_0 = 15.915$, $A_1 = 12.5$, $A_2 = 5.308$, $A_3 = 0.00$, $A_4 = -1.0638$,
    $A_5 = 0.00$, $A_6 = 0.45179$, $A_7 = 0.2118$, $A_8 = 0.1773$, $A_9 = 0.2125$

CHAPTER 15

1. (a) $x_1 = 1\frac{1}{5}$, $x_2 = 3\frac{1}{5}$, $P = 36$
    (b) Six basic solutions
    (c) Four feasible basic solutions

2. Produce $6\frac{2}{3}$ product A and $35\frac{5}{9}$ product B (or 7 product A and 36 product B).

4. Number of cakes $A = 0$, number of cakes $B = 12$, profit $= \$36$.

INDEX

INDEX

QUESTIONS

1. Test for convergence in Transcendental functions, does this go for all methods or only for Newton Raphson.

2. What about Bairstow's method for Polynomials with Real coefficients? or exam or not...?